FATHER-CHILD RELATIONS
Cultural and Biosocial Contexts

FOUNDATIONS OF HUMAN BEHAVIOR

An Aldine de Gruyter Series of Texts and Monographs

SERIES EDITOR

Sarah Blaffer Hrdy
University of California, Davis

FATHER-CHILD RELATIONS
Cultural and Biosocial Contexts

Barry S. Hewlett
EDITOR

ALDINE DE GRUYTER
New York

About the Editor

Barry S. Hewlett is Associate Professor of Anthropology and Adjunct Associate Professor of Tropical Medicine at Tulane University. The author of a monograph on Aka Pygmy fathers, he has also published several articles on parenting and child development in journals such as *American Anthropologist; Journal of Anthropological Research;* and *Man* (in the U.K.)

ALDINE DE GRUYTER
A division of Walter de Gruyter, Inc.
200 Saw Mill River Road
Hawthorne, New York 10532

The paper used in this publication meets the minimum requirements of American National Standard for Information Sciences—Permanence of Paper for Printed Library Materials, ANSI Z39.48-1984.

Library of Congress Cataloging-in-Publication Data
Father-child relations : cultural and biosocial contexts / Barry S. Hewlett, editor.
    p.   cm.—(Foundations of human behavior)
    Includes bibliographical references and index.
    ISBN 0-202-01188-7 (cloth : alk. paper)
    1. Fatherhood—Cross-cultural studies.   2. Father and child—Cross-cultural studies.   I. Hewlett, Barry S., 1950- .   II. Series.
HQ756.F369   1992
306.874'2—dc20   92-267
                                                                          CIP

Manufactured in the United States of America

10   9   8   7   6   5   4   3   2   1

Contents

List of Contributors

Laura Betzig

Department of Anthropology
Evolution and Human Behavior
    Program
University of Michigan

Anne Buchanan

Department of Anthropology
Pennsylvania State University

Victoria K. Burbank

Department of Anthropology
University of California, Davis

James S. Chisholm

Department of Applied Behavioral
    Sciences
University of California, Davis

Patricia Draper

Department of Anthropology
Pennsylvania State University

Karen Endicott

Department of Anthropology
Dartmouth College

Mark V. Flinn

Department of Anthropology
University of Missouri

Marcus B. Griffin

Department of Anthropology
University of Hawaii at Manoa

P. Bion Griffin

Department of Anthropology
University of Hawaii at Manoa

David J. Gubernick

Department of Psychology
University of Wisconsin

Raymond Hames

Department of Anthropology
University of Nebraska

Sara Harkness

Department of Human Development
and Family Studies
Pennsylvania State University

Barry S. Hewlett

Departments of Anthropology and
Tropical Medicine
Tulane University

Kim R. Hill

Department of Anthropology
Evolution and Human Behavior
Program
University of Michigan

A. Magdalena Hurtado

Department of Anthropology
Evolution and Human Behavior
Program
University of Michigan

William Jankowiak

Department of Anthropology
University of Nevada, Las Vegas

Gilda A. Morelli

Department of Psychology
Boston College

Robert L. Munroe

Department of Anthropology
Pitzer College

Ruth H. Munroe

Department of Psychology
Pitzer College

A. Bame Nsamenang

Institute of Human Sciences
Bamenda, Cameroun

Vishvajit Pandya

Department of Sociology and
Anthropology
Westminister College

Barbara B. Smuts

Department of Psychology and
Anthropology
Evolution and Human Behavior
Program
University of Michigan

Charles M. Super   Department of Human Development
                             and Family Studies
                             Pennsylvania State University

Edward Z. Tronick   Child Development Unit
                             Boston Children's Hospital

Paul Turke   Department of Anthropology
                             Evolution and Human Behavior
                                 Program
                             University of Michigan

Acknowledgments

It is a pleasure to gratefully acknowledge the generous assistance of Arlene Perazzini, managing editor at Aldine de Gruyter. She was able to pull the volume together while I conducted field research in Cameroon, Africa. I would also like to acknowledge and sincerely thank Sara Hrdy, Michael Lamb, Jane Lancaster, Cheri Hewlett, and Richard Koffler for their encouragement and assistance.

Introduction

Throughout much of Europe and America, the past 20 years has been a period of increased involvement by fathers in the direct care of their children (Lamb 1981; 1987). Contemporary American fathers are characterized by their nurturant and caregiving roles (Pleck 1984; Lamb 1987), while fathers during earlier stages of American history were characterized by their roles as moral teachers, breadwinners, or sex-role models (Pleck 1984). This increased paternal involvement has generated interest in the nature of fathers' roles and has resulted in a proliferation of popular and academic publications about fathers. The increase in fathering research has led Lamb (1987:xiii) to state that fathers are no longer the "forgotten contributors to child development" (Lamb 1975).

While the number of studies and publications about European and American fathers has increased exponentially since the early 1970s, relatively little is known about fathers in the rest of the world. The problem with focusing so much attention on predominantly white middle-class fathers from highly stratified societies is that the studies often suggest, implicitly or explicitly, that the patterns that are identified in the research are universal and natural, and, consequently, often become the basis for public policy. The American or European infant becomes the "universal" infant. For instance, current American research and literature indicate that father's participation in childbirth and father's playful interaction with infants or young children are natural or important aspects of the paternal role. Father's active participation in childbirth contributes to an easier delivery for his wife and facilitates infant–father bonding, which is in turn considered important for the infant's emotional and social development. Father's vigorous play with his infant is suggested to be the means by which the infant becomes attached to the father and the way in which the infant first learns social competence (i.e., the father's vigorous play is the first interactive style that is different from that of the mother, therefore the infant first learns how the deal with an alternative interactive style). Public policy changes have taken place as a result of these research findings. Hospitals and physicians now encourage if not expect fathers to participate in childbirth (prior to the 1970s hospital regulations excluded fathers from the delivery room), and pediatricians and child psychologists are emphasizing the importance of father's "quality" time (i.e., playful and caring attention to child) with his child, rather than the amount of time he spends with his child, so that secure child–father attachment takes place.

In the middle-class American and European cultural contexts, these are important aspects of father's role. Infants are usually placed in their own crib after birth, fathers are seldom around their infants, the father's role as cultural transmitter is minimized since the state provides education, and children leave the family when they go to college or get married. Consequently, participation in childbirth and playful interaction become important mechanisms by which child–father attachment can take place. But studies in non-Western populations indicate that these are not universal or natural features of the father's role. Fathers in non-Western populations are seldom present at childbirth and never direct the mother's birthing process (Hewlett and Hannon 1989), and the few studies that have investigated father's versus mother's interactive style with infants in non-Western populations indicate that vigorous play is not central to infant–father attachment (Hewlett 1991; Roopnairine, 1991). Cultural contexts in non-Western populations are often dramatically different: fathers often sleep with their wife and newborn shortly after birth, fathers are active cultural transmitters, especially with sons, and not all household members leave the family when they get married.

While cross-cultural studies question some of the European and American research, this does not mean that all aspects of father's role are culturally relative. Fathers in all parts of the world do share certain characteristics: fathers provide less direct caregiving than mothers (but there may be some fathers within a culture that take on primary caregiving), fathers are expected to provide at least some economic support for their children, and fathers are expected to support the mother economically and/or emotionally.

This volume aims to elucidate both the diversities and commonalities in the father's role. The volume identifies factors that influence intracultural and intercultural variability in the father's role, and describes how economic, ecological, ideological, and reproductive factors influence both intracultural and intercultural variability.

The volume has three distinct features. First, the volume examines the father's role in several natural and social environments. Hunting–gathering, horticultural, pastoral, and highly industrialized societies are represented; matrilineal, patrilineal, and bilateral descent systems are considered; societies known for their peaceful, nonviolent nature (e.g., Aka, Batek, Ongee) can be compared to societies known for their frequent and extensive warfare and violence (Yanomamo, Agta,

Ache). A diversity of natural environments is also represented: people that have adapted to tropical forest, desert, mountain, and island environments are included in the volume. Considerable emphasis is given to fathers in hunting and gathering societies (Chapters 2, 6, 7, 11, 12, 13, 14) because this way of life characterizes about 90% of human history and it is rapidly disappearing. If we are going to try and understand the nature of fathers' roles it seems that the few remaining hunter–gatherer populations may provide some invaluable clues.

While the volume spans tremendous cultural and environmental diversity, most of the populations are "preindustrial" or what anthropologists sometimes call traditional or band and tribal level societies in the sense that the populations are from relatively rural and some of the least economically developed areas of the world. The frequency and nature of contact with industrialized and hierarchical societies tend to be limited, but these societies are by no means isolated or untouched by industrialization; all of the societies participate in the world economy at some level and they are all part of contemporary nation-states.

The second distinguishing feature of the volume is that it recognizes the importance of understanding both biological and cultural forces that influence the father's role. Contributors in the first section of the volume examine the father's role in evolutionary or biosocial frameworks, while contributors to the second section analyze the father's role in symbolic and cultural contexts. Both sets of authors recognize that ideology and biology are intertwined; both together influence the father's behavior and the effects of his behavior.

The final distinguishing feature is that all of the contributors are fieldworkers. Their research has been field oriented, rather than library or laboratory oriented. Quantitative or qualitative descriptions of father's role are based on long-term naturalistic observations. All of the authors have lived intimately with the people they are writing about.

Investment versus Involvement

It is important to distinguish father (or male) involvement from investment. Contributors in the first section of the book utilize the term male or father investment, while contributors in the second section tend to use the term involvement. The term investment comes from evolutionary biology and refers to a broad range of activities that the father engages in that contributes to the survival of his offspring, and ultimately to the father's own reproductive success. Generally, two types are recognized—direct and indirect (Kleinman and Malcolm 1981). Direct investment refers to male activities and behaviors that have an immediate physical influence on the child's survival. Direct investment may include holding, grooming, providing food, actively transmitting cultural knowledge, giving gifts, property, or access to resources. Indirect forms of investment are the father's activities and behaviors that benefit the child, but the father would do regardless of the presence of the child. Defending and maintaining access to important food resources, providing the mother with economic or emotional support, or providing the child with an extensive kin network are but a few forms of indirect investment.

Father involvement, on the other hand, is essentially one type of father investment. Involvement refers to interaction with or proximity to the child. Again, there are generally two types of involvement—active and passive. Active involvement refers to holding, feeding, cleaning, or talking to the child, while passive involvement refers to touching, sleeping with, or being near the child. The term involvement is usually used by psychologists or those interested in cross-cultural human development because they are interested in how the father's presence/absence or level of involvement influences the child's emotional, cognitive, personality, or moral development.

Development of the Volume

I began a study of Aka Pygmy father–infant relations in 1984 because of the paucity of data on fathers in non-Western cultures that has been described above. Hundreds of articles and papers existed on white middle-class European and American fathers, but it is near impossible to locate data on fathers in the rest of the world.

While it was very difficult to find published data on fathers in non-Western settings, I knew that many anthropologists and psychologists who were working with non-Western populations must have some data on fathers because the quantitatve (behavioral observations) and qualitative (interviews, participant-observation) methods I used in the Aka father study were similar to those used in other anthropological and psychological studies. The idea for the volume emerged several years ago, but it was not possible to start this comparative study of fathers until the Aka study was completed. Shortly after writing up the Aka material I invited anthropologists and psychologists working with non-Western populations to analyze and publish their data on fathers. Preliminary versions of most chapters were first presented at the 1989 Annual Meeting of the American Anthropological Association in Washington, D.C.

THE FATHER'S ROLE IN BIOSOCIAL CONTEXT

The chapters in the first section of the book utilize evolutionary biology to evaluate the nature of the father's role in human populations. This theoretical perspective is often called "biosocial" because it is interested in how biological or evolutionary factors influence and interact with social-cultural factors. Evolutionary biologists are concerned with how individuals in any species adapt to a particular environment. The ability of an individual to adapt to an environment is generally measured by its reproductive success—how many offspring or genes it was able to leave behind in subsequent generations. Consequently, the chapters in the first section focus on the father's reproductive interests—having children, raising children to reproductive maturity, and finding and keeping a spouse.

The biosocial perspective contributes to a better understanding of the father's role in several ways. First, it recognizes a biological dimension to paternal behavior. Anthropologists characterize their discipline as holistic, in part, because it recognizes biological–cultural interactions, but are generally reluctant to utilize evolutionary biology to explain human behavior because it is said to be "reductionist." Daly and Wilson (1988) describe the nature of this biophobia in the social sciences. Evolutionary biology provides the theoretical framework and the analytical tools for investigating biological constraints on human behavior. Second, the evolutionary perspective provides a conceptual framework that contributes to a broad understanding of the father's role. Evolutionary biologists prefer the term male parental investment to father involvement. Investment refers to the multitude of ways in which males can contribute directly and indirectly to their children—providing, caregiving, training, inheritance, etc. The term involvement focuses on active caregiving and interaction and neglects the various other ways that fathers can contribute. The term male rather than father also indicates that men can and do invest in children who are not their own. Finally, the evolutionary approach emphasizes the unity or commonalities of humankind. The assumption of an evolved biological basis for human paternal behavior suggests that fathers worldwide will have common interests, concerns, and emotions. Fathers from all parts of the world are likely to have similar concerns about the safety, health, and development of their children, the paternity of their children, and tradeoffs between spending time with their children and doing things that attract and keep women (e.g., working to increase status, prestige or wealth).

Figure 1 places the father's reproductive interests in the life effort model utilized by evolutionary theorists (Williams 1975; Low 1978). The

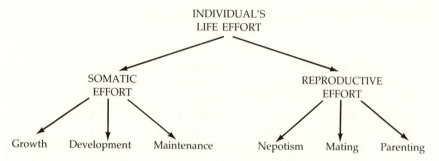

Figure 1. The father's reproductive interests in the life effort model.

model identifies two conceptually distinct categories—somatic and re-productive effort—that an individual engages in if it is to be biologically successful. Somatic effort refers to the risks and costs involved to ensure the physical survival of the individual—having shelter, protection from predators and conspecifics, obtaining food, keeping healthy, and so forth. Reproductive effort has to do with getting copies of one's self into subsequent generations. It is divided into three broad categories—parental effort (rearing children), mating effort (attracting, keeping, and guarding a spouse), and nepotistic effort (helping relatives besides one's own children). Several of the chapters indicate that there are problems with this model (Chapters 1, 7, and 8), especially with the mating effort-parenting effort dichotomy, and discuss the tradeoffs (costs and risks versus benefits) between survival and reproduction, growth and repro-duction, and providing parental care and having several children. Fathers that expend more parental effort than mating effort are some-times said to practice a "dad" reproductive strategy, while fathers with the reverse pattern are characterized as utilizing a "cad" reproductive strategy (Dawkins 1976; Draper and Harpending 1982).

Human males can generally enhance their reproductive success by spending more time in mating effort than in parental effort because males invest less in production than do females. A male's sperm is much smaller than the female's egg and males do not carry the fetus to term or lactate and nurse the infant. Since there is a higher cost to female reproduction, females are predicted to invest more in parental effort than are males. Males on the other hand tend to invest more time in mating effort and therefore compete with other males over available females. The intrasexual competition leads to considerable variance in males' reproductive success—some males gain status and prestige through competition and may attract several wives while other males may never have a wife because they do not have any resources. Chapters 3, 4, and 5 examine how intrasexual competition and father's wealth and status influence paternal caregiving.

Degree of genetic relatedness is also an important factor for evolutionary biologists. A father is predicted to be concerned about the paternity of his children and the degree of relatedness of children that he nurtures, supports, trains, and protects. Several of the chapters (1–4) discuss how paternity certainty or degree of relatedness influences intracultural variability in paternal care.

There is some ordering to the chapters in this section. Chapter 1 is the only chapter in the book that provides a cross-species perspective to male caregiving, and demonstrates that we can better understand human paternal behavior by examining nonhuman primate paternal behavior. It is also a major theoretical contribution to evolutionary biology. Chapters 2–5 identify several evolutionary factors that influence intracultural variability, while Chapters 6–8 move slowly away from a biosocial analysis of the father's role and move into conceptual frameworks of the next section of the book—the cultural context of the father's roles. Chapters 6–8 are especially nice transitions to the second section of the book because both biosocial and cultural paradigms are described and evaluated.

THE CULTURAL CONTEXT OF THE FATHER'S ROLE

The chapters in the second section of the book to a greater or lesser degree take biology for granted and focus on how cultural factors influence fathers' roles. To understand this theoretical perspective it is necessary to understand the concept of culture. Culture is knowledge that is transmitted generation to generation and has several distinguishing features: it is by nature ethnocentric, it influences an individual's physical and affective reality, and patterns how an individual classifies and organizes the world. Culture, of course, manifests itself in infinite ways. Super and Harkness (1986) describe three major aspects of culture as experienced by an individual at various life stages: (1) the physical and social setting of everyday life, (2) culturally regulated customs of care and rearing, and (3) the cognitive and affective orientations of parents and other caregivers (i.e., caregivers ideology and beliefs). A researcher interested in understanding the cultural factors that influence the father's role would have to know the place the father sleeps, eats, works in relation to his children, the availability of other caregivers, contexts in which fathers are expected to care for children, and the beliefs fathers have about children and their role as fathers. According to Super and

Harkness these three aspects of culture—demographic context, cultural practices, and ideology—can help to explain intracultural and intercultural diversity in fathers' roles.

The chapters in this section emphasize different components of the Super and Harkness model. Chapters 10 and 11 identify factors in the physical and social setting that contribute to the level and nature of father–child relations, Chapters 13 and 14 describe cultural practices that influence father–child relations, and Chapters 12, 15, and 16 emphasize how ideology or symbolic systems influence fathers' roles.

There are of course other cross-cultural human development models that identify important features of cultural context (Whiting and Whiting 1975; Whiting and Edwards 1988; LeVine 1977), but the Super and Harkness model is the most recent contribution and covers many of aspects of culture context identified in other models. Harkness and Super discuss some of these other models in Chapter 9.

The cultural perspective contributes to a better understanding of father's roles in several ways. First, it demonstrates how the father's role is often relative to culture context. Culture is by nature ethnocentric; individuals raised in a particular culture generally come to view their customs and ideology about the father's role as universal and natural. As previously described, Europeans and Americans perceive active participation in childbirth and vigorous interaction with children as not only highly desirable but as natural and universal aspects of the father's role. These are not necessarily universal or natural aspects of the father's role if non-Western cultural contexts are considered. Second, the cultural perspective demonstrates that ideology influences the father's actions. For instance, Chapter 9 by Harkness and Super indicates that U.S. and Kipsigis fathers are around their children about the same amount of time, but U.S. fathers are much more engaging with their children than are the Kipsigis fathers. U.S. fathers are more interactive because they feel that stimulating interaction with their children is an important part of their role.

The first three chapters of the second section use cross-cultural comparisons to examine the diversity and cultural context of fatherhood. The last of these three chapters that uses a comparative approach (Chapter 11) is exceptional in that both cultures live in the same tropical forest environment. Chapters 12–16 are ethnographic case studies of father–child relations. Chapters 12–14 explore the cultural context of father's role among three Asian tropical forest hunter–gatherer societies, while Chapters 15 and 16 describe how the father's role in Cameroon and Inner Mongolia is influenced by modernization and urbanization.

REFERENCES

Daly, M. and Wilson, M.I. 1988. *Homicide*. New York: Aldine de Gruyter.

Dawkins, R. 1976. *The Selfish Gene*. New York: Oxford University Press.

Draper, P., and Harpending, H. 1982. Father absence and reproductive strategy: An evolutionary perspective. *Journal of Anthropological Research* 38:255–273.

Hewlett, B. S. 1991. *Intimate Fathers: The Nature and Context of Paternal Infant Care*. Ann Arbor, MI: University of Michigan Press.

Hewlett, B. S., and Hannon, N. 1989. Myths about "natural" childbirth. Paper delivered at the annual meeting of the Society for Cross-Cultural Research, New Haven, CT.

Kleiman, D. G., and Malcolm, J. R. (1981). The evolution of male parental investment in mammals. In *Parental Care in Mammals*. D. G. Guberich and P. A. Klopper (Ed.), pp. 347–387. New York: Plenum Press.

Lamb, M. E. 1975. Fathers: Forgotten contributors to child development. *Human Development* 18:245–266.

———. 1981. *The Role of Father in Child Development*, 2d ed. New York: Wiley.

———. 1987. *Father's Role: Cross-Cultural Perspectives*. New York: Erlbaum.

LeVine, R. A. 1977. Child rearing as cultural adaptation. In *Culture and Infancy: Variations in the Human Experience*. P. H. Leiderman et al. (eds.). New York: Academic Press.

Low, B. S. 1978. Environmental uncertainty and the parental strategies of marsupials and placentals. *American Naturalist* 112:197–213.

Pleck, J. H. 1984. *Working Wives and Family Well-Being*. Beverley Hills, CA: Sage Publications.

Roopnairine, J. P. Father–infant interaction in India. *Developmental Psychology* (in press).

Super, C. M., and Harkness, S. 1986. The Developmental Niche: A conceptualization at the interface of child and culture. *International Journal of Behavioral Development* 9:545–69.

Whiting, B. B., and Edwards, C. P. 1988. *Children of different worlds: The Formation of Social Behavior*. Cambridge, MA: Harvard University Press.

Whiting, B. B., and Whiting, J. W. M. 1975. *Children of Six Cultures*. Cambridge, MA: Harvard University Press.

Williams, G. C. 1975. *Sex and Evolution*. Princeton: Princeton University Press.

PART I

Dad and Cad Reproductive Strategies:
Biosocial Context of Father's Role

Chapter 1

Male–Infant Relationships in Nonhuman Primates: Paternal Investment or Mating Effort?

Barbara B. Smuts and David J. Gubernick

Since natural selection favors behaviors that promote individual reproductive success, both males and females should be expected to direct caregiving to their own offspring rather than the offspring of other individuals. Because female mammals gestate and give birth, they can normally be certain which offspring are theirs. In contrast, males can never be absolutely certain of paternity, because their mates could have copulated with other males. This has led to the prediction that male care of offspring is most likely to evolve in species in which males can achieve high paternity certainty and thus increase the chances that their investment is directed toward their own young (Alexander et al. 1979; Barash 1982; Kurland and Gaulin 1984).

Although male care of infants is uncommon in mammals in general, it occurs in about 40% of primate genera (Kleiman and Malcolm 1981). High paternity certainty is the most common explanation given for the occurrence of male–infant care in nonhuman primates (Alexander and Noonan 1979; Bales 1980; Busse 1984; Kurland 1977; Redican 1976; but see Snowdon and Suomi 1982 for a different view). In this chapter, we evaluate several predictions derived from the paternity certainty hypothesis by examining differences between nonhuman primate species in the prevalence of male–infant care. As a further test of the paternity certainty hypothesis, we investigate differences between individuals within polygynous species in the extent of male care of young. We argue that the paternity certainty hypothesis does not provide an adequate explanation for patterns of male–infant care in nonhuman primates, and we present an alternative hypothesis to account for these patterns. We

1

conclude with some possible implications for the evolution of male–infant care in humans.

A careful formulation of the paternity certainty hypothesis states that high paternity certainty is a necessary, but not sufficient, condition for the evolution of male parental care; in addition, infants must also benefit from male care. Thus, interspecific variation in the importance of male care to infant survival (and, ultimately, to the infant's own reproductive success) could in theory account for some of the variation across species in patterns of male care. However, since almost no information is available on the effects of male care on infant survival in the wild, we cannot presently determine the role this variable plays in the evolution of male parental care in primates. In evaluating the paternity certainty hypothesis, therefore, we assume that interspecific variations in the benefits infants derive from male care do not obscure the expected relationships between paternity certainty and male care described below.

Paternity Certainty Hypothesis: Predictions

Several predictions follow from the paternity certainty hypothesis:

1. Male care of infants should be more prevalent in monogamous species because a single male typically monopolizes matings, and paternity certainty is therefore high.
2. Male care of infants should be more prevalent in species that live in one-male groups because a single male typically monopolizes matings, and paternity certainty is therefore high.
3. Male care of infants should be relatively rare in species that live in multimale groups because females typically mate with more than one male, and paternity certainty is therefore low.
4. In those multimale groups in which male care is observed, it should involve those infants most likely to be the male caregiver's offspring.

Below, we first evaluate predictions 1–3, which concern interspecific variation in the prevalence of male–infant care. We then evaluate the fourth prediction, which concerns variation in male care within particular species.

MALE CARE OF INFANTS: INTERSPECIFIC COMPARISONS

We evaluate the first three predictions listed above using data primarily from wild and free-ranging (provisioned) primates. Information from captive groups is included when it is especially relevant. These comparisons are necessarily based on qualitative information, since few studies provide quantitative information on rates of male–infant interactions that can be compared across species.

Male care of infants can be divided into two types: (1) direct care, where the male directs caregiving behaviors (such as carrying, holding, grooming, protection) toward particular infants, and (2) indirect care, where the male performs behaviors that could benefit infants (such as defending the group's territory or chasing away predators), but these behaviors are not directed toward any particular infant(s) (Kleiman and Malcolm 1981). Although indirect care may sometimes be important, it is in practice difficult to determine when male behavior such as territorial defense is designed to benefit infants and when such potential benefits are simply an incidental byproduct of behavior performed for other reasons, such as to exclude male rivals. Because of this difficulty, we focus our analysis on instances of direct male care.

To simplify comparison between species, we have used a dichotomous classification: presence or absence of male care (see Table 1 for details). We categorize species as *male care present* when adult males typically show either "intensive caretaking" or "affiliation," as defined by Whitten (1987). We categorize species as *male care absent* when males show either no care of infants or only "occasional affiliation" or "tolerance" (Whitten 1987). Male caretaking and affiliative behaviors include carry, protect, share food, co-feed (allow infant to feed in close proximity), groom, hold, and frequent close proximity.

Table 1 lists the presence or absence of male care in monogamous, one-male, and multimale groups of nonhuman primates. Table 1 is not exhaustive but includes all species in which it is known that male care is present, except for some marmosets and tamarins (see below).

*Prediction 1: Male Care Is More Prevalent
in Monogamous Species*

In general, prediction one is supported: most monogamous species show male care of infants (Table 1). In fact, in the monogamous species listed as having male care (such as owl monkeys and titi monkeys), all paired males show infant care, and they provide more extensive care than males in any other primate species except tamarins and marmosets, which are discussed further below. However, the gibbons represent a striking exception to this general pattern; within this family, only siamangs show direct male care. Several gibbon species have been well studied in the wild, and no evidence indicates that paternity certainty is lower for gibbon males than for males of the other monogamous species listed here (Robbins Leighton 1987). Thus, although male care is most

Table 1. Presence or Absence of Male–Infant Care in Relation to Mating
System in Selected Nonhuman Primates[a]

	Male care present	*Male care absent*
Monogamy	Owl monkey[1] Dusky titi monkey[2] Yellow-handed titi monkey[3] Siamang[4] Black howler monkey[5]	All gibbons (8 species)[15]
One-male groups	Mountain gorilla[6]	Gelada baboon[16] Hamadryas baboon[17] Hanuman langur[18] Banded leaf monkey[19] Dusky leaf monkey[20] Mentawai langur[21] Capped langur[22] Campbell's guenon[23] Lowe's guenon[24] Patas monkey[25]
Multimale groups	Saddle-back tamarin[7] Black-capped capuchin[8] Olive baboon[9] Yellow baboon[10] Chacma baboon[11] Barbary macaque[12] Stumptail macaque[13] Japanese macaque[14]	Sifaka[26] Red howler monkey[27] Common squirrel monkey[28] Rhesus macaque[29] Bonnet macaque[30] Long-tailed macaque[31] Vervet monkey[32] Chimpanzee[33]

Note: Species are classified as "male care present" when they show "intensive caretaking" or "affiliation"; species are classified as "male care absent" when they show "occasional affiliation" or "tolerance." Whitten (1987) defines these terms as follows: "Intensive
caretaking: males spend a large part of the day engaged in infant caretaking; although the
actual extent of male participation varies, males predictably perform some parental duties
for all infants"; "Affiliation: males spend part of the day engaged in affiliative interactions
with one or more specific infants; most males interact affiliatively with at least one infant";
"Occasional affiliation: males occasionally interact affiliatively with one or more infants,
but these associations are not characteristic of all males nor of any single male all of the
time"; "Tolerance: males permit infants to be near them but otherwise interact rarely with
infants" (p. 343). This table is not exhaustive, but it includes all species in which it is
known that male care is present, except for some tamarins and marmosets (discussed in
text). For many additional species living in one-male and multimale groups, no evidence of
male care, as defined here, exists.
   [a]References: [1]Wright (1984); [2]Wright (1984); [3]Kinzey (1981); Kinzey et al. (1977); Starin
(1978); [4]Chivers (1974); Chivers and Raemakers (1980); [5]Bolin (1981); [6]Fossey (1979, 1983);
Harcourt (1979); Harcourt and Stewart (1981); some groups have more than one adult
male; additional males usually do not breed; [7]Goldizen (1987, 1988); Terborgh and Goldizen (1985); [8]Escobar-Paramo (1989); Janson (1984, 1986); van Schaik and van Noordwijk
(1989); [9]Packer (1980); Ransom and Ransom (1971); Smuts (1985); Strum (1984, 1987);
[10]Altmann (1980); Stein (1984a,b); [11]Busse (1984); Busse and Hamilton (1981); [12]Burton
(1972); Deag (1974, 1980); MacRoberts (1970); Taub (1980b, 1984); [13]Estrada (1984); Estrada
and Sandoval (1977); Smith and Peffer-Smith (1984); [14]Itani (1959); Hasegawa and Hiraiwa

common and most intensive among monogamous primates, the paternity certainty hypothesis leaves unexplained some notable exceptions.

Prediction 2: Male Care Is More Prevalent in Species Living in One-Male Groups

The evidence in Table 1 does not support this prediction. With the exception of mountain gorillas, in none of these species does the breeding male show frequent caregiving or affiliative behavior toward infants, and in some species, males virtually never interact with infants at all (e.g., capped langurs, patas monkeys). Thus, the paternity certainty hypothesis does not explain patterns of male–infant relations in species breeding in one-male groups.

One possible objection to this conclusion is that, despite the one-male group structure, females in these species actually mate frequently with other males and hence paternity certainty is thereby reduced (cf. Alexander and Noonan 1979). In some cases, copulations with outside males do occur (e.g., patas monkeys: Chism and Rowell 1986; Harding and Olson 1986; redtail monkeys: Cords 1984; blue monkeys: Tsingalia and Rowell 1984; hanuman langurs: Hrdy 1977; Sommer 1988). In patas monkeys, for example, multimale influxes during the breeding season occur regularly, females mate promiscuously with several different males, and paternity certainty for the "resident" male is probably consistently quite low (Chism and Rowell 1986; Harding and Olson 1986). The situation for other "one-male" species appears to be more ambiguous. In blue monkeys and redtails, multimale influxes accompanied by promiscuous mating sometimes occur (Cords 1984; Henzi and Lawes 1988; Tsingalia and Rowell 1984), but their likelihood varies from year to year, depending on factors such as the number of females that are simultaneously sexually receptive and the local population density of extra-group males (Butynski 1982; Cords 1987; Henzi and Laws 1988).

(1980); Hiraiwa (1981); Takahata (1982a); the extent of male care varies considerably between different troops in this species, but in at least some troops, males show frequent affiliation (Itani, 1959); [15]Robbins-Leighton (1987); Wittenberger and Tilson (1980); [16]Dunbar (1984a); Mori (1979a); [17]Kummer (1968); [18]Hrdy (1976, 1977); in some habitats found in multimale groups; [19]Curtin (1980); in some habitats, found in multimale groups; [20]Curtin (1980); in some habitats, found in multimale groups; [21]Wittenberger and Tilson (1980); [22]Stanford (1989); [23]Galat-Luong and Galat (1979); [24]Bourliere et al. (1970); [25]Hall (1967); Loy and Loy (1987); [26]Jolly (1966); [27]Sekulic (1983); [28]Vogt (1984); [29]Breuggeman (1973); Taylor et al. (1978); Vessey and Meikle (1984); [30]Simonds (1965, 1974); Sugiyama (1971); [31]van Noordwijk and van Schaik (1988); Mitchell and Brandt (1972); [32]Struhsaker (1967); Whitten (1987); [33]Goodall (1986); Nishida (1983).

Observations to date indicate that in both blue monkeys and redtails, several years may pass in which the resident male monopolizes most matings (Butynski 1982; Cords 1987; Rudran 1978; Struhsaker and Leland 1979). Speaking of blue monkeys, Rowell (1988, p. 192) carefully concludes, "It is quite likely that resident males sire most of the offspring conceived in their group during their tenure, but it is by no means sure." A similar conclusion may apply to hanuman langur populations characterized by one-male groups. During most of the tenure of a given male, he monopolizes matings with the females in his group, but females do occasionally mate with outside males, especially during takeover attempts when an all-male band may invade the troop (Hrdy 1977; Sommer 1988). It is important to note that, contrary to the paternity certainty hypothesis, male care is consistently absent in the species mentioned above, even during those times when paternity certainty appears to be quite high.

In still other species that live in one-male groups, female copulation with males other than the adult breeding male appears to be extremely rare. For example, observers studying wild hamadryas baboons for several years saw no instances of adulterous mating (Sigg et al. 1982). Similarly, in gelada baboons, mating is usually restricted to a single male (Dunbar 1984b). Yet, in neither of these species does the breeding male show frequent affiliative interactions with his infants.

Until paternity is determined through genetic analysis, the frequency with which infants are fathered by nonresident males cannot be known with certainty, but our current knowledge of mating behavior indicates that, in many species that live in one-male groups, the resident male is usually the father of infants born in those groups. The virtual absence of male–infant care in these species does not support the paternity certainty hypothesis.

Prediction 3: Male Care is Relatively Rare in Species
Living in Multimale Groups

The presence of male care/affiliation in a number of species living in multimale groups is inconsistent with this prediction. Table 1 shows that patterns of male–infant relationships vary considerably in primates living in multimale groups characterized by female promiscuity (i.e., females typically mate with more than one male around the time of conception). In some species, such as rhesus macaques or vervet monkeys, males rarely interact with infants, which would appear to conform to the paternity certainty hypothesis. However, other species living in multimale groups, such as Barbary macaques and savanna baboons, show frequent affiliative male–infant interactions, despite low certainty of paternity. The paternity certainty hypothesis might account for instances of male care in these species if only one or two males monopolized matings. There is no evidence that this is the case; for example, in savanna baboons, which show male care, females typically mate with several males during the week of peak fertility (Hausfater 1975; Scott 1984; Smuts 1985). In addition, behavioral evidence indicates that Barbary macaques are more promiscuous than any other species listed in Table 1 (Small 1990; Taub 1980a). While in estrus, female Barbary macaques initiate and terminate a series of brief consortships that allow them to copulate, at least once, with virtually every sexually mature male in the group. Yet the males of this species frequently carry, hold, and protect infants, and they are, in fact, the only nonmonogamous species classified by Whitten (1987) as showing "intensive caretaking."

The saddle-back tamarins listed in Table 1 deserve special mention. The callitrichid primates (the tamarins and marmosets) all show elaborate male care of infants (Box 1975; Epple 1975; Hoage 1978; Terborgh and Goldizen 1985; Vogt et al. 1978), including extensive infant carrying, comparable to the male care shown by monogamous New World monkeys like owl monkeys and titi monkeys (Wright 1984). Until recently, callitrichids were considered monogamous, because all wild groups that had been observed contained only one breeding female, and captive animals appeared to breed most successfully when caged in pairs (Goldizen 1988). However, a detailed field study of individually recognized saddle-back tamarins showed that many groups included two males and one breeding female, and behavioral observations indicated that both males copulated and both males cared for the infants (Goldizen 1987; Terborgh and Goldizen 1985). Few data are available on the mating patterns of other callitrichids, but in both moustached tamarins (Garber et al. 1984) and emperor tamarins (Goldizen 1988), many groups contain more than one adult male, suggesting that polyandry may occur. Saddle-back tamarins are the only callitrichids included in Table 1, because, until more field data are available, we cannot reliably classify the breeding systems of the other species. The data available for saddle-back tamarins do not support the paternity certainty hypothesis, since extensive male care is shown by males even though paternity certainty is considerably reduced.

In summary, the paternity certainty hypothesis does not provide an adequate explanation for *interspecific* differences in the prevalence of male care of infants in nonhuman primates (see also Smuts 1985; Snowdon and Suomi 1982; Whitten 1987). This conclusion is supported, in particular, by the fact that several highly promiscuous species show considerably more frequent male care of infants than do any of the species breeding in one-male groups.

MALE–INFANT RELATIONSHIPS IN PROMISCUOUS SPECIES

Olive Baboons: A Case Study

The fourth prediction states that, within multimale groups, male care should reflect the degree of paternity certainty. In other words, males should care primarily for those infants they are most likely to have sired. This prediction is evaluated below, first, through a detailed case study of olive baboons and, second, by reviewing patterns of male care in several other species living in multimale groups.

Affiliative relationships between particular adult males and particular infants were a notable feature of the Eburru Cliffs group, a savanna baboon society studied between 1977 and 1983 near Gilgil, Kenya (Nicolson 1982; Smuts 1983a,b, 1985). These male–infant relationships were characterized by frequent close proximity, affiliative interactions such as greeting and grooming, and intimate physical contact including carrying, holding, and cuddling (Figure 1). Affiliative and care-giving interactions between males and infants were almost entirely restricted to these particular relationships. Infants showed fear toward, and avoided, all other males.

Males provided numerous, important benefits to the infants with whom they associated (Smuts 1985). They protected the infants against predation and potential infanticide by other baboon males (see also Packer 1980; Stein 1984b). They also allowed the infants to feed with them. Since adult males monopolized the best feeding sites, this association may have provided important nutritional benefits to rapidly growing infants (see also Altmann 1980; Stein 1984b). Males encouraged the infants to rest near them by engaging in spirited grunting duets, and they were very tolerant of infant proximity and physical contact during rest or play sessions.

In the Eburru Cliffs group, the male's relationship with the infant was closely tied to the male's relationship with the infant's mother (Figure 2). Quantitative analysis of data on male–female interactions showed that each female in the troop formed a long-term, special relationship, or "friendship," with one or two of the 18 adult males; different females had different males as friends. Friends groomed each other much more than other male–female dyads, had many more affiliative interactions, and spent a great deal of time in proximity, especially when the female was nursing a young infant. As a result of the male's friendship with the mother, he developed a long-term, protective relationship with her infant. Although only 12% of all possible adult male–adult female dyads in the troop were considered "friends," virtually all male–infant affiliative interactions involved males who were friends with the infant's

Figure 1. An adult male olive baboon from Eburru Cliffs troop holding the hand of an infant female with whom he has developed an affiliative relationship.

mother (Smuts 1985). With few exceptions, friendships involved males who had transferred from other groups and who were therefore unrelated to their female friends.

Friendship with the mother appeared to be a better predictor of male–infant relationships than was probability of paternity (Smuts 1985). Evidence for possible paternity was based on detailed observations of female mating behavior during the estrous cycle in which she conceived. At this time, females typically form a series of temporary but exclusive mating relationships, called consortships, with several different males. Males observed in consort with the female during the 7 days of peak fertility of her conception cycle were labeled "possible fathers." Using this criterion, most infants had two or three possible fathers. In 55% of the friendships, the male was a possible father of the female's current

Figure 2. Adult male (left) and adult female olive baboon "friends" asleep together.

infant, but in the remaining 45%, he had never been observed mating with the mother, and, in several cases, had not even been in the group when the infant was conceived.

Table 2 shows that friendship was a better predictor of male–infant relationships than was possible paternity. In 80% of the male–infant dyads where the male was a friend of the mother, the male showed affiliative behavior toward her infant, and this probability remained the same whether or not he was a possible father. Males who were possible fathers but who were not friends with the mother showed affiliative behavior toward the infant in only 25% of the dyads, while males who

Table 2. Effect of Possible Paternity and Friendship with the Infant's Mother on Male–Infant Affiliation in Eburru Cliffs Baboons

Male was friend	*Male was possible father*	*Number of dyads*	*Percent of dyads affiliative*
Yes	Yes	12	83.3
Yes	No	10	80.0
No	Yes	12	25.0
No	No	192	3.0

Note: Data from Smuts (1985).

were neither friends nor possible fathers showed affiliative behavior in only 3% of the dyads. These results indicate that (1) for a male, the existence of a prior friendship with the mother was both a necessary and sufficient condition for the development of an affiliative relationship with her infant and (2) being a probable father was likely to result in an affiliative relationship with the infant only if the male also had a friendship with the mother.

Thus, in the Eburru Cliffs group males sometimes formed close bonds with infants who were not their own offspring. Why did they do so? Data on consortships during the second-half of the study showed that adult males who had formed a prior friendship with the female had a significantly increased probability of mating with her in the future. Smuts (1985) argued that, in these baboons, males invested in infants not because those infants were likely to be their own (i.e., they had high paternity certainty), but because caring for infants increased the probability that the male would be chosen by the mother as a mate in the future (see also Seyfarth 1978). In other words, male–infant caregiving can be viewed as a form of "mating effort" rather than as "paternal investment." This hypothesis is developed further, below. First, however, we ask whether observations of other species living in multimale groups are consistent with the results presented above for Eburru Cliffs.

Male–Infant Relationships in Savanna Baboons
and Macaques

Affiliative relationships between particular adult males and infants, similar to those described above for Eburru Cliffs, have been observed in a number of baboon troops and in several species of macaques. However, quantitative data relating male–infant interactions to probability of paternity and to the males' social relationships with the infants' mothers are available in only a few cases, which are summarized in Table 3. We can use these data to test further the prediction that male care is related to a high probability of paternity.

In three of the six cases listed in Table 3, males developed affiliative relationships with infants significantly more often when they were likely fathers than when they were not, but in the other three cases, probability of paternity had no effect on male–infant relationships. Information is available on the males' relationships with the infants' mothers in four of the six cases. In all of these instances, affiliative bonds with mothers were significantly associated with the development of male–infant relationships. Most importantly, in the three cases that showed a positive relationship between probability of paternity and male–infant affiliation, researchers concluded from the evidence that the male's

Table 3. Male–Infant Affiliation, Paternity, and Male–Female Relationships
     in Savanna Baboons and Macaques

| Species[a] | Male–Infant Affiliation Related to: | | | |
	Special relationship with mother	Probability of paternity	Method of assessing paternity[b]	References
Olive baboon (w)	Yes	Yes	CC	Smuts (1983b, 1985)
Olive baboon (w)	—	No	CC	Packer (1980)
Yellow baboon (w)	Yes	Yes	CC	Altmann (1980); Stein (1984a,b)
Barbary macaque (p)	?[c]	No	MC	Kuester and Paul (1986)
Japanese macaque (p)	Yes	No	CB	Takahata (1982a); Gouzoules (1984)
Rhesus macaque (c)	Yes	Yes	G	Berenstain et al. (1981); Kaufman (1967)

Note: Even though rhesus males show only occasional affiliation with infants (Table 1), they are included here because this study provides information highly relevant to the paternity certainty hypothesis. Berenstain et al. (1981) define male–infant affiliation in terms of amount of time spent in close proximity.

[a] w, wild; p, free-ranging, provisioned; c, captive.

[b] CC, quantitative analysis of consort activity around the time the infant was conceived; MC, quantitative analysis of mating around the time the infant was conceived; CB, quantitative analysis of consort activity throughout the breeding season; G, genetic determination of paternity.

[c] Of seven studies on Barbary macaques, only two provide information on male–female relationships. MacRoberts (1970) reported that two subadult males who developed strong affiliative bonds with infants had special relationships with the infants' mothers. Small (1990) claimed that Barbary macaque males and females do not form special relationships but did not present data on proximity or social interactions of particular male–female dyads.

relationship with the mother was an even more important determinant of male–infant affiliation than was paternity (Berenstain et al. 1981; Smuts 1985; Stein 1984b). The research by Berenstain et al. (1981) is particularly noteworthy, because it is the only study that determined paternity through biochemical analysis. In a large, captive group of rhesus macaques, fathers and offspring were found in close proximity to one another more often than other male–infant dyads. However, "the effect of paternity disappeared when maternal association with males was controlled. . . . This result accords with the hypothesis that selective father–offspring association depends on the mother's relationship with males" (p. 1061).

Several other studies provide information that supplements the data summarized in Table 3. Strum argued that the male–infant affiliative relationships she observed in olive baboons were related to the males' social bonds with the infants' mothers (Strum 1987) and were unrelated to paternity (Strum 1984). Busse (1984) and Busse and Hamilton (1981) reported that instances of male–infant carrying in chacma baboons in the presence of other males ("triadic interactions") were related to both male–female bonds and to paternity. However, because their assessment of paternity was based on male dominance rank rather than mating activity, the role of paternity in male–infant carrying remains unclear. In a review of all published studies of triadic interactions in savanna baboons, Smith and Whitten (1988) concluded that "the most common denominator of triadic interactions is a close affiliative relationship of the carrier male, whether related or not, with the infant and its mother . . . [which] suggests that the cultivation and/or maintenance of special relationships with females may be central to triadic interactions" (p. 422). van Noordwijk and van Schaik (1988) reported increased proximity between probable fathers and infants in wild long-tailed macaques, but, like Busse and Hamilton (1981), they used male dominance rank to estimate probability of paternity. They did not provide a measure of male–female affiliation. In stumptailed macaques, in which males frequently interact in affiliative ways with infants, no data are available on the effect of paternity, but several studies suggest that the males' social relationships with mothers may influence male–infant affiliation (Estrada and Sandoval 1977; Estrada 1984; Smith and Peffer-Smith 1984).

In summary, in savanna baboons and macaques, the relationship between probable paternity (as assessed from mating activity) and male–infant affiliative relationships explains some, but by no means all, or even a major part, of the data. Although several studies report a link between probable paternity and male–infant affiliation, no studies have shown that probability of paternity influences male–infant affiliation independent of male–female bonds. When researchers have systematically examined both the male's social relationship with the infant's mother and paternity, they have concluded that the former is a more important determinant of male–infant affiliation. Below, we explore the implications of this finding in more detail. First, however, we briefly review data from two other primates relevant to the paternity certainty hypothesis.

Male–Infant Relationships in Vervets and Capuchins

Vervets are small African monkeys related to baboons and macaques that live in small groups with several adult males and females. Males typically show neither caretaking nor affiliative behaviors toward infants. Hauser (1986), however, examined the potential for male protection of infants by playing back tape recordings of infant distress calls to adult males in five groups of wild vervets. He found that some males attended to the call (measured by the duration of looking toward the speaker) significantly more than did other males. Paternity was estimated by frequencies of copulations with the infants' mothers during the season when the infants were conceived. Paternity certainty correlated positively and significantly with male response to infant distress calls.

It is possible, however, that a male's response to infant distress calls reflects the male's social relationship with the mother; if sexual and social relationships overlap extensively, as they do in baboons, this could account for the correlation Hauser (1986) found between mating behavior and male response. There is no evidence that male vervets form obvious friendships with females as male baboons and macaques do, but further study might reveal more subtle social preferences.

Laboratory data indicate, however, that the male vervet's response to infants is mediated by the mother's presence (Keddy Hector et al. 1989). Individual males and infants were removed from the group and allowed to interact briefly. The infant's mother was either present and visible behind a plexiglass partition, present behind a one-way mirror (so that she could see the male and infant but they could not see her), or absent. When they knew mothers were watching, alpha males directed significantly less agonistic behavior toward infants. Under these same conditions subordinate males (all unlikely fathers) showed significantly more affiliative behavior toward infants. When the mothers were subsequently given access to the males, the degree of agonism they showed toward the males correlated negatively and almost perfectly with the degree of affiliative behavior the males had shown toward their infants; in other words, females punished males who were not nice to their infants.

Whether or not the mother was present, alpha males who were likely fathers showed significantly more affiliative behavior toward infants than alpha males who were not likely fathers. However, subordinate males (unlikely fathers), contrary to the paternity certainty hypothesis, showed as much affiliative behavior toward infants as did alpha males, but only when they could see that the mothers were watching.

These data suggest that males behaved affiliatively toward infants to influence their relationships with the mothers—specifically, to reduce female aggression and perhaps also to increase the likelihood of future cooperative relations with particular females. Field data suggest that such reductions in female aggression could be important for males, since vervet females reject male suitors aggressively (Andelman 1985) and form aggressive coalitions to prevent males from joining their troops (Cheney 1983a,b). More data are needed to clarify the effects of paternity and male–female relationships on male–infant interactions in vervets.

Black-capped capuchins are the only nonmonogamous New World primates in which extensive male–infant affiliation has been described (Escobar-Paramo 1989; Janson 1984). Like vervets, they live in fairly small, multimale, multifemale groups. Janson (1984) found that all estrous females initiated copulations and showed strong and active preferences for mating with the alpha male around the time of conception. The alpha male was therefore the likely father of all infants in the group. He allowed these infants to feed near him, although he threatened other subordinate animals away. Since the alpha male monopolized the best feeding sites, his tolerance at food sources provided nutritional benefits to infants. In addition, he was observed defending infants against aggression from other troop members. Escobar-Paramo (1989) describes similar alpha male tolerance of infants during feeding, and she also reports that infants congregate around the alpha male during rest and play sessions. However, other males have been observed behaving affiliatively toward infants. van Schaik and van Noordwijk (1989) reported that during times of fruit scarcity, not only the alpha male, but other troop males as well, attracted females and their young by food calls and allowed them to eat the males' leftovers.

Janson argued that the alpha male's tolerance and protection of infants reflected paternity. In support, he cited one instance in which a newly dominant male was intolerant toward a juvenile sired before the male took over, but was later tolerant toward juveniles of similar age that he probably fathered (1984, p. 196). Although paternity certainty may influence male–infant relationships in black-capped capuchins, male–female relationships may also be important, as discussed further below.

Summary of Results within Species Living
in Multimale Groups

Contrary to the paternity certainty hypothesis, in all promiscuous species that show regular male–infant caregiving, males often care for infants they probably did not father. The relationship between likelihood of paternity and male–infant care varies. Male–infant care is not associated with paternity (as measured by mating behavior) in Barbary macaques (Kuester and Paul 1986), Japanese macaques (Gouzoules 1984), and some baboon groups (e.g., Packer 1980). In other baboon groups (e.g., Smuts 1985; Stein 1984a,b), paternity and male care are positively correlated, but paternity appears to be a less important determinant of male–infant relationships than the male's social relationship with the infant's mother. Vervet data suggest a possible role for paternity certainty, but they also show that male behavior toward infants is influenced by the mother's presence, independent of paternity certainty.

In all of these studies, paternity was estimated on the basis of sexual behavior; such estimates may not always reflect actual paternity (Stern and Smith 1984). Only one study (Berenstain et al. 1981) has combined biochemical analysis of paternity and data on male–infant relationships, and it clearly showed that the male's relationship with the mother influenced male–infant proximity, while paternity alone did not.

Taken together, these data suggest that patterns of male–infant relationships in species living in multimale groups often reflect the males' social relationships with the infants' mothers more than the males' genetic relationships to the infants. Below, we discuss this finding and develop further the mating effort hypothesis.

MALE–INFANT CAREGIVING AS MATING EFFORT

Males normally maximize reproductive success by mating with multiple females. Female reproductive success, in contrast, is limited primarily by time and energy demands, which can sometimes be reduced through male paternal assistance (Trivers 1972; Wittenberger and Tilson 1980). However, male investment in one female's offspring often reduces the male's chances of inseminating other females (Trivers 1972). For this reason, evolutionary theorists usually regard male efforts to obtain mates (i.e., mating effort) and male care of infants as alternative and opposing male reproductive strategies (see Hurtado and Hill, this volume). However, male care of young is not always an alternative to mating effort; it can sometimes represent a means by which males increase their mating success. Indeed, male care of infants represents mating effort rather than parental investment whenever selection favors male care because of the benefits males receive *in exchange for* this care rather than because of enhanced survivorship of their own infants. This does not mean that females or infants do not benefit from male care; in fact, they must do so, or else females would not be selected to engage in an exchange of benefits with males. We propose that male primates sometimes care for infants in response to female mate preferences for such caring males, or in exchange for other benefits provided by females (or occasionally by the infants themselves) that contribute to male mating success.

The mating effort hypothesis predicts that male care of and affiliation toward infants will be most likely when (1) infants can benefit from male care, (2) females (or infants) can control and offer important benefits to males, and (3) females (or infants) have opportunities to compare the behavior of different males and then, on the basis of this comparison, distribute benefits to some males but not others.

The benefits females provide males in exchange for male care, affiliation, or protection of their infants can vary within and between species. In olive baboons, males gain increased mating opportunities with the mothers of affiliated infants (Seyfarth 1978; Smuts 1985). Males can also gain benefits directly from affiliated infants who cooperate with the males during tense interactions with other males, thereby reducing the males' vulnerability to attack (Collins 1986a,b; Packer 1980; Stein 1984a,b; Strum 1984).

In rhesus and Japanese macaques, friendship with females and their infants generally does not increase a male's mating opportunities with those females (Chapais 1981, 1983a; Takahata 1982a,b). However, male macaques appear to receive substantial benefits from agonistic alliances with affiliated females. Among rhesus macaques, female intervention in male–male disputes can strongly influence male–male dominance relationships (Chapais 1983b). Female interventions also appear to affect male status in Japanese macaques (Koyama 1970), and female aggression—or lack of it—can determine the fate of a new male attempting to enter a group (Fedigan 1976; Packer and Pusey 1979). In 10 captive groups of vervet monkeys in which the alpha males were experimentally removed, bonds with high-ranking females predicted the identity of the new alpha males while male rank did not (Raleigh and McGuire 1989). In macaques as well, bonds with high-ranking females can be especially important in helping a male to achieve and/or maintain high rank (Chapais 1983b; de Waal 1989). The importance of developing ties with influential females may explain why male macaques (Auerbach and Taub 1979; Gouzoules 1975; Hendy-Neely and Rhine 1977) and vervets (Keddy Hector et al. 1989) sometimes bias their affiliative interactions toward the infants of high-ranking females.

The third condition listed above suggests that male care for infants as a form of mating effort should be more common when females are in a position to dispense benefits among more than one male on the basis of the males' behavior toward infants. In species that live in one-male groups, such as hamadryas baboons, mountain gorillas, or hanuman langurs, such opportunities for female choice are probably normally more limited than in species that live in multimale troops, where females can routinely interact with, and compare, several different males. The mating effort hypothesis is thus entirely consistent with the fact that male–infant caregiving is more common in polygamous primates living in multimale groups than it is in those living in one-male groups.

However, even in species living in one-male groups, females sometimes have opportunities to choose between different males. Such female choice may help to explain several findings that are not consistent with the paternity certainty hypothesis. For example, in gelada baboons, young male "followers" sometimes attempt to join one-male breeding units. If successful, the follower may eventually succeed in luring a few females away to form a unit of his own. Followers cultivate special relationships with females and infants of the unit, even though those infants are not their own. Mori (1979b) has suggested that follower males attempting to join a breeding unit care for infants to develop intimate bonds with the infants' mothers. In addition, Dunbar (1984a) suggested that the infants themselves may provide benefits to the male, by either buffering aggression from the breeding male or soliciting agonistic support from the mother. If such bonds with infants facilitate group membership, and group membership, in turn, facilitates future breeding, then the follower's treatment of infants represents a form of mating effort.

Similarly, in one-male groups, even though the male is probably the father of all of the infants, he may develop special relationships with particular infants. This appears to be the case for gorillas, at least in captivity (Tilford and Nadler 1978). In this instance, the male's special relationship with an infant mirrored his special relationship with the infant's mother. In the wild, the breeding male might cultivate such preferential relationships to reduce the chances that one of his females will transfer to another male, a hypothesis currently under investigation (Sicotte 1989).

Mating Effort versus Paternity Certainty:
Future Directions

Evaluating the mating-effort versus paternity-certainty hypotheses will often be difficult, because, under certain conditions, both selective forces can produce a strong positive correlation between male care and high paternity certainty for very different reasons. Suppose, for a moment, that paternity certainty is driving male–infant caregiving in a multimale primate species, such as savanna baboons. The result will be that most males will care for infants likely to be their own. However, assume now that mating effort is driving male–infant caregiving in the same species, and assume, furthermore, that this strategy is very often successful in increasing male mating opportunities with the infant's mother in the future. If so, then these males may also end up caring for their own offspring, because they continue to invest mating effort in particular females who then reward them by mating with them again. Thus, we wish to emphasize that the demonstration of a positive correlation between male–infant caregiving and high probability of paternity is not sufficient evidence, in and of itself, to conclude that male–infant caregiving represents paternal investment rather than mating effort.

Janson's (1984) study of black-capped capuchins, mentioned earlier, provides an instructive example. Janson argues that, because of the nature of the capuchins' diet, alpha males can monopolize the best food sources and can therefore offer females and infants important benefits that other males cannot. This, in turn, selects for females who prefer the alpha male as a mate. Janson argues that the ability of the alpha male to discriminate against offspring sired by other males facilitates the evolution of female preferences for alpha males. However, given the strong role played by female choice in this system, one could just as easily argue that by discriminating in favor of alpha males who invest in their infants, females could facilitate the evolution of male–infant care. In other words, the correlation between high paternity certainty and male care for infants could simply be a byproduct of consistent female choice for the mate who offers them the greatest benefits, an argument that is consistent with Janson's own analysis of this species' mating system. If so, then the male–infant relationship could represent male mating effort as well as paternal investment.

The mating-effort hypothesis may apply even to monogamous species, in which it is usually assumed that high paternity certainty, along with the need for biparental care, favors male investment in young. However, high paternity certainty could be a result, as well as a cause, of male care of offspring in monogamous species. That is, evolution may have favored male investment in young mainly because such investment greatly enhanced the probability that the mother would continue to mate, more or less exclusively, with the investing male.

To evaluate these hypotheses we will need to go beyond simple correlations between male–infant caregiving and paternity certainty to look more closely at the development of male–infant relationships, the male's relationships with the infants' mothers, and the benefits females (and infants) provide males, including mating opportunities. We should also pay special attention to male–infant relationships involving newcomers to the social group, or newly matured males, or males that are in the process of cultivating a new relationship with a female, because it is under these circumstances that the predictions of the two hypotheses are most likely to diverge. Finally, in some cases, especially when male–female relationships are relatively stable, it may not be possible to distinguish between the two hypotheses based on observations alone, and experimental manipulation may be required. The experiments of Keddy Hector et al. (1989) with captive vervets, described above, indicate that the experimental approach is likely to be extremely rewarding.

Clearly, both the paternity-certainty hypothesis and the mating-effort hypothesis require that infants benefit from male care. As noted earlier, we have not investigated how the infant's need for male care influences male–infant caregiving, because few data relevant to this issue are available. It is important to point out, however, that even if a considerable proportion of the interspecific variation in the prevalence of male care could be explained by interspecific variation in the degree to which infants benefit from such care, we would still be left with the question: To what extent does male–infant care represent paternal investment, and to what extent does it represent mating effort? Our review of the evidence suggests that increased survivorship of their own infants (paternal investment) is not a sufficient explanation for male care in many primates, and that males who care for infants often do so because they receive important benefits from females, including increased mating opportunities.

CONCLUSION: IMPLICATIONS FOR HUMAN MALE–INFANT RELATIONSHIPS

The evidence cited here calls into question the hypothesis that male–infant caregiving in nonhuman primates is primarily a form of paternal investment and suggests, instead, that male–infant care is sometimes a form of mating effort. This hypothesis has important implications for understanding the evolution of male–infant relations in humans and may help explain cross-cultural and interindividual variation in male care of young.

Extensive male investment in infants supposedly did not evolve in our hominid ancestors until males could be reasonably certain that they were investing in their own offspring (e.g., Alexander and Noonan 1979; Lovejoy 1981; Symons 1979). Thus paternity certainty has been considered a critical selective force favoring the evolution of male care in humans. In addition, the development of a pair-bonded, or monogamous, mating system in which females restricted their mating to a single male is viewed as a crucial evolutionary step that allowed males, for the first time, to make a significant contribution to the welfare of mothers and infants (Alexander and Noonan 1979; Lovejoy 1981; Strassman 1981; Symons 1979; Turke 1984).

We have already documented the inadequacy of the paternity certainty hypothesis as a complete explanation for the evolution of male care of young in nonhuman primates. We suggest that male–infant care in humans initially evolved as a form of mating effort rather than paternal investment. Furthermore, we suggest that male care was not a consequence of increased paternity certainty, but rather led to increased paternity certainty as a result of female choice for investing males. Thus male care was probably not initially a consequence of monogamy, but rather preceded and favored the evolution of pair bonds.

If male care of infants in nonhuman primates is better understood as a form of mating effort, which entails a mutually advantageous, reciprocal relationship between a male and female, then it is likely that hominid males made significant contributions to the welfare of mothers and infants long before the evolution of the pair bond. It is also possible that, even in modern humans, care and protection of women and children by men sometimes represents mating effort rather than paternal investment.

For example, the Aka pygmies of the Central African Republic display the highest rates of male care of young documented for any human society (Hewlett 1988, and this volume). The primary subsistence activity of the Aka is net hunting, which, to be successful, requires intimate cooperation between a husband and wife team. Hewlett (1988, and this volume) suggests that males provide infant care (predominantly in the camp setting) in order to obtain females' assistance in net hunting (in the forest), whereas females may select men that demonstrate the willingness and ability to care for children (Hewlett 1988). Hewlett notes further that high status males with more resources invest less direct care in their infants than do low status males with fewer resources. This suggests the possibility that in the Aka, and perhaps in other human societies as well, low status males may try to compensate for their reduced attractiveness as mates by offering females additional investment in infants (Strassman 1981).

Similarly, male interest in children during courtship may increase the male's chances of marrying the child's mother. Flinn (this volume) found in a rural Trinidad village that when a female is single and has a child, a prospective husband interacts more with the child before he marries the mother than after they are married, suggesting that males invest in young to enhance their mating opportunities. This is consistent with common lore among men that the best way to "get in good" with a woman with children is to be kind to her children. This phenomenon has also been observed among the Ache foragers of Paraguay, in which males sometimes invest in young not their own to increase their future mating opportunities (Hill, personal communication).

At the very least, the mating effort hypothesis should encourage those studying male–infant relationships in humans to pay attention to variables they might not otherwise consider, such as the nature of male–female relationships (Gubernick 1991), opportunities for female mate choice, the nature and extent to which females and offspring can offer benefits to males, and how these variables may influence male investment in infants.

ACKNOWLEDGMENTS

We thank Barry Hewlett for organizing the symposium that led to this volume, and we thank Jeanne Altmann, Stuart Altmann, Dorothy Cheney, Sarah Hrdy, Robert Seyfarth, and Robert Smuts for very helpful feedback on this manuscript.

REFERENCES

Alexander, R. D. 1974. The evolution of social behavior. *Annual Review of Ecological Systems* 5:325–383.

Alexander, R. D., and Noonan, K. M. 1979. Concealment of ovulation, parental care, and human social evolution. In *Evolutionary Biology and Human Social Behavior: An Anthropological Perspective*. N. A. Chagnon and W. Irons (Eds.), pp. 430–461. North Scituate, MA: Duxbury Press.

Alexander, R. D., Hoogland, J. L., Howard, R. D., Noonan, K. M., and Sherman, P. W. 1979. Sexual dimorphism and breeding systems in pinnipeds, ungulates, primates, and humans. In *Evolutionary Biology and Human Social Behavior: An Anthropological Perspective*. N. A. Chagnon and W. Irons (Eds.), pp. 402–435. North Scituate, MA: Duxbury Press.

Altmann, J. 1980. *Baboon Mothers and Infants*. Cambridge, MA: Harvard University Press.

Andelman, S. 1985. Ecology and reproductive strategies of vervet monkeys (*Cercopithecus aethiops*) in Amboseli National Park, Kenya. Ph.D. dissertation, University of Washington.

Auerbach, K. G., and Taub, D. M. 1979. Paternal behavior in a captive "harem" group of cynomolgus macaques (*Macaca fascicularis*). *Laboratory Primate Newsletter* 18:7–11.

Bales, K. B. 1980. Cumulative scaling of paternalistic behavior in primates. *American Naturalist* 116:454–461.

Barash, D. 1982. *Sociobiology and Behavior*, 2nd ed. Elsevier, NY.

Berenstain, L., Rodman, P. S., and Smith, D. G. 1981. Social relations between fathers and offspring in a captive group of rhesus monkeys *(Macaca mulatta)*. *Animal Behaviour* 29:1057–1063.

Bolin, I. 1981. Male parental behavior in black howler monkeys *(Alouatta palliata pigra)* in Belize and Guatemala. *Primates* 22:349–360.

Bourliere, F., Hunkeler, C., and Bertrand, M. 1979. Ecology and behavior of Lowe's guenon *(Cercopithecus campbelli Lowei)* in the Ivory Coast. In *The Old World Monkeys*. J. Napier and P. Napier (Eds.), pp. 297–333, New York: Academic Press.

Box, H. O. 1975. A social developmental study of young monkeys *(Callithrix jacchus)* within a captive family group. *Primates* 16:155–174.

Breuggeman, J. A. 1973. Parental care in a group of free-ranging rhesus monkeys *(Macaca mulatta)*. *Folia Primatologica* 20:178–210.

Burton, F. D. 1972. The integration of biology and behavior in the socialization of *Macaca sylvana* of Gibraltar. In *Primate Socialization*. F. E. Poirier (Ed.), New York: Random House.

Busse, C. D. 1984. Triadic interactions among male and infant chacma baboons. In *Primate Paternalism*. D. M. Taub (Ed.), pp. 186–212. New York: Van Nostrand Reinhold.

Busse, C. D., and Hamilton, W. J., III. 1981. Infant carrying by male chacma baboons. *Science* 212:1281–1283.

Butynski, T. M. 1982. Harem male replacement and infanticide in the blue monkey *(Cercopithecus mitis stuhlmanni)* in the Kibale Forest, Uganda. *American Journal of Primatology* 3:1–22.

Chapais, B. 1981. The adaptiveness of social relationships among adult rhesus monkeys. Ph.D. Thesis, University of Cambridge.

Chapais, B. 1983a. Adaptive aspects of social relationships among adult rhesus monkeys. In *Primate Social Relationships: An Integrated Approach*. R. A. Hinde (Ed.), pp. 286–289. Oxford: Blackwell.

Chapais, B. 1983b. Structure of the birth season relationship among adult male and female rhesus monkeys. In *Primate Social Relationships: An Integrated Approach*. R. A. Hinde (Ed.), pp. 200–208. Oxford: Blackwell.

Cheney, D. L. 1983a. Extra-familial alliances among vervet monkeys. In *Primate Social Relationships: An Integrated Approach*. R. A. Hinde (Ed.), pp. 278–286. Oxford: Blackwell.

Cheney, D. L. 1983b. Proximate and ultimate factors related to the distribution of male migration. In *Primate Social Relationships: An Integrated Approach*. R. A. Hinde (Ed.), pp. 241–249. Oxford: Blackwell.

Chism, J. L., and Rowell, T. E. 1986. Mating and residence patterns of male patas monkeys. *Ethology* 72:31–39.

Chivers, D. J. 1974. The Siamang in Malaya. *Contributions to Primatology* 4: 1–335.

Chivers, D. J., and Raemakers, J. J. 1980. Long-term changes in behaviour. In: *Malayan Forest Primates: Ten Years' Study in Tropical Rain Forest*. D. J. Chivers (Ed.), pp. 1–335. New York: Plenum Press.

Collins, D. A. 1986a. Interactions between adult male and infant yellow baboons *(Papio c. cynocephalus)* in Tanzania. *Animal Behaviour* 34:430–443.

Collins, D. A. 1986b. Relationships between adult male and infant baboons. In *Primate Ontogeny, Cognition, and Social Behaviour.* J. G. Else and P. C. Lee (Eds.), pp. 205–218. Cambridge: Cambridge University Press.

Cords, M. 1984. Mating patterns and social structure in redtail monkeys *(Cercopithecus ascanius). Zeitschrift für Tierpsychologie* 64:313–339.

Cords, M. 1987. Forest guenons and patas monkeys: Male–male competition in one-male groups. In *Primate Societies.* B. B. Smuts, D. L. Cheney, R. M. Seyfarth, R. W. Wrangham, and T. T. Struhsaker (Eds.), pp. 98–111. Chicago: University of Chicago Press.

Curtin, S. H. 1980. Dusky and banded leaf monkeys. In *Malayan Forest Primates.* D. J. Chivers (Ed.), pp. 107–145. New York: Plenum Press.

Deag, J. M. 1974. A study of the social behavior and ecology of the wild Barbary macaque, *Macaca sylvanus L.* Ph.D. dissertation, Bristol University.

Deag, J. M. 1980. Interactions between males and unweaned Barbary macaques: Testing the agonistic buffering hypothesis. *Behaviour* 75:54–81.

Dunbar, R. I. M. 1984a. Infant-use by male gelada in agonistic contexts: Agonistic buffering, progeny protection, or soliciting support? *Primates* 25:28–35.

Dunbar, R. I. M. 1984b. *Reproductive Decisions.* Princeton: Princeton University Press.

Epple, G. 1975. Parental behavior in *Saguinus fuscicollis* spp. (Callithricidae). *Folia Primatologica* 24:221–238.

Escobar-Paramo, P. 1989. Social relations between infants and other group members in the wild black-capped capuchin *(Cebus apella).* In *Field Studies of New World Monkeys. La Macarena, Columbia.* 2:57–63.

Estrada, A. 1984. Male–infant interactions among free-ranging stumptail macaques. In *Primate Paternalism.* D. M. Taub (Ed.), pp. 56–87. New York: Van Nostrand Reinhold.

Estrada, A., and Sandoval, J. M. 1977. Social relations in a free ranging troop of stumptail macaques *(Macaca arctoides):* Male care behavior I. *Primates* 18:793–813.

Fedigan, L. M. 1976. A study of roles in the Arashiyama monkeys *(Macaca fuscata). Contributions to Primatology* 9:1–95.

Fossey, D. 1979. Development of the mountain gorilla *(Gorilla gorilla berengei):* The first thirty months. In *The Great Apes.* D. A. Hamburg and E. R. McCown (Eds.), pp. 139–186. Menlo Park, CA: Benjamin/Cummings.

Fossey, D. 1983. *Gorillas in the Mist.* Boston: Houghton Mifflin.

Galat-Luong, A., and Galat, G. 1979. Conséquences comportementales des perturbations sociales repetées sur une troupe de Mones de Lowe *Cercopithecus campbelli Lowei* de Côte d'Ivoire. *Terre et Vie* 33:4–57.

Garber, P. A., Moya, L., and Malaga, C. 1984. A preliminary field study of the moustached tamarin monkey *(Saguinus oedipus geoffroyi). Folia Primatologica* 42:17–32.

Goldizen, A. W. 1987. Facultative polygyny and the role of infant-carrying in wild saddle-back tamarins. *Behavioral Ecology and Sociobiology* 20:99–109.

Goldizen, A. W. 1988. Tamarin and marmoset mating systems: Unusual flexibility. *Trends in Ecology and Evolutionary Biology* 3:36–40.

Goodall, J. 1986. *The Chimpanzees of Gombe: Patterns of Behavior.* Cambridge, MA: Harvard University Press.

Gouzoules, H. 1975. Maternal rank and early social interactions of infant stumptail macaques, *Macaca arctoides. Primates* 16:405–418.

Gouzoules, H. 1984. Social relations of males and infants in a troop of Japanese monkeys: A consideration of causal mechanisms. In *Primate Paternalism.* D. M. Taub (Ed.), pp. 127–145. New York: Van Nostrand Reinhold.

Gubernick, D. J. 1991. Biparental care and male–female relations in mammals. In *Protection and Abuse of Young in Animals and Man.* S. Parmigiani, B. Svare, and F. vom Saal (Eds.). London: Harwood Academic Publishers (in press).

Hall, K. R. L. 1967. Social interactions of the adult male and adult females of a patas monkey group. In *Social Communication among Primates.* S. A. Altmann (Ed.), pp. 261–280. Chicago: University of Chicago Press.

Harcourt, A. H. 1979. Social relationships between adult male and female mountain gorillas in the wild. *Animal Behaviour* 27:325–342.

Harcourt, A. H., and Stewart, K. J. 1981. Gorilla male relationships: Can differences during immaturity lead to contrasting reproductive tactics in adulthood? *Animal Behaviour* 29:206–210.

Harding, R. S. O., and Olson, D. 1986. Patterns of mating among male patas monkeys *(Erythrocebus patas)* in Kenya. *American Journal of Primatology* 11:343–358.

Hasegawa, T., and Hiraiwa, M. 1980. Social interactions of orphans observed in a free-ranging troop of Japanese monkeys. *Folia Primatologica* 33:129–158.

Hauser, M. D. 1986. Male responsiveness to infant distress calls in free-ranging vervet monkeys. *Behavioral Ecology and Sociobiology* 19:65–71.

Hausfater, G. 1975. Dominance and reproduction in baboons. *Contributions to Primatology* 7:1–150.

Hendy-Neely, H., and Rhine, R. J. 1977. Social development of stumptail macaques *(Macaca arctoides):* Momentary touching and other interactions with adult males during the infants' first 60 days of life. *Primates* 18:589–600.

Henzi, S. P., and Lawes, M. 1988. Strategic responses of male Samango monkeys *(Cercopithecus aethiops)* to a decline in the number of receptive females. *International Journal of Primatology* 9:479–495.

Hewlett, B. S. 1988. Sexual selection and parental investment among Aka pygmies. In *Human Reproductive Behaviour: A Darwinian Perspective.* L. Betzig, M. Borgerhoff Mulder, and P. Turke (Eds.), pp. 263–276. Cambridge: Cambridge University Press.

Hiraiwa, M. 1981. Maternal and alloparental care in a troop of free-ranging Japanese monkeys. *Primates* 22:309–329.

Hoage, R. J. 1978. Parental care in *Leontopithecus rosalia rosalia*: Sex and age differences in carrying behavior and the role of prior experience. In *The Biology and Conservation of the Callitrichidae.* D. G. Kleiman (Ed.), Washington, D.C.: Smithsonian Institution Press.

Hrdy, S. B. 1976. The care and exploitation of nonhuman primate infants by conspecifics other than the mother. In *Advances in the Study of Behavior.* J. Rosenblatt, R. Hinde, E. Shaw, and C. Beer (Eds.), Vol. 6, pp. 101–158. New York: Academic Press.

Hrdy, S. B. 1977. *The Langurs of Abu: Female and Male Strategies of Reproduction.* Cambridge, MA: Harvard University Press.

Itani, J. 1959. Paternal care in the wild Japanese monkey, *Macaca fuscata. Primates* 2:61–93.

Janson, C. H. 1984. Female choice and mating system of the brown capuchin monkey *Cebus apella* (Primates: Cebidae). *Zeitschrift für Tierpsychologie* 65:177–200.

Janson, C. H. 1986. The mating system as a determinant of social evolution in capuchin monkeys *(Cebus).* In *Primate Ecology and Conservation.* J. G. Else and P. C. Lee (Eds.), pp. 169–179. Cambridge: Cambridge University Press.

Jolly, A. 1966. *Lemur Behavior.* Chicago: University of Chicago Press.

Kaufman, J. H. 1967. Social relations of adult males in a free-ranging band of rhesus monkeys. In *Social Communication among Primates.* S. A. Altmann (Ed.), pp. 73–98. Chicago: University of Chicago Press.

Keddy Hector, A. C., Seyfarth, R. M., and Raleigh, M. J. 1989. Male parental care, female choice and the effect of an audience in vervet monkeys. *Animal Behaviour* 38:262–271.

Kinzey, W. E. 1981. The titi monkeys, genus *Callicebus.* In *Ecology and Behavior in Neotropical Primates.* A. F. Coimbra-Filho and R. A. Mittermeier (Ed.), Vol. 1. Rio de Janeiro: Academia Brasileira de Ciencias.

Kinzey, W. E., Rosenberger, A. L., Heisler, P. S., Prowse, D. L., and Trilling, J. S. 1977. A preliminary field investigation of the yellow-handed titi monkey. *Callicebus torquatus torquatus,* in northern Peru. *Primates* 18:159–181.

Kleiman, D. G., and Malcolm, J. R. 1981. The evolution of male parental investment in mammals. In *Parental Care in Mammals.* D. G. Gubernick and P. H. Klopfer (Eds.), pp. 347–387. New York: Plenum Press.

Koyama, N. 1970. Changes in dominance rank and division of a wild Japanese monkey troop in Arashiyama. *Primates* 11:335–390.

Kuester, J., and Paul, A. 1986. Male–infant relationships in semifree-ranging Barbary macaques *(Macaca sylvanus)* of Affenberg Salem/FRG: Testing the "male care" hypothesis. *American Journal of Primatology* 10:315–327.

Kummer, H. 1968. *Social Organization of Hamadryas Baboons.* Chicago: University of Chicago Press.

Kurland, J. A. 1977. Kin selection in the Japanese monkey. *Contributions to Primatology* 12:1–145.

Kurland, J. A., and Gaulin, S. J. C. 1984. The evolution of male parental investment: Effects of genetic relatedness and feeding ecology on the allocation of reproductive effort. In *Primate Paternalism.* D. M. Taub (Ed.), pp. 259–308. New York: Van Nostrand Reinhold.

Lovejoy, C. O. 1981. The origin of man. *Science* 211:341–350.

Loy, K. M., and Loy, J. 1987. Sexual differences in early social development among captive patas monkeys. In *Comparative Behavior of African Monkeys.* E. L. Zucker (Ed.), pp. 23–37. New York: Alan R. Liss.

MacRoberts, M. H. 1970. Social organization of Barbary apes *(Macaca sylvanus)* on Gibraltar. *Journal of Physical Anthropology* 33:83–100.

Mitchell, G. D., and Brandt, E. M. 1972. Paternal behavior in primates. In *Primate Socialization.* F. E. Poirer (Ed.), New York: Random House.

Mori, U. 1979a. Development of sociability and social status. *Contributions to Primatology* 16:125–154.

Mori, U. 1979b. Individual relationships within a unit. *Contributions to Primatology* 16:93–124.

Nicolson, N. A. 1982. Weaning and the development of independence in olive baboons. Ph.D. Thesis, Harvard University.

Nishida, T. 1983. Alloparental behavior in wild chimpanzees of the Mahale Mountains, Tanzania. *Folia Primatologica* 41:1–33.

Packer, C. 1980. Male care and exploitation of infants in *Papio anubis*. *Animal Behaviour* 28:521–527.

Packer, C., and Pusey, A. E. 1979. Female aggression and male membership in troops of Japanese macaques and olive baboons. *Folia Primatologica* 31:212–218.

Raleigh, M. J., and McGuire, M. T. 1989. Female influences on male dominance acquisition in captive vervet monkeys, *Cercopithecus aethiops sabaeus*. *Animal Behaviour* 38:59–67.

Ransom, T. W., and Ransom, B. S. 1971. Adult male–infant relations among baboons *(Papio anubis)*. *Folia Primatologica* 16:179–195.

Redican, W. K. 1976. Adult male–infant interactions in nonhuman primates. In *The Role of the Father in Child Development*. M. E. Lamb (Ed.), pp. 345–385. New York: Wiley.

Ridley, M. 1978. Paternal care. *Animal Behaviour* 26:904–932.

Robbins Leighton, D. 1987. Gibbons: Territoriality and monogamy. In *Primate Societies*. B. B. Smuts, D. L. Cheney, R. M. Seyfarth, R. W. Wrangham, and T. T. Struhsaker (Eds.), pp. 135–145. Chicago: University of Chicago Press.

Rowell, T. E. 1988. Beyond the one-male group. *Behaviour* 104:189–201.

Rudran, R. 1978. Socioecology of the blue monkey *(Cercopithecus mitis stuhlmanni)* of the Kibale Forest, Uganda. *Smithsonian Contributions to Zoology* 249:1–88.

Scott, L. M. 1984. Reproductive behavior of adolescent female baboons *(Papio anubis)* in Kenya. In *Female Primates: Studies by Women Primatologists*. M. Small (Ed.), pp. 77–100. New York: Alan R. Liss.

Sekulic, R. 1983. Spatial relationships between recent mothers and other troop members in red howler monkeys. *(Alouatta seniculus)*. *Primates* 24:475–485.

Seyfarth, R. M. 1978. Social relationships among adult male and female baboons, II. Behavior throughout the female reproductive cycle. *Behaviour* 64:227–247.

Sicotte, P. 1989. Female migration and differential social development in infant mountain gorillas. *Anthroquest* 40:3–4.

Sigg, H., Stolba, A., Abegglen, J. J., and Dasser, V. 1982. Life history of hamadryas baboons: Physical development, infant mortality, reproductive parameters and family relationships. *Primates* 23:473–487.

Simonds, P. E. 1965. The bonnet macaque in South India. In *Primate Behavior: Field Studies of Monkeys and Apes*. I. DeVore (Ed.), pp. 175–196. New York: Holt, Rinehart, & Winston.

Simonds, P. E. 1974. Sex differences in bonnet macaque networks and social structure. *Archives of Sexual Behavior* 3:151–166.

Small, M. F. 1990. Promiscuity in Barbary macaques. *American Journal of Primatology* 20:267–282.

Smith, E. O., and Peffer-Smith, P. G. 1984. Adult male-immature interactions in captive stumptail macaques *(Macaca arctoides)*. In *Primate Paternalism*. D. M. Taub (Ed.), pp. 88–112. New York: Van Nostrand Rinehold.

Smith, E. O., and Whitten, P. L. 1988. Triadic interactions in savanna-dwelling baboons. *International Journal of Primatology* 9:409–424.

Smuts, B. B. 1983a. Dynamics of special relationships between adult male and female olive baboons. In *Primate Social Relationships: An Integrated Approach*. R. A. Hinde (Ed.), pp. 112–116. Oxford: Blackwell.

Smuts, B. B. 1983b. Special relationships between adult male and female olive baboons: Selective advantages. In *Primate Social Relationships: An Integrated Approach*. R. A. Hinde, (Ed.), pp. 262–266. Oxford: Blackwell.

Smuts, B. B. 1985. *Sex and Friendship in Baboons*. Hawthorne, NY: Aldine.

Snowdon, C. T., and Suomi, S. J. 1982. Paternal behavior in primates. In *Child Nurturance:* Volume 3. *Studies of Development in Nonhuman Primates*. H. Fitzgerald, J. Mullins, and P. Gage (Eds.), pp. 63–108. New York: Plenum.

Sommer, V. 1988. Male competition and coalitions in langurs *(Presbytis entellus)* at Jodhpur, Rajasthan, India. *Human Evolution* 3:261–278.

Stanford, C. 1989. The capped langur in Bangladesh: Ecology and behavior of a colobine living in one-male groups. Ph.D. dissertation, University of California, Berkeley.

Starin, E. D. 1978. Food transfer by wild titi monkeys *(Callicebus torquatus torquatus)*. *Folia Primatologia* 30:145–151.

Stein, D. M. 1984a. The ontogeny of infant-adult male relationships during the first year of life for yellow baboons *(Papio cynocephalus)*. In *Primate Paternalism*. D. M. Taub (Ed.), pp. 213–243. New York: Van Nostrand Reinhold.

Stein, D. M. 1984b. The Sociobiology of Infant and Adult Male Baboons. Norwood, NJ: Ablex.

Stern, B. R., and Smith, D. G. 1984. Sexual behavior and paternity in three captive groups of rhesus monkeys *(Macaca mulatta) Animal Behaviour* 32: 23–32.

Strassman, B. I. 1981. Sexual selection, paternal care, and concealed ovulation in humans. *Ethology and Sociobiology* 2:31–40.

Struhsaker, T. T. 1967. Social structure among vervet monkeys *(Cercopithecus aethiops)*. *Behaviour* 29:83–121.

Struhsaker, T. T., and Leland, L. 1979. Socioecology of five sympatric monkey species in the Kibale Forest, Uganda. In *Advances in the Study of Behavior*. J. S. Rosenblatt, R. A. Hinde, C. Beer, and M. C. Busnel (Eds.), Vol. 9, pp. 159–228. New York: Academic Press.

Strum, S. C. 1984. Why males use infants. In *Primate Paternalism*. D. M. Taub (Ed.), pp. 146–185. New York: Van Nostrand Reinhold.

Strum, S. C. 1987. *Almost Human*. New York: Random House.

Sugiyama, Y. 1971. Characteristics of the social life of bonnet macaques *(Macaca radiata)*. *Primates* 12:247–266.

Symons, D. 1979. *The Evolution of Human Sexuality*. New York: Oxford University Press.

Takahata, Y. 1982a. Social relations between adult males and females of Japanese monkeys in the Arashiyama B troop. *Primates* 23:1–23.

Takahata, Y. 1982b. The socio-sexual behavior of Japanese monkeys. *Zeitschrift für Tierpsychologie* 59:89–108.

Taub, D. M. 1980. Female choice and mating strategies among wild Barbary macaques *(Macaca sylvanus)*. In *The Macaques: Studies in Ecology, Behavior and Evolution*. D. G. Lindburg (Ed.), pp. 287–344. New York: Van Nostrand Reinhold.

Taub, D. M. 1980b. Testing the 'agonistic buffering' hypothesis. I. The dynamics of participation in the triadic interaction. *Behavioral Ecology and Sociobiology* 6:187–197.

Taub, D. M. 1984. Male caretaking behavior among wild Barbary macaques *(Macaca sylvanus)*. In *Primate Paternalism*. D. M. Taub (Ed.), pp. 20–55. New York: Van Nostrand Reinhold.

Taylor, H., Teas, J., Richie, T., and Southwick, C. 1978. Social interactions between adult male and infant rhesus monkeys in Nepal. *Primates* 19:343–351.

Terborgh, J., and Goldizen, A. 1985. On the mating system of the cooperatively breeding saddle-backed tamarin *(Saguinus fuscicollis)* *Behavioral Ecology and Sociobiology* 16:293–299.

Tilford, B., and Nadler, R. D. 1978. Male parental behavior in a captive group of lowland gorillas *(Gorilla gorilla gorilla)*. *Folia Primatolgica* 29:218–228.

Trivers, R. L. 1972. Parental investment and sexual selection. In *Sexual Selection and the Descent of Man, 1871–1971*. B. Campbell (Ed.), pp. 136–179. Chicago: Aldine.

Tsingalia, H. M., and Rowell, T. E. 1984. The behaviour of adult male blue monkeys. *Zeitschrift für Tierpsychologie* 64:253–268.

Turke, P. W. 1984. Effects of ovulatory concealment and synchrony on protohominid mating systems and parental roles. *Ethology and Sociobiology* 5:33–44.

van Noordwijk, M. A., and van Schaik, C. P. 1988. Male careers in Sumatran long-tailed macaques *(Macaca fascicularis)*. *Behaviour* 107:24–43.

van Schaik, C. P., and van Noordwijk, M. A. 1989. The special role of male *Cebus* monkeys in predation avoidance and its effect on group composition. *Behavioral Ecology and Sociobiology* 24:265–276.

Vessey, S. H., and Meikle, D. B. 1984. Free-living rhesus monkeys: Adult male interactions with infants and juveniles. In *Primate Paternalism*. D. M. Taub (Ed.), pp. 113–126. New York: Van Nostrand Reinhold.

Vogt, J. L. 1984. Interactions between adult males and infants in prosimians and New World Monkeys. In *Primate Paternalism*. D. M. Taub (Ed.), pp. 346–376. New York: Van Nostrand Reinhold.

Vogt, J. L., Carlson, H., and Menzel, E. 1978. Social behavior of a marmoset *(Saguinus fuscicollis)* group, 1: Parental care and infant development. *Primates* 19:715–726.

de Waal, F. B. M. 1989. *Peacemaking in Primates*. Cambridge, MA: Harvard University Press.

Whitten, P. L. 1987. Infants and adult males. In *Primate Societies*. B. B. Smuts,

D. L. Cheney, R. M. Seyfarth, R. W. Wrangham, and T. T. Struhsaker (Eds.), pp. 343–357. Chicago: University of Chicago Press.

Wittenberger, J. F., and Tilson, R. L. 1980. The evolution of monogamy: Hypotheses and evidence. *Annual Review of Ecological Systems* 11:197–232.

Wright, P. C. 1984. Biparental care in *Aotus trivirgatus* and *Callicebus moloch*. In *Female Primates: Studies by Women Primatologists*. M. Small (Ed.), pp. 60–75. New York: Alan R. Liss.

Chapter 2

Paternal Effect on Offspring Survivorship among Ache and Hiwi Hunter–Gatherers: Implications for Modeling Pair-Bond Stability

A. Magdalena Hurtado and Kim R. Hill

The effects of father absence on child morbidity and mortality constitute an area of considerable interest in the medical and social sciences (Desai 1970; Franklin and Vial 1981; Marchione 1980; Brown 1973; Lancaster 1988 and references therein; Epenshade 1979; Daly and Wilson 1985; Berklov and Sklar 1976; Jason et al. 1983; Golding et al. 1986; Skjaerven and Irgens 1988). The few studies that have been conducted indicate that there are large differences in the effects of father absence on child survivorship across societies. In some populations the absence of fathers leads to a decrease in child health while in others paternal abandonment may lead to an increase or to no change in the health of offspring (see Lancaster 1988). For example, some studies show that in modern economies with well-developed health care systems child survivorship is negatively affected by the absence of fathers (e.g., Sweden, see Skjaerven and Irgens 1988), while in less developed countries child survivorship is sometimes positively associated with father absence (e.g., Dominican Republic, Brown 1973). Interestingly, this high variation in paternal effects on child health across human populations is paralleled by a rich diversity in human mating systems.

In recent years, anthropologists specializing in human behavioral ecology have become increasingly interested in the relationship between mortality in offspring and the differential distribution of parental care and male and female mating strategies (Draper and Harpending 1982; Kaplan and Hill 1985a; Harpending and Draper 1986; Pennington and

Harpending 1988; Borgerhoff Mulder 1988; Hewlett 1988). Child mortality is of particular interest in human behavioral ecology because it is an important component of reproductive success or biological fitness.

In this chapter we report preliminary analyses of the relationship between father absence and child mortality in two groups of hunter–gatherers: the Ache of Eastern Paraguay and the Hiwi of Southwestern Venezuela. We also present a preliminary model of the relationship between *paternal effectiveness in reducing child mortality* and marital pair-bond stability. The comparative analysis of Ache and Hiwi foragers is particularly revealing due to extreme differences in the socioecologies of these two hunting and gathering societies.

Even though we focus primarily on the anthropological literature on mating systems, it is important to note that a number of more sophisticated and comprehensive models of male and female desertion of mates have been proposed by biologists (see Trivers 1972; Maynard Smith and Ridpath 1972; Maynard Smith 1977; Parker and McNair 1978; Murray 1984, 1985; Brown 1987). Due to the primarily anthropological focus of this introduction to comparative research on Ache and Hiwi mating systems, we will not incorporate these more exhaustive models in this chapter. There is nevertheless considerable overlap between the causal components considered in our analyses and in the behavioral ecology literature on mating systems (Trivers 1972; Maynard Smith and Ridpath 1972; Maynard Smith 1977; Parker and McNair 1978; Murray 1984, 1985; Brown 1987).

THEORY

A key aspect of human mating systems is male reproductive strategies. Modern evolutionary theory allows us to generate useful general predictions regarding the conditions under which fathers might be expected to allocate most of their resources into raising few offspring with one spouse, and the conditions under which they might be expected to invest heavily in obtaining mates instead of providing paternal care. However, the predictions are at present too general and difficult to translate into rigorous hypothesis testing because adequate data collection on most variables of interest minimally requires frequent sampling over the entire life span of subjects.

Males among sexually reproducing organisms have three general alternatives for investment of time and energy: improving their own survivorship and growth (somatic investment), obtaining copulations (mating investment—MI), and increasing offspring survivorship (parental investment—PI).[1] Since somatic investment is mainly important because of its long-term effects on both mating and parenting success, we can focus primarily on the way total fitness is affected by a male's decisions concerning resource allocation to parenting versus mating investment. The total amount of resources (i.e., time, energy, food, wealth, etc.) that males have available to invest in parenting or mating is finite such that investment in parental care is expected to compete with investment in securing many mates. On average, natural selection is expected to favor individuals who allocate investment in mating and parenting in ways that yield a higher number of surviving offspring than the number that could be potentially produced via alternative allocations of mating and parenting investment.

Harpending and Draper's (1986) theoretical work on pair-bond stability in humans is an important step toward specifying conditions under which human males might prefer to invest most of their time and resources in parenting, or conversely, invest mainly in obtaining matings (see also Kleiman and Malcolm 1981; Lovejoy 1981). They have proposed a pair-bond stability model describing how differences in the effects of paternal abandonment on child survivorship across socioecologies may explain men's preference for stable monogamous unions over the frequent desertion of their mates and vice versa. Specifically, they propose that in societies in which father absence results in significantly lower offspring survivorship, pair-bond stability will be high. At the other extreme, higher divorce rates will be favored in situations where the presence of fathers in the households has a negligible or negative effect on the survivorship of their offspring.

The hypothesized relationship between the effects of paternal investment on offspring survival and resultant pair-bond stability in a given socioecological context is a function of the fitness gains associated with an additional unit of paternal investment versus an additional unit of mating investment. When an additional unit of paternal care yields less of a fitness increase than would an equal investment in obtaining copulations, males are expected to seek matings rather than continue to invest in offspring. Under extreme conditions where paternal investment does not increase offspring survivorship, it is expected that males will direct all of their resources into mating. On the other hand, some conditions may favor high parental investment, which should often lead to high pair-bond stability. This is because high levels of paternal investment probably preclude frequent male desertion of mates since father's ability to increase child survivorship probably occurs along several dimensions that require continual presence and much of an individual's time, energy, and resources (i.e., human fathers simultaneously protect their children from harm by conspecifics or predators, feed and teach their children valuable social, economic, and other skills, and provision and protect mates such that they can be more effective mothers in turn). Consequently, under conditions in which fathers can positively affect child survivorship, it is expected that high levels of marital stability will result in highest fitness.

The pair-bond stability model is a useful starting point for identifying specific socioecological conditions that might be expected to affect the fitness payoffs of paternal abandonment and the fitness payoffs of paternal care. These two variables are probably independently affected by aspects of the physical and social environment in important ways. The payoff to mating investment, for example, is likely to be affected by the adult sex ratio and female fertility (Harpending and Draper 1986). In contexts characterized by an abundant number of females with high fertility, there are many opportunities for a temporarily mated male to produce more offspring with other unencumbered females. On the other hand, paternal care-independent and care-dependent causes of child mortality may represent important determinants of the fitness payoffs to paternal care. High child mortality due to paternal care-independent causes (e.g., some infectious diseases) favors abandonment because there is little fathers can do to reduce child mortality. However, when child mortality is primarily due to paternal care-dependent factors (e.g., protection from conspecifics, nutritional deficiencies), stable monogamous unions may be favored (Harpending and Draper, 1986:46).

In summary, the simple model of pair-bond stability described above assumes that male fitness is a function of two important components, male parental and mating investment and their respective payoffs, such that:

$$F_m = (MI) \times (M) + (PI) \times (P) \tag{1}$$

where F_m = fitness of males

MI = investment of resources in obtaining copulations (mating investment)

M = fitness payoff per unit of mating investment (MI)

PI = investment of resources to effect offspring survival (parental investment)

P = fitness payoff per unit of paternal investment (PI)

and that pair-bond stability is directly proportional to PI/MI.

Thus, if the left side of Equation (1) is to be maximized, it is argued that the level of pair-bond stability can be predicted by the relative size of the M and P components in the formula. When M stays relatively constant, the model suggests that changes in the payoff to paternal investment *(P)* can be used to predict pair-bond stability. Increases in *P* should lead to increases in *PI*, and complementary, inevitable reductions in the mating investment component *(MI)*. Thus, if pair-bond stability is a function of *PI/MI*, increased payoffs to parenting will lead to increased pair-bond stability. When specific socioecological factors are taken into account it becomes apparent that the size of the *M* and the *P* components are in turn determined by subsistence opportunities, disease ecology, female fertility, group composition, and other such factors.

BACKGROUND

The Ache[2] are a native population of Paraguay who until recently were full-time foragers (Hill and Hurtado 1989). By the end of the 1970s, four distinct macrogroups of Ache had made contact with local Paraguayans and government officials. At contact, three of these groups were rather small with 35–65 individuals each. The remaining group, the Northern Ache, however, were more numerous with approximately 600 individuals just prior to contact. Recall by informants suggests that the median size of a band was 48 people; the range on a given day was 3 to 160. The Northern Ache, who are the focus of this study, made peaceful contact between 1971 and 1978 and subsequently settled as part-time agricultural farmers in several reservations (Hill and Hurtado 1989).

The Northern Ache traditionally foraged in an area approximately 18,500 km², between 54–56° west and 24–25° south. This area is drained to the west by the Paraguay River and to the East by the Parana River. It is characterized by rolling hills covered with tropical forest vegetation and grasslands surrounded by stands of palms. The Ache hunt and gather primarily in the forest. Precipitation in Eastern Paraguay is highly unpredictable from month to month and from year to year. The mean annual precipitation is approximately 1600 mm. Temperature changes predictably across seasons with mean low temperatures ranging from approximately 10°C in the cold season to 20°C in the warm season.

Descriptions and analyses of foraging behavior (Hawkes et al. 1982; Hill 1987), hunting (Hill and Hawkes 1983; Kaplan and Hill 1985b), food sharing (Kaplan et al. 1984), men's and women's time allocation (Hill et al. 1985; Hurtado et al. 1985) and child development (Kaplan and Dove 1986) among Ache hunter–gatherers have been published over the past decade.

The Hiwi are hunter–gatherers of Southwestern Venezuela. They live in the extremely seasonal neotropical savannas of the Orinoco River

Basin where a larger population of closely related Guahibo-speaking populations reside. Although all the Guahibo-speaking populations refer to themselves as "Hiwi," here the term Hiwi is used exclusively to refer to the hunting and gathering bands of the Guahibo population, as no other adequate label is available. The local criollo populations use the term "Cuiva," which has strong derogatory connotations.

The Hiwi territory is confined to the drainages of the upper Cinaruco, Capanaparo, Ariporo, Agua Clara, and Meta Rivers. The main territory of the Venezuelan Hiwi is confined to areas contiguous to the Cinaruco River (see Hurtado and Hill 1990b).

Close to 90% of the precipitation falls during the months of May–November followed by an intervening period of severe moisture stress between January and March. During these dry months, monthly precipitation averages fall below 25 mm (Hurtado and Hill 1990) and often there is no rain in January and February. The ecological consequence of this rainfall regime is marked fluctuations in the temporal and spatial distribution, the biomass, and productivity of plants and animals. In the past, the Hiwi coped with these fluctuations by moving as much as 150 km from one food patch to another over a huge range that included three river drainages in Venezuela and Colombia. This transhumancy has recently been greatly constrained by the presence of military forces in the area, and by cattle ranching.

Changes in temperatures across seasons are less drastic than fluctuations in precipitation. Temperatures range between an average daily maximum of 37.7°C in March to an average daily minimum of 19°C in December (Hurtado and Hill 1990).

The population size of the Venezuelan and Colombian Hiwi hunter–gatherers is approximately 800 individuals (Hurtado and Hill 1987). Venezuelan and Colombian Hiwi bands visit one another primarily during the dry season when nocturnal traveling across savannas is less arduous than in the wet season. The size of the Venezuelan Hiwi population was 290 individuals in 1988 (Hurtado and Hill 1990b). These 290 individuals form two semipermanent residential bands. The bands form very large camps including all members of the band during much of the year, but also break up into smaller bush camps for periods of up to 4 weeks at a time. The two residential settlements are located near the Cinaruco river within a 4-hour walk of each other on a reserve bounded by two rivers and an incipient cattle ranch: 12,058 hectares set aside in 1971 by presidential decree.

The larger band (188 individuals) is settled in the middle of a dry savanna next to the local indian services office. We studied the more isolated, smaller band (102 individuals) that lives in the gallery forest along the Cinaruco River. Its central place has been moved several times over the past 20 years.

Socioecological Differences in Paternal Care-Dependent Child Mortality

Obtaining adequate measures of the difference in the relative contribution of paternal care-dependent and care-independent child mortality between societies is methodologically challenging. To date we can only guess about how the Ache and Hiwi population might differ along these lines. Food consumption among the Ache is high relative to the Hiwi (Hill et al. 1984; Hurtado and Hill 1987), and the food sharing pattern of the Ache generally ensures that no individual undergoes severe nutritional stress (Kaplan et al. 1984). The forest environment of Ache foragers appears to contain more insect pests and dangerous animals than the grassland savana of Venezuela. Ache foragers also live in new uncleared forest camps each day whereas the Hiwi inhabit well cleared permanent villages during much of the year. Consequently, in the Ache case careful monitoring of children is crucial to child survivorship. However, this is probably a more important determinant of maternal care than paternal care strategies (Hurtado 1985; Hurtado et al. 1985; Hurtado and Hill 1990a). Ache men spend relatively little time holding, playing, grooming, or carrying their children and spend most of the day hunting or in other activities. Men tend to take care of infants and children when their wives leave camp for water, firewood, or to gather food, and usually do very little childcare when the children's mother is in camp (see Hill 1983).

Among the Ache, fathers appear to play a more important role in protecting their offspring from the infanticidal/homicidal attacks of conspecific adult males (Hill 1990). The positive effects of men's hunting ability on child survivorship that we have previously reported (Kaplan and Hill 1985a) may be due in part to the better treatment that the children of good hunters receive from the other men in the band than to the food that fathers share with their offspring (Kaplan and Hill 1985b).

In contrast, among the Hiwi food consumption levels are relatively low, and paternal food provisioning seems to be a key determinant of child survivorship, particularly during long seasons of food scarcity when men hunt and gather close to 90% of the food consumed (Hurtado and Hill 1990b). This paternal provisioning may be crucial for breaking the cycle of frequent microbial intestinal disease bouts associated with increasing levels of malnutrition, and ultimately death. It is our impression that gut infections and diarrhea are much more common and serious health hazards to Hiwi children than they are for Ache children (Hurtado et al. 1988). Unlike Ache fathers, Hiwi men spend considerable amounts of time taking care of their children (unpublished data). Men frequently hold infants and carefully monitor older children when women engage in food processing activities, manufacturing, and foraging. Nevertheless, Hiwi fathers do not spend as much time taking care of the young as do women on average. Preliminary analyses suggest that paternal food provisioning probably has a greater effect on child survivorship than does this kind of direct paternal care. Among the Hiwi, men whose caloric return rates per hour spent searching and acquiring food is higher than the median for all hunters have more surviving offspring than hunters whose rates fall below the median (unpublished data).

In summary, even though paternal care-dependent causes of child mortality appear to be important in both Ache and Hiwi society, the types of care required from fathers to prevent death in offspring are very different. Ache fathers may influence their children's long-term health to a great extent by building alliances via hunting partnerships with other men, whereas Hiwi fathers may gain more from putting much of their time and energy into making sure that their own children consume a reasonably sufficient and constant diet across all seasons of the year.

Socioecological Differences in Mating Opportunities

The neotropical forests of Eastern Paraguay and the llanos (savannas) of Venezuela and Colombia are very different habitats. Seasonal fluctuations in rainfall and food availability are more extreme for the Hiwi of Venezuela than for the Ache of Paraguay. Thus, while foraging opportunities change dramatically across the year for Hiwi foragers, they are fairly constant for the Ache year round (see Hill et al. 1984; Hurtado and Hill 1990). In the Ache environment, foods of different types are relatively evenly distributed across time and space. Even though single meat and vegetable resources can be patchily distributed and differ in availability across the year, their distribution in time and space overlaps considerably across a vast territory with very low population density (Hill et al. 1984). In contrast, the Hiwi environment is extremely patchy with plant and animal resources found in discrete clumps mainly along river banks and streams or in transitory areas between the gallery forest and the savanna (Hurtado and Hill 1988; Hurtado and Hill 1990b). There are few areas that have the preferred combination of abundant root and fruit patches, as well as lagoons with rich supplies of fish, capybara, alligators, and turtles in the dry season and effective population densities are high.

Associated with differences in forest cover and seasonality we find large differences in the social systems of Ache and Hiwi hunter–gatherers. While territorial defense plays a minor role in Ache society, it seems to constitute a major factor in the distribution, size, and warfare patterns of Hiwi bands. Hiwi territories appear to be discrete with well-defined boundaries. Bands seem to have exclusive rights to these territories, with violations poorly tolerated.

Low levels of territorial defense and amicable interband relations among the Ache facilitate considerable movement of individuals across bands and increases the pool of mates for individuals of marriageable age. Even though the Ache live in small bands ranging in size between 7 and 30 individuals, movement across bands in combination with a total population size of approximately 600 individuals increases the mating opportunities that are open to men. An unmarried Ache man can always find a potential female mating partner by simply visiting each foraging band in turn. In contrast, the Hiwi population with a total size of approximately 800 individuals is extremely endogamous. Marriage across bands occurs rarely and visiting is often dangerous or impossible. Consequently, the mating pool is considerably smaller for individuals of marriageable age at any given point in time among the Hiwi than is the case for the Ache.

Low seasonal fluctuations in food supply and higher levels of protein and caloric consumption may be responsible for higher female fertility rates among the Ache than among the Hiwi. This difference in the socioecologies of Hiwi and Ache foragers also affects the difference in the number of potential mating partners for males of the two groups. The Ache have a high fertility population with a positive growth rate and a very young population age structure (Hill 1990). This disproportionately inflates the number of individuals in the younger age groups with respect to older age groups. The size of the younger female cohorts will in turn affect the number of potential female partners that are available to men in the population because females become incorporated into the mating system several years before males. The Hiwi on the other hand are characterized by low fertility with a negative population growth rate (Hurtado and Hill 1987), a relatively old population age structure, and fewer mating opportunities available to men than is the case for the Ache.

Lastly, differences in the availability of reproductive-age females between the Hiwi and the Ache population is exacerbated by differences in the adult sex ratio for each population. Among the Hiwi, mating opportunities available to males are greatly reduced by a high male-biased sex ratio from birth through middle age. This is due in part to high female infanticide rates apparently caused by women's strong preference for sons over daughters (Hurtado and Hill 1987). The Ache, in contrast, show a male-biased sex ratio in the junior age grades, but a relatively even sex ratio in most adult categories (see Table 1).

Differences in levels of mating opportunities between Ache and Hiwi bands permeate other aspects of social organization in interesting ways.

While there is little segregation in space by sex among the Ache, interactions among nonspouses in the Hiwi community are quite restricted. Ache men and women who are not married to each other are frequently seen having long private conversations or spending time together in tactile contact even in public. Among the Hiwi mixed sex interaction among unmarried individuals is almost completely absent and tactile contact between unmarried adults of different sexes has never been observed. In addition, when Hiwi men and women that are not married to one another converse, they face opposite directions and speak in a loud voice, so that their conversation may be overheard by all band members. Married couples, on the other hand, do not follow these behavioral restrictions and spend considerable amounts of time in close proximity to one another and converse privately for hours at a time facing each other.

Differences in levels of mating opportunities between the Ache and the Hiwi occur alongside marked contrasts in marital stability. While serial monogamy and extra marital promiscuity is very common among the Ache, stable lifetime monogamous unions with almost no extramarital copulation is the normative mating pattern among the Hiwi.

The differences in mating systems are reflected in the roles of Ache and Hiwi fathers. Even though men do almost all the hunting in both societies, the Ache share most of the meat they acquire outside the nuclear family (Kaplan et al. 1984). Ache men not only acquire food for their spouses and children but also for all other individuals that are in their residential band. This food sharing is associated with high levels of male–male cooperation in hunting as opposed to cooperation among spouses. In contrast, Hiwi men share most of the meat and other foods they acquire with their spouse and offspring only (Lyles et al. 1990), and spouse cooperation in foraging activities is commonly observed. In addition, while Ache men specialize almost exclusively in hunting throughout the year, Hiwi men not only do all the hunting but also gather most of the fruit consumed during the late dry/early wet season, and do considerable amounts of childcare in the late wet season when women gather large amounts of tubers (Hurtado and Hill 1990a). Thus, while in the former season, husbands free their wives from strenuous foraging activities, in the latter season they free them from the burden of having to care for small infants and children during food collecting trips. Women, in turn, very frequently accompany their husbands on hunting outings. Even though the women do not kill prey, they help their husbands with the paddling and steering of canoes while they shoot game along the river bank. In summary, economic and other kinds of cooperation between spouses appears to be more common among the Hiwi than among the Ache.

METHODS

The data presented in this paper were collected over a period of 10 years by Hill and Hurtado. A demographic interview developed by Hill in 1981 is the main source of data in this study. The same interview was used in both the Ache and Hiwi populations, however, interviews with Ache individuals were conducted without the help of translators whereas among the Hiwi, it was necessary to use a bilingual (Hiwi/Spanish) informant. The investigators have not yet developed the necessary language skills to carry out complicated interviews without assistance.

The interviews are designed to record the following reproductive experiences of all men and women in the population: live births of own children, names of an individual's mates over the course of a lifetime, and dates of divorce, dates and causes of death for children, dates of death or divorce for each child's parents, and a large number of other variables not relevant to this study. Individuals were also asked the same questions about their deceased and living siblings. Reproductive events and their outcomes were recorded for each ego in chronological order and coded for computer analyses.

The Ache data set for this study consists of information on 832 births provided by 161 reproductive histories of individual women. The Hiwi data set is substantially smaller with information on 135 births recorded in 23 reproductive history interviews. The methodology used to determine the dates of birth and death, or divorce of all individuals mentioned in interviews is quite elaborate and thoroughly described in Hill (1990). Here it is sufficient to mention that most dates were assigned based on information provided by relative age lists and known calendar dates and reference to previously dated events.

This method to determine ages in combination with questions concerning causes of death and the survival/marital status of fathers provided the necessary information to measure child mortality by age, and as a function of the marital and survivorship status of father, as well as population-level divorce rates and female total fertility rates. Standard life table analyses were used to estimate the survivorship rates of children to different ages, lx, as a function of characteristics of their parents' marriage or father's death. Pearson and Mantel–Haenszel χ^2 tests for statistical significance and one-tailed probability values less than or equal to 0.05 were used to test alternatives against null hypotheses.

Because the Ache have gradually become settled agricultural farmers in the past two decades, we report only precontact, retrospective demographic data. Thus, the Ache data set is censored at 1970, the last year that all Ache individuals lived as uncontacted hunter–gatherers. In contrast, we analyzed the entire Hiwi data set, which represents the precontact and postcontact periods. This is because the Hiwi have maintained an almost intact foraging economy in spite of considerable exposure to outsiders since the late 1950s.

RESULTS

The Ache before Contact

The Effects of Father's Death on Child Survivorship. Among Ache hunter–gatherers, the probability of child survivorship tends to be lower when father dies than when father lives. This is true for all children up to 10 years of age at which point paternal mortality ceases to have an effect on child survivorship (n = 294 births; Figure 1). However, in our sample, this difference is statistically significant only in the 1- to 5-year interval [Pearson's χ^2 = 44.2; p (one-tailed) = 0.04] with children without fathers experiencing a risk of death 2.6 times higher than children with fathers. In all the other intervals, there is no statistically significant effect, primarily due to high mortality for all children in the first interval and a very small paternal effect in later intervals [0–1 year Pearson's χ^2 = 0.83, p = 0.49; 5–10 year Pearson's χ^2 = 2.36, p (one-tailed) = 0.1149]. The effect of father's death on child survivorship is, however, highly significant when all age strata are examined [Mantel–Haenszel χ^2 = 4.48, p (one-tailed) = 0.017].

The Effects of Divorce on Child Survivorship. Similarly, parental divorce within the first year of life and in subsequent 5-year intervals also leads to higher child mortality than when no parental divorce is experienced (n = 292 births; Figure 2). Again, at age 10 and beyond, the marital status of parents appears to have little impact on subsequent survivorship. Between birth and 1 year of age, the effect of divorce on child survivorship is highly significant [Pearson's χ^2 = 13, p (one-tailed) = 0.0001]. In this age interval, children who experience parental divorce are 2.6 times more likely to die than children who do not get divorced. In the 1- to 5-year interval the effects of divorce are also significant [Pearson's χ^2 = 5.8, p (one-tailed) = 0.007] with children of divorce parents being 2.9 times more likely to die than children whose parents stay together. Not surprisingly, the effect of divorce on child survivorship is highly significant when all age strata are examined [Mantel–Haenszel χ^2 = 10.2, p (one-tailed) = 0.0007].

Parental divorce leads to increases in mortality from certain causes but not others (Figure 3). When the analyses is stratified by cause of death, it was found that children who experience parental divorce between birth

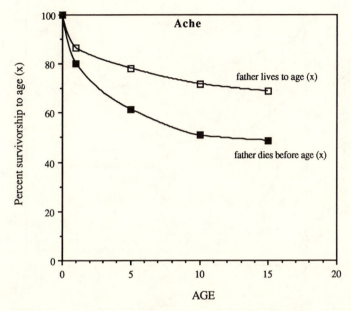

Figure 1. Percent of children who survive to a specified age as a function of whether their father lives until they reach that age or dies before they reach that age. This is equivalent to the lx calculation in demographic analyses and calculated as the product of age specific probabilities of survival (px) through each age interval as a function of whether father does or does not survive to the end of that interval. Probability of survival through an interval px = number of children who survive an interval/number of children who enter an interval.

and 1 year of age are more frequently victims of sickness, homicide, and capture in raiding by Paraguayans than children whose parents stay together [Pearson's χ^2 = 3.8, p (one-tailed) = 0.0021; Pearson's χ^2 = 7.7, p (one-tailed) = 0.0055; and Pearson's χ^2 = 8.9, p (one-tailed) = 0.0028, respectively]. Children whose parents were divorced before their first birthday were not more likely to die at birth or from accidental causes. In later age strata, only differences in mortality due to illness reach statistical significance [1–5 years Pearson's χ^2 = 7.3, p (one-tailed) = 0.0003], although mortality rates from homicide and capture in warfare are consistently higher in children whose parents are divorced. When all age strata are combined the effect of parental divorce on the probability of death from sickness, homicide, and capture in warfare are all statistically significant [Mantel–Haenszel χ^2 = 2.98, p (one-tailed) = 0.042; Mantel–Haenszel χ^2 = 3.1, p (one-tailed) = 0.04; and Mantel–Haenszel χ^2 = 3, p (one-tailed) = 0.042, respectively]. Thus children whose

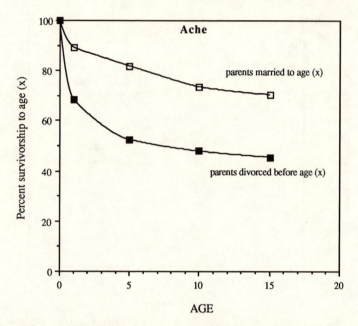

Figure 2. Percent of children who survive to a specified age as a function of
    whether or not their parents stay married until they reach that age (calcu-
    lated as described for figure 1).

parents get divorced are more vulnerable to sickness, homicide, and
capture in warfare, but not to accidental causes of death.

Pair-Bond Stability. In addition to a very high effect of father absence
on child mortality, the Ache show very high levels of pair-bond instability. A small sample of postreproductive women report an average of
12.1 spouses to date (SD = 4.3, *n* = 8). The number of spouses a woman
has had increases as a function of age throughout her reproductive years
(Figure 4). It is therefore not at all surprising that 25% of all Ache
children ever born grew up with a divorced parent. Paternal losses due
to death by the time children reach 15 years of age are experienced at a
lower rate (20%) (Figure 5).

Hiwi Hunter–Gatherers

The Effects of Father's Death and Parental Divorce. Due to small sample
sizes, we were unable to stratify statistical analyses of child mortality
among the Hiwi by divorce status of parents and father's death, and by

percent death from each cause by age 15

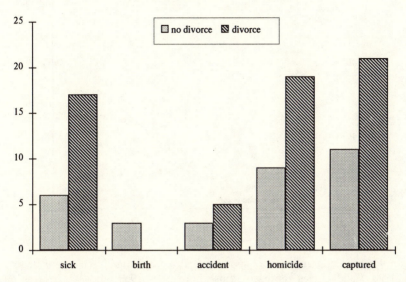

Figure 3. Percent of children ever born who die from each of five causes before the age of 15 years depending on whether their parents stay married until they reach their 15th birthday, or divorce before that time. Causes of death are: died from sickness; died at birth; died in an accident; was a victim of infanticide/homicide; and captured in warfare. The ultimate fate of children captured in warfare is generally unknown.

cause of child's death and age group. Consequently, in this data set, "father absence" is operationalized as both divorce and father's death. All analyses are limited to a single age interval: from birth to 5 years.

Analyses show that father's death and divorce have less of an effect on child mortality in the Hiwi than in the Ache population. Between birth and 5 years of age, Hiwi children whose fathers die and whose parents divorce are only 1.1 times more likely to die than children whose fathers live and stay married. This difference is not statistically significant at the 0.05 level [Pearson's χ^2 = 2.2, p (one-tailed) = 0.08; n = 107 births].

Pair-Bond Stability. Interestingly, only 8% of Hiwi children in our sample experienced the dissolution of their parents' marriage by the time they reached 5 years of age. The comparative rate for the Ache is considerably higher (17%). In contrast to the Ache women, Hiwi women report an average of only 1.7 husbands by the end of their reproductive careers (n = 23 women).

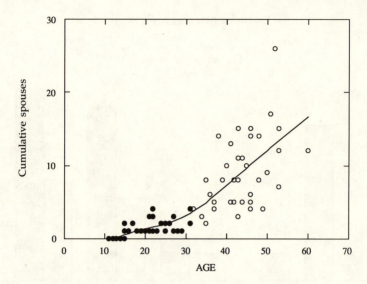

Figure 4. Cumulative number of spouses reported by women who were alive in
1990. Solid circles represent those born after 1960 whose marriages all
occurred on reservations.

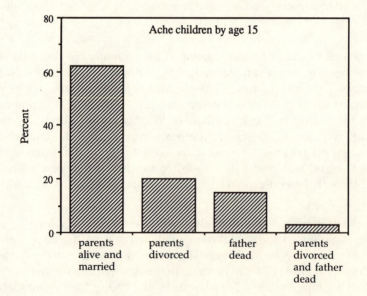

Figure 5. Probability of different family outcomes by the age of 15 for Ache
children.

DISCUSSION

In the anthropological literature it has been proposed that under conditions where father presence has a strong positive effect on child survivorship, long-term stable monogamous unions will be favored over less stable marriages while paternal abandonment is expected to be common under conditions where father presence has no effect or has a negative effect on the survivorship of offspring. The findings of this study run contrary to these expectations. Even though father absence has a strong negative effect on child survivorship among the Ache, pair-bonds are highly unstable in this group of hunter–gatherers. In contrast, father absence appears to have a very small impact on child survivorship among the Hiwi, and yet pair-bonds in this group are quite stable.

Thus, our data do not support the model proposing that parents are more likely to stay married when father absence makes a big difference in child survivorship. This can either mean that the hypothesized relationship is invalid, or that the conditions under which we might expect the relationship to be significant have not been adequately specified in the anthropological literature (but see Maynard Smith 1977; Murray 1984).

Problems with the Current Formulation of the Pair-Bond Stability Model

The simplest formulation of the pair-bond stability model as proposed by Harpending and Draper (1986) and described in the introduction implicitly assumes that

1. The payoffs to mating investment in various societies are all approximately equal.
2. Paternal effects on child survivorship lead to an increase or decrease in the amount of paternal investment *(PI)* that males provide to offspring.
3. The amount of investment that males put into mating *(MI)* is a complementary response to the amount of paternal investment because investment in parenting and mating requires mutually exclusive use of time and resources.
4. Increasing levels of parental investment lead to an increase in pair-bond stability and decreasing levels of parental investment lead to a decrease in pair-bond stability.

Under these assumptions, if Equation (1) roughly captures the components of male fitness, and if fitness is to be maximized, it does appear that increased paternal effects on child survivorship should lead to higher pair-bond stability.

We would like to examine one obvious difficulty with these assumptions, namely, that the first assumption is almost certainly invalid. As the model is theoretically derived and expressed in Equation (1), payoff to paternal investment is not the only independent variable in the model. Nevertheless, for the sake of simplification, payoffs from mating investment have been treated as invariant in the simplest predictions about pair-bond stability (Harpending and Draper 1986). While we sympathize with the attempt to simplify the model and make straightforward testable predictions, we believe that it is more likely that the payoffs from mating investment and paternal investment are both determined by socioecological factors that are independent of one another and that the payoffs from mating and paternal investment are both important independent determinants of pair-bond stability.

When two independent variables such as mating and paternal investment payoffs independently participate in the causal pathway of an outcome, they frequently interact on the dependent variable (in this case, pair-bond stability). Interaction occurs when the magnitude of the effect of one independent variable on a dependent variable changes according to the values of the second variable and vice versa (see Neter et al. 1985). With respect to the problem of pair-bond stability, this means that the amount of variance in pair-bond stability in a system that is explained by paternal investment payoffs may change depending on the level of mating investment payoffs. Considering the possibility of interaction effects allows us to examine and specify the conditions under which a univariate relationship is likely to be present, absent, weak, or strong at different levels of other independent factors.

Ache and Hiwi group composition data allow us to illustrate the potential problems of interaction between the two independent variables (P and M) and pair-bond stability. The Ache and Hiwi not only vary in paternal effects on child survivorship but also on the number of mating opportunities that are open to males at any one point in time. One very crude estimate of potential differences in the mating opportunities open to males across these two groups is the ratio of females of reproductive age to reproductive adult males in the population. This ratio is determined by mortality and fertility schedules characterizing a population at different points in time and the age-specific sex ratios in the population. This ratio of females per male of reproductive age is higher in the precontact Ache population (1.13) than in the Hiwi population (0.72) over the past 30 years (see Table 1): Ache men appear to have experienced a social situation where there has been higher availability of potential fecund mating partners than seems to be the case for Hiwi men.

Table 1. Calculation of the Parenting/Mating Index

	Parameter	1970 (precontact) ACHE	1987 HIWI
a	Number of females 15–40 years of age	122	18
b	Number of males 20–55 years of age	108	25
c	Female/male ratio ($= a/b$)	1.13	0.72
d	Female total fertility rate	7.8	5.4
M	Fertility units per male ($= c \times d$)	8.8	3.9
e	Child survivorship with father	0.86	0.57
f	Child survivorship without father	0.53	0.52
P	Relative increase in child survivorship with father and without father ($= e/f$)	1.6	1.1
I	Parenting/mating index ($= P/M \times 100$)	18.2	28.2

It is therefore possible that the relationship between paternal effectiveness and pair-bond stability is tempered by the relatively higher levels of mating opportunities that are open to Ache men. At high levels of mating opportunities the steepness of the slope defined by the relationship between paternal effects on child survivorship and marital stability may be lower than at low levels of mating opportunities for men (see Figure 6). Consequently, in the Ache system, the fitness benefits to be gained from changing mates frequently may be considerably higher than the payoffs associated with investing in one mate and her offspring only, even though paternal abandonment leads to high offspring mortality.

In contrast, low levels of mating opportunities may create the necessary conditions for the effects of father absence on child survivorship to strongly influence levels of marital stability. In this situation, *any* difference in child survivorship might select for high levels of pair-bond stability. Hence, in this hypothetical example, the Ache represent point D in Figure 6 while the Hiwi represent point A.

It is evident that to adequately test this interaction hypothesis we would need data on several societies with high, medium, and low levels of mating opportunities and high, medium, and low levels of paternal effects on child survivorship. The information on the Ache and the Hiwi provides only two extreme points in a much larger comparative data set.

Qualitative Predictions about Pair-Bond Stability Using a Simple Model

Faced with sparse comparative data, we can at least attempt to evaluate the potential explanatory value of the simple model described in the introduction, through qualitative means. In this model we adhere to

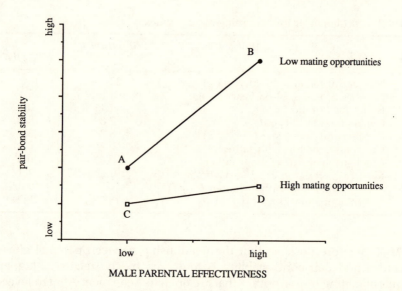

Figure 6. A hypothetical model describing the relationship between male parental effectiveness (increase in survivorship as a function of father's parental
investment) and pair-bond stability as a function of the level of mating
opportunities. In the model there is an interaction effect between father
effectiveness and mating opportunities such that father effectiveness only is
a strong determinant of pair-bond stability when mating opportunities are
low.

assumptions 2–4 in the previous section, and to the simple formulation
of male fitness as expressed in Equation (1). We can then estimate the
relative differences in the payoffs from parenting versus mating investment for the Ache and the Hiwi to assess the prediction that pair-bond
stability should be higher when the relative payoffs to parenting versus
mating are higher. A measurement of the potential parenting versus
mating investment payoffs given certain relevant parameters is possible
with our demographic data and is shown in Table 1.

Using demographic data we calculate a "parenting/mating index" and
estimate this parameter for different societies as follows:

I = parenting/mating index = $P/M \times 100$
P = payoff to parental investment
M = payoff to mating investment

where P is
estimated as

$$P = \frac{\text{offspring survivorship to adulthood with father}}{\text{offspring survivorship without father}}$$

and M is
estimated as

$$M = \frac{(\text{number reproductive females}) \times (\text{total fertility rate})}{\text{number of reproductive males}}$$

Thus, an estimate of potential male mating investment payoffs can be calculated by multiplying the ratio of reproductive females per male times the total female fertility rate (see Table 1). This number represents the fertility increment potential for a male if he could sire the average number of children given that he obtains access to an average share of females in the population. We term this estimate of the mating payoff "fertility units per male." The estimate of paternal investment payoff, or *P*, that we use is based on the reported difference in survivorship for children whose fathers stay with their mothers or abandon them.[4] Finally, the ratio of the relative risk of survivorship to fertility units per male can be used to estimate the relative payoffs of parenting to mating investment in a group. We have labeled this measurement the "parenting/mating index."

Among the Ache, the parenting/mating index is lower (18.2) than the Hiwi index (28.2) (Table 1). This is primarily due to the fact that both the ratio of reproductive age females to adult males (1.3) and the female total fertility rate (7.8) are higher among the Ache than among the Hiwi (0.72 and 5.4, respectively). Thus, the number of "fertility units per male" is considerably higher among the Ache (8.8) than among the Hiwi (3.9). Consequently, even though the relative increase in survivorship for offspring in father-present versus father-absent families is higher among the Ache (1.6) than among the Hiwi (1.1), it is not sufficiently high to make the parenting/mating index higher for the Ache than for the Hiwi. Using the parenting/mating index numbers as a guide, we might expect pair-bond stability to be higher in the Hiwi than in the Ache, just as we observe. Unfortunately, this model does not allow us to make quantitative predictions about how much higher the divorce rate should be among the Ache.

The quantitative estimates of male mating opportunities and potential payoffs from mating investment presented above are particularly useful because they are independent measurements of the levels of marital instability that we are trying to explain. This is an important issue to address since it can be easily argued that one reason why mating opportunities are so high among the Ache is *because of* high divorce rates, which produce many potential sexual partners, rather than vice versa. This circularity can be avoided in our model because neither the age structure of the population nor female fertility rates are necessarily determined by divorce rates.

In summary, the age structure of the Ache population and high female fertility may greatly increase the fitness payoffs associated with male mating investment relative to payoffs associated with paternal investment relative to the Hiwi population. The socioecological conditions necessary to favor pair-bond *instability* appear to be met in the

Ache population while the opposite seems to be the case among the Hiwi.

The model we have presented here generates some interesting hypotheses worthy of future investigation. Levels of mating opportunities not only vary across societies, but are also likely to vary across categories of men within societies. The model predicts that individual differences in the effects of father absence on child survivorship should be a stronger predictor of marital stability among men who have fewer mating opportunities than among men who have more mating opportunities.

CONCLUSION

Analyses of the fitness outcomes of paternal abandonment and its marital correlates among Ache and Hiwi hunter–gatherers suggest that the effect of father absence on child mortality is only one of several component causes of pair-bond stability. Another important component in determining marriage patterns is the fitness payoff that males can gain by investing time and energy into having more than one mating partner. Data analyses suggest that among the Ache father absence has a negative effect on child survivorship and nevertheless pair-bonds are highly unstable. In contrast, among the Hiwi father absence has a relatively small effect on child survivorship and yet most marriages last a lifetime. Previous models have proposed that positive paternal effects on child survivorship should be correlated with high levels of marital stability and vice versa but our data do not meet these predictions. Instead we propose that the interacting effects of levels of mating opportunities and paternal effect on marital stability need to be considered.

This attempt to develop a multivariate model of pair-bond stability requires considerable theoretical improvement. It nevertheless points to the present scarcity of adequate multivariate models, and for the need to incorporate the exhaustive and universal models proposed by behavioral ecologists, in studies of human mating systems and human behavior in general (see Maynard Smith and Ridpath 1972; Maynard Smith 1977; Parker and McNair 1978; Murray 1984, 1985; Brown 1987). Multivariate analyses can be extremely useful in the study of complex relationships between socioecological variables, fitness, and human behavior. The utility of single variable models for explaining human behavioral patterns is likely to be extremely limited and should be invoked only when supported by strong theoretical inference.

NOTES

1. In theory parental investment includes any investment that increases the survivorship or mating success of offspring at the cost of the parent's ability to invest in other offspring (Trivers 1972). We have chosen to ignore effects on offspring mating success in this chapter to simplify the models presented.

2. The ethnographic present for the Ache is the precontact period. The ethnographic present for the Hiwi is both the precontact and postcontact periods.

3. We chose age categories based on data concerning the age span over which males and females normally reproduce. Since few Hiwi women reproduce beyond age 40, we chose that as our cutoff point even though many Ache women reproduce beyond that age.

4. In theory, paternal effectiveness should be measured based on the effect of divorce, not father death, since we are modeling the behavioral decision about whether to abandon a pair-bond, not whether or not to die.

REFERENCES

Berkov, B., and Sklar, J. 1976. Does illegitimacy make a difference? A study of the life chances of illegitimate children in California. *Population and Development Review* 2(2):201–207.

Borgerhoff Mulder, M. 1988. Behavioral ecology in traditional societies. *Trends in Ecological Evolution* 3:260–264.

Brown, J. L. 1987. *Helping and Communal Breeding in Birds.* Princeton: Princeton University Press.

Brown, S. E. 1973. Coping and poverty in the Dominican Republic: Women and their mates. *Current Anthropology* 14:555.

Daly, M., and Wilson, M.I. 1985. Child abuse and other risks of not living with both parents. *Ethology and Sociobiology* 6:197–210.

Draper, P., and Harpending, H. 1982. Father absence and reproductive strategy: An evolutionary perspective. *Journal of Anthropological Research* 38:255–273.

Epenshade, T. J. 1979. The economic consequences of divorce. *Journal of Marriage and the Family* 41(3):615–625.

Franklin, D. L., and Vial, I. 1980. *Food and Nutrition Policies: Does Women's Time Matter?* Chapel Hill, NC: Sigma One Corporation.

Golding, J., Henriques, J., and Thomas, P. 1986. Unmarried at delivery. II. Perinatal morbidity and mortality. *Early Human Development* 14(3–4):217–227.

Harpending, H., and Draper, P. 1986. Selection against human family organization. In *On Evolutionary Anthropology: Essays in Honor of Harry Hoijer 1983.* B. J. Williams (ed.), pp. 100–107 Undena: UCLA.

Hawkes, K., Hill, K., and O'Connell, J. 1982. Why hunters gather: Optimal foraging and the Ache of eastern Paraguay. *American Ethnologist* 9:379–98.

Hewlett, B. 1988. Sexual selection and paternal investment among Aka pygmies. In L. Betzig, M. Borgerhoff-Mulder, and P. Turke (Eds.), *Human Reproductive Behavior*, pp. 263–276. Cambridge: Cambridge University Press.

Hill, K. 1983. Men's subsistence work among Ache hunter-gatherers of Eastern Paraguay. Ph.D. Dissertation, University of Utah.

Hill, K. 1987. Foraging decisions among Ache hunter-gatherers: New data and implications for optimal foraging models. *Ethology and Sociobiology* 8:1–36.

Hill, K., and Hawkes, K. 1983. Neotropical hunting among the Ache of eastern Paraguay. In *Adaptive Responses of Native Amazonians*. R. Hames and W. Vickers (Eds.), pp. 139–188. New York: Academic Press.

Hill, K., and Hurtado, A. M. 1990. Hunter-gatherers of the new world *American Scientist* September–October:437–443.

Hill, K., and Hurtado, A. M. 1991. The evolution of premature reproductive peuescence and menopause in human females: An evaluation of the "grandmother hypotheses." *Human Nature* 2(4):313–350.

Hill, K., Hurtado, A. M., Hawkes, K., and Kaplan, H. 1984. Seasonal variance in the diet of Ache hunter-gatherers of eastern Paraguay. *Human Ecology* 12:145–180.

Hill, K., Kaplan, H., Hawkes, K., and Hurtado, A. M. 1985. Men's time allocation to subsistence work among the Ache of eastern Paraguay. *Human Ecology* 13:29–47.

Hurtado, A. M. 1985. Women's subsistence strategies among Ache hunter-gatherers of eastern Paraguay. Ph.D. dissertation, University of Utah.

Hurtado, A. M., and Hill, K. R. 1987. Early dry season subsistence ecology of the Cuiva (Hiwi) foragers of Venezuela. *Human Ecology* 15(2):163–187.

Hurtado, A. M., and Hill, K. R. 1991. Food gathering among Hiwi women hunter-gatherers: Implications for the sexual division of labor. *Human Ecology*, to be submitted.

Hurtado, A. M., and Hill, K. R. 1990. Seasonality in foragers: A study of variation in the diet, work effort, fertility and the sexual division of labor among the Hiwi of Venezuela. *Journal of Anthropological Research* 46(3):293–345.

Hurtado, A. M., Hawkes, K., Hill, K., and Kaplan, H. 1985. Female subsistence strategies among Ache hunter-gatherers of eastern Paraguay. *Human Ecology* 13:1–28.

Hurtado, A. M., Hurtado, I., and Hill, K. R. 1988. Ecologia del comportamiento y estado de salud en una población indigena de los llanos venezolanos: Estudios preliminares. Proceedings of the seminar Aspectos antropólogicos y sociológicos de la atención primaria de salud en el Territorio Federal Amazonas CAICET. Manuscript, IVIC, Caracas, Venezuela.

Jason, J. M., Carpenter, M. M., and Tyler, C. W. 1983. Underrecording of infant homicide in the United States. *American Journal of Public Health* 73:195–197.

Kaplan, H., and Dove, H. 1986. Infant development among the Ache of eastern Paraguay. *Developmental Psychology* 13(2):321–328.

Kaplan, H., and Hill, K. 1985a. Hunting ability and reproductive success among male Ache foragers. *Current Anthropology* 25:113–115.

Kaplan, H., and Hill, K. 1985b. Food sharing among Ache foragers: Tests of explanatory hypotheses. *Current Anthropology* 26:223–245.

Kaplan, H. K., Hill, K., Hawkes, K., and Hurtado, A. 1984. Food-sharing among the Ache hunter-gatherers of eastern Paraguay. *Current Anthropology* 25:113–115.

Kleiman, D. G., and Malcolm, J. R. 1981. The evolution of male parental investment in mammals. In *Parental Care in Mammals*. D. J. Gubernick and P. H. Klopfer (eds.), pp. 347–387. New York: Plenum.

Lancaster, J. B. 1988. Evolutionary and cross-cultural perspectives on single-parenthood. In *Interfaces in Psychology: Sociobiology and the Social Sciences*. R. W. Bell and N. J. Bell (Eds.), pp. 63–72. Lubbock, TX: University Press.

Lovejoy, O. C. 1981. The origin of man. *Science* 211:340–350.

Lyles, R. B., Hill, K. R., and Hurtado, A. M. 1990. Preliminary quantitative analyses of food sharing patterns among the Hiwi of Venezuela. Manuscript: Department of Anthropology, University of Michigan.

Marchione, T. J. 1980. Factors associated with malnutrition in the children of western Jamaica. In *Nutritional Anthropology*. N. W. Jerome, R. F. Kandel, and G. H. Pelto (Eds.), p. 223. Pleasantville, NY: Redgrave.

Maynard Smith, 1977. Parental investment: A prospective analysis. *Animal Behavior* 25:1–9.

Maynard Smith, J., and Ridpath, M. G. 1972. Wife sharing in the Tasmanian native hen: A case of kin selection? *American Naturalist* 106:447–452.

Murray, B. G. 1984. A demographic theory on the evolution of mating systems as exemplified by birds. *Evolutionary Biology* 18:71–140.

Murray, B. G. 1985. The influence of demography on the evolution of monogamy. In *Avian Monogamy*, Ornithological Monographs No. 37. P. A. Gowaty and D. W. Mock (Eds.). Washington, D.C.: American Ornithologists' Union No.

Neter, J., Wasserman, W., and Kutner, M. H. 1985. *Applied Linear Statistical Models: Regression, Analysis of Variance and Experimental Designs*. Illinois: Irwin.

Parker, G. A., and Macnair, M. R. 1978. Models of parent-offspring conflict. I. Monogamy. *Animal Behavior* 26:97–110.

Pennington, R., and Harpending, H. 1988. Fitness and fertility among Kalahari !Kung. *American Journal of Physical Anthropology* 77:303–319.

Skjaerven, R., and Irgens, L. M. 1988. Perinatal mortality and mother's marital status at birth in subsequent siblings. *Early Human Development* 18(2–3):199–212.

Trivers, R. L. 1972. Parental investment and sexual selection. In *Sexual Selection and the Descent of Man*. B. Campbell (Ed.). London: Heinemann.

Chapter 3

Paternal Care in a Caribbean Village

Mark V. Flinn

Family relationships and household composition vary widely in Caribbean societies. Nuclear (biparental), single parent (usually mother), and extended grandparental households are common. Male parental behavior is highly variable, with some fathers providing extensive resources and care for their children, while others provide little or none (Clarke 1957). This wide range of parent–offspring relationships provides a "natural experiment" for comparative analysis of factors influencing family structure.[1]

This chapter examines patterns of male parental behavior in "Grande Anse," a rural village in north-central Trinidad. The objective is to better understand individual strategies of parenting. Factors considered in the analysis include (1) age and sex of offspring, (2) genetic relatedness to child (step vs. genetic relationships), (3) residence and marital status of father and mother, (4) age of father, and (5) material resources (land and income) controlled by father.

THE VILLAGE OF GRANDE ANSE

The village of Grande Anse is located on the northern coast of Trinidad. It is isolated from the more heavily populated and economically developed central and western areas of the country by the steep and densely vegetated slopes of the Northern Range, which rise directly from the sea. Most of the 342 inhabitants live in the small pocket of relatively level alluvial deposits from the Grande Anse river. The surrounding hillsides are cultivated with cocoa, coffee, bananas, and citrus as cash crops, and cassava, corn, dasheen, and vine tubers as subsistence items. Further inland the topography is too severe for efficient cultivation. Most of this land is undeveloped government forest reserve.

The village founders arrived about 1860 from Venezuela in small sailing canoes (Harrison 1979). Later, immigrants rowed or sailed from the nearby (40 km) island of Tobago. By 1900 the community was thriving, with most villagers owning or squatting on plots of land, cultivating cocoa and subsistence crops. During the cocoa boom of the early 1900s outside interests purchased tracts of land and employed village labor. However, the cocoa market crashed during the 1920s and never recovered. Workers were laid off, and the smaller cocoa plots abandoned. Diversification into other crops such as coffee, citrus, and bananas helped to maintain the agricultural base of the village, but it never returned to the prosperity of the early cocoa days. Census data indicate that the village population has slowly declined, largely due to emigration to more developed areas (Harrison 1979).

There are a variety of ways to make a living in Grande Anse. Some are more lucrative than others. Most villagers have several part-time occupations, such as cocoa cultivation, fishing, carpentry, road work (government job), and shopkeeping. A majority of adults have rights to cultivated land and spend some effort growing cash crops (e.g., cocoa, coffee) and subsistence crops. But the profits are slim and the work is hard so cultivation is the primary occupation of very few villagers (about 13% of adult males, 8% of adult females).

METHODS AND FIELD TECHNIQUES

Five types of data were gathered that are useful for testing hypotheses about father–offspring relationships: (1) behavioral observations, (2) genealogies, (3) residence, (4) land ownership and income, and (5) marital/mating relationships.

Day-to-Day Behavior

I collected data on day-to-day behavior with a "behavioral observation route instantaneous scan sample" procedure (cf. Altmann 1974; Munroe et al. 1983; Johnson 1978; Gross 1984; Hames 1979). Scan data are useful for the study of parent–offspring relationships because they can provide objective measures of behavior that would be difficult or unreliable to obtain by questionnaire techniques (cf. Draper 1975, 1976; Blurton-Jones 1972; Hames 1988; Flinn 1988b).

The behavior scan procedure was as follows: I traveled a set of 4.7-km route through the study site once or twice daily, starting at a randomly determined time and place on the route. The route went through the entire village, passing within 20 meters of each inhabited house and each community structure (e.g., church, cricket field, water outlets). Observability was excellent because people were usually outside during the day, and even when inside they were almost always visible because houses typically consist of one or two rooms with open large doors and windows. Each time an individual was observed, I recorded (with a notebook and/or tape recorder) the time, location, individual, and behavior. This information was coded within 48 hours onto computer format sheets. For each 'observation,' the date, time, one of 1375 location codes, one of 480 individual identification numbers, and one or more of 475 behavior codes were numerically recorded for computer analysis. For example, on February 11, 1980 at 9:53 AM I observed Hubert M. in his household's front porch holding Chirnal M. (his 1-year-old daughter) who was asleep. This observation was coded:

Date	Time	Location	Individual	Behavior
110380	0953	0787	0782	348
110380	0953	0787	0785	754

I recorded about 33,000 observations in the above fashion over a period of six months (173 scan routes on 152 days). Of these observations, 24,577 form the data base used in this chapter. I have excluded observations recorded during the first two weeks of the procedure, observations recorded during scan routes in which fewer than 50% of the villagers were observed, observations of visitors to the village, and observations of unidentified individuals.

Three measures of parent–offspring behavior are computed from the scan data: (1) The *proportion of behavioral interactions* occurring between parent and offspring was determined by dividing the number of observed interactions between parent and offspring by the total number of observations of the parent. This provides an estimate of the proportion of time a parent interacts with an offspring. (2) The *proportion of caretaking* interactions was determined by dividing the number of "caretaking" interactions (feeding, holding, cleaning, watching, playing, teaching, changing diapers, and other general "babysitting"[2] activities) by the total number of observations of potential caretakers. This provides an estimate of the proportion of time different individuals spend in direct care of offspring. (3) The *proportion of agonistic behavioral interactions* occurring between parent and offspring was determined by dividing the number of observed "agonistic" interactions between parent and offspring by the total number of interactions between parent and offspring. Agonistic interactions are defined as those behaviors that involved

physical or verbal combat (e.g., "spanking" or "arguing") or expressions of injury inflicted by another individual (e.g., "screaming in pain
or anguish" or "crying"). 26 of the 475 behavior codes were included in
this category (Flinn 1988a, Appendix). Of the total of 24,577 observations of all villagers, 1218 (4.8%) involved agonistic interactions. Most of
these were verbal behaviors (92.5%). Of the total of 5343 observations of
parent–offspring interactions, 318 (6%) were agonistic. Most of these
were verbal behaviors (299, or 94%). As a frame of reference, I subjec-
tively consider the level of observable agonism in Grande Anse families
to be about equal to American middle-class families. Although agonistic
interactions probably reflect a conflict of interests, some agonistic interactions might be nepotistic, or at least mutually beneficial in the long
term. For example, a parent may spank a child to instruct it to not repeat
a behavior that could be dangerous to the child, such as walking into the
street, or pulling a pot from on top of the stove. From the scan data, it is
difficult to distinguish nepotistic agonistic interactions from non-nep-
otistic agonistic interactions. The rate of agonistic interactions is used
here as a reasonable, albeit imperfect, indicator of the level (degree) of
conflict between individuals. I was unaware of any instances of what
would be called "physical child abuse," i.e., serious injury inflicted on a
child by a parent (Daly and Wilson 1980; Gelles and Lancaster 1987)
during the period of the fieldwork.

Because I gathered genealogies early on in the fieldwork and hence
knew some of the paternity assignments, it is possible that my observations of step versus genetic offspring were biased. However, the objective nature of the scan technique, and the complex results for which I
had no conscious preconceptions, suggest that it is unlikely that the
observations were biased. Replication with "blind" observers could
provide more reliable results.

Genealogical Information

Genealogical information is used to determine ages of individuals and
identities of relatives and nonrelatives (genetic parents and stepparents).

To collect genealogies I interviewed informants from each household,
usually adult females, obtaining names, genealogical relationships,
ages, and current residences of all relatives (blood and affinal) they
could remember (see Chagnon 1974). These interviews were well received. On returning from interviews, I assigned unique identification
numbers to each individual collected in the genealogies and put all of
the above information on 3×5 inch index cards for each individual.
Discrepancies and questionable paternity assignments were checked by

additional interviews. I found it useful to seek redundant information from several informants to allow for cross-checking (Chagnon 1974). Genealogical information was analyzed by computer (in the United States) for cross reference with behavioral data.

To the best of my knowledge the genealogies that I collected are correct as understood by the villagers; there may be a few errors of which they were unaware or about which I was deceived. In four cases some villagers held differing opinions; these cases involved potential cuckoldry unknown to the males, who assumed they were the fathers. For obvious reasons I did not challenge the supposed father's account. However in three of the four cases I was convinced by accounts from other informants that cuckoldry had occurred, and put the reported cuckolder down as the genetic father in the genealogies. These four cases do not affect the statistical significance of any results presented in this chapter. I estimate that the genealogies are at least 95% accurate. Lacking paternity exclusion tests, I cannot verify this.

An offspring's *genetic parents* are defined as the individuals believed to have provided the egg and sperm that resulted in the offspring. A *stepparent* is defined as a genetically unrelated (via direct descent to the child), co-residential (see below) spouse (mate) of an offspring's genetic parent. All coresidential step parents were males, i.e., stepfathers, because children usually stay with their mother after a marital dissolution. In the few cases ($N = 6$) where children stayed with their father, either the father remained single, or the children moved out to stay with grandparents or on their own when their father acquired a new spouse.

Residence and Household Composition

Information about where individuals resided in the village was obtained by interview and corroborated by incidental observation. Some individuals had multiple residences. For example, several children stayed with their grandparents or other relatives while their parent(s) were away working outside of the village. And some mating relationships involved part-time cohabitation (and, hence, part-time parenting). *Coresident* parent–offspring dyads are defined as those that sleep in the same house together more than 90% of the time and regularly eat meals in the same house.

At the time of the fieldwork, there were 112 "households" (residential units) in the village. Of these households 57 involved parent–offspring and/or grandparent–grandoffspring dyads. Five households were composed exclusively of genetic mother–offspring dyads (single mothers). Four households were composed exclusively of genetic father–offspring dyads (single fathers with older sons). Twelve households were composed exclusively of genetic mother and genetic father–offspring dyads (nuclear families). Five households had, in addition to genetic mother–offspring dyads, stepfather–offspring dyads, but no genetic father–offspring dyads. Fourteen households had both stepfather–offspring and genetic father–offspring dyads, involving 27 stepoffspring and 29 genetic offspring (i.e., some of the children in the household were sired by the resident male, but some were not). These 14 households with both step and genetic father–offspring relationships are especially useful for investigation of the effects of genetic relatedness on father–offspring relationships.

Twelve households included multiple generation maternal families, i.e., an adult female (ages ranged from 18 to 34) living with her parents and her offspring. Two households included multiple generation paternal families, i.e., an adult male living with his parents and his offspring. No multiple generation families had a coresident stepparent or stepgrandparent. Two households had grandparent–grandoffspring dyads but no parent–offspring dyads, and one household had a grandmother–grandoffspring dyad but no parent–offspring dyads.

There were 147 coresidential genetic parent–offspring dyads, 28 part-time coresidential genetic parent–offspring dyads, and 56 nonresidential genetic parent–offspring dyads in the village. There were 36 coresidential stepfather–offspring dyads, and 21 nonresidential stepfather–offspring dyads. There were no coresidential stepmother–offspring dyads. There were no cases of coresidential polygamy.

About 41% (26 out of 63) of the young adults (females aged 18–28 years old, males aged 20–30 years old) had both genetic parents living in the village, 27% (17 of 63) had only a genetic mother living in the village, 16% (10 of 63) had only a genetic father living in the village, and 16% (10 of 63) had no genetic parents living in the village. Of the young adults 43% (27 of 63) did not have a genetic father resident in the village. These figures are consistent with other studies of rural Caribbean populations (e.g., Clarke 1957; Otterbein 1966; M. Smith 1962).

Resource Control

To test the hypothesis that resources influence male parental behavior, associations between parental behavior and land and income are analyzed. To simplify the analysis, land ownership and income are defined as dichotomous variables. About half of the adult village males were from households with rights to six or more acres of land ($N = 24$), and half were from households with less than six acres ($N = 29$). About half ($N = 27$) had incomes greater than $4000 T.T. per year, and half ($N = 26$) had incomes less than $4000 T.T.

Information about economic assets and occupations were collected by interview (e.g., What land do you own, rent, cultivate? What major possessions do you own—house, mule, radio? How much do you earn from selling cocoa?). This survey was conducted directly with informants at their place of residence, and, in some cases, was corroborated by interviews with other villagers. Government land ownership maps were useful for corroborating information about land ownership (especially the precise size of landholdings, or at least the government's measurement of the acreage) and for establishing patterns of 'legal' inheritance.

In this chapter land ownership is used as a measure of *heritable* resources and income is used as a measure of *temporary* resources. This distinction is based on the observations that (1) land ownership was much more stable over time than income or ownership of other material items, (2) land was the most valuable resource inherited by most villagers, and (3) land was measured more accurately and reliably than other economic assets. I use household land as a measure of individual land ownership because land is worked jointly by household family members, the benefits are distributed among household family members, and land is not always "owned" by specific individuals (for discussion of land tenure in Caribbean societies, see Besson 1979). No adjustment for the number of household members was made because this was difficult to do appropriately, and because there seemed no reason why not adjusting for household size would bias the results for or against any of the hypotheses tested.

Marital/Mating Relationships

Collection of mating histories occurred over the entire period of the field study, and overlapped with collection of genealogies. For both sets of data I found it useful to seek redundant information from several informants, to allow for cross-checking (Chagnon 1974). An additional source of information was the registry of births. This was not very reliable because it systematically avoided illegitimacy by ascribing paternity to a woman's legal husband. The registry was, however, useful for acquiring birth dates. Information about recent and current mating relationships was much more reliable and complete than that for past relationships, partly because informants' memories were fresher, and partly because they were observable at the time of the study.

The mating–courting relationships analyzed in this paper were widely recognized by the villagers, were readily observable (i.e., coresidence), or were deduced from the genealogies (i.e., relationships that produced one or more offspring). In almost all cases these three sources of information overlapped and were congruent.

Some individuals had multiple residences. For example, a number of children would stay with their grandparents or other relatives while their parent(s) were away working outside of the village. And some mating relationships involved part-time cohabitation. *Coresident* mates are defined as unrelated adult male–female pairs that sleep in the same house together more than 80% of the time, regularly eat meals together, and reportedly are sexual partners.

General Remarks

The data analyzed in this paper are complete for each villager. That is, behavior (scan sample), genealogies of at least two generations in depth, residence, household land and income, and marital–mating relationships are known for each of the 342 individuals in the village population.

RESULTS AND DISCUSSION

General Patterns of Parent–Offspring Interactions

This first section provides a brief overview of parent–offspring relationships in Grande Anse. The objective is to provide background information that will allow better understanding of analyses of individual variation in paternal behavior that are presented in following sections.

Fathers in Grande Anse help their offspring in a number of different ways. Direct care of infants and young children includes activities such as holding, feeding, cleaning, playing, teaching, changing diapers, and other general "babysitting" activities. Fathers contribute indirectly by providing resources such as food and money. For older offspring, fathers may give important economic, social, and political support. And, finally, fathers may leave inheritances of land and savings for their offspring. Male parental effort appears to have important effects on offspring well-being, including mate competition (Flinn 1986). Women are reluctant to raise offspring without male support; infant children of single mothers are much more likely to have health problems, frequently resulting in "adoption" by grandparents or other relatives.

Figure 1 presents the frequencies of observed interactions among different kin. Genetic parent–offspring interactions account for a substantial portion (35.6%) of the total number of observed interactions.

Figure 2 illustrates the relative amounts of time that infants are cared for by different relatives. Mothers are the most important caretakers, although infants also spend a considerable amount of time with grand-

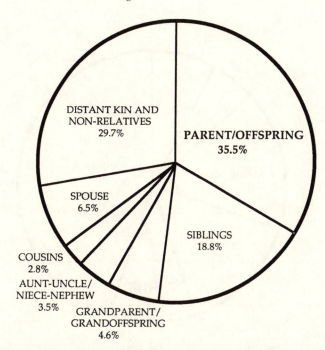

Figure 1. Kinship interactions. Behavioral observation data illustrating the proportion of interactions that individuals spend with different categories of
kin. Data are dyad referenced from complete scan data set (i.e., each
interaction is identified as involving one type of dyad—parent–offspring,
cousin–cousin, etc.). These data suggest that individuals spend a substantial amount of time with their relatives. Parent–offspring interactions are
especially common.

parents, siblings, and fathers. Males generally are less important caretakers than females in comparable age and kinship categories (i.e.,
mothers are more important than fathers, aunts are more important
than uncles, sisters more important than brothers, etc.).

Figure 3 compares rates of caretaking in households with and without
resident fathers. Infants in households with a resident father were
observed in caretaking interactions more frequently than infants in
households without a resident father. Infants in these "father-absent"
households received less care from all types of caretakers (mothers,
siblings, etc.) except grandparents. This is partly because their mothers
were burdened with more economic responsibilities, and partly because
there were fewer potential caretakers in father-absent households (cf.
Munroe and Munroe 1971; Borgerhoff Mulder and Milton 1985; Hames
1988). Mothers without coresident males tend to live with their parents,

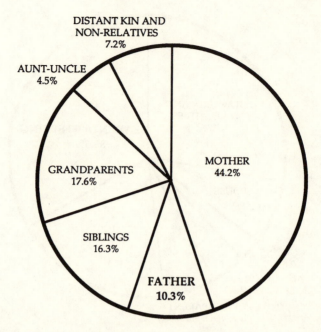

Figure 2. Infant and early childhood (0–4 years) care interactions. Behavioral observation data illustrating the proportion of care interactions that children aged 0–4 spend with different categories of kin.

especially if they are young, hence the importance of grandparental caretaking in father-absent households.

Figure 4 presents the frequencies of interaction by offspring age among the four gender combinations of genetic parent–offspring dyads: mother–daughter, mother–son, father–daughter, and father–son.

Mothers have higher proportions of interaction with offspring during infancy (aged 0–12 months) than do fathers (coresident mothers range = 14–67%, mean = 31.9%; fathers range = 0–9%, mean = 3.3%). This sex difference in parental care is reduced, but still substantial, during early childhood (coresident mothers range = 8–36%, mean = 22.9%; fathers range = 0–17%, mean = 4.2%). Mother–daughter dyads have the highest rates of interaction for post-infant age categories, indicative of the importance of this relationship throughout childhood, adolescence, and adulthood (Flinn 1988c, 1989). Mother–son interactions, in contrast, sharply decline during the adolescent years, and remain at low levels during adulthood.

Fathers interact slightly more with adolescent and adult offspring than with infants and preadolescents. Father–daughter dyads have the highest rates of interaction during late adolescence. This may involve "guarding" of the daughter to prevent her from developing suboptimal

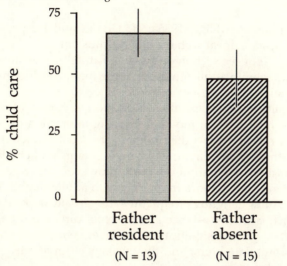

Figure 3. Comparison of rates of child care in father-resident and father-absent households. Behavioral observation data indicate higher rates of child-care interactions with all types of caretakers in households with coresident fathers. Sample includes all households with children aged 0–4. $\overline{X}$ or mean = 67.9% and SE = 9.5% for father-resident households (black bar). $\overline{X}$ or mean = 48.8% and SE = 11.2% for father-absent households (striped bar). $\chi^2 = 13.2$, $p < 0.01$. Eleven of 13 father-resident households had equal or higher rates of child care interaction than father-absent households. Average age of father-resident children is 2.42 years, father-absent children is 2.37 years. 95% confidence intervals are shown by vertical lines.

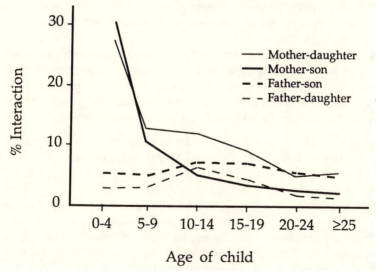

Figure 4. Parent–child interaction rates by age and gender.

mating relationships (Flinn 1988a; cf. Draper and Harpending 1982). Father–son dyads appear to have a fairly constant rate of interaction in all age groups (but see section on "Age of Father"). The rates of interaction maintained with adult sons seem quite high, considering that most of these relationships are not coresident.

These results indicate sexual specialization in parent–offspring interactions. The high rates of mother–offspring interaction during the 0–5 age category reflect the fact that mothers are usually much more important than fathers in the day-to-day care of infants and children of both sexes. Interactions with adult offspring, however, show gender biases. Mothers interact much more frequently with adult daughters than with adult sons. Adult daughters frequently are partially dependent on their mothers for financial assistance and for child care. On the other hand, mothers often receive significant help (e.g., with household chores) from their adult daughters, and they usually seem to relish taking care of their grandchildren.

Fathers interact more frequently with their sons than with their daughters, particularly after the offspring have moved out into a house of their own. The higher rates of interaction with adult sons than daughters are partly due to cooperative economic activities, such as growing cocoa on family land, but fathers and sons are also more likely to engage in social activities together, such as drinking beer or playing checkers.

These patterns of parent–offspring interaction are common in many human societies (cf. Ainsworth 1967; Whiting and Whiting 1975; Katz and Konner 1981; Lamb 1981; Hames 1988; Levine et al. 1988; Whiting and Edwards 1988; Werner 1989ab; Cronk 1989). There is, however, individual variation. Some fathers spend much more time with their children than do others.

The objective of the following sections is to examine factors that affect individual parenting strategies in Grande Anse. Factors considered in the analysis include (1) genetic relatedness (step versus genetic relationships), (2) marital status and residence of mother and father, (3) age of father, and (4) material resources (land and income) controlled by father.

Step versus Genetic Relationships. Inclusive fitness theory (Hamilton 1964) posits that some probability of genetic relatedness between caregivers (putative fathers) and care-receivers (putative offspring) is a necessary condition for the evolution of paternal care (Alexander 1974; Irons 1979; Daly and Wilson 1981; Kurland and Gaulin 1984; Lamb et al. 1985, 1987). The mechanisms whereby humans ascertain paternity are uncertain, but may include (1) monitoring and controlling sexual activity, e.g. "mate guarding" (Daly et al. 1982; Buss 1988; Flinn 1988a), (2) analysis of physical, olfactory, and behavioral resemblance, i.e., "phenotype matching" (Sherman and Holmes 1985), and (3) other social and environmental cues, such as residential proximity. Regardless of the precise mechanisms, paternity, and non-paternity, appear to be universally recognized in human societies (e.g., Kurland 1979).[3]

Given the recognition of paternity and non-paternity, evolutionary logic suggests the hypothesis that *male parental investment is preferentially distributed to genetic offspring*[4] as compared to unrelated children sired by other males (Daly and Wilson 1980; Wilson et al. 1980). This hypothesis can be tested by examining paternal behavior of step and genetic fathers.

Step and genetic parent–offspring relationships are compared using two measures of behavior: (1) proportion of interactions, and (2) proportion of agonistic interactions.

Figure 5 compares the proportion of interaction between genetic fathers and genetic offspring with the proportion of interaction between stepfathers and stepoffspring in those households where both genetic

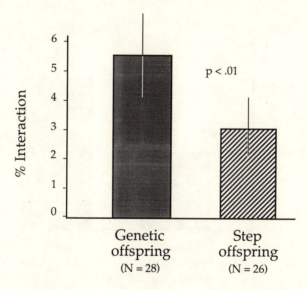

Figure 5. Comparison of interaction rates in step versus genetic relationships. Behavioral observation data indicate that stepfather–child relationships have lower rates of interaction than genetic father–child relationships. Subjects are from households with both step and genetic relationships. $\overline{X}$ or mean = 5.5% and SE = 0.64% for genetic relationships (black bar). $\overline{X}$ or mean = 3.1% and SE = 0.47% for steprelationships (striped bar). χ^2 = 7.1, $p < 0.01$. Fourteen of 14 households had equal or lower proportions of interaction in step versus genetic relationships. Average age of step children is 7.46 years, genetic children is 7.57 years. 95% confidence intervals are shown by vertical lines.

offspring and stepoffspring are present. Here the male parent has the 'choice' of interacting with his genetic offspring or with his stepoffspring, all in the same household, so the effect of residence is controlled. To control for age effects, the oldest stepoffspring and the youngest genetic offspring were removed from the sample, resulting in an average age of 5.9 years for step offspring and 5.8 years for genetic offspring (see Flinn 1988b for specific ages and genders of offspring in these households).[5] The data indicate that males interact more frequently with their genetic offspring than they do with their stepoffspring.

Figure 6 indicates that the proportion of agonistic interactions is higher with stepoffspring than with genetic offspring. These data suggest that the types of interaction are different in step and genetic relationships (cf. Gelles and Lancaster 1987; Giles-Sims 1984; Ihinger-Tallman 1988).

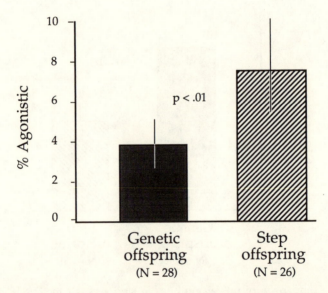

Figure 6. Comparison of rates of agonistic interactions in step versus genetic father–child relationships. Behavioral observation data indicate higher rates of agonistic interactions among stepfather–child relationships. Subjects are from households with both step and genetic relationships. $X = 3.9\%$ and SE $= .54\%$ for genetic relationships (black bar). $X = 7.8\%$ and SE $= 1.2\%$ for steprelationships (striped bar). $\chi^2 = 10.4$, $p < 0.01$. Fourteen of 14 households had equal or lower proportions of agonistic interactions in genetic versus steprelationships. Average age of stepchildren is 7.46 years, genetic children is 7.57 years. 95% confidence intervals are shown by vertical lines.

Land inheritance information provides an additional insight into parent–offspring relationships. In the past 40 years, no land in the village was inherited by a stepoffspring, except for two cases of indirect inheritance through the mother (man dies, leaves land to his wife, who leaves the land to her children, some of whom were not the man's) and one case involving a lack of related heirs. Some wills specify genetic offspring as heirs, excluding step offspring; informants mentioned that this usually was unnecessary because the legal code states that land shall be inherited by "seed."

Informants uniformly agreed that step parent–offspring relationships generally were less amicable than genetic parent–offspring ("blood") relationships, and that this was "natural." However, they often mentioned variability in step relationships, usually by contrasting particular relationships with which they were familiar. Men with stepchildren made a number of interesting comments to me. Most stepfathers indicated that they "cared" more for their blood offspring, because it "was just so," or because "we are more like each other," or "resemble one another." One father indicated that he cared for his wife's children from a previous relationship equally to "his own." Indeed, he seemed proud of this, and made special mention of the Christmas presents he had given his stepchildren. Interestingly, the stepchildren were not to inherit land from their stepfather because his "family would not go for that. It was my father's land and my grand[parents'] before that." The observations (scan data) of interactions between this male and his step and genetic offspring were consistent with results presented in Figures 5 and 6 (i.e., his behavior was inconsistent with his oral account), suggesting that what people do and what they say they do may be different. This illustrates a possible advantage of systematic behavioral observation and the use of multiple informants (Bernard 1988). Such discrepancies between expressed beliefs and actual behavior suggest that differential treatment of step and genetic offspring may result from sub-conscious decision making.

Current research in rural Dominica using radioimmunoassay of saliva indicates that in general, stepchildren have higher levels of cortisol—a hormone related to levels of stress—than genetic children (Flinn and Durbrow 1990; Flinn and England 1991). It is not clear, however, whether higher stress levels of stepchildren result from conflict with step parents, or from lack of parental support mediating stress from other causes (school, squabbles with friends, work). Regardless, coresidence with genetic father appears to have important health consequences for children (Marchione 1980; Flinn et al. 1992).

Non-residential Father–Child Relationships. Fathers sometimes do not reside with their children as a consequence of divorce, separation, or

"casual" mating relationships. These nonresidential father–child relationships are particularly sensitive to influence by other family members, such as mother, mother's new spouse, and father's new spouse.

Figure 7 compares the interaction rates of nonresidential father–child
relationships according to whether father has acquired a new coresidential mate (i.e., stepmother to the child). Fathers with new mates interact
less frequently with their children from previous mating relationships.
These data suggest that a father's new mate influences him not to see his
children, perhaps in part because she is jealous of his ex-spouse. Conflicts between current and ex-spouses are common, and reportedly concern matters of child support.

Figure 8 compares the interaction rates of nonresidential father–child
relationships according to whether mother has acquired a new coresidential mate (i.e., stepfather to the child). Fathers interact less frequently with their children from previous mating relationships if their
ex-spouses have acquired new mates. These data suggest that a mother's new mate influences the father not to see his children. Interestingly,
some men expressed concerns about support for their stepchildren
(from the genetic father), because such support was thought to be
associated with continuation of a sexual relationship with their mother.
They (stepfathers) were jealous of their mate's ex-spouses providing
money. On the other hand, men usually do not want their own money
being used to support stepchildren either. The best solution, from the
perspective of stepfathers, is for stepchildren to move out to their
grandparents (cf. Sanford 1975).

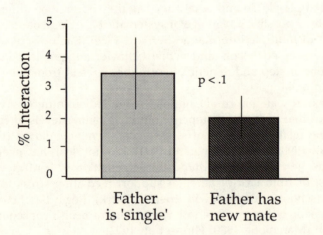

Figure 7. Effect of father's marital status on nonresidential father–child relationships.

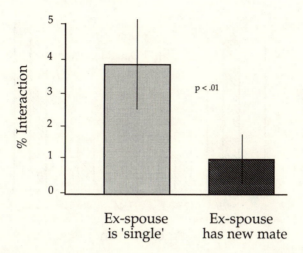

Figure 8. Effect of marital status of mother (ex-spouse) on interaction rates in nonresidential father–child relationships.

The influence of other family members on father–child relationships contributes to the complexity of male allocation strategies. Fathers frequently find themselves in a bind between their obligations to a new wife (particularly if they have children), and obligations to a previous wife. Indeed, such pressures are mentioned as the critical factor preventing concurrent polygynous relationships. Other family and kin (e.g., nephews and nieces) may pose additional competition for a male's time and resources.

Age of Father. Age may have an important effect on male parenting. Young males are likely to have different opportunities and goals than older males. In this section behavioral data are analyzed to determine if age is associated with paternal behavior.

Figures 7–9 illustrate frequencies of interaction between fathers and offspring of different ages and genders. A general pattern is evident. Figure 9 indicates that young fathers (<25 years) and old fathers (>54 years) interact more frequently with infant and juvenile offspring (<10 years) than do middle-aged fathers (25–54 years). Conversely, Figure 11 indicates that middle-aged fathers interact more frequently with older sons (>20 years) than do old fathers. Figure 10 suggests an intermediary relationship with teenage offspring (10–20 years).

Several factors may contribute to this age-related pattern. First, young and old fathers generally seemed less 'busy' than middle-aged fathers. Young and old fathers are less likely to be employed full-time than middle-aged fathers (Flinn 1983), and hence have more time to spend

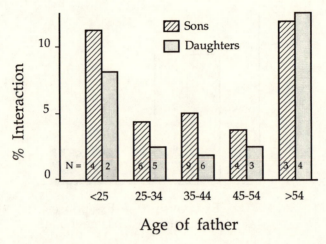

Figure 9. Paternal interaction with offspring <10 years old.

caretaking infants. Middle-aged fathers spend more time with older sons in cooperative economic and social activities than do old fathers, because old fathers are less likely to be engaged in such activities, and perhaps because sons receive more benefit from such interactions if their fathers are younger (i.e., middle-aged). Reciprocity may be particularly important in middle-aged father–older son relationships. Age related patterns of male parental behavior also may be related to economic factors in complex ways. For example, families with large land holdings may benefit from increased father–older son cooperation.

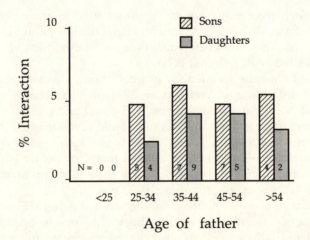

Figure 10. Paternal interaction with offspring 10–20 years old.

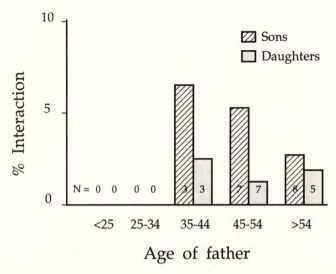

Age of father

Figure 11. Paternal interaction with offspring > 20 years old.

Material Resources (Land and Income) Controlled by Father. Parenting may be viewed as part of a reproductive strategy (e.g., Irons 1988). Individuals allocate time, energy, resources, and risk (referred to as "effort") toward a number of possible goals (Figure 12). A critical allocation decision for males is the relative distribution of effort to mating and parenting (e.g., Hewlett 1988; Hill and Kaplan 1988ab).

Resources controlled by males may influence allocation decisions. Some resources may be more useful for attracting and maintaining mating relationships (mating effort), whereas other resources may be more useful for helping children (parental effort). Land and income are

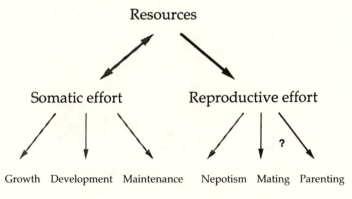

Figure 12. Resource allocation strategy.

important resources with different effects on male reproductive strategies (Flinn 1986).

Both land and income are associated with male reproductive success (Figure 13). Income is a better predictor of the number of mates with whom males reproduced; that is, high income males tend to have children by more women than do low income males (Figure 14). Money is an important resource for acquiring "outside" (extramarital) relationships; in contrast, land is not liquid and cannot be used as "gifts" to an outside woman. Income is also important for maintaining existing marital relationships. Poor men are more likely to lose their mates to other, more wealthy men. Occupations that provide erratic income (e.g., temporary road work) contribute to marital instability.

Land is associated with marital stability. Landed males tend to maintain mating relationships for longer periods than do males with little or no land (Figure 15). The increased marital stability of landed males may result in part from the steady income provided by cash crops, but the potential for land inheritance by children was commonly mentioned to be an important incentive for women to stay with their mates. Landed males were reportedly more concerned with their mate's fidelity, because they wanted to ensure that their land went to their "own" offspring (Flinn 1988a). Hence the "heritability" of land, as opposed to the "liquidity" of income, affect male reproductive strategies differently. In brief, income appears to have higher utility as mating effort, whereas land may have higher utility as parental effort. This suggests that income and land may influence patterns of paternal care.

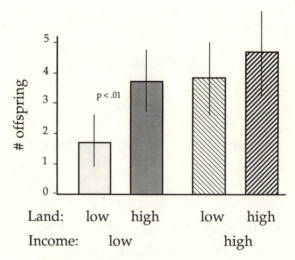

Figure 13. Resources and male reproduction.

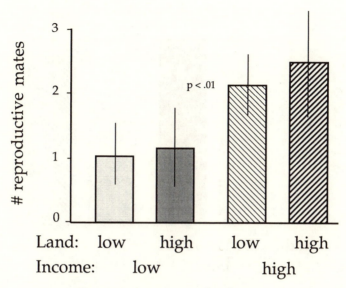

Figure 14. Resources and polygyny.

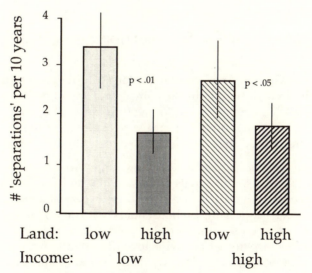

Figure 15. Resources and marital stability.

Figure 16 indicates that landed males interact more frequently with their children than do males with little or no land. Income appears to have little effect on father-child interaction rates. These data are consistent with the hypothesis that land influences males to allocate resources towards parental effort.

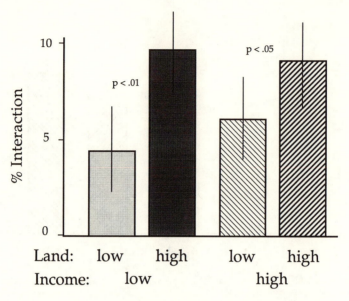

Figure 16. Resources and paternal care.

SUMMARY AND CONCLUDING REMARKS

Fathers in Grande Anse make important contributions to the welfare of their children, although they usually do not spend much of their time (range = 0–17%, average = 4.2%) involved in direct care of infants and preadolescents. Data examined in this paper suggest that paternal behavior is influenced by at least five factors summarized below.

1.   *Age and sex of offspring.* Fathers in Grande Anse interact differently with infants versus adolescents versus adults, and sons versus daughters. Fathers are not as involved as mothers in caretaking of infants and preadolescents, especially in households with alternative caretakers, such as grandparents, aunts, or older sibs. There is little or no sexual specialization in paternal behavior towards infants; fathers treat their infant sons and daughters similarly. Fathers and mothers spend nearly equivalent amounts of time with adolescent and adult children, and sexual specialization is apparent. For example, fathers commonly exert influence over their teenage daughter's mating relationships (Flinn 1988a), and fathers interact more frequently with their adult sons than with their adult daughters. All single-father households ($N = 4$) involved adolescent or adult sons.

2. *Genetic relatedness to offspring.* Males distinguish among step and genetic children and usually interact more frequently and less agonistically with their genetic children than with their stepchildren (Flinn 1988b). Coresidence with genetic father appears to provide important benefits for children.

3. *Residence and marital status.* Coresidence facilitates father–offspring interactions. Fathers interact more frequently with offspring if they (father and offspring) live together. Nonresidential father–offspring relationships are significantly influenced by other kin ties, especially the presence of new spouses. Father–offspring interactions are less frequent when the father has acquired a new "wife," and/or when the mother has acquired a new "husband." This may be due to avoidance behavior between ex-spouses and/or their new mates, and new spouses (stepparents of the children) inhibiting paternal care. Nonresidential relationships with children older than 20 years, however, are not significantly affected by new spouses.

4. *Age of father.* Young fathers (<25 years) and old fathers (>54 years) interact more frequently with infant and juvenile offspring (<10 years) than do middle-aged fathers (25–54 years). Conversely, middle-aged fathers interact more frequently with older sons (>20 years) than do old fathers. These data suggest that age affects male time allocation strategies.

5. *Land ownership and income.* Both land and income are associated with male reproductive success. Income is a better predictor of the number of mates with whom males reproduced; that is, high income males tend to have children by more women than do low income males. Land is associated with marital stability. Landed males tend to maintain mating relationships for longer periods than do males with little or no land. Landed males spend a greater proportion of their time involved in paternal care than do males with little or no land. Income appears to have little effect on father–child interaction rates. These results are consistent with the hypothesis that land influences males to allocate resources towards parental effort, whereas income influences males to allocate resources towards mating effort.

The individual differences in paternal behavior suggested by the data are generally consistent with the hypothesis that males adaptively allocate their time and resources. Paternal investment is high when potential benefits to offspring are high and costs to father are low. Paternal investment is low when potential benefits to offspring are low and costs to father are high. Unfortunately, we have little understanding of specific psychological and other proximate mechanisms associated with these aspects of variation in paternal behavior (Petrovich and Gewirtz

1985). Hopefully the chances of identifying such mechanisms are improved by knowledge of what their functions might be.

NOTES

1. For example, Besson 1979; Clarke 1957; Gonzalez 1969; Goody 1975; Otterbein 1966; Rodman 1971; M. Smith 1962; R. Smith 1957.
2. "Watching" and "babysitting" involved situations in which the caretaker was within 10 meters of a child and was "responsible" for the infant's temporary well-being. These codes included situations in which a child was sleeping and a caretaker was involved in some other activity (e.g., sewing), but was still attentive to the child, as indicated by position and/or behavior such as looking at the child.
3. Those societies in which paternity is not acknowledged, or downplayed relative to maternity, are characterized by mating systems in which confidence of paternity is likely to be low (Flinn 1981).
4. I use the term "genetic offspring" rather than "natural offspring" or "biological offspring" because stepoffspring are no less "natural" or "biological." In all cases genetic offspring are putative, being based on reported genealogical relationships (see Methods); no paternity exclusion data are available. Nepotistic behavior is expected to be based on the proximate mechanisms associated with paternity identification rather than genetic relatedness per se (Alexander 1979; Daly and Wilson 1983; Flinn 1988b; Sherman and Holmes 1985; Symons 1979).
5. Controlling for age effects is difficult because the gender and age-specific patterns of parent–offspring interaction are different for step and genetic relationships—see section V. Hence a simple age-weighting would not be valid. The samples used in Figures 5 and 6 are adjusted by removal of the youngest and oldest offspring such that the mean ages of the two groups being compared are nearly equal. In all cases the results are significant with and without this adjustment.

REFERENCES

Ainsworth, M. 1967. *Infancy in Uganda. Infant Care and the Growth of Love.* Baltimore: Johns Hopkins Press.
Alexander, R. D. 1974. The evolution of social behavior. *Annual Review of Ecology and Systematics* 5:325–383.
———.1979. *Darwinism and Human Affairs.* Seattle: University of Washington Press.
Altmann, J. 1974. Observational study of behavior: sampling methods. *Behaviour* XLIX:227–266.
Bernard, H. R. 1988. *Research Methods in Cultural Anthropology.* Beverly Hills: Sage.

Besson, J. 1979. Symbolic aspects of land in the Caribbean: The tenure and transmission of land rights among Caribbean peasantries. In *Peasants, plantations and rural communities in the Caribbean*. M. Cross and A. Marks, (Eds.), pp. 86–116. Department of Sociology, University of Surrey, and Department of Caribbean Studies, Royal Institute of Linguistics and Anthropology.

Betzig, L., and Turke, P. 1986. Parental investment by sex on Ifaluk. *Ethology and Sociobiology* 7:29–37.

Blurton-Jones, N. 1972. (Ed.) *Ethological Studies of Child Behavior*. Cambridge: Cambridge University Press.

Borgerhoff Mulder, M., and Milton, M. 1985. Factors affecting infant care in the Kipsigis. *Journal of Anthropological Research* 41:231–262.

Buss, D. M. 1988. From vigilance to violence: Tactics of mate retention in American undergraduates. *Ethology and Sociobiology* 9:291–317.

Chagnon, N. A. 1974. *Studying the Yanomamo*. New York: Holt, Rinehart & Winston.

Clarke, E. 1957. *My Mother who Fathered me*. London: Allen & Unwin.

Cronk, L. 1989. Low socioeconomic status and female-biased parental investment: the Mukugodo example. *American Anthropologist* 91:414–429.

Daly, M., and Wilson, M. I. 1980. Discriminative parental solicitude: A biological perspective. *Journal of Marriage and the Family* 42:277–288.

_____. 1981a. Abuse and neglect of children in evolutionary perspective. In *Natural selection and social behavior: Recent research and new theory*, R. D. Alexander, D. W. Tinkle (Eds.), pp. 405–416. New York: Chiron Press.

_____. 1981b. Child maltreatment from a sociobiological perspective. *New Directions for Child Development* 11:93–112.

Daly, M., Wilson, M. I., and Weghorst, S. J. 1982. Male sexual jealousy. *Ethology and Sociobiology* 3:11–27.

_____. 1983. Sex, evolution, and behavior (2nd edition). Boston: Willard Grant Press.

_____. 1987. Risk of maltreatment of children living with stepparents. In *Child abuse and neglect*, R. Gelles and J. Lancaster (Eds.), pp. 215–232. Hawthorne, New York: Aldine de Gruyter.

Draper, P. 1975. Cultural pressure on sex differences. *American Ethnologist* 2(4):602–616.

_____. 1976. Social and economic constraints on child life among the !Kung. In *The Kalahari hunter-gatherers*, R. B. Lee, I. DeVore (Eds.). Cambridge: Harvard University Press.

Draper, P., and Harpending, H. 1982. Father absence and reproductive strategy: An evolutionary perspective. *Journal of Anthropological Research* 38:255–273.

Flinn, M. V. 1981. Uterine vs. agnatic kinship variability and associated cousin marriage preferences. In *Natural selection and social behavior: Recent research and new theory*, R. D. Alexander, D. W. Tinkle (Eds.), pp. 439–475. New York: Chiron Press.

_____. 1983. Resources, mating, and kinship: The behavioral ecology of a Trinidadian village. Ph.D. thesis, Department of Anthropology, Northwestern University. Ann Arbor, MI: University Microfilms.

————. 1986. Correlates of reproductive success in a Caribbean village. *Human Ecology* 14(2):225–243.

————. 1988a. Mate guarding in a Caribbean village. *Ethology and Sociobiology* 9:1–29.

————. 1988b. Step and genetic parent/offspring relationships in a Caribbean village. *Ethology and Sociobiology* 9:335–369.

————. 1988c. Parent-offspring interactions in a Caribbean village: Daughter guarding. In *Human reproductive behaviour*. L. Betzig, M. Borgerhoff Mulder, P. Turke (Eds.), pp. 189–200. London: Cambridge University Press.

————. 1989. Household composition and female reproductive strategies. In *Sexual and reproductive strategies*, A. Rasa, C. Vogel, E. Voland (Eds.), pp. 206–233. London: Chapman.

Flinn, M. V., and Durbrow, E. 1990. Factors associated with childhood stress as measured by radioimmunoassay of cortisol levels in saliva. *American Journal of Physical Anthropology* 81:222.

Flinn, M. V., and England, B. 1991. Childhood stress as measured by radioimmunoassay of cortisol levels in saliva. *American Journal of Physical Anthropology* supplement 12:73.

Flinn, M. V., England, B., and Beer, T. 1992. Health condition and corticosteroid stress response among children in a rural Dominican village. *American Journal of Physical Anthropology*.

Gelles, R., and Lancaster, J. 1987. (Eds.) *Child Abuse and Neglect: Biosocial Dimensions.* Hawthorne, NY: Aldine de Gruyter.

Giles-Sims, J. 1984. The stepparent role: Expectations, behavior, and sanctions. *Journal of Family Issues* 5:116–130.

Gonzalez, N. S. *Black Carib household structure.* Seattle: University of Washington Press, 1969.

Goody, E. 1975. Delegation of parental roles in West Africa and the West Indies. In *Socialization and Communication in Primary Groups*, T. R. Williams (Ed.), pp. 125–158. The Hague: Mouton.

Gross, D. 1984. Time allocation: A tool for the study of cultural behavior. *Annual Review of Anthropology 1984* 13:519–558.

Hames, R. 1979. Relatedness and interaction among the Ye'kwana: A preliminary analysis. In *Evolutionary biology and human social behavior*. N. Chagnon, W. Irons, (Eds.), pp. 238–250. North Scituate, MA: Duxbury Press.

————. 1988. The allocation of parental care among the Ye'kwana. In *Human Reproductive Behaviour*. L. Betzig, M. Mulder, P. Turke (Eds.), pp. 237–252. London: Cambridge University Press.

Hamilton, W. D. 1964. The genetical evolution of social behavior I. and II. *Journal of Theoretical biology* 7:1–52.

Harrison, D. H. 1979. The changing fortunes of a Trinidad peasantry: A case study. In *Peasants, plantations and rural communities in the Caribbean*. M. Cross and A. Marks, (Eds.), pp. 54–85. Department of Sociology, University of Surrey, and Department of Caribbean Studies, Royal Institute of Linguistics and Anthropology.

Hewlett, B. S. 1988. Sexual selection and paternal investment among Aka pygmies. In *Human Reproductive Behaviour*. L. Betzig, M. Mulder, P. Turke (Eds.). London: Cambridge University Press, pp. 263–276.

Hill, K., and Kaplan, H. 1988a. Tradeoffs in male and female reproductive strategies among the Ache: Part 1. In *Human Reproductive Behaviour*. L. Betzig, M. Mulder, P. Turke (Eds.), pp. 277–290. London: Cambridge University Press.

———. 1988b. Tradeoffs in male and female reproductive strategies among the Ache: Part 2. In *Human Reproductive Behaviour*. L. Betzig, M. Mulder, P. Turke (Eds.), pp. 291–306. London: Cambridge University Press.

Ihinger-Tallman, M. 1988. Research on stepfamilies. *Annual Review of Sociology* 14:25–48.

Irons, W. 1979. Investment and primary social dyads. In *Evolutionary biology and human social behaviour*. N. Chagnon, W. Irons (Eds.), pp. 181–212. North Scituate, MA: Duxbury Press.

———. 1983. Human female reproductive strategies. In *Social behavior of female vertebrates*, S. Wasser, M. Waterhouse (Eds.). New York: Academic Press, pp. 169–213.

———. 1988. Parental behavior in humans. In *Human Reproductive Behaviour*. L. Betzig, M. Mulder, P. Turke (Eds.), pp. 307–314. London: Cambridge University Press.

Johnson, A. W. 1978. *Quantification in Cultural Anthropology*. Stanford: Stanford University Press.

Katz, M. M., and Konner, M. 1981. The role of the father: An anthropological perspective. In *The role of the father in child development* (2nd edition), M. Lamb (Ed.), pp. 155–185. New York: John Wiley & Sons.

Kurland, J. 1979. Paternity, mother's brother, and human sociality. In *Evolutionary biology and human social behavior*. N. Chagnon, W. Irons, (Eds.), pp. 145–180. North Scituate, MA: Duxbury Press.

———, Gaulin, S. J. C. 1984. The evolution of male parental investment: Effects of genetic relatedness and feeding ecology on the allocation of reproductive effort. In *Primate Paternalism: An evolutionary and comparative view on male investment*, D. M. Taub (Ed.), pp. 259–308. New York: Van Nostrand Reinhold.

Lamb, M. E. 1981. (Ed.) *The role of the father in child development* (2nd edition). New York: John Wiley & Sons.

Lamb, M. E., Pleck, J. H., and Charnov, E. L. 1985. Paternal behavior in humans. *American Zoologist* 25:883–894.

Lamb, M. E., Pleck, J. H., Charnov, E. L., and Levine, J. A. 1987. A biosocial perspective on paternal behavior and involvement. In *Parenting across the lifespan: Biosocial dimensions*, J. B. Lancaster, J. Altmann, A. S. Rossi, L. R. Sherrod (Eds.), pp. 111–142. Hawthorne, NY: Aldine de Gruyter.

Levine, R. A., Miller, P. M., West, M. M. 1988. (Eds.). *Parental Behavior in Diverse Societies*. San Francisco: Jossey-Bass Inc.

Marchione, T. J. 1980. Factors associated with malnutrition in the children of western Jamaica. In *Nutritional Anthropology*. N. Jerome, R. Kandel, and G. Pelto (Eds.). Pleasantville, NY: Redgrave.

Munroe, R. H., and Munroe, R. L. 1971. Household density and infant care in an East African Society. *Journal of Social Psychology* 85:3–13.

Munroe, R. L., Munroe, R. H., Michealson, C., Koel, A., Bolton, R., and Bolton, C. 1983. Time allocation in four societies. *Ethnology* 22:355–70.

Otterbein, K. F. 1966. *The Andros Islanders.* Lawrence: University of Kansas.

Petrovich, S. B. and Gewirtz, J. L. 1985. The attachment learning process and its relation to cultural and biological evolution: Proximate and ultimate considerations. In *The psychobiology of attachment and separation,* M. Reite and T. Field (Eds.), pp. 259–291. New York: Academic Press.

Rodman, H. 1971. *Lower class families.* London: Oxford University Press.

Sanford, M. 1975. To be treated as a child of the home: Black Carib child lending in a British West Indian Society. In *Socialization and Communication in Primary Groups,* T. R. Williams (Ed.), pp. 159–181. The Hague: Mouton.

Sherman, P. W., and Holmes, W. G. 1985. Kin recognition: issues and evidence. In *Experimental behavioral ecology and sociobiology,* B. Holldobler and M. Lindauer (Eds.). Sunderland, MA: Sinauer.

Smith, M. G. 1962. *West Indian family structure.* Seattle: University of Washington Press.

Smith, R. T. 1957. *The Negro family in British Guiana.* New York: Humanities Press.

Symons, D. 1979. *The evolution of human sexuality.* Oxford: Oxford University Press.

Werner, E. E. 1989a. Children of the Garden Island. *Scientific American* April 1989:106–111.

———— 1989b. High risk children in young adulthood: a longitudinal study from birth to 32 years. *American Journal of Orthopsychiatry* 59:72–81.

Whiting, B., and Edwards C. P. 1988 *Children of different worlds: The formation of social behavior.* Cambridge: Harvard University Press.

————, and Whiting, J. 1975. *Children of six cultures: A psycho-cultural analysis.* Cambridge: Harvard University Press.

Wilson, M., Daly, M., and Weghorst, S. 1980. Household composition and the risk of child abuse and neglect. *Journal of Biosocial Science* 12:333–340.

Chapter 4

Variation in Paternal Care Among the Yanomamö

Raymond Hames

The aim of this chapter is to document and attempt to explain variation in paternal investment in offspring in four Yanomamö villages. Paternal investment is broadly defined: it ranges from simple childcare (e.g., holding, feeding, comforting) to provisioning (time allocated to food production and other economic activities). I argue that variation in paternal care can be understood only in relation to variation in maternal care. This is because parental investment in offspring is a cooperative activity involving both parents. In addition, I will demonstrate that parental investment is specialized between the sexes with one sex or the other dominating particular types of parental investment.

BACKGROUND

It is well known and amply documented (Whiting and Whiting 1975; Babchuck et al. 1985; West and Konner 1986) that females provide more care to infants and children than do males. However, most studies measure care as the amount of time allocated to feeding, nursing, holding, or simply childcare (Lamb et al. 1987). Evolutionary theory in its emphasis on parental investment (Trivers 1972) forces one to look at all forms of effort allocated to increasing an offspring's chances of survival and reproduction. Thus, care would also include provisioning (production of food and other resources necessary for survival and reproduction) and other forms of investment that Hewlett (this volume) refers to as "indirect care." Recent applications of parental investment theory (see below) have led to the development of useful hypotheses to explain differential parental investment.

In their review of research on paternal care West and Konner (1986) note that males in sedentary polygynous societies are much less likely to engage in childcare than males in mobile (e.g., hunter–gatherers) monogamous societies. A further refinement of that generalization has been made and developed by Draper (1988) and Draper and Harpending (1989) in a number of publications based on Dawkins' (1976) "Dad" (high parental investment males) and "Cad" (high mating effort males) dichotomy. To sharpen this distinction, Draper and Harpending distinguish between two types of societies, largely based on the father's role in the family's social environment and economy. In father-absent societies, mothers provide a large portion of resources needed by offspring, the father is distant, absent, or aloof from mother and child, the marital system is polygynous, and marital ties tend to be fluid. In father-present societies, fathers provide a large portion of resources needed by offspring, the father eats, sleeps, and interacts frequently with family members, the marital system is monogamous, and marital ties are enduring. There are other factors that differentiate father-absent and father-present societies (see Draper and Harpending 1989: 349–351) such that these polar types grade over a multivariate continuum. The primary factors that locate a society on this continuum are the degree to which females are able to independently provision themselves and offspring and the degree to which males differentially allocate reproductive effort into parental and mating components.

Using the Draper–Harpending scheme it is clear that the Yanomamö fall closer to the father-absent end of the continuum [compare Chagnon's ethnographic descriptions (1983) to Draper and Harpending's criteria (1989: 349–351)]. In quantitative terms, Yanomamö males spend less time in proximity maintenance and active childcare (see below) compared to father-present groups such as the Aka Pygmies studied by Hewlett (1988, 1991). One important prediction of this generalization is that fathers in father-absent societies invest less in all forms of parental investment than mothers. This descriptive hypothesis will be investigated by looking at three different measures of parental investment among the Yanomamö: childcare, proximity maintenance, and provisioning (labor or indirect care) as they are affected by sex, marital status, number of dependents, and nursing status of mother.

METHODS

Measurement of Behavior

Time allocation data from six different Yanomamö villages were collected from 1985 to 1987 in three field sessions of approximately 3 months duration each. The Yanomamö are a relatively unacculturated population inhabiting the Venezuelan and Brazilian Amazon. On average, village population ranges in size from about 40 to over 200. The village itself *(shabono)* is built in the form of a large circular lean-to with an uncovered central plaza.[1] Family living quarters are not individually partitioned by walls. Thus, the activities of all other families are in full view of any family (see Chagnon 1974 for schematic drawings of villages). Subsistence is gained—in standard Amazonia way—through shifting cultivation of plantains and root crops (chiefly manioc and taro) and through the foraging activities of hunting, gathering, and fishing. Although gardening provides the major sources of calories, two to three times more hours per day are allocated to foraging activities (Hames 1989). In this chapter, data from four of the six villages studied are analyzed.

Sampling of behavior in four different villages was a result of field exigencies and an attempt to determine the degree to which time allocation measures varied between villages. The villages of Mishimishimaböwei and Bisaasi were sampled in 1986 while the villages of Rakoiwä and Krihisiwä were sampled in 1987. As shown below, many of the measures of parental investment differ from village to village and the interpretation of these differences may be relatable to the unique situation of each village. Each of the villages is described below.

The village of Mishimishimaböwei is located in the headwaters of the Mavaca River. Although it is the most isolated of all villages (4 to 5 days travel from the nearest mission) in the sample it has been the subject of numerous articles, books, and films by Chagnon (e.g., 1974 and references therein). During the time allocation study in 1986 approximately one-half of the village was on trek *(wayumi)*, occupying an old garden about 2 day's walk distant.

The villages of Krihisiwä and Rakoiwä are located 1 day's walk inland from the Orinoco River. These villages are separated by a 10 minute walk. Collectively they are known as Sheroanä, but they currently occupy separate residences owing to dispute between the two headmen, Krihisiwä and Rakoiwä.

The village of Bisaasi-teri (or Mosuu-teri) is located directly across the Orinoco River from the Salesian Mission at Mavaca, and occupies the confluence of the Mavaca and Orinoco Rivers. For the Yanomamö, this village is highly acculturated (Chagnon 1983). Nearly all school age children attend the mission school, adults frequently trade with the missionaries, and several young adults are employed by the mission in a variety of tasks ranging from elementary school teaching to manual labor.

Behavioral sampling occurred in February and March, the middle of the dry season. During this time the Yanomamö frequently trek and engage in long distance hunting in preparation for multivillage feasts *(reahu)*. Indeed, during the behavior-sampling period nearly all the able-bodied men in the villages of Krihisiwä, Rakoiwä, and Mishimishima-böwei engaged in overnight *heniyomou* hunting lasting from 3 to 5 days. Although I sampled behavior during these periods, *heniyomou* days have been deleted (for males and females) in the present analysis for two simple reasons. First, the goal of this chapter is to determine relative contributions of parental investment from both sexes. Including *heniyomou* hunting days in the analysis would have overrepresented female contributions to childcare and underestimated male contribution because the frequency at which men engaged in *heniyomou* hunting during the sampling period is much greater than what normally occurs in a yearly cycle. Second, since all able-bodied men are encouraged to participate in *heniyomou* hunting, variance in time allocated to labor would be reduced.

Some sociodemographic attributes of the villages are presented in Table 1. Two things should be noted about this table. In two of the villages there are polyandrous males. Among the Yanomamö polyandry usually involves a polygynous male sharing one of his wives with a younger male. The Yanomamö refer to this as *yädöa*, which means to add oneself, whether one is male or female, to a current marriage. In the analysis these males are counted as monogamous. In a number of cases the number of monogamous or polygynous males and females may not agree with the number in some of the analyses. This is due to a variety of considerations such as nonresident (visitor) status and too few observations (e.g., leaving the village to visit another during the sampling period). Also, in several villages there are preteen girls married to mature males. These couples are not included in the analysis. Married couples were defined as those who had never married offspring residing with them.

All measures of parental investment were gained through scan sampling (Altmann 1974; Johnson 1975). At random hours of the day the behavior, location, time, and interaction of all individuals within the *shabono* (village) and its immediate environs were recorded. If an indi-

Table 1. Sociodemographic Attributes of Yanomamö Villages

Village	Monogamous		Polygnous		Polyandrous	
	Males	*Females*	*Males*	*Females*	*Males*	*Total*
Mishimishi	16	16	7	14	3	56
Krihisiwä	8	9	4	8	1	30
Rakoiwä	8	7	2	5	1	24
Bisaasi	20	20	4	8	0	52

vidual was absent from observation because he or she was in the forest hunting, gathering, gardening, or fishing this was recorded using the same variables as scans of individuals observed within the village (Hames 1979). For the four villages, a total of 11,912 observations were recorded for an average of 48 observations per individual. Observations were made between 0600 and 1959 hours, a period of 780 minutes or 13 hours. Thus, hours or minutes allocated to various activities may be estimated by multiplying the percentages in the tables and figures by 13 hours or 780 minutes. Clearly, important childcare activities occur outside the hours of observation and collection of such data would be revealing. Nevertheless, the hours chosen reflect the typical time of settling down to sleep and rising in the morning.

In addition, I accompanied numerous groups of Yanomamö into the forest while they hunted, fished, gathered, and gardened. During these forays scans were performed every 5 to 10 minutes on all group members using the same variables as the in-village scans. Analysis of this data set is not reported here.

In the analyses presented below I have decided against pooling all villages into a single analytic sample. The tabular data presented below show moderate to sometimes considerable variation between villages in labor time. Much of this variation is undoubtedly related local environmental differences. Therefore, the desirability of statistically controlling for such "village effects" precludes pooling.[2]

Classification of Caretaking Behavior

At its most general level parental investment may be defined "as any investment by the parent in an individual offspring that increases the offspring's chance of surviving (and hence reproductive success) at the cost of the parent's ability to invest in other offspring" (Trivers 1972: 139). For the purposes of this chapter, I have divided parental investment into three categories: (1) childcare, (2) proximity maintenance, and (3) economic provisioning. Children who are the objects of care are those less than 10 years of age. Although somewhat arbitrary, I chose this limit analysis of direct care in all four villages reveals that children beyond this age rarely receive direct childcare (Figure 1).

Childcare is simply the amount of time an individual allocates to interactive behaviors such as nursing, feeding, holding, and socializing with children.

In the field, proximity maintenance was measured by the frequency that caretakers (in general, an individual older than the child) are found to be *touching* (e.g., child sitting in lap), *adjacent* to (< 1 m), *observant* of (> 1 m but < 2 m), *distant*, (> 2 m but < 5), and *nonproximate* to (> 5 m) a

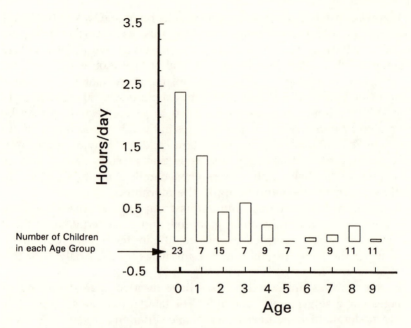

Figure 1. Physical care of children in hours/day by age.

child less than 10 years of age. In measuring proximity maintenance, the location of the active or passive caretaker is the issue and *not* the caretaker's behavior relative to a child. For example, a mother nursing a child would be scored as touching proximity and so would a father who holds a child's hand as they walk. In the discussion of proximity maintenance to follow, degree of proximity is not considered but rather the frequency at which mothers or fathers were proximate (touching, adjacent, observant, or distant) or nonproximate to a child.

I must stress that all measures of childcare and proximity maintenance come from behavioral observations made in the village. Childcare and proximity maintenance occur outside the village when children accompany their parents on gardening, gathering, and fishing excursions. These data have yet to be analyzed. However, preliminary results of behavior outside the village indicate that while the *differences* between the sexes in time allocated to direct care and proximity maintenance are similar to what is found in the village, levels of both variables *increase* dramatically for both sexes.

Economic provisioning is amount of resources produced for investment in children and it is measured by the amount of labor a male or female allocates to basic subsistence tasks. Obviously, not all resources produced are bound for investment in offspring. Some are consumed by producers and some are given to nonfamily members (see Figure 11 and below). Unfortunately, it is impossible to disaggregate this measure in terms of fractions devoted for self, mate, offspring, and others.

General Patterns of Parent–Child Interaction

Patterns of direct childcare for adult males and females differ in a number of fundamental ways. Infants and children to the age of about 3 are carried in a sling normally made of homespun cotton that is shaped like a broad belt and is hung over the left shoulder, extending to the wearer's right hip. The sling supports the child's buttocks and lower back and the wearer's left arm cradles the rest of the body. In this position, an infant has easy access to the breast and may nurse on demand. It is extremely rare for a man to use a sling. When a man carries a child he simply places the child on a hip, or higher up on the upper abdomen or lower chest if the child is very young.

A very large fraction of childcare is simply child holding or carrying. When women carry or hold children they frequently engage in a variety of activities such as food preparation, cotton spinning, or transporting burdens. Males very rarely engage in alternative activities (except for conversation) while holding or carrying children. They tend to direct their full attention to children by playing with them, verbalizing, or fondling (e.g., nuzzling the stomach, neck, or chest). This dichotomy is even stricter for activities that take place outside of the village: men never carry children when collecting firewood, gardening, hunting, gathering, or fishing, while women frequently do.

The amount of direct care a child receives declines dramatically with age. This relationship for all villages (based on 106 children < 10 years) is shown in Figure 1. Infants, or those less than a year, average 2.5 hours of direct care per day. For children between 2 and 3 years there is a sharp decline in care that corresponds to the cessation of nursing (I have no observational records of children nursing beyond the age of 3). Child-care declines dramatically to much less than one-half hour after age 4. Interestingly, this is the age when children are no longer carried to the garden and when they are increasingly left at home when their mothers work in forest or garden.

ASSUMPTIONS

In the analysis to follow I have assumed that mothers and fathers are the primary investors in children. In a previous study on the neighboring Ye'kwana I demonstrated that nonparent individuals (brothers, sisters, grandparents) provide childcare (Hames 1988). This also is true for the Yanomamö. However, the goal of this chapter is to document paternal care and I believe that it can be most simply accomplished by focusing on fathers and by comparing them to mothers. A more complex analysis might show that low investment by some mothers or fathers may not mean low care or investment received by a child but rather unencumbered kin or other family members may be investing in that child. This type of analysis is planned for the future.

DETERMINANTS OF INVESTMENT

Sex of investor, number of dependent offspring, presence of highly dependent offspring (i.e., nursing child), and marital status (polygynous or monogamous) are factors hypothesized to determine levels of parental investment. Below I describe the theoretical rationale for hypothesizing these factors as determinants of differential parental investment.

Sex of Investor

It follows from Trivers' (1972) model of parental investment that Yanomamö females should invest more in childcare than Yanomamö males. There are two basic reasons for this. First, female reproduction is more limited than a male's such that the cost of loss of an offspring is greater for females than for males. Second, males in polygynous societies such as the Yanomamö may more profitably enhance their reproductive success by expending effort in acquiring another mate. While this option is theoretically available to women (polyandry), following it is less likely to enhance a woman's reproductive output significantly, and it may lead to abandonment of paternal investment in her offspring because a male without sole sexual access would doubt his paternity. It should be clear that Trivers' model does not preclude paternal care—it predicts only that maternal investment should be greater (see Lamb et al. 1988; Lancaster and Lancaster 1983 for detailed theoretical justification of male–female differences in investment).

Number of Dependent Offspring

Children are incapable of providing their own subsistence and require some degree of nurturing and care from adults. Therefore, it should be obvious that the greater number of dependent children a couple have the greater amount of time mothers and fathers must allocate to all forms of investment. For the Yanomamö, I define dependent children as those who are less than 10 years of age. This age division is not arbitrary. Boys and girls generally begin to make significant contributions to the household economy after the age of 10 in the areas of food production and preparation and, as I have already noted, direct childcare all but ceases when a child is older than 10 years.

This prediction rests on the assumption that households are economically independent and self-sufficient, an assumption made explicit in Chayanovian analyses of labor effort and consumer/producer ratios (Hames 1988). For the Yanomamö this assumption does not hold. Food resources and labor are widely exchanged between households (Hames 1989, below, and Figure 12; Saffirio and Hames 1983). Although Yanomamö households are not totally independent, household personnel, in most cases, provide the bulk of economic resources for their members. Therefore, it is reasonable to predict that number of dependents will be correlated with the labor efforts of productive adults.

Nursing Status

Since nursing children demand more car than nonnursing children it is perhaps obvious that nursing women should allocate more time to childcare than nonnursing women. Likewise one would predict that men with nursing wives would allocate more time to childcare. The latter prediction is reasonable if childcare of nursing children is shared proportionately and is not the exclusive domain of women.

My previous research on the Ye'kwana women indicated a negative correlation between nursing frequency and labor time (Hames 1988: 247); and research on the Ache (Hurtado et al. 1985) has demonstrated that nursing women allocate less time to labor than women who do not nurse. Ache males with dependent children allocate more time to care and less time to hunting (controlling for efficiency) (Hill and Kaplan 1988: 284) than men without dependent offspring. A nursing child is frequently nonambulatory or partially ambulatory, which forces the caretaker to work with a child in a sling or interrupt work in order to care for the child. Both factors decrease work efficiency and leave less time available for labor (Hurtado et al. 1985). This requirement is especially stringent in the neotropical forest where sources of environmental trauma abound (insects, thorns, and open fires). It should be noted that my Ye'kwana research (Hames 1988) indicates that Ye'kwana males did not increase their work loads (provisioning) in response to their wives' decreased work load. These relationships are examined for the Yanomamö.

Marital Status

In the four villages sampled, from 17 to 29% of all married males are married polygynously and the corresponding figure for females ranges from 29 to 47% (Table 1). Marriage status and consequent variation in male parental investment may be the result of simple economic factors or reflect different reproductive strategies. From a simple economic perspective, polygyny in relation to parental investment has different implications for men and women. For co-wives it means that the economic services and paternal care of their husband must be shared. If polygynous males work no harder or more efficiently than monogamous males, then polygynous females receive economic services and paternal care of their offspring at half the rate of monogamous females. Therefore, polygynous females would have to work harder to compensate for low paternal investment. For polygynous men, it means that they have twice as many spouses and more children to support. Therefore, they must allocate more time to paternal investment or render it more efficiently if they are to provide investment equal to monogamous males. Both of these predictions not only assume that mothers and fathers are primary caregivers but also assume that no food resources from other households subsidize their investment in offspring.

However, the marriage status of males may mark different reproductive strategies. As described above in the Draper–Harpending model, monogamous males should devote more time to paternal investment because it is a superior allocation of their reproductive effort. Polygynous males, on the other hand, should devote more time to mating effort since it has a higher payoff than parental effort (see Hurtado and Hill, this volume, for an extended discussion of this issue). As developed by Draper and Harpending (1989), these predictions are designed to account for differential allocation of parental and mating effort made by males in polygynous and monogamous societies. As an extension of this model, it would be useful to determine whether it can predict variation in parental effort among monogamous and polygynous males within a polygynous society such as the Yanomamö. For the Yanomamö the question becomes, do monogamous males allocate more time to paternal investment (specifically, childcare and labor) than polygynous males? And do polygynous males allocate more time to mating effort (e.g., status maintenance activities that allow them to hold onto plural wives and gain others)? Hewlett (1988) demonstrates for the foraging Aka that polygynous men invest less time in paternal investment (care and proximity maintenance, but not necessarily provisioning) than monogamous males.

RESULTS

Sex

In all four village populations females allocate significantly more time to childcare than do males (Figure 2). It should be noted that in nearly all cases the standard deviation is greater than the mean. In three of the four villages women allocated significantly more time to labor (provisioning) than did males (two-tailed t test $p < 0.025$, Figure 3). If childcare and labor are combined this sum is a fair index to total amount of parental effort. In three of four villages females allocate significantly (two-tailed t test, $p < 0.01$) more time to parental effort than males (Figure 4).

Dependents

In only two (Mishimishimaböwei and Krihisiwä) of the four villages (Table 2) is there a significant positive correlation between number of dependents and the labor time of fathers (Figures 5 and 6). And in those

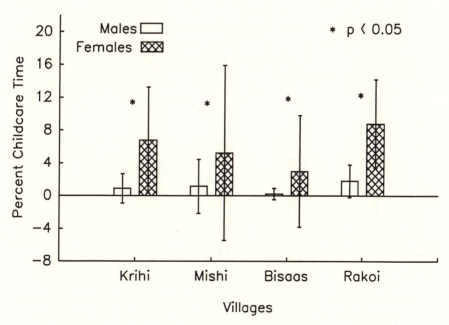

Figure 2. Percent time allocated to childcare for males and females.

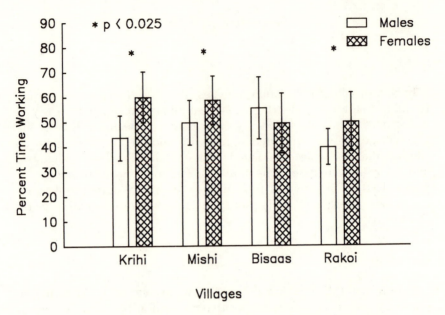

Figure 3. Percent time allocated to labor for males and females.

Figure 3. Percent time allocated to labor for males and females.

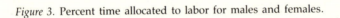

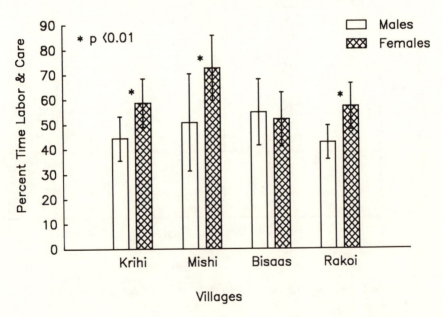

Figure 4. Percent time allocated to labor and care for males and females.

Table 2. Correlation (Pearson's *r*) of Indirect Investment and Number of Dependents by Village for Males and Females by Marriage Status

	Males			Females		
Village	Polygynous	Monogamous	All	Polygynous	Monogamous	All
Mishimishi	−0.12	0.51*	0.44**	−0.28	−0.32	−0.28
Krihisiwä	0.82	0.45	0.63**	−0.08	−0.49	−0.29
Bisaasi	−0.46	0.05	−0.16	−0.85	−0.23	−0.39
Rakoiwä	1.0	0.33	0.28	0.55	0.50	0.44

* *p* < 0.05, two-tailed, *t* test.
** *p* < 0.025, two-tailed, *t* test.

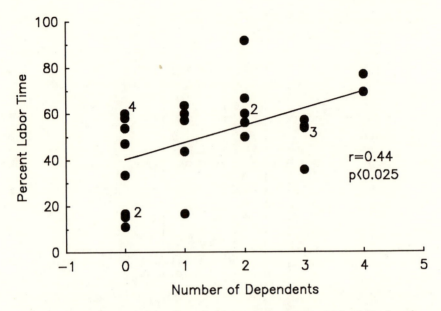

Figure 5. Time allocated to indirect investment by Mishimishimaböwei males.

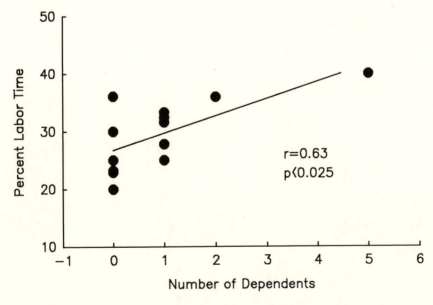

Figure 6. Time allocated to indirect investment by Krihisiwä males.

two villages, female labor time and number of dependents are negatively, but nonsignificantly, correlated. For males and females in the other two villages (Rakoiwä and Bisaasi) the correlation between labor time and number of dependents is not significant.

In all villages, there is no correlation between time allocated to childcare and number of dependent children for males or females. As is demonstrated below, the lack of relationship between childcare and number of dependents is attributable to the practice of investing high levels of care only to nursing children or children less than 3 years of age.

Nursing

Childcare and Nursing Status. In three of four villages (Table 3) nursing females allocate significantly more time to childcare than do nonnursing women, but in none of the villages do husbands of nursing wives allocate more time to childcare than husbands of nonnursing wives. That nursing women allocate significantly more time to care than nonnursing women is undoubtedly the result of the high rates of care received by children less than 3 years of age (Figure 1). That a father's participation in childcare is independent of his wife's nursing status strongly indicates that childcare is the special domain of a mother.

Labor and Nursing Status. In three of the four villages nursing women work significantly less than nonnursing women (Figure 7 and Table 4) but only in one of four villages (Figure 8 and Table 4) do men with nursing wives work more than men with nonnursing wives. This means that in most cases women with highly dependent children are working less than women without highly dependent children, a finding consonant with my Ye'kwana research (Hames 1988) and research on the Ache (Hurtado et al. 1985). In the village of Mishimishimaböwei husbands apparently compensate for their wives' reduced workload by

Table 3. Percent Time Allocated to Childcare by Nursing Status of Women and Nursing Status of Husband's Wives

| Village | Female | | Males | |
	Nursing	Not nursing	Nursing	Not nursing
Mishimishi	6.68 (±4.1)*	1.77 (±2.0)	2.11 (±3.1)	0.9 (±1.1)
Krihisiwä	12.67 (±8.2)*	4.28 (±3.9)	1.57 (±2.8)	0.0 (±0.0)
Bisaasi	8.91 (±11.1)*	0.65 (±1.1)	0.25 (±0.8)	1.79 (±0.7)
Rakoiwä	8.50 (±5.9)	10.42 (±6.0)	4.5 (±3.8)	1.26 (±1.2)

*$p < 0.05$, two-tailed, t test.

Table 4. Percent Time Allocated to Labor (Provisioning) by Nursing Status of Women and Nursing Status of Husband's Wives

	Females		*Males*	
Village	*Nursing*	*Not nursing*	*Nursing*	*Not nursing*
Mishimishi	62.9 (±18.9)*	73.3 (±14.8)	59.9 (±13.5)*	38.4 (±13.8)
Krihisiwä	45.3 (±6.2)*	54.8 (±8.8)	43.5 (±11.3)	43.1 (±8.8)
Bisaasi	39.6 (±12.8)*	49.5 (±12.6)	43.8 (±10.3)	38.0 (±13.8)
Rakoiwä	60.9 (±10.0)	60.2 (±6.8)	54.4 (±6.4)	54.7 (±15.3)

*$p < 0.05$, two-tailed t test.

working more. However, in the villages of Bisaasi, Rakoiwä, and Krihisiwä no compensation occurs: husbands of nursing wives do not work more than husbands of nonnursing wives. This problem is dealt with in the discussion section.

Proximity Maintenance

In the analysis below, active (e.g., feeding a child) and passive (e.g., keeping an eye on a child while doing something else) forms of prox-

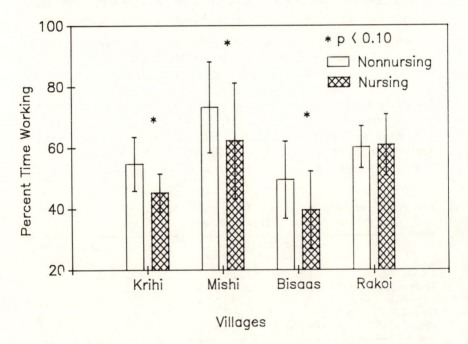

Figure 7. Percent time allocated to labor for nursing and nonnursing women.

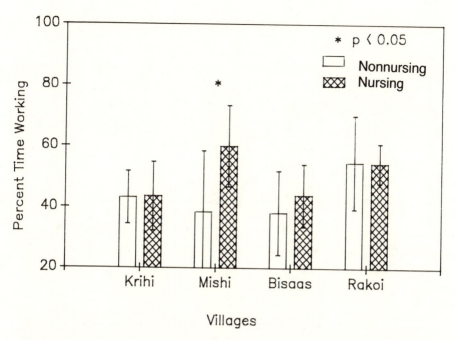

Figure 8. Percent time allocated to labor for males with nursing and nonnursing wives.

imity maintenance are combined. Proximity measures are scored only for observations made in the village. As a result, men have a lower probability of being seen in proximity with a child because they spend approximately 40% of their time in the forest compared to approximately 25% for women. Although proximity was noted for mothers, fathers, others, and no one, only proximity measures for mothers and fathers are compared. Finally, Mishimishimaböwei is the only village analyzed.

In Mishimishimaböwei mothers allocated 32% (4.16 hours/day) of their time in close proximity to children less than 10 years of age while fathers allocated 4.3% (0.56 hours/day) of their time. The difference is highly significant (*t* test, two-tailed, $p < 0.0001$). The difference is true for all age groups except for children of 5 years of age. In this case the difference between mothers and fathers is not significantly different even though males allocated 9.4% of their time compared to 7.5% for mothers.

Overall the amount of time that an adult is in close proximity to a child declines significantly with age ($r = -0.854$, $p < 0.001$). While this relationship holds for mothers (Figure 9, $r = -0.8154$, $p < 0.001$) there is no correlation between age of child and proximity to father ($r = -0.035$, $p = 0.9832$). To some extent the extremely low level of prox-

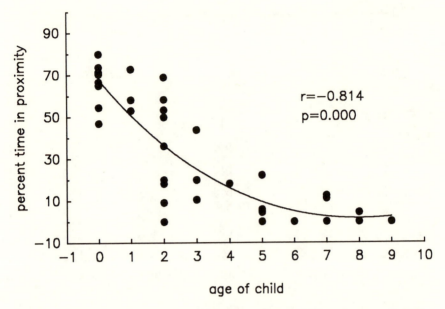

Figure 9. Percent time mothers are in proximity to children by age of child.

imity to children manifested by fathers is an artifact of the analytic procedure. For example, if a set of data records indicated that the mother was nursing her child and the father was less than a meter distant then the mother would be recorded as proximate and the father not. In other studies (e.g., Hewlett 1988) proximity measures the frequency at which one person or several people are within a particular distance from a child or infant. Therefore, the measures of proximity use here may be best interpreted as measuring the most proximate individual to the child.

Marital Status

Childcare and Labor. Table 5 reveals that although monogamous fathers allocate more time to childcare in three of the four villages the differences are not significant. For labor time, the same pattern is found in Table 6: in three of the four villages monogamous males work more than polygynous males, but the differences are not significant (Figure 10).

For women the same lack of statistical significance for time allocated to labor for polygynous and monogamous females is evident (Table 7 and

Table 5. Percent Time Allocated to Care by Monogamous and Polygynous
Fathers

| | Marriage type | | | | | |
| | Monogamous | | | Polygynous | | |
Village	N	Mean	SD	N	Mean	SD
Krihisiwä	8	0.975	±1.89	4	0.0	±0.0
Rakoiwä	7	2.800	±3.1	2	1.0	±1.3
Bisaasi	19	0.256	±0.75	4	0.0	±0.0
Mishimishi	16	0.781	±3.12	7	1.18	±3.125

Table 6. Percent Time Allocated to Labor by Monogamous and Polygynous
Fathers

| | Marriage Type | | | | | |
| | Monogamous | | | Polygynous | | |
Village	N	Mean	SD	N	Mean	SD
Krihisiwä	8	37.82	±11.91	4	29.45	±17.41
Rakoiwä	7	35.33	±12.10	2	28.7	±17.67
Bisaasi	19	48.21	±15.14	4	41.9	±13.81
Mishimishi	16	38.86	±16.71	7	51.51	±13.62

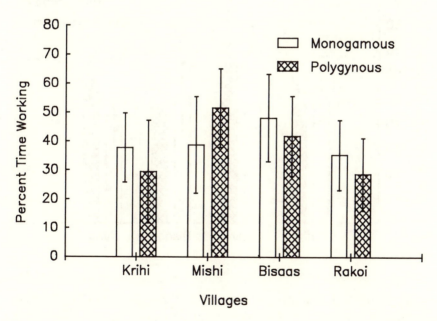

Figure 10. Percent time allocated to labor for monogamous and polygynous
males.

Table 7. Time Allocated to Labor by Monogamous and Polygynous Mothers

| | Marriage type | | | | | |
| | Monogamous | | | Polygynous | | |
Village	N	Mean	SD	N	Mean	SD
Krihisiwä	8	54.17	±12.947	8	47.63	±8.31
Rakoiwä	7	43.32	±13.48	4	57.60	±9.67
Bisaasi	19	50.84	±13.55	8	46.15	±8.57
Mishimishi	16	68.93	±12.46	13	64.35	±21.23

Figure 11), even though in three of the four villages monogamous females work more than polygynous females. From a simple Chayano-vian perspective one would have expected polygynous females to work more than monogamous females, but they do not. Although the Draper–Harpending model makes no clear predictions on labor time allocation differences between monogamously and polygynously married women, polygynous women should perhaps be working more since they are married to husbands who allocate more time to mating effort than to parental effort.

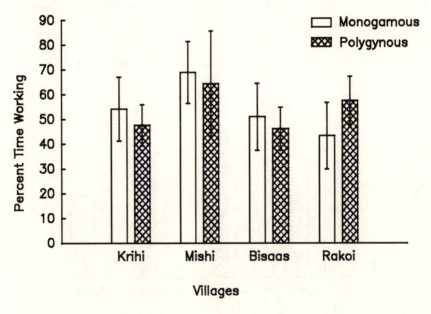

Figure 11. Percent time allocated to labor for monogamous and polygynous females.

DISCUSSION AND CONCLUSION

The research presented here leads to no firm conclusions about variation in paternal care or the interaction between paternal and maternal care but some trends are evident. The results suggests that other factors such as full household composition and exchange relationships may provide useful independent variables to account for male variation in parental investment.

I had hoped to show that time allocated to labor or childcare would be responsive to the number of dependents a couple has. For both sexes labor time should increase with the number of dependents. In the four villages analyzed, there was a positive correlation between number of dependents and time allocated to labor by fathers. But in only two of the four cases presented were the correlations significant. In the case of mothers, two of the four correlations were negative and two were positive but none was close to statistical significance.

The lack of better than expected fit between dependents and childcare may be the result of labor activities of other household members, food exchange patterns, and age-related changes in work capacity. The variable presence of other household members (e.g., siblings older than 10 years, grandparents, and in-laws) contributes labor to the household and these inputs may obscure the relationship between parental labor and number of dependents. This is readily apparent in the village of Bisaasi-teri where old polygynous men have many dependents but do little labor. These households frequently contain childless married daughters and son-in-laws who contribute to the household economy. Some households may be subsidized through food exchanges. For example, in four of the villages sampled, on average, 40% of all garden food consumed by any family member was produced outside of his/her household (Figure 12). Highly subsidized households, therefore, would have lower labor requirements. Finally, the results suggest that male provisioning investment is more sensitive to number of dependents than that of females.

In three of the four villages nursing mothers worked significantly less than nonnursing mothers. However, only in one village (Mishimishima-böwei) did husbands with nursing wives work significantly more than husbands of nonnursing wives. This indicates that diminished female capacity or ability for labor is not fully compensated for by husbands through increased labor time. Again, variability in household composition and exchange practices may account for this lack of reciprocity. Overall these results suggest that female time allocated to labor is more sensitive to presence of a nursing child than is male labor allocation.

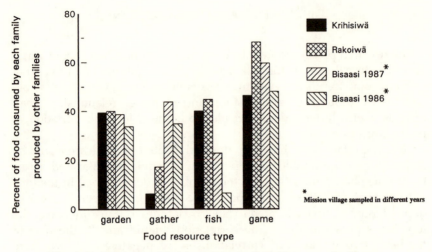

Figure 12. Patterns of food sharing in four Yanomamö villages.

In all of the villages mothers allocated more time to childcare than fathers. While this result is not surprising from any theoretical perspective, the magnitude of the difference perhaps is (see Babchuck et al. 1984 for comparative data). In fact, fathers are so disassociated from childcare that I would predict that more care is allocated to his dependent offspring by his older offspring and female kin and affines, a finding that would be consistent with the distribution of alloparental care among the Ye'kwana (Hames 1988) and the Agta (Goodman et al. 1985). In three of the four villages females allocated significantly more time to labor and total care (labor plus direct childcare). The clearly emergent pattern is one of female specialization in childcare and a female-dominated but biparental sharing of childcare.

For males and female neither the Draper–Harpending nor Chayanovian model of time allocation is supported. This lack of association between marital status and childcare and labor may be the result of the fluid marriage system, unmeasured forms of investment, or food exchange patterns.

The marriage situation among the Yanomamö is fluid (Chagnon 1982). Over the course of a male's lifetime he may alternate from monogamy to bachelorhood and then back to monogamy and later polygyny. Some monogamous males at the time of this study may have been allocating more time to mating effort than parental effort in an attempt to acquire another wife. Therefore, it does not necessarily follow that monogamous males, relative to polygynous males, should allocate more time to paternal effort.

How to classify particular behaviors as instances of mating or parental effort is problematic. In the behavioral literature, fighting other males for mating rights and mate guarding (Flinn 1988) provide direct observational evidence for mating effort. For the Yanomamö and other groups the sociocultural system may provide a guide for the classification of mating effort. Among the Yanomamö, grooms, especially young grooms, are required to provide a period of bride service for 1 to 2 years (Chagnon 1983). During this time the groom must work assiduously for his parents-in-law before gaining full marital rights. In some cases, the father-in-law strictly regulates sexual access of the groom to his daughter. In addition, the marital arrangement may break down during this period (Chagnon, personal communication). For the Yanomamö bride service may be seen as a form of institutionalized mating effort.

On the other hand, a male may expend a tremendous amount of time hunting, gathering, fishing, and gardening. If he is married and has many dependent children then one might wish to conclude that the product of these resources go to wife and offspring, that is they are fair indices of parental investment. But to complicate matters, the sharing of food resources occurs intensively between families: anywhere from 5 to 70% of all resources consumed by a family unit are produced by other families in the village (Hames 1990; Saffirio and Hames 1984). Figure 12 graphically shows this pattern by documenting the percent of food (by type) consumed by a family that was produced by other families in several of the villages.[3] It is entirely possible that males may divert some food resources to families with marriageable females to better position themselves for marriage. It is also possible that high status polygynous males (polygyny being a good index of status) are able to receive more food than they give.

That polygynous males invest less in childcare but not significantly less than monogamous males is contrary to predictions I derived from the Draper–Harpending model and to the empirical findings of Hewlett (1988), who found that polygynous males engaged in less paternal investment than monogamous males among the Aka. However, it is highly possible that all males, regardless of their marital status, are devoting considerable time to mating effort. Monogamous males do so to gain another wife and polygynous males do so to gain a third or fourth wife. Therefore, the monogamy–polygyny distinction may not distinguish different investment patterns but rather marks current success in the mating game.

This finding also has implications beyond paternal investment. For the Yanomamö and perhaps other highly polygynous groups with no accumulable wealth (e.g., Tiwi) it suggests that individual male economic performance is not the basis of polygyny (Chagnon n.d.). At this point what leads to polygyny among the Yanomamö is not clear, but the likely candidate may be differential abilities in the political realm (Chagnon 1988).

I conclude with a methodological note. Theoretically compelling models of reproductive effort (e.g., Trivers, 1971) are notable for their generality and clarity but they may be difficult to apply in the field for two reasons. First, I argued that parental investment operationally not only encompasses childcare but also proximity maintenance and economic provisioning. Actually, it theoretically encompasses much more such as risks of injury parents may sustain to protect children or effort they may expend in assisting them in finding a mate (e.g., provisioning bride price or dowry). In the case of the Yanomamö, we may have to look further into the costly politics of intimidation and negotiation by a young man's father who seeks to arrange a marriage for his son (Chagnon, 1988). It may be the case that a father's parental effort on behalf of his son to acquire a mate may be much greater than direct care or provisioning when his son was young.

Second, just as importantly and perhaps more easily solvable is the need to clearly specify the context in which behavioral observations were made. Measures of childcare in this chapter are measures of care received and given in the village (see also Tronick et al., 1987; and comments by Hewlett 1989). In superior studies, investment includes care inside and outside the village (e.g., Hewlett, 1988). Measures of proximity maintenance (see above) is also fraught with similar problems as well as the behavior sampling technique employed (e.g., focal person continuous vs. instantaneous scans [Martin & Bateson, 1988]). As a result, cross-cultural comparisons are difficult to make. I would conclude that methodological rigor and clarity are just as important as hypotheses development in our attempts to evaluate Darwinian models of human behavior.

NOTES

1. Villages at higher elevations frequently have enclosed plazas.
2. I am preparing a publication that specifically deals with variation in labor time allocation of polygynous and monogamous couples using pooled data that controls for village effects.
3. Data on food exchange was collected following the procedures first introduced by Kaplan and Hill (1985). To summarize, if, in the course of behavioral scan sampling, an individual was observed eating the following additional information was noted: item eaten, producer, and consumer. The data in Figure 12 measure the frequency that individuals were observed to consume food that was produced by someone other than a fellow family member.

ACKNOWLEDGEMENTS

I would like to thank Ana Magdalena Hurtado, Kim Hill, and Barry Hewlett for their useful comments on the manuscript. Research for this chapter was funded by the National Science Foundation (grant # BNS 8411669).

REFERENCES

Altmann, J. 1974. The observational study of behavior. *Behaviour* 48:1–41.

Babchuck, W., Hames, R., and Thompson, R. 1985. Sex differences in the recognition of infant facial expressions of emotion: The Primary caretaker hypothesis. *Ethology and Sociobiology* 6:89–101.

Chagnon, N. 1974. *Studying the Yanomamo.* New York: Holt, Rinehart & Winston.

Chagnon, N. 1982. Sociodemographic attributes of nepotism in tribal populations: man the rule breaker. In *Current Problems in Sociobiology.* Kings College Sociobiological Group (Eds.), pp. 291–318. Cambridge: Cambridge University Press.

Chagnon, N. 1983. *Yanomamo: The Fierce People.* New York: Holt, Rinehart & Winston.

Chagnon, N. 1988. Life histories, blood revenge, and warfare in a tribal population. *Science* 239:985–992.

Chagnon, N. n.d., 1989. HBES paper. First Annual Human Behavior and Evolution Society Meetings Northwestern University, August 16–19.

Draper, P. 1989. African marriage systems: Perspectives from evolutionary ecology. *Ethology and Sociobiology* 10:145–169.

Draper, P., and Harpending, H. 1988. A sociobiological perspective on the development of human reproductive strategies. In *Sociobiological Perspectives on Human Development.* K. MacDonald (Ed.), pp. 340–372. New York: Springer-Verlag.

Hames, R. 1979. Interaction and relatedness among the Ye'kwana: A preliminary analysis. In *Evolutionary Biology and Human Social Behavior.* N. Chagnon and W. Irons (Eds.), pp. 201–219. North Scituate, MA: Duxbury Press.

Hames, R. 1988. The Allocation of parental care among the Ye'kwana. In *Human Reproductive Behaviour.* L. Betzig, M. Borgerhoff Mulder, and P. Turke (Eds.), pp. 237–254. Cambridge: Cambridge University Press.

Hames, R. 1989. Time, efficiency, and fitness in the Amazonian protein quest. *Research in Economic Anthropology* 11:43–85.

Hames, R. 1990. Sharing among the Yanomamo, the effects of risk. In *Risk and Uncertainty in Tribal and Peasant Economies.* E. Cashdan (Ed.), pp. 89–105. Boulder, CO: Westview Press.

Hewlett, B. 1988. Sexual selection and paternal investment among the Aka pygmies. In *Human Reproductive Effort*. L. Betzig, M. Borgerhoff Mulder, and P. Turke (Eds.), pp. 263–276. Cambridge: Cambridge University Press.

Hewlett, B. 1989. Multiple caretaking among African Pygmies. *American Anthropologist* 91:186–188.

Hewlett, B. 1991. Intimate Fathers: The Nature and Content of Aka Pygmy Paternal Infant Care. Ann Arbor, Mi: University of Michigan Press.

Hill, K., and Kaplan, H. 1988. Tradeoffs in male and female reproductive strategies among the Ache: Part 1. In *Human Reproductive Behavior: A Darwinian Perspective*. L. Betzig, M. Borgerhoff Mulder, and P. Turke (Eds.), pp. 277–289. Cambridge: Cambridge University Press.

Hill, K., Kaplan, H., and Hurtado, M. 1985. Men's time allocation to subsistence work among the Ache of eastern Paraguay. *Human Ecology* 13:29–47.

Hurtado, M., Hawkes, K., Hill, K., and Kaplan, H. 1985. Female subsistence strategies among Ache hunter-gatherers of eastern Paraguay. *Human Ecology* 13:1–28.

Johnson, A. 1975. Time allocation in a Machiguenga community. *Ethnology* 14(3):301–310.

Kaplan, H., and Hill, K. 1985. Food sharing among Ache foragers: Test of explanatory hypotheses. *Current Anthropology* 26:223–245.

Lamb, M., Pleck, J., Charnov, E., and Levine, J. 1987. A biosocial perspective on paternal behavior and involvement. In *Parenting Across the Lifespan: Biosocial Perspectives*. J. Lancaster, J. Altmann, A. Rossi, and L. Sherrod (Eds.). pp. 68–91 Chicago: Aldine.

Lancaster, J., and Lancaster, C. 1983. Parental investment: The hominid adaptation. In *How Humans Adapt*. D. Ortner (Ed.), pp. 33–69. Washington, DC: Smithsonian Institute Press.

Saffirio, G., and Hames, R. 1983. The forest and the highway. In *Working Papers on South American Indians #6 and Cultural Survival Occasional Paper #11* (joint publication). K. Kensinger and J. Clay (Eds.), pp. 1–52. Cambridge, MA: Cultural Survival Inc.

Trivers, R. 1972. Parental investment and sexual selection. In *Sexual Selection and the Descent of Man: 1871–1971*. B. Campbell (Ed.), pp. 136–179. Chicago: Aldine.

Tronick, E., Morelli, G., and Winn, S. 1987. Multiple caretaking of Efe (Pygmy) infants. *American Anthropologist* 89:96–106.

West, M., and Konner, M. 1986. The role of the father: An anthropological perspective. In *The Role of the Father in Child Development*. M. Lamb (Ed.), pp. 185–217. New York: Wiley.

Whiting, B., and Whiting, J. 1975. *Children of Six Cultures*. Cambridge: Harvard University Press.

Chapter 5

Fatherhood by Rank on Ifaluk

Laura Betzig and Paul Turke

"The baby is king in Ifaluk."
Burrows and Spiro (1957: 274)

Ifaluk fathers are doting fathers. Almost no one who has lived on Ifaluk and written about it has forgotten to mention that the men there love children (e.g., Burrows and Spiro 1957; Bates and Abbott 1958; Turke and Betzig 1985). Although the figures are few, and the methods are seldom the same, fathers on Ifaluk seem to spend as much or more time with their children as fathers in other traditional cultures spend with theirs (Betzig 1992a).

Much more clearly, there is a great deal of variability among fathers on Ifaluk itself. Many things contribute to that variability; one of the most important is the father's rank. The vast majority of traditional societies left at the end of the twentieth century are small and relatively egalitarian. Ifaluk is one of the few ranked societies left.

There are limits on how much care fathers can give to their children. Lately, those limits have been explained in terms of life history theory (see Low 1978; Alexander and Borgia 1979; review in Betzig 1988a). Because one can do only so many things at a time, the amount of effort devoted to caring for children must be constrained by the amount devoted to solving other problems, specifically, staying alive and finding a mate. Hewlett in particular has found that paternal care within an Aka band declines with the number of a father's wives (Hewlett 1986, 1988, 1989). In theory, and in practice in many hunting and gathering societies, men who devote a lot of effort to mating have no choice but to devote little effort to parenting. Across foraging cultures polygyny, an index of mating effort, appears to vary inversely with paternal care, one measure of a father's parental effort (Katz and Konner 1981; Hewlett 1988). As long as the amount of effort each man has to spend is roughly

111

the same, he who spends more time mating will typically have less to spend parenting.

Things get especially interesting when all men's effort is not equal. Many things might make for such inequality, including longevity. But the most dramatic differences are likely to follow from exploitation. A century ago, Engels defined exploitation as "surplus-labour, labour beyond the time required for the labourer's own maintenance, and appropriation by others of the product of this surplus-labour" (in the *Anti-Dührung*, quoted in Terray 1975: 94). In other words, exploitation is the use of one man's labor by another. According to Engels (1884) and Marx, who got their anthropology from Morgan (1877), exploitation was absent before the advent of the state. The anthropological evidence of the last hundred years, has, however, been consistently to the contrary. Exploitation probably exists in every society (e.g., Terray 1972; Betzig 1986, 1988b, 1992a).

By appropriating the fruits of others' labors, a powerful man can spend more effort staying alive, finding mates, *and* caring for his children (Betzig 1988a: 5). In human societies more than any other societies, this kind of exploitation gets to be extreme. Until very recently, the larger the culture, the greater the differences in power, and the greater the degree of exploitation. There are plenty of examples. Typically, in the nineteenth-century African Kingdom of Barotsi, chiefs liberally levied labor from men, women, and children. The fields of one Barotsi king, Lewanika, "which cover the country, are cultivated by forced labourers. . . . From top to bottom of the social scale the chiefs have the power of levying labour, and the unhappy labourer, who often belongs to several masters, must at the first requisition abandon his or her personal work, and can attain neither food nor payment" (Bertrand 1899: 274). Similarly, in Uganda in the last century, kings enlisted subordinate chiefs to help them find mates. The Ganda king "made a levy on the country for girls who in due course became his wives" (Roscoe 1911: 205). Landlords and chiefs throughout Uganda held marriage councils, choosing virgin girls between the ages of 12 and 17, of whom they sent the most attractive to the king (Kagwa 1934: 68). Finally, in many "civilized" societies, parents in power have got wet nurses, nannies, tutors, and others to help bring their children up (e.g., Betzig 1992b; Hrdy, 1992).

As in other places and times, Ifaluk chiefs may have advantages in acquiring what it takes to stay alive, to find a mate, and to care for their children. Chiefs have, and traditionally have had, several energetic advantages. Data on redistribution make it clear that chiefs take in more food in many ways (see below). In spite of that, they tend to spend less time physically at work than their subjects, and in the past were spared a significant risk—when the men of Ifaluk went to war, chiefs typically stayed behind (Betzig and Wichimai 1990).

Traditionally, chiefs were free too to devote more effort to finding mates. Polygyny has been prohibited since early in this century. In the past, though, the size of a man's harem paralleled the extent of his power on Ifaluk, as in virtually every traditional society (Betzig 1986). Polygyny on Ifaluk was a prerogative of chiefs (Burrows and Spiro 1957: 302). Even as late as our 1983 study, chiefs tended to marry more often than their subjects, though they took their extra wives in sequence rather than all at once. Overall, the 85 Ifaluk commoner males who lacked chiefly rank included a sum of just 13 previous spouses in their reproductive histories; at the same time, four former wives are listed in the reproductive histories of just eight men of rank (Betzig 1988b: 57). This difference is not significant. There is, though, a significant difference in the amount of time men with and without rank get to spend with their wives (Betzig 1988b: 58). A man who spends more time with his wife may arguably restrict her access to other prospective mates (e.g., Flinn 1988).

Finally, chiefs are now, and may always have been, better able to provide parental care for their children. Even as late as the 1980s the children of Ifaluk's chiefs, their likely successors, and men paid to work as teachers or health care aides were provided more food and direct care by their fathers and mothers, and more care by adoptive parents as well. What follows elaborates on each of these results.

RANK ON IFALUK

Like the atolls Darwin sighted from aboard the Beagle, Ifaluk probably began as a reef around a volcanic island that was eventually submerged (Darwin 1842). Ifaluk now is a ring of coral in the Western Pacific about 1 mile across, and more than a thousand miles from Australia, the nearest continent. By the standards of most ranked societies Ifaluk is tiny. Its two inhabited islets, Falalop and Falachig, total only about half a square mile in land area, and supported a full time population in 1983 of just 446. By recent historical standards, even that number is high. Devastating typhoons and epidemics have probably always kept the population in flux (e.g., Burrows and Spiro 1957).

For centuries the people of Ifaluk, and of other atolls in the Western Caroline archipelago, sent canoes loaded with tribute every year to Yap, the nearest "high" island to the west (Lessa 1950). Ifaluk's inhabitants and other Caroline atoll dwellers, or "outer islanders," were all low caste members of the Yapese Empire (de Beauclair 1964). That form of tribute more or less stopped in the 1920s, when the Japanese put an end to long distance sailing (Lessa 1950). Ifaluk and other western Caroline islands are now a part of Yap State of the Federated States of Micronesia, and have been since 1981.

On Ifaluk itself, the indigenous system of rank is relatively uninfluenced by outside forces. Two groups of men are now distinct from the rest of Ifaluk's fathers. First are its chiefs, that is, holders of Ifaluk's highest traditional rank; second are the men now paid to teach in the island school or to work in the island dispensary, usually men of high-ranking lineages as well (Wichimai, personal communication). There are now, as there traditionally have been, five major matriclans on Ifaluk (e.g., Burrows and Spiro 1957). The head of the highest ranking clan, Hofalu, was traditionally called *ubut*, or "king"; he or she had ultimate jurisdiction over atoll affairs. Heads of the second and third ranking clans, Saufelachig and Manauglifach, were called *tamol*, or "chief"; they sat in council with the *ubut* in determining island-wide politics. Historically, the power of these three was sufficiently great that they could take, or ask a sorcerer to take, a "bad" subject's life (cf. Cantova 1728). The head of the fourth ranking clan, Chapifelu, was traditionally messenger to, and among, these three chiefs; and the head of the last ranking clan, Sauwel, was king-maker, performing magic when it was time for a new chief to succeed (Betzig and Wichimai 1990).

As of 1983, Ifaluk's *ubut* was a woman, reportedly for lack of suitable male heirs. Although she had a private voice in political matters, she was publicly represented by her "executor," an elder man of her clan. Manauglifach, the third-ranking clan, had no head at all, and had not had for a generation due to a lack of suitable heirs of either sex. Each of the other three clans was headed by a man. During a follow-up trip in 1986 and 1987, four men were identified by concensus as the most likely successors to Ifaluk's chiefs. Each of these men must be a member of the highest ranking lineage within his clan. In the analyses that follow, the three male chiefs, the one male executor, and the four successors are all considered men of high traditional rank. So are 13 men being paid in 1983 to teach full-time in Ifaluk's elementary school, or to act as health care aides in its dispensary. These positions were lucrative and coveted; again, they too generally went to men of high lineage rank (Wichimai, personal communication).

PROVIDING FOOD

Food from Fathers

Men on Ifaluk still make their living, to a large extent, communally. The bulk of the diet on Ifaluk comes from taro; but the business of planting, harvesting, and cooking taro belongs to women. Men fish. Although fishing can be done individually with traps, line, and spear, individual fishing is discouraged, and communal fishing encouraged, in the island-wide meetings regularly presided over by chiefs (see Burrows and Spiro 1957; Turke 1985; Betzig 1988b). Most of the fish consumed on Ifaluk appears to be caught by the collective efforts of every able-bodied man and boy.

Between August and November of 1983, we watched five collective catches of mackerel just off Falalop islet. At least that many again, both of mackerel and of other fish, were known to have occurred during that time but were not completely observed. Following each catch, the fish were hauled ashore in canoes and individually counted. Redistribution followed. At first an equal number of fish was allocated to every man, woman, and child on the islet. In other words, most of Ifaluk's fathers brought home exactly the same number of fish to every mouth in their households. Inevitably, though, a few fish remained after all had an equal share. These fish, along with any larger fish caught in the nets, always went to chiefs. On average over the five catches we measured, members of the chiefly household on Falalop islet got 179% as many fish, in pounds per person, as did members of subjects' households; this is a significant difference (Figure 1; Betzig 1988b: 52–53).

Chiefs also get forms of tribute we were unable to quantify. The Saufelachig chief, for instance, is given 10 baskets of breadfruit per household, one bottle of palm wine per man who cut it, and fish from trolling expeditions once yearly from Falachig village. Fines levied in

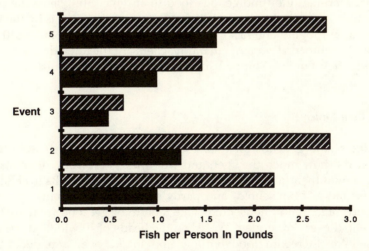

Figure 1. Fish received by the household of the highest ranking chief on Falalop islet (striped bars) versus all other households (solid bars) following five collective catches and redistributions. (Source: Betzig 1988b).

punishment still go directly to chiefs; and privileges in etiquette, including the first and best shares of food at feasts, persist (Betzig 1988b).

Successors, chiefs of the next generation, take in no tribute but may pass on other material advantages to their daughters and sons. Being members of the highest ranking lineages within their clans they probably have privileged access to the fruits of atoll property. Though the size, quality, and tenure hierarchy associated with every plot of land on Ifaluk has yet to be determined, it is likely that people of rank on Ifaluk enjoy advantages in each of these respects (see Alkire 1974 on nearby Woleai atoll). Second, being heirs apparent, successors may have attracted mates of equally high rank and so with similar privileged access to atoll water and land.

Finally, teachers and health care workers on Ifaluk take in unprecedented wealth in the form of cash. Salaries in 1983 were in the vicinity of $100 a week; these were used primarily to buy provisions off the field trip ship. That ship, the *Microspirit*, has been Ifaluk's sole connection with the outer world since the end of long distance sailing by canoe. The *Microspirit* makes an irregular circuit of the Western Caroline Islands, roughly every 6 weeks, departing from Yap. A representative of each of the three biggest stores in Yap's capitol, Colonia, makes that circuit with a limited supply of goods. These include luxury items like vodka, coffee, and cigarettes, and staples like sugar, flour, and rice. There is no electricity on Ifaluk, and there are of course plenty of rats, insects, and other parasites, so food storage is not an easy task. Everybody on Ifaluk still depends primarily on indigenous food to survive. Still, since the only other form of cash income available to the people of Ifaluk is by the sale of copra, at roughly one sack per extended family household, at $10 per sack (in 1983) per *Microspirit* circuit, teachers and health aids are able to provide their families shipped supplies in much greater bulk than anyone else.

Food from Others

Ifaluk's kids get most of their food from someone other than their father. But how much they get, and who they get it from, depends on the extent of their father's kin network, on the ratio of adults to children in their father's household, and partly on their father's rank.

On average, Ifaluk households take food to or get food from another household every other day. We asked the heads of 10 widely dispersed households to record food outflow and intake over a period of 12 consecutive days in October 1983. Altogether, we got data on 42 pairs of households, taking part in 84 separate food sharing events.

In the course of this kind of food sharing, children are most likely to get food from the households of close kin. We computed a mean genealogical relatedness between households on Ifaluk by averaging the genealogical relatedness between every pair of people living in every pair of households. Households that shared food over the course of these 12 days were related, on average, more than twice as closely as households which did not, a significant difference (Betzig and Turke 1986a: 398). As a result, children of fathers with more close kin on the island may be more likely to consume other households' food.

Food is also more likely to flow from households with higher producer to consumer ratios. That is, families with many adults and few dependents tend to give food more often; families with few adults and many children tend to get food more often (Figure 2; Betzig and Turke 1986a). These differences increase with the consumers' youth. Food-receiving households tend to have a higher ratio of children under 16 to adults 16 and over than food-giving households, though this difference is not significant. However, the ratio of children under 6 to adults is significantly higher in food-receiving households; so is the ratio of infants born in 1983 to adults (Betzig and Turke 1986a). All over the island, then, Ifaluk's adults cooperate to provision the families of young children.

Finally, the flow of food between households depends in part on rank. Of the 84 food-sharing events recorded, seven involved food flowing from commoner households to the households of male chiefs;

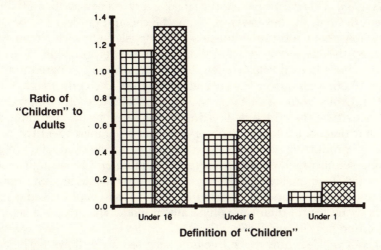

Figure 2. Ratio of food consumers to producers in food giving (vertical hatch) and food receiving (diagonal hatch) households. (Source: Betzig and Turke 1986a).

three involved food flows from chiefly households to commoners. Another three involved food flows to the house of the female *ubut*; food flowed from the *ubut*'s household to other households once. These differences are not significant (Betzig and Turke 1986a: 398). However, chiefs' households did give food away to households roughly three times more closely related to them, on average, than households which gave food to them, another significant difference (Betzig and Turke 1986a; Betzig 1988b: 53–55). Children of chiefs, then, may receive more food than other children when food is shared among households on a daily basis; more information is needed to be certain. Chiefs' children are, though, more likely than other men's children to get food from distantly related relatives, and to give food in return to close kin.

PROVIDING DIRECT CARE

Labor and Leisure

In spite of the fact that they take in more food, Ifaluk's chiefs have the advantage of working less often, at least in activities that we could quantify, than other men. We made an attempt to measure labor and leisure on a daily basis by making a randomly timed walk on a set circuit of Falalop, the larger of Ifaluk's two inhabited islets, over a period of 48 consecutive days from September to November 1983 (see Betzig and Turke 1985). This circuit passed the site of every major activity on Ifaluk; it went through the taro swamp, along the coconut groves, and beside every household and canoe house on Falalop islet. On each circuit, we recorded the identity and activity of everyone seen on sight. Two of Ifaluk's chiefs live on Falalop islet; their behavior was compared to that of the 10 other men over 50 on Falalop who lacked chiefly status. Of a total of 39 observations of these two chiefs, 69% were of "nonproductive" activities. These included resting, eating, walking, or grooming. At the same time, of a total of 310 observations of other men over fifty, 59% were of "productive" activities. These included textile production (e.g., making sennit rope), construction (e.g., building and repairing canoes and traps), food quest (e.g., fishing and coconut harvesting), and transport (e.g., hauling canoes). In short, compared to men of the same age, chiefs spend less of their time physically at work. This, too, is a significant difference (Betzig 1988b: 55–56).

It is not yet clear how much free time successors are allowed. The one successor living on Falalop islet was at work 11 of the 17 times we saw him; this is not significantly different from the pattern among men without rank (Betzig 1988b: 59).

Extra leisure time is not, on the other hand, a perk for salaried men. Four of the 13 men being paid for full-time work were also residents of Falalop; all of them worked, however, on Falachig islet, the site of both the dispensary and the Ifaluk school. Each of these men was obliged to work 5 days a week. Though they were seldom if ever likely to have been engaged in physical labor, their work certainly kept them away from home, and, for the most part, away from their children.

Childcare by Rank

Ifaluk's chiefs, on the other hand, appear to have been free to spend more time caring for their children. "Quality time" may be a much better measure of direct childcare than the number of hours parents are able to spend with their children; but "quality" is a hard thing to get a handle on. As many have already said (especially Lutz 1988), negative affect is uncommon on Ifaluk. We saw parents threaten their children with punishment only four times in 4 months. Interestingly, in every case we eventually found out that these parents were keeping their children away from danger, for example, out of the water or out from under a coconut palm when fruit was being cut.

In any case, because "quality" care is so difficult to measure, we measured the amount of time parents spent with their children instead. Even here there are obvious problems. For instance, when are parents actually "with" their children (see, e.g., Altmann 1974)? In our study, "association" was defined to include people who were aggregated (i.e., in close proximity), engaged in the same activity (e.g., collecting fish at opposite ends of a seine), or communicating verbally or nonverbally. This measure has the drawback of being somewhat subjective; it has the advantage of being less arbitrary than some more objective measures. Our measure of association on Ifaluk during instantaneous scans correlates well with measures of proximity within 5 m during focal scans (see Betzig et al. 1989); it also correlates with our measures of sharing food. Members of Ifaluk households who share food with one another associate significantly more often than members of households who do not (Betzig and Turke 1986b: 34).

On our 48 circuits of Falalop islet, we were able to collect association data on both fathers of high rank, one chief and one successor, who lived on Falalop with children under age 16. We also followed two fathers of salaried status, one teacher and one health care aide, and 11 commoner fathers with coresident genetic children. Every one of these fathers was living with his wife; and in every case these wives were the genetic mothers of their husband's children.

Children of high ranking fathers, and children of paid fathers, spend a higher fraction of their time in the company of at least one adult (Figure 3). The 12 coresident children of the four paid Falalop fathers were without an adult 16 or older 40% of the time; the 9 children of the two ranked fathers on Falalop were seen without an adult 46% of the time; while the 37 children of other Falalop fathers were without an adult 53% of the time. One of these differences is significant (χ^2 = 2.275, p = 0.1315 for ranked versus other; χ^2 = 4.182, p = 0.0409 for paid versus other). Parents, rather than other adults, make up this difference. When they were with adults, at least one of those adults was the mother or father in ranked families 81% of the time, in paid families 73% of the time, and in other families just 54% of the time. These are significant differences (χ^2 = 18.459, p < 0.0001 for ranked versus other; χ^2 = 5.113, p = 0.0237 for paid versus other).

The ages of these children could, of course, account for a portion of the differences. Younger children are more likely to get adult attention, and chiefs and teachers appear to have slightly younger children. The mean age (in years) of children of ranked fathers in this sample is 5.00, of paid fathers 4.00, and of other fathers 6.00. These differences are small and insignificant, but they could bias the results.

To control for age effects such as these, we focused on the amount of time parents spent with children born in 1983, the year of our study. This included both sets of parents of rank, one of the four set of parents with salaried status, and two sets of parents with neither salary nor rank. We found that, altogether, high ranking fathers were with their

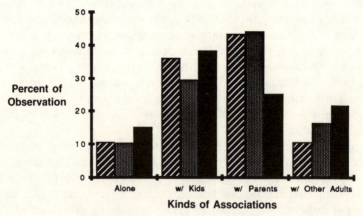

Figure 3. Percent of times children of ranked (striped bars), paid (speckled bars), and other (solid bars) fathers were seen alone, with other children only, with their parents, or with other adults (see text).

infant children 15 of the 45 times we saw those fathers, or exactly one-third of the time. On the other hand, neither the paid father nor either of the two other fathers was seen with his infant even once. Because mother–infant interaction is so much more frequent, the comparison among mothers may be even more dramatic. Wives of fathers of rank were with their infants 31 of 44 times or 70% of the time we saw them; the wife of the salaried father was with her infant 3 of 13 times we saw her or 23% of the time; and wives of fathers without status were with their infants 4 of 25 times we saw them or just 16% of the time. Clearly, the wives of men of rank spend significantly more time with their infant children than wives of paid or of any other fathers ($\chi^2 = 18.913$, $p < 0.0001$ for ranked versus other; $\chi^2 = 9.359$, $p = 0.0022$ for ranked versus paid). These results are consistent with comparisons of observations on mothers' and fathers' associations with all of their children (Figure 4). Again, fathers of rank spend significantly more with their children than either paid fathers or other fathers ($\chi^2 = 9.464$, $p = 0.0021$ for ranked versus other; $\chi^2 = 5.617$, $p = 0.0178$ for ranked versus paid). And again the same is true, to an even greater degree, of their wives ($\chi^2 = 23.336$, $p < 0.0001$ for ranked versus other; $\chi^2 = 11.857$, $p = 0.0006$ for ranked versus paid).

Ranked fathers on Ifaluk, then, spend more of their time with their children. So do their wives. That might be in part because they are freed from having to provide for themselves and their children to some extent. For chiefs the traditional tribute system, perks received in connection with fish redistribution, and the regular flow of food between house-

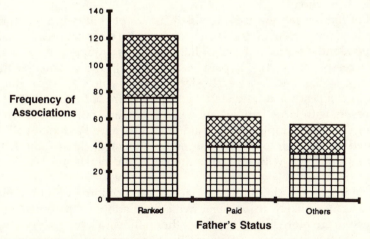

Figure 4. Number of times mothers (vertical hatch) and fathers (diagonal hatch) were seen in association with their children (see text).

holds might all lighten their workloads enough to make it easier to spend free time with children. For successors privileged access to productive atoll plots might lighten the load in similar ways. Paid men, on the other hand, work for their money in places far removed from their families by Ifaluk standards. It is less clear why the wives of men with income should not be relatively free to dote on their infants and other children.

PROVIDING ADOPTIVE CARE

Adoption by Rank

Last but not least, fathers of high rank may be better able to adopt their children out. People with power might exploit their peers by taking in what they need to feed their families, or by farming their families out. On Ifaluk, as on other islands, adoption might serve the latter function (cf. Lambert 1970).

As has often been pointed out, adoption in Oceania is widespread (e.g., Brady 1976). On Ifaluk, prospective adoptive parents approach natural parents before the birth of a child and bear gifts, in the form of food and a handwoven mat, at the time of birth. After that, adoption on Ifaluk can involve childcare in many different degrees. It can be little more than a formality, or children may be taken in and raised for years by their adoptive parents. In every case, children know who both their genetic and adoptive parents are; that made it easy to find out who was adopted to whom.

All of Ifaluk's fathers are more likely to adopt children in when they have fewer children of their own at home. This relationship holds, independently, for all but one of Ifaluk's status groups; it is significant for successors (n = 4), for paid men (n = 13), and for men without status (n = 85); and it is nearly significant for chiefs (n = 4). But the slope is steepest for higher status groups (Figure 5; Betzig 1988c: 115). Successors with large families are more likely than fathers of any other category to have adopted more children out than in. Paid men with lots of children of their own are the second most likely to adopt their children out; men without status are next, and chiefs are last (Betzig 1988c).

More important, though, is the fact that the children of high ranking men are more likely to be *living* with their adoptive parents. Again, successors are more likely than any other fathers to have children living with adoptive parents; and again, they are more likely to farm their children out as the number of their children went up (Figure 6; Betzig 1988c). Paid men with lots of kids are second most likely to have

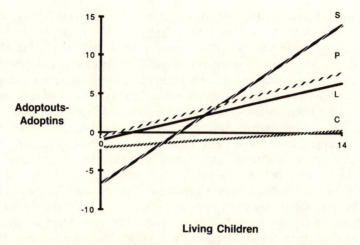

Figure 5. Net number of children adopted out for chiefs (C), successors (S), paid (P), and relatively low status (L) fathers. All adoptive relationships are included here. (Source: Betzig 1988c.)

children farmed out to adoptive parents; chiefs are third, and in this case men without status are last. All of these slopes are statistically significant except that for the small sample of chiefs (Betzig 1988c).

It may seem reasonable to assume that children who live with their adoptive parents are getting more parental care from them; but that assumption might not always hold (see Silk 1990). Some economists

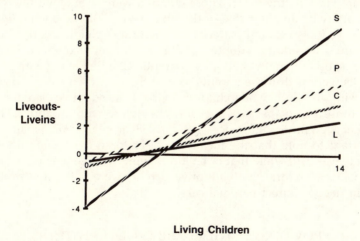

Figure 6. Net number of children living out with adopted parents for chiefs (C), successors (S), paid (P), and relatively low-status (L) fathers. Only coresident adoptions are included here. (Source: Betzig 1988c).

have argued that wealth often flows upward through the generations (e.g., Caldwell 1982). If it does, then Ifaluk men of rank may be losing rather than gaining by adopting their children out. It is difficult, of course, to determine at what point children become self-supporting, that is, when they stop being net consumers and become net producers. As far as we have been able to tell, though, on the basis of interviews, participant observations, and systematic observations of labor and leisure at all ages, resources on Ifaluk consistently flow downward from old to young (Turke 1985, 1988, 1989). Accordingly, having long-lived parents yields a statistically significant reproductive advantage (Turke 1985; Turke and Betzig 1985). The best evidence we have that the children of high status men are getting at least as much care from their adoptive parents comes from comparing ages. The children of paid men living with adoptive parents were significantly younger, i.e., more in need of care, than the children of men without status who were living with adoptive fathers and mothers. On the other hand, children adopted *to* chiefs and successors were older, i.e., less in need of care, than children adopted to other men (Betzig 1988c: 117).

Childcare by Adoption

Nor were children living with adoptive parents any more likely than children living with genetic parents to be left alone, or to be left without an adult. Altogether, the 58 children on Falalop living with genetic parents were seen 13% of the time alone, and 50% of the time without an adult. The figures for the 10 Falalop children living with adoptive parents are virtually the same. Those children were seen alone 13% of the time, and with an adult 48% of the time (Figure 7). The one interesting difference in association patterns between these children is that, when they are with adults, adopted children tend more often to be with someone other than their adoptive parents. Children living with genetic parents were with those parents 65% of the time they were in association with an adult, while children living with adoptive parents were with those parents 44% of the time they were with an adult. This is another significant difference ($\chi^2 = 7.038$, $p = 0.0080$). Finally, it is important to note that the mean age of children living with adoptive parents was 7.10 while that of children living with genetic parents was just 5.43. So children with adoptive parents were older, and probably less in need of direct parental care.

PROVIDING FATHERS ARE PROLIFIC FATHERS

The extra food Ifaluk chiefs take in is allocated to their households as wholes. Chiefs' wives and children are better provisioned. This differ-

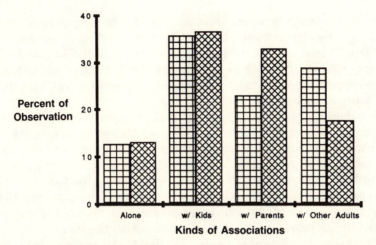

Figure 7. Percent of time children living with genetic parents (vertical hatch) versus children living with adoptive parents (diagonal hatch) were seen alone, with other children only, with their parents (genetic in the first case, adoptive in the second), or with other adults (see text).

ence, along with differences in direct parental care, and in care provided through adoption, may account for the fact that Ifaluk men with rank tend to be producing children at a faster rate than men without. Compared to the 85 Ifaluk men without status, Ifaluk's three male chiefs and the executor for the *ubut* have fathered more, though not significantly more, children, controlling for age. This is especially remarkable since two of these men appear to be sterile.

Chiefs of the next generation, that is, the four likely successors, are on the other hand fathering significantly more children than men without rank (Betzig 1988b: 57; see too Turke and Betzig 1985). Successors' ability to get more parental care through adoption may be one particularly important means to that end.

By far the most prolific fathers on Ifaluk, though, are salaried fathers. Their age-specific fertility is higher than that for any other group; that difference is achieved, in part, by shorter intervals between their children's births (Turke and Betzig 1985). In turn, higher fertility rates may be made possible, in part, by the better provisions afforded by a cash income.

DISCUSSION

The evidence suggests that some exploitation may take place in even the simplest human societies. As Chagnon cleverly pointed out over a decade ago, even where resources are equally shared per head, men with bigger families come off better (Chagnon 1979). Even notoriously "egalitarian" hunters, like the Paraguayan Ache (Hill and Kaplan 1988), may very well be exploitive in these terms. Better hunters may actually be exploiters if the extra meat they provide the band is less than their own dependents consume (Betzig 1992a).

In a majority of societies, then, a minority of men may have what it takes to spend extra effort both on finding a mate *and* on being a parent. That extra effort may come from exploitation even more than by their own harder or more efficient labors. On Ifaluk, fathers of chiefly rank tend to have attracted more mates, and spent more time with them; at the same time they have produced more children, and provided their children with more direct and indirect care than commoner fathers. Exploitation appears to have been a means to all these ends.

As exploitation goes up, so might both the size of a man's harem and the privileges he provides his children (e.g., Betzig 1992b). Gifford, in a section called "Special treatment of children of chiefs," provides one of many examples from ancient Tonga. Typically, Tonga chiefs kept harems of hundreds of women. At the same time, unlike commoner children, chiefs' daughters and sons had the privilege of living apart from their parents in houses of their own. Chief's daughters kept separate houses within their father's enclosures, and were cared for by one or more old women, and by several attendant girls. Chief's sons lived in separate houses, sometimes even in separate enclosures, attended by several boys, old women, and old men. A chief's daughter did a little sweeping, but no cooking, and looked elaborately after her complexion. "Orange juggling was one of her pastimes" (Gifford 1929: 129).

Because the father's role *is* so potentially important, women appear to have been selected to choose mates for their ability to provide parental care (e.g., Buss 1989). Men, on the other hand, may be able to attract more mates *to the extent* that they are willing to care more for children. Exploitation, more than anything else, makes both bigger harems and better childcare possible at once. And it makes humans an important exception. Among other organisms, the tradeoffs between spending effort on mating and spending effort on caring for offspring are relatively clear (e.g., Low 1978). In fact, as Darwin (1871: 581) noted, and as Trivers (1972: 56) and others have elaborated, concentration on mating versus parenting essentially defines sex differences; in almost all cases, males devote more effort to mating and females more to parenting.

Time, more than anything else, is likely to be a limiting factor. Chiefly fathers on Ifaluk are able to spend more time with their children; but this is probably an exception. Polygynous chiefs in Ifaluk's past, like polygynous chiefs, kings, and emperors in most of history's societies, inevitably spent less and less time with each of their children as they had more and more of them. But, like Ifaluk chiefs of the present, they were probably well positioned to provide parental care of many other kinds, including better food, better protection, and better direct care by their mothers or others. Like the size of their harems, the care they provided each of their children is likely to have come courtesy of somebody else's labor.

ACKNOWLEDGMENTS

Thanks first of all to the people of Ifaluk, particularly Pakalmar, Wichimai, and Yangrelbug, and our interpreters Yangitelmes, Hagilmai, and Yangespai. Thanks too to the Wenner-Gren Foundation, the National Geographic Society, and the NIMH for providing support to L. B., and to the National Science Foundation, the Leakey Foundation, the Population Council, and the Michigan Society of Fellows for supporting P. T. Thanks to Barry Hewlett for encouraging words.

REFERENCES

Alexander, R. D., and Borgia, G. 1979. On the origin and basis of the male-female phenomenon. In *Sexual Selection and Reproductive Competition in Insects*. M. F. Blum and N. Blum (Eds.), pp. 417–440. New York: Academic Press.

Alkire, W. 1974. Land tenure in the Woleai. In *Land Tenure in Oceania*. H. P. Lundsgaarde (Ed.), pp. 99–137. Honolulu: University of Hawaii Press.

Altmann, J. 1974. The observational study of behavior. *Behaviour* 48:1–41.

Bates, M., and Abbott, D. 1958. *Coral Islands*. New York: Scribner's.

Beauclair, I. de. 1964. Caste and class on Yap. *Bulletin of the Institute of Ethnology, Academia Sinica* 14.

Bertrand, A. 1899. *The Kingdom of the Barotsi*. London: T. Fisher Unwin.

Betzig, L. 1986. *Despotism and Differential Reproduction: A Darwinian View of History*. New York: Aldine.

———. 1988a. Mating and parenting in Darwinian perspective. In *Human Reproductive Behaviour: A Darwinian Perspective*. L. Betzig, M. Borgerhoff Mulder, and P. Turke, (Eds.), pp. 3–20. Cambridge: Cambridge University Press.

———. 1988b. Redistribution: Equity or exploitation? In *Human Reproductive Behaviour: A Darwinian Perspective*. L. Betzig, M. Borgerhoff Mulder, and P. Turke, (Eds.), pp. 49–63. Cambridge: Cambridge University Press.

———. 1988c. Adoption by rank on Ifaluk. *American Anthropologist* 90:111–119.

———. 1992a. *Of Human Bonding*. Manuscript under review.

———. 1992b. Sex, succession, and stratification in the first six civilizations. In *Stratification*. L. Ellis, (Ed.), in press.

Betzig, L., Harrigan, A., and Turke, P. 1989. Childcare on Ifaluk. *Zeitscrift für Ethnologie* 114:161–177.

Betzig, L., and Turke, P. 1985. Measuring time allocation: Observation and intention. *Current Anthropology* 26:647–50.

———. 1986a. Food sharing on Ifaluk. *Current Anthropology* 27:397–400.

———. 1986b. Parental investment by sex on Ifaluk. *Ethology and Sociobiology* 7:29–37.

Betzig, L., and Wichimai, S. 1990. A not so perfect peace: A history of conflict on Ifaluk. *Oceania* 6:240–256.

Brady, I. 1976. *Transactions in Kinship*. Honolulu: University of Hawaii Press.

Burrows, E., and Spiro, M. E. 1957. *An Atoll Culture*. Westport, CT: Greenwood Press.

Buss, D. 1989. Sex differences in human mate preferences: Evolutionary hypotheses tested in 37 cultures. *The Behavioral and Brain Sciences* 12:1–49.

Caldwell, J. 1982. *The Theory of Fertility Decline*. New York: Academic Press.

Cantova, J. 1728. Lettre du P. Jean Cantova, March 20, 1722. *Lettres Edifiantes et Curieuses* 18:188–247. Translation courtesy of Father Francis Hezel.

Chagnon, N. A. 1979. Is reproductive success equal in egalitarian societies? In *Evolutionary Biology and Human Social Organization*. N. A. Chagnon and W. Irons (Eds.), pp. 374–401. North Scituate, MA: Duxbury Press.

Darwin, C. 1842. *The Structure and Distribution of Coral Reefs*. London: Murray.

———. 1871. *The Descent of Man and Selection in Relation to Sex*. London: Murray.

Engels, F. 1884. *On the Origin of the Family, Private Property, and the State*. New York: International Publishers.

Flinn, M. V. 1988. Mate guarding in a Caribbean village. *Ethology and Sociobiology* 9:1–28.

Gifford, E. 1929. *Tongan Society*. Honolulu: The Bishop Museum.

Hewlett, B. S. 1986. Intimate fathers: Paternal patterns of holding among Aka pygmies. In *Father's role in cross-cultural perspective*. M. E. Lamb (Ed.). New York: Erlbaum.

———. 1988. Sexual selection and paternal investment among Aka pygmies. In *Human Reproductive Behaviour: A Darwinian Perspective*. L. Betzig, M. Borgerhoff Mulder, and P. Turke (Eds.), pp. 263–271. Cambridge: Cambridge University Press.

———. 1989. Multiple caretaking among African Pygmies. *American Anthropologist* 90:186–191.

Hill, K., and Kaplan, H. 1988. Tradeoffs in male and female reproductive strategies among the Ache. In *Human Reproductive Behaviour: A Darwinian Perspective*. L. Betzig, M. Borgerhoff Mulder, and P. Turke, (Eds.), pp. 277–305. Cambridge: Cambridge University Press.

Hrdy, S. B. 1992. Fitness tradeoffs in the history and evolution of delegated mothering with special reference to wet-nursing, abandonment and infanticide. In *Darwinian History*. L. Betzig (Ed.). Special issue of *Ethology and Sociobiology*, in press.

Kagwa, A. 1934. *The Customs of the Baganda*. New York: Columbia University Press.

Katz, M., and Konner, M. 1981. The role of the father: An anthropological perspective. In *The Role of the Father in Child Development*. M. Lamb (Ed.), pp. 189–222. New York: Wiley.

Lambert, B. 1970. Adoption in the Nortern Gilbert Islands. In *Adoption in Eastern Oceania*. V. Carroll (Ed.), pp. 261–291. Honolulu: University of Hawaii Press.

Lessa, W. 1950. Ulithi and the outer native world. *American Anthropologist, 52*: 27–52.

Low, B. S. 1978. Environmental uncertainty and the parental strategies of marsupials and placentals. *American Naturalist* 112:197–213.

Lutz, C. 1988. *Unnatural Emotions*. Chicago: University of Chicago Press.

Morgan, L. H. 1877. *Ancient Society*. New York: International Publishers.

Roscoe, J. 1911. *The Baganda*. London: Macmillan.

Silk, J. B. 1990. Human adoption in evolutionary perspective. *Human Nature* 1:25–52.

Terray, E. 1972. *Marxism and 'Primitive' Societies*. New York: Monthly Review.

——— . 1975. Classes and class consciousness in the Abron Kingdom of Gyaman. In *Marxist Analyses and Social Anthropology*. M. Bloch (Ed.), pp. 85–135. New York: Wiley.

Trivers, R. 1972. Parental investment and sexual selection. In *Sexual Selection and the Descent of Man*. B. Campbell (Ed.), pp. 136–179. New York: Aldine.

Turke, P. 1985. Fertility Determinants on Ifaluk and Yap: Tests of economic and Darwinian hypotheses. Ph.D. Dissertation, Northwestern University, University Microfilms, Ann Arbor, Michigan.

——— . 1988. Helpers at the nest: Childcare networks on Ifaluk. In *Human Reproductive Behaviour: A Darwinian Perspective*. L. Betzig, M. Borgerhoff Mulder, and P. Turke, (Eds.), pp. 173–188. Cambridge: Cambridge University Press.

——— . 1989. Evolution and the demand for children. *Population and Development Review* 15:61–90.

Turke, P., and Betzig, L. 1985. Those who can do: Wealth, status, and reproductive success on Ifaluk. *Ethology and Sociobiology* 6:79–87.

Chapter 6

If You Have a Child You Have a Life: Demographic and Cultural Perspectives on Fathering in Old Age in !Kung Society

Patricia Draper and Anne Buchanan

In raising the topic of fathering in different cultures, one typically thinks of a father's relationships with his young children. The importance of mothers and fathers to children is assumed by everyone, regardless of the type of society that is being considered. Everyone knows that children mature slowly and require years of physical support and tutelage before they can be independent. The biology and psychology of our slow release from immaturity have put their imprint on all human social systems with direct implications for the ubiquity of family organization, marriage, and the asymmetries of gender roles. Everyone understands the importance of parents (or their surrogates) to children; but what of the importance of adult children to elderly parents? In this chapter we present normative and demographic data from a study of the !Kung San of the Kalahari Desert. The findings indicate the extreme cultural preoccupation with parent–adult child relationships and the strong empirical association that exists for older people between having more rather than fewer adult offspring and surviving into old age.

The topic of parent–adult child relationships has received less attention than parent–young child relationships both in modern societies and in traditional ones though the imbalance is beginning to be corrected (Ikels 1983, 1989; Keith 1985; Fry 1988; Rubeinstein 1990; Rubeinstein and Johnsen 1982; Sokolovsky 1990). Among members of western cultures the importance of adult children to their parents is less widely assumed for a number of economic and technological reasons. In the West, parents and adult children are typically not economically interdependent, though their social and emotional ties are strong (Foner 1984; Riley 1988; Hagestad 1984; Neugarten 1974). Other institutions related to retirement and various forms of social entitlement enable older adults to be self-supporting, even though they may no longer be gainfully employed (Kohli 1985, 1986; Neugarten 1982). This relieves adult offspring of providing daily support for elderly parents. In much of North America and parts of Europe the ethic of independence is strong. Both adult children and their parents take pride in not having to be supported by the other (Clark 1969; Clark and Anderson 1967). The value on independence extends to separate residence with both adult children and older parents preferring to have separate domiciles.

The economic emancipation of the generations is further stabilized by technological advances available in modernized societies. The many labor-saving and prosthetic devices available to older people make the elderly less dependent on the physical services of their grown children. Although older people everywhere have reduced physical strength, in modern communities they can drive cars, ride elevators, and compensate for physical declines with eyeglasses and medications. This enables large number of older adults to remain socially and economically active in their communities without the direct and personal assistance of younger kin. The falling fertility associated with industrialized countries is balanced by reduced mortality and most older people who have had children can expect their children will be available to them in their declining years.

In nonindustralized societies parent–child ties retain their practical, economic significance over the life span. Across the reach of three or more generations, the interdependence of family members of different ages is the norm (Treas and Logue 1986). Older parents continue to live with one or more of their grown children in an extended family setting. Production and distribution are managed within the kindred and local community and, as a consequence, a person's economic sustenance cannot be separated from his or her personal relationships. Intergenerational relations among family members of different ages is typically more hierarchical than the case in western societies. Property, whether symbolic or real, is controlled by elders who in their turn depend on the labor of their descendants. Just as the generations are not economically emancipated in simpler societies, the low development of technology means that older people are not buffered from the physical losses of aging. Older people are literally dependent on the human energy of others, and specifically on the physical labors and services of their younger kin. The high fertility is often explained by people in traditional societies both by the need to replace children lost to high levels of mortality and by the need to have children as a form of old age insurance.

This chapter focuses on the ties between older parents (particularly fathers) and their adult children among the !Kung San. The !Kung are a

Southern African population whose cultural traditions include hunting and gathering. In the context of the issues raised above there are several reasons for looking at intergenerational relations in this population. First, kinship and marriage are the primary media through which social and economic life is organized and so parent–child relations remain important throughout the life course. Second, the technological resources available to the !Kung are extremely limited, which means that human labor is essential and that the physically infirm must be directly assisted by younger people. Third, the !Kung, have unusually low fertility in comparison with other African populations. !Kung women have a completed fertility of an average of 4.5 to 5 children (Howell 1979). This fact, coupled with the high childhood and adult mortality found in remote areas of the world, means that old people cannot assume that if they survive into old age they will have children to help them.

Population planners have often noted that in Third World countries, high rates of childhood mortality lead to the desire on the part of parents for large numbers of children. Parents argue that they must have large numbers of children to ensure that some will survive to provide for the old age of the parents. In the present study we ask the question: "Does having surviving adult children promote the survivorship of old parents?" The question has special significance for the !Kung and low fertility has important implications for the dynamics of intergenerational relations in their society as will be specified more fully below.

The proportion of a population that is "old" is influenced by its birth rate. High levels of fertility lead to broad based age-sex pyramids in which old people constitute a small proportion of the total population size. Low fertility groups, on the other hand, are characterized by steep–sided or columnar age–sex pyramids in which the old and the not yet old constitute relatively large proportions of the total population. Among the !Kung in the late 1980s about 13% of the population was 60 or more years of age (in comparison with a figure of 4% elderly for the population of the entire country of Botswana). This high proportion of elderly among !Kung was proceeded not from unusual longevity among old people but as the effect of low fertility. Table 1 shows the percentages of !Kung by age categories. A brief ethnographic summary of the !Kung will provide background for discussion.

ETHNOGRAPHY

The !Kung live in northwestern Botswana, Africa. A substantial literature describing this population has accumulated in recent years (Marshall 1976; Howell 1979; Lee 1979; Lee and DeVore 1976; Yellen 1977).

Table 1. Age Structure of !Kung Living in the "Home Area" of Botswana, 1987–88[a]

Age	Number	Percentage of total home area population
<1	27	4
1– 3.9	42	5
4– 5.9	64	8
6– 9.9	68	9
10–12.9	51	6
13–18.9	67	9
19–29.9	126	16
30–44.9	116	15
45–59.9	111	14
60+	104	13

[a] The "Home Area" is between /Ai/Ai in the South and /Obesha in the North, Namibian border to the West and Mahito to the East. The total Home Area !Kung population included in this study was 776.

These sources deal primarily with !Kung social organization, economy, demography, and archaeology. There has been relatively little scholarly attention to the subject of aging and intergenerational relations among the !Kung, although Biesele and Howell (1981), Rosenberg (1989), and Draper and Harpending (1991) are recent additions. Most writing on the !Kung describes them as hunter–gatherers, yet in recent decades many !Kung have had increasing contact with non-!Kung peoples owing to the intrusion of culturally distinct pastoral peoples such as the Tswana and Herero into areas previously occupied primarily by !Kung [see also Denbow and Wilmsen (1986) and Wilmsen (1989)]. In the past !Kung lived by a variety of economic strategies. Some !Kung, some of the time, lived in nomadic bands and subsisted primarily by hunting and gathering. Other groups of !Kung, for varying periods of time, lived as servants to Bantu-speaking pastoralists. Today, all of the !Kung of western Botswana have become permanently settled around year-round water sources and they live by a combination of gardening, stock raising, hunting and gathering, and a government distribution of famine relief foods. They live in small villages ranging in size from about 10 to 30 or more people related to each other by kinship and marriage. Except for irregular food relief from the government, the !Kung subsist on foods they provide themselves. Because of the remoteness of the area and lack of economic development, there are virtually no wage–paying jobs to be had in the region. !Kung know the value of money but about the only regular source of cash income is through the sale of craft items, purchased two or three times per year by a government-subsidized craft buyer who tours the area, buying beaded jewelry, traditional bow, arrow, and quiver kits, and hand-carved wooden figurines.

Whether living as hunter–gatherers or as clients to pastoralists, the elderly !Kung were limited in their ability to provide security for their old age. As mobile foragers, !Kung did not accumulate durable property and therefore older people could not accrue rights in property that then gave them leverage and influence over younger kin. Leverage through property is a gerontocratic strategy seen to varying degrees in agricultural and pastoral societies, and has led to the often justified stereotype of the revered elder in primitive society (Simmons 1945, 1960; Cowgill and Holmes 1972).

Foraging, with its requirements of frequent moves, put a premium on the individuals' physical strength and endurance and acted as an additional leveling or antiage stratifying device. Particular old people, for example, those with admirable personal qualities and especially those with numerous surviving younger relatives, were well treated and respected. Other elders without kin and an accumulation of social credits fared poorly. However, in times of dire necessity, old people who could not keep up on the march were eventually abandoned regardless of their personal circumstances. In general, !Kung values, like those of many cultures found in precarious circumstances, did not stress respect and deference to the aged as a social category (Glascock 1982, 1983; Sharp 1981).

The rigors of the hunting–gathering life exacted its toll by middle age and men felt the brunt of senescence more acutely than women as hunting and tracking were physically more rigorous than the gathering work of women. By their 40s and 50s, !Kung men began to rely increasingly on the hunting abilities of younger men due to their failing eyesight and physical vigor.

Among the settled !Kung living as servants to Bantu pastoralists, the physical demands of daily living were reduced for older !Kung, but, like the elders living in the foraging groups, they were not able to amass a material basis for high status. Settled !Kung who worked for Bantu could not accumulate sufficient wealth in the form of domestic stock to become independent food producers and to live without the patronage of the pastoral people. Thus as among the foragers, elderly settled !Kung were dependent on their younger kin. Lacking control of economic resources, they could not command respect or support from their juniors but relied on good will and personal ties with their children. As they aged the settled !Kung men were less able to do the physically demanding work required by their patrons such as stock watering, cattle droving, and fence construction.

NORMATIVE AND DEMOGRAPHIC DATA

Two types of data are used in the discussion of intergenerational and father–child relations among the !Kung. The first type of data is normative and was collected in the form of interviews with adult !Kung about the experience of aging and the importance of children for the social support of elderly parents.[1] The second type of data is demographic and is based on over 300 reproductive interviews collected in 1987–1988. These data pertain to characteristics of !Kung population structure and the proportions of !Kung in various age and sex classes who have living parents or living adult offspring. These two types of data, normative and demographic, are distinct but mutually relevant. A purpose of this chapter is to juxtapose what people say about aging and the importance of having children with the reality (of a different sort) of the actual existence of parent–adult child dyads in the !Kung communities.

The data sets show interrelated facts. The demographic data show that the experience of fathering is extremely variable among !Kung men, much more so than mothering is for women. A substantial number of interviewed men claim they have never been fathers. Many other men, though they have had children by their wives in the past, nevertheless, spend much of their adult life without surviving children. These demographic patterns will be detailed below. The normative interview data show that men (and women) are intensely aware of the relationship between what we in the western world call "successful aging" and having surviving adult offspring. A particularly telling response by many !Kung, regardless of their age, came to one of the central questions asked in the survey: "What is it that allows an old person to have a good life?" Most people answered, "If you have a child, you have a life." In other words, respondents ignored the issue of what contributed to the quality of an old person's life and talked about survival to old age.

Findings from Demographic Data

A good place to begin in understanding fathering in !Kung society is to understand aspects of the population structure. Father–adult child relationships can be looked at in two ways: from the point of view of men who are or are not fathers and from the point of view of adult children who do or do not have a male parent. Table 2 shows the percentage of adults who have living fathers.[2] It can be seen that the probability of having a living father declines sharply with age. Whereas 76% of people of the "young adults" (19–29 years) have living fathers, by "late middle age" (45–59 years) only 15% of adults of this age have

Table 2. Percentage of Adults with Living Parents

Age	Fathers alive		Mothers alive	
	n	%	*n*	%
19–29	122/161	76	120/161	75
30–44	77/160	48	88/160	55
45–59	18/122	15	35/123	29
60+	3/107	3	6/107	6

living fathers. For "old adults" (60 years and over) only 3% of the population have living fathers.

The decline in survivorship of fathers, from the vantage point of offspring, is steeper than for mothers. The higher attrition on fathers (from the vantage point of adult children) is to be expected given that in this society men are 5–10 years older than their first wives, and even older than the women they marry subsequently, following divorce or widowhood. In comparison with mothers, fathers have fewer shared years with their children.

Not all men become fathers in their life times. Figure 1 shows the percentage of men who never had a child. Notice particularly the two older age groups, "old" and "mid-aged old." Fourteen percent of the

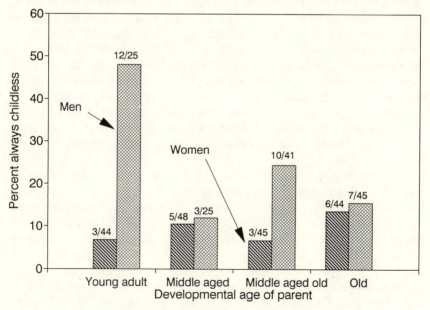

Figure 1. Percent adults always childless, by age and sex.

men over the age of 60 years say they have never fathered children. An even higher 24% of the "middle-aged old" men (45–59 years) say the same. For the most part these ever childless men are not men with abnormal personal characteristics or unusual marital histories. Some had had one life-long wife with whom they had produced no children; others had had several unions, all of which were barren. The large percentage (48%) of younger men aged 19–29 who have never fathered a child would not have been unusual in earlier decades as men this age were in many cases still unmarried or married to women too young to bear children. The same chart shows comparable figures on the percentage of ever childless women. Whereas older cohorts of women were similar to men, the "middle-aged old" age group of women (45–59 years) has a much lower percentage (7%) of members who have never given birth. Overall, the fact that about one-seventh of the oldest men have *never* had children and about one-quarter of the next youngest cohort of men have *never* had children underscores the significance !Kung informants attach to the issue of having children and the meaning of these children for one's old age.

High childhood and adult mortality coupled with low overall fertility can mean that many men reach their late years with no surviving children. Figure 2 shows the percentage of men who were childless at the time of the interviews in 1987–1988. These figures include both the "ever childless" and those men who have had children but lost them to death.[3] Thirty-one percent of men 60 years or over had no children surviving at the time of the interview; for "middle-aged old" men (45–59 years) the comparable figure is 34%. Some of the men of the 45–59 year age range may eventually father children either by their current wives or by younger men to whom they are not yet married, but their chances are slim. Most men 45 years or over are in marriages of long standing with women who are already at or near the end of their child-bearing ages.[4] In former times childless, middle-aged men might have married younger women. Today these opportunities are increasingly limited, as will be explained below.

The opportunity to be a father is not the same as the opportunity to be a mother. This inequality stems from several sources. In the past low levels of polygyny (around 5%) meant that younger men had more difficulty finding wives in their own group or had to wait until more mature women became widowed or divorced to begin their own parental careers. By marrying older women they were able to take advantage of a smaller number of a woman's reproductive years and consequently fathered fewer children than their mates bore. In the present, living in settled villages, the !Kung have much more frequent contact with members of non-!Kung ethnic groups such as Tswana and Herero, men-

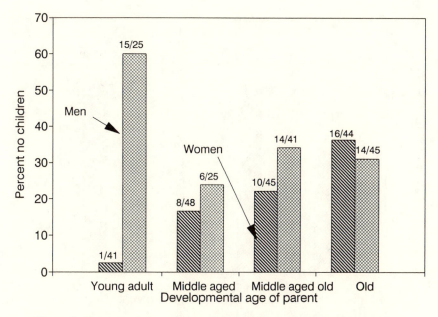

Figure 2. Percent adults with no living children at time of interview.

tioned formerly. One consequence of this culture contact is more frequent sexual unions between !Kung women and non-!Kung men (Bailey 1988). Figure 3 shows the average number of births by sex and age group of the parent. Notice that with the exception of the older age groups (people who were in prime child-bearing ages well before 1950 and who are now 60 years and over), the gap between the numbers of children born to men and women consistently favors women. For people 60 years and over, however, men and women have had approximately the same average number of children.[5] In the three younger age groups, women consistently outreproduce men. Eventually some of the men of the "young" group (19–29 years) and "middle aged" (30–44 years) group will make up their fertility shortfall in future years when they marry younger women. However, as Figure 4 shows, their prospects as a cohort are not good.

As stated above, there are undoubtedly several factors operating to produce these sex differences in completed fertility. However, in recent years the percentage of children of non-!Kung paternity is steadily increasing. !Kung men are losing out in reproductive opportunity because !Kung women mate with non-!Kung men (Bailey 1988). Figure 4, showing the percent of mixed-race children born to women of different age groups, makes the point that there has been a strong secular trend in

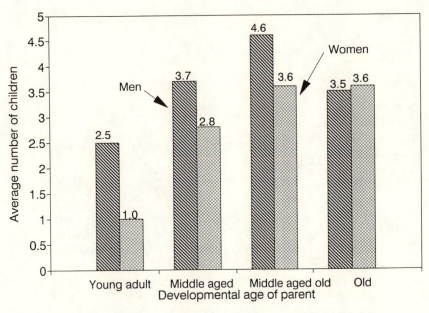

Figure 3. Average number of births by sex and age of parent.

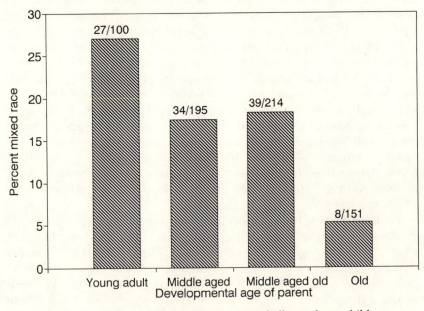

Figure 4. Mixed race children as percent of all ever-born children.

recent years whereby !Kung women bear mixed-race children. Whereas 4% of the children born to older women were of mixed parentage, the percentages jump substantially for women of later cohorts who bear approximately 20% of their children to non-!Kung fathers. The sex difference in reproductive success is sharpest between the "old" and "mid-aged old" cohorts. The oldest women of the "mid-aged old" were 59 years in 1988, which would mean a birth year of about 1929 for the oldest members of this cohort. Their prime reproductive years would have been in the late 1940s and 1950s, precisely the time period during which there was a marked build-up in the number of Bantu colonists in the western Kalahari (Lee 1979: 82–84). We suggest that the large discrepancy between male and female reproductive success (seen in cohorts younger than 60) is the result of reproductive competition from Bantu men.

This competition has intensified in succeeding decades. Twenty-seven percent of the children born to the youngest women (19–29 years) are of mixed parentage. As !Kung are the lowest ranking ethnic group in the local status hierarchy, !Kung men via liaisons with Tswana or Herero women have contributed essentially nothing to the births of mixed-race children. !Kung men lacked property, influence, and cattle. They cannot pay bridewealth fees necessary for marriage in the Bantu custom and they are not taken seriously as paramours or as potential husbands by Bantu women or their senior kin.[6]

To summarize, these data show several interesting patterns. Among !Kung adults there is a steep decay with age in the probability of having a living father (or mother). But this does not mean that there are practically no old people in the population. On the contrary, as seen in Table 1, about 13% of the population are over the age of 60 years and another 14% are aged 45–59 years. (There are no sex differences in the percentages of males and females surviving to any of the age groups.) However, many of these older people have no living offspring, either because they never had children, or because the children they had died. For men these percentages of being "always childless" are higher than for women. Further, with the apparently strongly established secular trend in outmatings by women, the opportunity to father will continue to be problematic as the pool of eligible partners of their own ethnic group diminishes.

At present young !Kung women do not permanently marry out and become incorporated in Bantu families. Instead !Kung women establish only informal liaisons with Bantu men. Mixed-race children born to these unions are reared by their mothers in the villages of the maternal grandparents. In some cases these women later settle down with !Kung men who stepfather the wife's child. In other cases the women remain unmarried and have successive children by various Bantu men who live permanently or semipermanently in the area with their herds and Bantu relatives.

FINDINGS FROM NORMATIVE INTERVIEW DATA

In response to a battery of questions about intergenerational relations and how people viewed the later stages of life, !Kung informants of all ages showed a great deal of unanimity. People stressed in every conceivable context that the physical declines of age are inevitable and that aging makes a person vulnerable to death unless younger kin (especially children) are available. Examples of some of the questions asked of 105 adults are listed below:

- "What are some of the good and bad things about being the different ages?"
- "How are people of the same age similar?"
- "What is it that makes people of different ages different?"
- "What age group do you think (you) are in?"
- "What is it like for older people? Is it good for them? Bad for them?"
- "Think of an old person you know. What is his life like? Why?"
- "If an old person has a good life, what makes it good?"
- "If an old person has a bad life, what makes it bad?"

These questions were designed to elicit values about the stages of adult development in !Kung society and to focus people's answers on how people experience their own age and age transitions and their relations with people of different ages. The answers were coded into four categories depending on whether the informant mentioned (1) physical and health issues, (2) economic issues, (3) social issues having to do with social support and quality of relations with others, or (4) personal issues having to do with the person's individual characteristics of temperament, character, or philosophy of life. Table 3 shows the distribution of rateable responses according to the age group of the informant and the category of response.[7] Sex differences are not reported as men and women responded similarly.

One of the questions asked of all interviewees was, "What makes life bad for an old person?" (the informant was asked to think of a particular known elder in framing the response). Regardless of the age of the informant, people overwhelmingly stressed the importance of issues of health and loss of physical stamina. !Kung were universally preoccupied with the physical disabilities associated with aging and, in the context of

Table 3. Percentage of Responses to the Question "What Makes Life Bad for an Old Person?" by Category

Age	Poor physical health (%)	Inadequate material well-being (%)	Not having child or young kin (%)
19–29	69	10	8
30–44	61	10	11
45–59	33	12	30
60+	55	5	30

Note: The total number of responses to this question was 135.

the extreme technological simplicity of their lives, this preoccupation was understandable. Failing eyesight, lack of strength, joint ailments, and chest sickness were commonly mentioned. On the average about one-half of the responses across age groups mentioned topics having to do with the physical condition of the person. The agreement among people of widely different ages on this topic is to be expected in respondents such as these. Living in small villages and age-heterogeneous family groupings, young and old can see first hand what aging means. In small, face to face communities of this type there is no "generation gap" at least with respect to attitudes and beliefs about the aging process.

Next in importance as responses to the question, "What makes life bad for a (particular) old person?" were comments on the relationships that the old person had with his younger kin. Thirty percent of the responses by people in the two oldest age groups were of the type: "He has no child to help him . . . his child(ren) are dead . . . his children are not supportive." It is worth stressing that the questions, as framed, did not ask specifically about parent–child relationships. However, answers to many of the questions about old age, aging, and the relationships among people of different ages consistently stressed the interdependence of elders and youngers, parents and children. Informants spontaneously and consistently mentioned that one of the most important factors that affected the welfare of an older person was whether he or she had a child to provide care.

Another question about old age was phrased more abstractly. Whereas the previous question asked about what contributed to the quality of life for a particular old person, another question was phrased "What is good (bad) in general about the later stages of life?" In this case the informant was not asked to have a particular person in mind. Again there was substantial uniformity in responses as can be seen in Table 4. Close to 40% of informants in most age groups mentioned the importance of having a child or a younger relative to provide care. The

Table 4. Percentage of Respondents Who Believe Having
a Child or Young Kin is Important in Old Age

Age	Percentage
19–29	38
30–44	26
45–59	40
>60	40

Note: The total number of responses to the question "What is
good about old age?" was 97.

younger respondents and the oldest ones were about equally likely (38
versus 40%) to say "having a child makes life good" or "not having a
child means you are close to death" in your later years.

In summary, in asking about age, and age transitions, and the quality
of life in old age, old people stress the significance of physical condition
and having adult children. There was a strong continuity across the age
groups of nearly all issues. The interview material indicates that !Kung
think of old age as a period of inevitable dependency that is ameliorated
only by having a grown child who will provide food and shelter. It is
worth remarking that the two themes that emerged most strongly from
the interview texts: one's physical health and whether one has a grown
child are both circumstances over which members of this society have
little if any control.

The normative data make clear the significance of morbidity and
childlessness for old age. The emphasis on the physical disabilities
associated with aging are associated with the value put on adult children. Children are the prostheses for old age. The demographic data
point up the precariousness and unpredictability of whether one will
reach old age at all and whether one will have children to help should
one live that long. Many people, and more men than women, end up in
late middle age and old age without a child. If there is such cultural
consistency in the opinion about the value of adult children to old men,
what are the actual risks associated with having no children or only a
few children?

*The Relationship between Numbers of Surviving Children
Born to a Father and the Probability That the Father
Survives into Older Ages*

On the basis of reproductive interviews with 318 !Kung ranging in age
from 19 to over 90 years it was possible to ask whether there is a
correlation between having children (more children rather than fewer)

and surviving into old age for fathers (and mothers). In conducting the demographic interviews, Draper asked adults about their own reproductive histories and about the reproductive histories and status (alive or dead) of the interviewees' two parents. From these data it was possible to arrange all subjects along two dimensions: (1) Did or did not the interviewee have a living mother and/or father? (2) Did the interviewee have a small sib set (two or fewer surviving sibs) or a large sib set (three or more surviving sibs)? These two types of information are almost sufficient to determine whether there is a relationship in this data set between the numbers of a parent's children and the probability of that parent surviving into old age.

However, the issue of the age of the informant's mother or father (or more precisely the number of child-bearing years the parent achieved regardless of whether the interviewee's parent was alive or dead at the time of the interview) is a confounding factor, since the older the age attained by an informant's parent, the greater the opportunity that parent had had to bear children. Said another way, fathers and mothers who die young will typically leave behind small rather than large offspring sets. In this case, death of the parent cannot be attributed to the possible help (or lack thereof) that he or she received from the adult children.

Anyone who has struggled with demographic issues in relation to data from nonliterate populations will be familiar with the problems we confront in doing these analyses. !Kung do not know their own calendar ages, they do not know their parents or their sibs ages, and do not know what age their parents or sibs were when and if they have died. On the other hand, !Kung almost without exception know other useful information. They can explain (1) whether their parents, sibs, and children are alive or dead; (2) the order in which individuals were born to the same mother or father, and (3) the approximate developmental age of an individual. This latter information is readily given by informants about people who are not able to be directly observed or interviewed. !Kung say, "So-and-so is about the same age as so-and-so over there" (pointing to an individual that both the informant and the interviewer know).

As a way around these problems we decided to group parents by age on the basis of the age of his or her oldest surviving child. We included only those children born to the parents of informants who were adolescents or older. We imposed this constraint on the grounds that only older children could be a significant help to their parents whereas younger children were drains on the energy and resources of parents. By grouping informants' parents on this basis we were comparing parents who were at least comparable by the age attained by the oldest surviving child born to that parent. This technique is obviously imprecise, but was devised as a means for overcoming the many unknown factors about the parents of interviewees, many of whom were dead and many of whom, if they were still living were not themselves interviewed, nor necessarily living in the research area. For these reasons we could not, with confidence, directly assign the parents of interviewees a probable chronological age.

We could assume, in general, that parents of interviewees whose eldest living children were of comparable age had logged roughly comparable numbers of years in the child-bearing ages, even though some of these parents had died by the time one or more of their adult children were interviewed. We recognized that using the age of eldest surviving child as a proxy for parental age ignores the possibility that other, earlier born children of a given parent may have died previously, leading to an underestimate of the parent's age. However, this source of error should operate in a nonbiasing way for all parents of interviewees, both those dead and those still living.

Given the complexity of these ways of linking data, and given the number of variables considered simultaneously (interviewee's parents alive or dead, number of parent's surviving offspring, and age of eldest surviving offspring), we provide a discussion of how to "read" Figures 5 and 6. The paired histograms marked "old" in Figure 5 refer to the

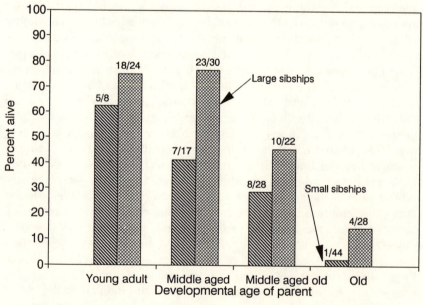

Figure 5. Fraction of fathers alive by age of oldest living child.

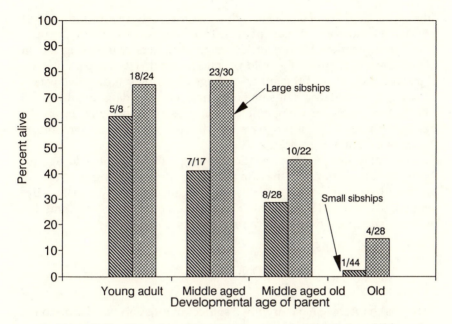

Figure 6. Fraction of mothers alive by age of oldest living child.

percent of fathers alive at the time of interview whose oldest surviving child is 60 years or over. The rightmost histogram of the pair located at "Old" refers to the percent of fathers alive who were fathers of large (>2) surviving offspring sets. The adjacent cross-hatched histogram refers to the percent of fathers alive at the time of interview who had fathered small (≤2) surviving offspring sets. In the case of fathers classified as "old," only 6% of fathers of large offspring sets survive at all. Zero percent of the fathers of interviewees who are members of smaller offspring sets have survived. Notice that as you read Figure 5 from right to left, the difference between the paired histograms is in the same direction, meaning that fathers of differing ages (based on the ages of eldest living child) are more likely to be alive if they have more rather than fewer living adult children.

The paired histograms located at "Middle-aged old" refers to the percent of fathers alive at the time of interview whose oldest surviving child is 45–59 years. The rightmost histogram of the paired histograms marked "Middle-aged old" refers to the percent of fathers alive who were fathers of large (>2) surviving offspring, and so on for the other age categories. About 20% of the fathers of interviewees survive who are fathers of large surviving offspring sets (of which the eldest surviving child is 45–59 years old). This compares with 16% of the fathers surviving who are fathers of small surviving offspring sets (of which the eldest surviving child is 45–59 years of age). The discrepancy in survivorship is much more marked for the survivorship of fathers of offspring sets in which the eldest surviving child is "middle aged" (30–44 years of age). Approximately 80% of the fathers of large offspring sets are alive versus about 25% of the fathers of small offspring sets. The data for fathers fall short of significance. Comparable data, presented in Figure 6, on the relationship between surviving adult children and the survivorship of mothers do reach significance.[8]

These data indicate a correlation among surviving into old age for both fathers and mothers, having surviving adult offspring, and having more rather than fewer such offspring. !Kung interviewees state, unequivocally, that old parents must be nurtured by their children and that without such care from children survival is difficult.

CONCLUSION

In this chapter we have used two sources of inference for discussion of fathering and parent–adult child relations in !Kung society. Where relevant, comparable data on mother and their connections to living adult children have been included for those interested in sex differences among age cohorts. The demographic data indicate that although the !Kung San living in western Botswana are unlike many populations in the Third World in having a large percentage of the population over the age of 60 years, this does not necessarily mean that old people are directly connected to multigenerational linkages by having living adult children. Over 12% of the elderly men have never had children and due to high levels of child and adult mortality. Many men (almost 31%) become childless by the age of 60 or more years, having outlived their own children. The future prospects of !Kung men for creating and solidifying family ties through marriage and child bearing are not good. In recent decades, partly due to economic changes among the !Kung themselves, but also due to increased daily contact with members of other ethnic groups, increased numbers of !Kung children have been born who are fathered by men of socially and economically superior ethnic groups. Thus, !Kung men are losing out in the opportunity to marry, to father children with women of their own ethnic group, and to benefit from the support of their grown children when they reach old age.

A second source of inference about fathering and intergenerational relations came from interviews with over 100 adults on age, age transitions, and relations with members of other age groups. When older

!Kung men and women are asked about their own old age and that of other old people, they are overwhelmingly agreed that having one or more adult children for support in old age is the most important ingredient for not only the quality of old age but survivorship into old age. Informants of all ages claim that having children together with the importance of one's own bodily strength are the most critical components of successful aging. While acknowledging that having adult children for support would logically promote well being and longevity among the aged, we turned to demographic data collected in 1987 and 1988 for possible empirical confirmation of this association. We found a strong association, significant for mothers but not for fathers, between surviving into older ages and having more than two surviving adult offspring.

NOTES

1. These data were collected as part of a multi cultural study of adult development and aging. The research was supported by a grant National Institute of Aging, Grant: AG03110 to Christine Fry and Jennie Keith.

2. These data are generated from interviews with 318 adults of both sexes who lived in the !Angwa, /Ai/Ai, and N!aun!au and /Obesha valleys of northwestern Botswana. Subjects are grouped into four age categories that correspond to "young adulthood," "young middle age," "older middle age," and "old age." !Kung do not know their own ages but it is possible to assign ages to informants and to other living people named by informants on the basis of inference from known historical dates, previous age assessments by Nancy Howell, and informant reports about which individuals were born at approximately the same time.

3. The numbers on which these data are based are smaller than numbers in the previous charts, due to the fact that only individuals who were directly interviewed themselves are included.

4. Middle-aged and postmenopausal !Kung women typically remain with their husbands when they have passed the age of childbearing. This practice is unlike the pattern found in many Bantu societies in which middle-aged women often leave their husbands and return to live with their adult children.

5. It is interesting to note that the pattern of equal parity for men and women is the same for the parents of the oldest informants. This suggest that in the recent past, for two generations born in the 1920s and the late 1890s the pattern of outmating by !Kung women has not been in place. These data are based on interviews with living old people about the numbers of children born to their mothers and fathers (Harpending and Draper 1990).

6. See Bailey (1988) for a discussion a general pattern of hypergynous marriages by hunter–gatherer women with the men of neighboring food-producing groups.

7. Notice that the numbers of rateable responses to some questions exceeds the number of informants ($n = 105$). This is because some informants mentioned more than one topic.

8. The test of statistical significance that we used was logistic regression. This technique is used when the investigator is interested in assessing the effects of categorical variables on a dichotomous "response" variable. Logistic regression indicates the effect of a variable on the log odds of the outcome event with all other variables held constant. The results show the magnitude of the increase or decrease in the log odds given one unit change in the regressor variable.

The effects of age of parent and sibship size on the log odds of parents survival to the present were tested by the model:

$$\text{Prob(Parent is Dead)} = \frac{1}{1 = \exp(b0 + b1 \times 1 + b2 \times 2)}$$

where b0 is a constant, b1 and b2 are regression coefficients for the variables sibship size ($\times 1$) and developmental age of oldest living child ($\times 2$), respectively. This is a standard logistic regression. Thus,

n[Prob(Parent Alive)/Prob(Parent Dead)] = b0 + b1 $\times$ 1 + b2 $\times$ 2
is a multivariate linear regression.

The best fitting model was the simplest; the effect of the interaction of sibship size and age of oldest child was not significant for mothers or fathers, so that only simple linear terms were included in the final model. The results of the analysis show that for fathers, the odds of dying significantly increase with age of the oldest living child (odds ratio = 2.22, 95% confidence interval = 1.5–3.3), but are not significantly affected by sibship size (odds ratio = 0.93, 95% confidence interval = 0.8–1.1). For mothers, the odds of dying also increase significantly with the age of the oldest living child (OR = 2.6, 95% confidence interval = 1.7–3.1), but are significantly affected by sibship size as well. The odds of dying for mothers with more than two children are significantly less than for mothers with two or fewer children (OR = 0.77, 95% confidence interval = 0.7–0.9).

REFERENCES

Bailey, R. C. 1988. The significance of hypergyny for understanding subsistence behavior among contemporary hunters and gatherers. In *Diet and Subsistence: Current Archaeological Perspectives*. B. V. Kennedy and G. LeMoine (Eds.), pp. 57–65. Calgary: University of Calgary.

Biesele, M., and Howell, N. 1981. The old people give you life. In *Other Ways of Growing Old. Pamella*. T. Amoss and S. Harrell (Eds.), pp. 77–98. Stanford, CA: Stanford University Press.

Clark, M. 1969. Cultural values and dependency in later life. In *Dependence and Old People*. R. Kalish (Ed.). Ann Arbor: University of Michigan, Occasional papers in Gerontology.

Clark, M., and Anderson, B. 1967. *Culture and Aging: An Anthropological Study of Older Americans*. Springfield, IL: Thomas.

Cowgill, D. O., and Holmes L. D. (Eds.). 1972. *Aging and Modernization*. New York: Appleton-Century-Crofts.

Denbow, J., and Wilmsen E. 1986. The advent and course of Pastoralism in the Kalahari. *Science* 234:1509–1515.

Draper, P., and Harpending, H. 1991. Work and aging in two African societies: !Kung and Herero. In *Occupational Performance in the Elderly*. B. R. Bonder (Ed.). Philadelphia, PA: Davis, in Press.

Foner, N. (1984). *Ages in Conflict: A Cross-Cultural Perspective on Inequality between Old and Young*. New York: Columbia University Press.

Fry, C. 1988. Comparative research in aging. In *Gerontology: Perspectives and Issues*. K. Ferraro (Ed.). New York: Springer.

Glascock, A. P. 1982. Decrepitude and death-hastening: The nature of old age in Third World societies. *Studies in Third World Societies* Publication 22:43–65.

Glascock, A. P. 1983. Death-hastening behavior: An expansion of Eastwell's thesis." *American Anthropologist* 85:417–421.

Hagestad, G. O. 1984. The continuous bond: A dynamic multigenerational perspective on parent-child relations between adults. In *Parent-child Relations in Child Development*. M. Perlmutter (Ed.), Vol. 17. The Minnesota Symposium on Child Psychology.

Harpending, H., and Draper, P. 1990. Estimating the parity of parents: Application to the history of infertility among the !Kung of southern Africa. *Human Biology* 62(2):195–203.

Howell, N. 1979. *Demography of the Dobe Area !Kung*. New York: Academic Press.

Ikels, C. 1983. *Aging and Adaptation: Chinese in Hong Kong and the United States*. Hamden, CT: Archon Books.

Ikels, C. 1989. Ideological aspects of age structuring. In *Social Structure and Aging: Comparative Perspectives on Age Structuring in Modern Societies*. D. Kertzer, J. Meyers, and K. W. Schaie (Eds.). Hillsdale, NJ: Erlbaum.

Keith, J. 1985. Age in anthropological research. *In Handbook of Aging and the Social Sciences*. R. Binstock and E. Shanas (Eds.), pp. 231–263. New York: Van Nostrand Reinhold.

Kertzer, D., and Keith J. (Eds.). 1984. *Age and Anthropological Theory*. Ithaca: Cornell University Press.

Kohli, M. 1985. Social organization and subjective construction of the life course. In *Human Development and the Life Course*. A. B. Sorensen et al. (Eds.). Hillsdale, NJ: Erlbaum.

Kohli, M. 1986. The world we forgot: A historical review of the life course. In *Later Life: The Social Psychology of Aging*. V. W. Marshall (Ed.), pp. 271–303. Beverly Hills: Sage.

Lee, R. B. 1979. *The !Kung San: Men, Women, and Work in a Foraging Society*. Cambridge: Cambridge University Press.

Lee, R. B., and DeVore, I. (Eds.). (1976). *Kalahri Hunter–Gatherers*. Cambridge, MA: Harvard University Press.

Marshall, L. 1976. *The !Kung of Nyae Nyae*. Cambridge, MA: Harvard University Press.

Neugarten, B. L. 1974. Age groups in American society and the rise of the young-old. *Annals of the American Academy of Political and Social Science* 415:187–199.

Neugarten, B. L. 1982. Policy for the 1980's: Age or need entitlement? In *Age or Need*. B. L. Neugarten (Ed.). Beverly Hills: Sage.

Riley, M. W. 1988. On the significance of age in sociology. In *Social Structure and Human Lives*. M. White Riley (Ed.), pp. 49–64. Newbury Park, CA: Sage.

Rosenberg, H. G. 1989. Complaint discourse, aging, and caregiving among the !Kung San of Botswana. In *The Cultural Context of Aging: Worldwide Perspectives*. J. Sokolovsky (Ed.), pp. 19–42. New York: Bergin & Garvey.

Rubenstein, R. L. (Ed.). 1990. *Anthropology and Aging: Comprehensive Reviews*. Dordrecht: Kluwer Academic.

Rubenstein, R. L., and Johnsen P. T. 1982. Toward a comparative perspective on filial response to aging populations. In *Aging and the Aged in the Third World*. Part I. *Studies in Third World Societies* (No. 22). J. Sokolovsky (Ed.). Williamsburg, VA: College of William and Mary.

Sharp, H. S. 1981. Old age among the Chipewyan. In *Other Ways of Growing Old: Anthropological Perspectives*. P. T. Amoss and S. Harrell (Eds.), pp. 99–109. Stanford, CA: Stanford University Press.

Simmons, L. W. 1945. *The Role of the Aged in Primitive Society*. New Haven: Yale University Press.

Simmons, L. W. 1960. Aging in preindustrial societies. In *Handbook of Social Gerontology*. C. Tibbitts (Ed.), pp. 62–91. Chicago: University of Chicago Press.

Treas, J., and Logue, B. 1986. Economic development and the older population. *Population and Development Review* 12(4):645–673.

Wilmsen, E. 1989. *Land Filled with Flies: A Political Economy of the Kalahari*. Chicago: University of Chicago Press.

Yellen, J. E. 1977. *Archeological Approaches to the Present*. Orlando, FL: Academic Press.

Sokolorski, J. J. (Ed.). 1990. The cultural content of aging: World wide perspectives, New York: Bergen and Garvey.

Chapter 7

Husband–Wife Reciprocity and the Father–Infant Relationship among Aka Pygmies

Barry S. Hewlett

Aka fathers provide more direct care and are near their infants more than fathers in any other human population that has been investigated. Aka fathers are within an arms reach (i.e., holding or within 1 m) of their infant more than 50% of a 24-hour period (Table 1) and Aka fathers hold their very young infants during the day at least five times more than fathers in other human populations (Table 2). While Aka father care is extensive, it is also highly context dependent—fathers provide at least four times as much care while they are in the camp setting than they do while out of camp engaged in economic activity (e.g., out on the net hunt or in the villagers' fields) (Figure 1).

Previous publications (Hewlett, 1988, 1991) have emphasized how female travel on the net hunt contributes to the high level of Aka paternal involvement. Unlike most other forms of hunting, the net hunt involves both women and children. This means Aka women and men walk the same 5–15 km during the day. In most preindustrial populations, women gather or farm near the camp or village, while men travel far away to hunt or trade. In societies where women gather or farm near the camp or village older siblings of the infants are often the second most important caregivers of the infants (Weisner and Gallimore 1977). Among the Aka, however, older siblings do not provide infant care even though they are on the net hunt because older siblings cannot carry infants long distances on the hunt. Older siblings can sit and hold an infant while a mother collects or farms, but they cannot carry an infant long distances. The energetic demands of walking may also explain why the few grandmothers that are around do not help with infant care as

153

Table 1. Average Percentage of Time an Aka Father is within an Arm's Reach of His Infant

	6:00 AM–6:00 PM		6:30 PM–9:00 PM		9:00 PM–6:00 AM (est.)		Total	
	Minutes	*% of time*	*Minutes*	*% of time*	*Minutes*	*% of time*	*Minutes*	*% of time*
Average time holding	57	7.9	35	23.3	0.0	0	92	6.5
Average time in proximity	54	7.5	42	28.3	540.0	100.0	636	45.1
Total	111	15.4	77	51.6	540.0	100.0	728	51.6

154

Table 2. Father Infant Holding in Foraging Populations (Camp Setting Only)

Population	Age of infants (months)	Father holding (% of time)	Source
Aka Pygmies	1–4	22.0	Hewlett (1991)
Efe Pygmies	1–4	2.6	Winn et al. (1990)
Gidgingali	0–6	3.4	Hamilton (1981)
!Kung San	0–6	1.9	West and Konner (1976)

much as is found in other populations. Aka fertility is also high (total fertility rate is 6.3) and infants are nursed for 2–4 years. This means most Aka women 18–45 years of age have a nursing infant–child, and there are only a few adult women without children who might help women with young children. The weight of infant/weight of adult female ratio is also high by cross-cultural standards (Table 3), which means that carrying an infant (and basket full of meat and other collected foods) is especially demanding for Aka women. Efe pygmy women also have a high weight of infant/weight of adult female ratio, and may be a contributing factor to their extensive multiple caregiving (Winn et al. 1990; Morelli and Tronick, this volume). The energetic demands on Aka mothers during the net hunt help to explain, in part, why Aka fathers are likely to help out with infant care while the family is out on the net hunt—Aka women need the assistance of another adult to help carry the

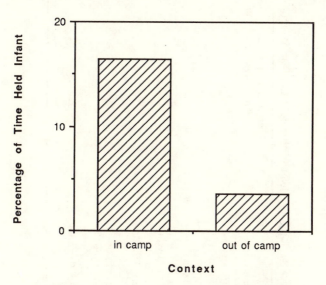

Figure 1. The context of Aka fathers' infant holding.

Table 3a. Ratio of Mean Birthweight to Mean Weight of Adult (18–45) Women in Various Populations

Population	Mean birthweight of infants (kg)	Mean weight of women (kg)	Ratio (%)	Reference
Turkish (Istanbul)	3.4	57.1	5.9	Neyzi et al. (1987)
Filipino	3.0	50.5	5.9	Adair and Popkin (1988)
American (Philadelphia)	3.4	60.9	5.8	Cronk et al. (1986)
Peru Lowland (Lima)	3.2	62.7	5.1	Frisancho et al. (1977)
Peru Highland (Cuzco)	3.1	54.6	5.7	McClung (1969)
Egyptian	3.3	56.1	5.9	Afifi (1985)
Bantu and Sudanese (NE Zaire)	2.9	54.2	5.4	Vincent et al. (1962)
Aka Pygmies	2.8	42.2	6.6	Hewlett (unpublished)
Efe Pygmies	2.6	38.0	6.8	Bailey (1991 and personal communication)

Table 3b. Ratio of Mean Adult Women's (18–45) Weight to Mean 1 Year Old's Weight in Various Populations

Population	1 year old weight (kg)	Adult (18–45) women's weight (kg)	Ratio (%)	Reference
Nonafrican				
Czechoslovakia	10.2	67.3	15.1	Kapalin et al. (1969); Prokopec (1972)
Bundi (New Guinea Highlands)	7.7	49.9	15.4	Malcolm (1970, 1969)
Kaiapit (New Guinea Lowlands)	7.6	53.0	14.3	Malcolm (1969)
African				
Egyptian (rural village)	7.8	56.1	13.9	Afifi (1985)
Nigeria (Ibadan—well-off)	9.6	64.6	14.8	Janes (unpublished; in Eveleth and Tanner 1976)
Nigeria (Ibadan—slum)	8.1	52.9	15.3	Janes (unpublished; in Eveleth and Tanner 1976)
Turkana (rural Kenya)	7.9	48.1	16.4	Little et al. (1983)
Somali (urban Somalia)	8.0	50.3	15.9	Gallo and Mestriner (1980)
Gambia (rural village)	7.3	52.2	14.0	McGregor et al. (1961); McGregor and Smith (1952)
Aka Pygmies	7.5	42.2	17.5	Hewlett (unpublished)
Efe Pygmies	7.3	38.8	18.8	Bailey (personal communication)

Table 4. Mother's Activity While Father Is Holding Infant

Mother's activity	% of time
Left camp to collect firewood or water	24
Food preparation	32
Net hunting	18
House maintenance	7
Idle	12
Other (includes talking to others and eating)	8

infant during the hunt, and Aka men are essentially the only adults available to help out. While Aka fathers *do* provide exceptionally high levels of infant care while out on the net hunt or engaged in other economic activity outside of the camp—Aka fathers do just as much infant holding outside of camp while engaged in economic activity as fathers in other foraging populations provide while sitting around in camp (about 3–4% of the holding; see Table 2 and Figure 1) when they are *not* engaged in economic activity—Aka fathers are much more likely to provide caregiving while they are in camp while the mother is engaged in food preparation or collecting firewood or water (Table 4). Women in most societies prepare the food and collect the firewood, but seldom do they receive any assistance with infant care from men while they are doing these activities. There are numerous societies (including our own) where women could use some help with infant care while they prepare food or clean the house, but in most societies men do not help out with infant care even though they are not engaged in any productive activity and are close by to help out. Older siblings or other adult women are often called on to help out. Older siblings are available in the Aka camp, but it is the father who provides most of the assistance with infant care.

The energetic constraints mentioned above do not help explain why Aka fathers provide exceptionally high levels of infant care in camp. Hewlett (1991) has suggested that husband–wife relations are central to understanding Aka fathers infant caregiving, but has not provided data to support the contention. This chapter quantitatively and qualitatively describes the diversity, nature, and frequency of Aka husband–wife interactions and how this relationship influences father–infant caregiving.

HUSBAND–WIFE RELATIONS AND INFANT CARE

Psychologists have indicated for some time that marital relations and parent–child relations are interdependent, but the psychologists' studies have focused almost exclusively on how marital relations influence mothering. Happily married mothers feel more pleased and competent in their maternal role (Goldberg and Easterbrooks 1984; Cox et al. 1985; Heinicke 1985) and relate more positively to their infants (Oates and Heinicke 1985; Meyer 1988). More recently psychologists have examined how marital relations influence fathering and have found that marital closeness is related to level of father's involvement (Belsky et al. 1989) and father's positive attitudes and warm feelings about his infant (Easterbrooks and Emde 1988). While the psychologists have identified a relationship between marital and parent–child relations, they seldom try to explain why husband–wife relations are linked to parent–child relations. Most studies simply imply an emotional-affective "spillover" effect (Engfer 1988), that is, if husband–wife relations are warm and close then this sensitivity will spillover into parent–child relations.

This chapter builds on the psychological studies by identifying factors in the marital relationships that are linked to father involvement among Aka Pygmies. The chapter hypothesizes that as the number, frequency, and cooperative nature of activities that husband and wife participate in together increases, the level of father involvement increases. Aka husband and wife frequently engage in a number of different types of activities that often require husband and wife to actively cooperate. Husband and wife share extensively as a result of the frequency and nature of their interaction. Infant caregiving is one part of husband–wife reciprocity. Fathers are active infant caregivers when they are not engaged in economic activity and the mother could use some assistance (e.g., she is preparing food, collecting firewood or water).

This hypothesis is a synthesis of reciprocal altruism theory, social organization of work theory, and the concept of many stranded relations from economic anthropology. Reciprocal altruism theory is important because it helps to explain why frequency of interaction is an important component of reciprocity. Evolutionary biologists indicate that two genetically unrelated individuals are likely to practice reciprocal altruism (i.e., share and help each other out) when there is a high likelihood that the individuals will see each other again and there is a high likelihood of receiving something in return for sharing (generally greater than that which is given) (Alexrod and Hamilton 1981; Irons 1979). Reciprocal altruism is sometimes referred to as tit-for-tat theory or "you scratch my back and I'll scratch yours." According to this neo-Darwinian theory, one is likely to share with neighbors or fellow workers because there is a high likelihood that one will see them again and there is a chance of getting something slightly greater in return for sharing or helping out. Reciprocal altruism also implies that an increase in the frequency of interaction generates greater familiarity between two individuals (Cosmides and Tooby 1989); that is, the individuals are better able to read and understand each other needs, desires, and expectations and are therefore able to share and support each other in a number of different ways (e.g., economically, socially, emotionally). But the key variables with this theoretical orientation are not emotional attachment or physical attraction, but the frequency of face-to-face interaction and the likelihood of receiving something in return.

Research by Arensberg (1937) and Johnson and Johnson (1975) on the social organization of work has demonstrated that the nature of husband–wife interactions during the work process contributes to the equality/inequality in male–female relations. "Where men and women cooperate in the productive sphere, the sexes are reciprocal, and there is clear recognition of the importance of women" (Johnson and Johnson 1975:635). Johnson and Johnson describe the great amount of time Machiguenga men and women spend in cooperative work effort in the fields, and link this to the generally high equality between men and women in the society. The social organization of work studies are important because they demonstrate the importance of the *nature* of husband–wife interaction, not just the frequency of that interaction.

Wolf (1966: 81) used the terms "manystranded" and "single stranded" to describe peasant social and economic relations.

> The image underlying this terminology is that of a cord, consisting either of many strands of fiber twisted together or of one single strand. A manystranded relation is built up through the interweaving of many ties [economic, social and symbolic], all of which imply one another. . . . The various relations support one another. A coalition built up in terms of such a variety of relations gives men security in many different contexts.

Wolf describes how unilineal descent groups and the compadre system in Latin America have manystranded social and economic relations. Wolf's concept of manystranded is useful in this discussion of husband–wife reciprocity because it suggests that the *variety* of interactions and their linkages are important factors in understanding reciprocity. Husband–wife reciprocity may be influenced by the *diversity* of activities they do together as well as the frequency and nature of those activities.

A synthesis of these theories and terms suggests that husband–wife reciprocity may be influenced by the frequency of face-to-face interaction, the number of different things they do together, and the nature of that time together. Husband and wife are predicted to share and help each other out more when they spend a lot of time together, cooperate in their activities, and do many kinds of activities together.

How is husband–wife reciprocity linked to the level of father's infant caregiving? Infant caregiving is only one of many tasks that is potentially shared by husband and wife. When husband and wife help each other out frequently in a number of different contexts, fathers are predicted to help out more with infant care. Fathers are providing the care in exchange for assistance the mother has or will provide in other contexts. Father's caregiving is a form of "generalized" reciprocity (Sahlins 1972) in that the timing and level of reciprocal help from his wife are nonspecific. But due to the frequency, nature, and diversity of husband–wife relations he knows that reciprocity will eventually take place.

THE AKA

The Aka are hunter–gatherer–traders of the tropical forest regions of the southern Central African Republic (CAR) and northern People's Republic of the Congo (PRC). There are about 30,000 Aka (8,000 in CAR and 22,000 in PRC) in the region. The Aka families in this study are associated with the Bokoka section of Bangandou village; there are approximately 300 Aka associated with Bokoka and 769 farmers, primarily Ngandu peoples, who live in this section of the village. The Aka spend about 80% of their time hunting and gathering, but are transitional hunter–gatherers in the sense that some 50% of their diet comes from domesticated village products (Bahuchet 1989). They acquire these village products primarily through extensive trade relations with traditional village partners—hunted meat and other forest products are traded for manioc and other village products. The term many stranded relations, discussed above, applies to Aka–villager exchange because their relations are multidimensional—i.e., there are social and symbolic dimensions as well as economic ones. For instance, villagers and Aka contribute to and participate in each other's funerals and clan dances. Aka today also acquire some of their domesticate foods from their own small fields deep in the forest. The average camp has 25–35 individuals and the Aka move camp three or four times during the year. Fertility and mortality are both high—women average 6.3 live births during their lifetime and one-fifth of the infants die before reaching 12 months, primarily of infectious and parasitic diseases.

The net hunt is the most common subsistence activity during the year. Each nuclear family usually has a net made of forest fibers 20–50 m in length and 1 m high, and there are usually 6–8 nets in a camp of 25–35 individuals. The husband usually carries the net and lays it out while his wife sets up and secures the net so animals cannot crawl underneath or jump over the net. The 6–8 nets are connected to each other so as to make a circle or semicircle. Once the family net is set up the husband goes to the center of the nets while his wife stands behind a tree on the inside of the circle of nets next to the family net. When all the nets are set up, a signal is given and the men in the center of the nets start to walk toward their family nets as they yell and scream and pound the ground with logs to try and startle the nocturnal duikers, the primary game animals of the net hunt. If a duiker is spotted it is chased toward the net and the husband yells to the wife the movements of the animal. She waits behind the tree until the duiker passes her, at which time she screams and scares the animal into the net. She tackles the duiker and grabs a nearby log to kill it. She has usually killed the duiker by the time the husband arrives at the net. For some larger species of duiker (i.e., over 40 kg) the husband or other nearby males and females usually arrive in time to help kill the animal. While this is the primary way of organizing the net hunt there are several other formats (e.g., role of men and women reversed) (Bahuchet 1985). Infants usually stay with their mother and older children go wherever they wish. After each cast of the nets there is a 15- to 45-minute rest period and there are 5–15 casts of the net during the day. Game that is captured in the family net is shared with other camp members in two ways. The husband or wife gives specific sections of the animal to others who directly contributed to the capture of the animal (e.g., helped jump on animal in net or helped the family set up the net), or after the wife prepares a pot of stew with the duiker, she sends out small bowls of the stewed meat to most, if not all, the other households in the camp.

While to net hunt takes place throughout the year, it is least likely to take place during the season of heavy rains (September–October) when cross-bow, small traps, and spear hunting predominate, the caterpillar and honey seasons (August and May), or while camp members are in the village to work for villagers.

The Aka are patrilineal and generally practice virilocality except for a few years after marriage when the male provides bride service in his wife's family camp. Kinship terms are basically generational. The Aka are fiercely egalitarian in that there are a number of mechanisms to maintain social and economic equality (Hewlett 1991). Sharing, cooperation, nonviolence, and autonomy are but a few of the Aka core values.

AKA HUSBAND–WIFE RELATIONS AND FATHER INVOLVEMENT

Aka husband and wife participate together in a wide range of activities. Table 5 lists the diversity of activities that husband and wife participate in together and the general nature and frequency of that time together. Husband and wife may work or participate within the larger group or they may go out alone together. Husband and wife participate in the camp net hunt as well as go out alone together to collect fruits or caterpillars and to hunt small animals with string snares. Husband and

Table 5. Number, Relative Frequency, and Nature of Husband–Wife Interactions in Subsistence and Social Activities

Activity	Frequency activity takes place[a]	Frequency husband and wife do this together[b]	Nature of interaction
Subsistence activities			
Net hunt	2	1	Cooperation
Collect fruits, termites, leaves, caterpillars, ignames	2	1	Cooperation and Association
Fish	5	1	Cooperation
Make palm oil for villagers	3	2	Cooperation
Clear, plant, harvest villager's fields	3	2	Cooperation
Hunt with small traps (small nets, snares)	4	2	Association
Capture animals by hand (pangolins, turtles)	3	2	Cooperation
Bow and arrow or cross-bow hunt	3	3	Cooperation
Food preparation	1	3	Association
Butcher and divide game animals	2	3	Association
Social and other activities			
Eat	1	1	Association
Sleep	1	1	Association
Move camp	5	1	Association
Travel to visit friends or relatives	4	2	Association
Childcare	1	3	Association
Drink palm wine	3	3	Association
Dance and sing	1	3	Association
Leisure	1	3	Association

[a] 1, almost every day; 2, 4–6 days per week for 8–9 months per year; 3, 2–5 days per week for 3–4 months per year; 4, 10–20 times during the year; 5, 3–10 times during the year.

[b] 1, almost always when this activity occurs; 2, about 50% of the time this activity occurs; 3, about 25% of the time this activity occurs.

wife are together for a wide range of both social and economic activities. They hunt and gather together as well as dance, sing, and relax together. They also sleep close together in a remarkably narrow bed (about 50–70 cm wide). Husband and wife see and actively work with their spouse in a number of different contexts. The diversity of interactive contexts contributes to the manystranded nature of the husband–wife relationship and provides security to the relationship. Security is developed as husband and wife see and learn how to respond to and count on each other in these diverse contexts.

Table 5 also distinguishes cooperative from associative interaction. Cooperative interaction means that frequent communication and interdependence between husband and wife contribute substantially to the efficiency and effectiveness of the task or activity. For instance, husband and wife have to be able to communicate easily and quickly on the net hunt to get the game into the net. Association means that husband and wife are together, but their tasks or activities are parallel and not dependent on one another. For instance, husband and wife eat, sleep, and work in villagers' fields together, but these activities will take place easily regardless of the presence of the other spouse. While I do not have quantitative data on the frequency of cooperative versus associative work effort, it is clear that Aka husband and wife spend a considerable amount of time in cooperative work effort since the net hunt is the most common subsistence activity throughout the year.

Limited quantitative data do exist on the frequency of Aka husband–wife interaction. Father-focal behavioral observations were conducted as part of the father–infant study mentioned earlier (Hewlett 1991). Each of the 15 fathers were followed for 12 daylight hours (6 AM–PM), and every 15 minutes the following were recorded: (1) all individuals within 1 m of the father (but not being held by the father), (2) the father's nearest neighbor—the closest individual within 10 m of the father (but not being held by the father), and (3) the availability of his infant and wife (within view, within hearing distance, or out of area).

The frequency of Aka husband–wife interaction is exceptional in a number of ways. First, husband and wife were within view of each other 46.5% of the time during daylight hours. If one considers that once the sun goes down everyone is in camp and husband and wife are certainly within view, and that husband and wife sleep together, husband and wife are within view of each other 72% of a 24-hour period. Second, the husband's nearest neighbor was his wife 17.8% of the daylight hours, and his wife was the first or second most frequent nearest neighbor for 13 of the 15 focal fathers. Finally, the husband's spouse was within 1 m of him 10% of daylight hours, and his wife was the first or second most proximal individual in 9 of the 15 focal fathers. Again, these percentages would increase dramatically during evening hours.

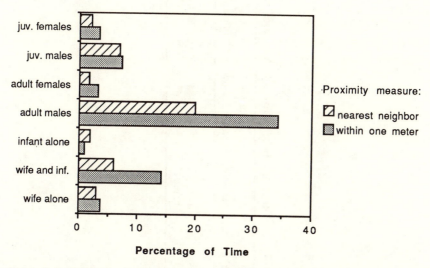

Figure 2. Individuals that were nearest neighbor or within 1 m of Aka fathers.

While Aka men are near their wives frequently, it is misleading to suggest that Aka men spend most of their time with their wives. As Figure 2 demonstrates, Aka men spend most of their time in the company of other adult men or young boys. Also, Aka husband and wife are very close, but they do not hold hands, kiss or hug, or show other signs of affection in public. Husband and wife will tease, joke, and engage in physical play with each other.

The Aka husband–wife relationship is close, diverse, and cooperative, but how is it directly related to the level of paternal involvement? Table 6 examines the statistical relationships between the amount of time fathers held their infants and how frequently they were close to their infants and wives. The table demonstrates that father's holding is not related to how often he is available, nearest neighbor, or within 1 m of his infant, but father's holding almost reaches significance for the amount of time that mother is nearest neighbor, and does reach significance for the amount of time that mother is within 1 m. These results were somewhat unexpected as the average amount of time the focal infant and wife are nearest neighbor and within 1 m of the father is very similar. Table 7 lists the father's proximity scores for the wife and infant, and indicates that there is tremendous variability between individuals and that the wife and infant values for each individual can be very different even though the means are very similar. Overall, these limited data are consistent with the hypothesis that as husband–wife time together increases father involvement in infant/childcare is also likely to increase.

Table 6. Correlations between Father's Holding of Infant and Proximity Measures of Mother and Infant Proximity Measures

	Infant			Mother		
	Availability	Nearest neighbor	Proximity	Availability	Nearest neighbor	Proximity
Correlation to father's holding						
r	0.002	0.205	0.285	0.085	0.488	0.611
p	0.990	0.531	0.303	0.760	0.062	0.015

166

Table 7. Percentage of Time the Focal Father's Wife
or Infant are Within 1 m

	Mean % of time in proximity	
Father number	Wife	Infant
1	06.1	02.4
2	02.5	02.1
3	18.4	16.7
4	08.2	01.1
5	00.0	01.0
6	02.1	11.4
7	22.4	08.1
8	26.5	16.3
9	00.0	00.0
10	08.3	04.1
11	08.4	09.8
12	10.2	13.6
13	08.2	03.4
14	00.0	03.8
15	28.6	19.6
Mean	10.0	07.6

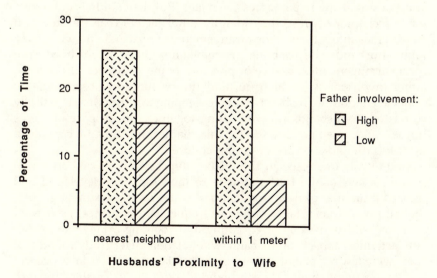

Figure 3. Level of father's involvement with infant and mother's proximity.

A relationship between frequency of husband–wife proximity and level of father involvement is especially pronounced when the wives' proximity to the four fathers who showed high levels of infant involvement (i.e., held their infants more than 2 hours during daylight hours on average) is compared to the wives' proximity of the 11 other fathers (i.e., held their infant less than 40 minutes during daylight hours on average). Involved fathers are within 1 m of their spouses almost three times more frequently than the other fathers (Figure 3). The differences are statistically significant [holding-proximity: $\chi^2(1) = 23.9$, $p < 0.01$; holding-nearest neighbor: $\chi^2(1) = 10.9$, $p < 0.01$].

CROSS-CULTURAL PATTERNS OF HUSBAND–WIFE RELATIONS AND FATHER INVOLVEMENT

Whiting and Whiting (1975) and Broude (1983) have utilized the standard cross-cultural sample (SCCS) (Murdock and White 1969) to examine husband–wife relations. Both studies indicate that there is a constellation of sociocultural factors that is linked to "aloof" versus "intimate" husband–wife relations. The Whitings were primarily interested in explaining why husband and wife room apart in some societies, and found that husband and wife room apart when the society needs warriors to protect property. According to the Whitings, the rooming apart and other aspects of "aloof" husband–wife relations have the psychological effect of producing hyperaggressive males. But their study is of interest for this chapter because they identify other factors that are linked to aloof versus intimate rooming arrangements of husband and wife. They found husband–wife rooming arrangements linked to husband–wife eating arrangements, absence or presence of men's houses, the level of father involvement in childcare, and the presence or absence of the father at childbirth. Husband and wife sleeping together was statistically correlated to husband and wife eating together, the absence of men's houses, and, most importantly for this chapter, having father involved in childbirth and the care of young children.

Broude was interested in the relationship between sexual and nonsexual aspects of the husband–wife relationship. She developed and utilized a number of new cross-cultural codes on the sexual (e.g., premarital sex, extramarital sex, divorce frequency, impotence, newlywed customs) and nonsexual (e.g., eating and rooming arrangements, leisure activities) aspects of husband–wife relations. Her study found that there were few correlations between the sexual and nonsexual aspects of husband–wife relations. The study did identify three "clusters" of variables, one of which is of interest to this chapter. Similar to the Whitings' findings, her cluster 3 shows strong correlations between men's houses, husband–wife eating, husband–wife rooming, husband–wife leisure activities, and husband attendance at birth. Unfortunately, she did not include a measure of father involvement in childcare in her study. Table 8 averages Broude's codes for husband–wife eating, sleeping, and leisure activities for the 37 societies in the SCCS with all three of her codes as well as Barry and Paxson's (1971) code for level of father involvement in infancy in these societies. Again, there is a statistical relationship between father involvement and husband–wife proximity.

DISCUSSION

This chapter has tried to understand (1) why Aka fathers provide substantially more direct infant care in the camp setting rather than out on the net hunt when there are good ecological-energetic reasons for increased paternal caregiving; and (2) why Aka fathers provide more direct infant care than fathers in any other known society. The chapter suggests that to understand the level of father involvement among the Aka or any other society it is necessary to examine the frequency, nature, and diversity of husband–wife interaction. As the frequency and cooperative nature of different husband–wife interactions increase the level of father involvement is predicted to increase. Qualitative data described the cooperative nature of Aka husband–wife interaction and the number of different activities that husband and wife participated in

Table 8. Relationship between Husband–Wife Proximity and Father Involvement in 37 Societies

	Father involvement score[a] for number of societies	
	2–3	4–5
Mean score of husband–wife proximity[b]		
1.0–1.5	4	10
1.6–3.0	17	6

[a] This score comes from Barry and Paxson (1971): 2–3, fathers have little or some physical and emotional proximity to infants; 4–5, fathers have regular or frequent physical and emotional proximity to infants.

[b] This score is the average of the following three scores from Broude (1983): husband–wife eating arrangments, husband–wife rooming arrangements, and husband–wife leisure time activities. *Note:* A score of 1 on any of these measures means that husband and wife eat, sleep, or have leisure activities together, while a score of 3 means they are not together for these activities.

together. Intracultural and intercultural quantitative data demonstrated a correlation between the level of father involvement and husband–wife proximity. Father involvement increases as the amount of time husband and wife spend together increases.

But what are the mechanisms by which husband–wife interaction increases paternal care? Psychologists generally indicate that when the husband–wife relationship is warm and close (implying that physical and emotional proximity are closely linked) that the emotional togetherness spills over into the father–infant relationship. Marital satisfaction leads to greater paternal care. Emotional satisfaction is central to white middle-class Euroamerican marriages because the Euroamerican family is so mobile, nucleated, isolated, and far away from relatives so that emotionally close relationships are hard to come by. The psychologist's explanation makes sense in the Euroamerican context, but it is not as useful for explaining Aka husband–wife relations. Aka are of course very mobile, but they move with or to family, and share emotions and experiences with many people they have known since childhood. Husband–wife emotional satisfaction is not as critical for Aka as it is for Euroamericans. While not a primary factor among the Aka, very low marital satisfaction could lead to a decrease in the level of paternal care because the father would spend more time away from camp and his infant to look for a new wife. But the marital satisfaction hypothesis also means that Aka marriage satisfaction should be substantially greater than what is found in other societies since most all Aka fathers provide substantially more paternal care than fathers in other societies, such as Efe and !Kung, where paternal care is much lower. There is no evidence to suggest that the Aka experience greater marital satisfaction than couples in other societies—arguments, divorce, and extramarital relations are common.

Surprisingly, I have been unable to locate psychological studies that suggest that increased husband–wife interaction leads to father–infant attachment. If a father is around his infant more frequently because he has a close relationship with his wife, it is possible that he may become "attached" to the infant. It is clear that infants become attached to both mothers and fathers (Ainsworth 1977; Lamb 1981) either by providing regular nurturing care or vigorous play, but little research has focused on mother or father attachment to the infant. The father may become involved because he is near the infant more often, becomes familiar with the infant's communication system, and possibly derives some emotional satisfaction out of the relationship. This hypothesis suggests father caregiving increases when the husband–wife relationship is close because the father becomes attached to the infant and wants and enjoys being near his infant. This explanation helps to explain part of the increased involvement of Aka fathers. Aka fathers intrinsically enjoy their infant caregiving role and seek interaction with their infants. For instance, Table 4 was used earlier in the chapter to indicate that fathers usually take care of infants when the mother is busy with other tasks, but the table also demonstrates that 20% of the time the father holds the infant the mother is *not* engaged in economic activity (i.e., she is idle, talking with others, or eating). Aka fathers also pick up and hold infants simply because they want to hold the infant (Hewlett 1991).

Marital satisfaction and father attachment to his infant may help to explain some of the increase in father caregiving associated with increased husband–wife interaction, but husband–wife reciprocity is most likely the prime factor that leads to increased paternal involvement among the Aka. The Aka are unique cross-culturally because both men and women participate in net hunting most of the year. This regular subsistence activity means that husband and wife see each other most of the day and that they have to cooperate extensively to be successful. These are the two criteria necessary for high levels of reciprocal altruism—frequent interaction and the likelihood of receiving something in return. The frequent cooperative nature of husband–wife interaction is important because it means that there is regular give and take between husband and wife. One consequence of the frequent and cooperative interaction is that Aka husband and wife know how to read each other extremely well. They can communicate quickly, easily, and nonverbally. Their familiarity with each other contributes to their ability to help each other out. There are numerous tasks that take place out on the net hunt—setting up the net, chasing game, singing, childcare, collecting fruits, etc.—and most identify men or women as primarily responsible for the task (e.g., men carry the net and women carry the basket and infant). But husband and wife help each other out with these various tasks because they are together often, give and take throughout the day, know when each is tired and needs assistance, and know that there is a high likelihood that their help will be reciprocated. The generalized reciprocity continues to take place when the family returns to camp. Fathers help out extensively in infant care in the camp because it is not energetically demanding or costly (especially by comparison to mother's carrying the infant on the hunt) because they usually sit and hold the infant, they can continue their conversations with other adult males in camp (a common activity of males when they return to camp), it helps out their wives while they are preparing food or collecting water or firewood, and there is a high likelihood that their help will be reciprocated soon—often the next day out on the net hunt.

From an evolutionary or Darwinian perspective, male parental care is considered part of parenting effort (see introduction for an overview).

Smuts and Gubernick (this volume) question this view, and make a convincing argument that in some contexts male caregiving may be mating effort. This chapter, on the other hand, suggests something contrary to both propositions—in given contexts male care may be part of somatic effort (i.e., subsistence effort). Aka men may hold and take care of their infants as part of generalized and extensive reciprocal relations with their wives. Specifically, Aka men may take care of infants in exchange for assistance in subsistence activities (primarily the net hunt).

If father's infant caregiving is part of parental effort, father's direct care should enhance infant survival. While it is clear that Aka infants with no father are at much greater risk of death by comparison to infants with fathers (Aka infants born without an identified father die within 6 months), it is not clear how caregiving directly increases survival. For instance, 4 of the 15 study infants died before their fifth birthday. Two of the infants had very involved fathers and 2 of the infants had relatively inactive fathers. While certainly not enough data to draw any conclusion, it made me question the idea that direct care was an essential part of parental effort. Subjective observations suggest that infant mortality is not linked to the level of paternal involvement. Most infants and young children with fathers seem to survive or die at the same rate regardless of the level of their father's direct caregiving. There are also other African Pygmy populations in similar environments where fathers provide minimal amounts of direct care (Winn et al. 1990) and the infant mortality levels are substantially lower. Other aspects of father's role may be more critical for infant and child survival—e.g., providing and cultural transmission.

Smuts' and Gubernick's hypothesis that in some contexts male–infant care may be mating effort rather than parenting effort helps to explain some features of Aka paternal care. Aka men without many kinship resources provide the greatest levels of direct care to their infants (Hewlett 1988). This suggests that an Aka man with few resources is willing to help out more with infant care in order to maintain the marriage. Aka men with many kinship resources are able to keep their wives by providing them with help and security from many relatives (the number of relatives the husband has is important because the Aka are virilocal). Aka men with fewer resources do not have this option and infant care therefore becomes part of mating effort rather than parenting effort. Male–infant caregiving is also a regular part of Aka life and all Aka women are likely to select men who publicly demonstrate sensitive caregiving. Men therefore have something to gain (extramarital affairs, new wife) by exhibiting sensitive caregiving in public. But this chapter suggests that husband–wife reciprocity is central to understanding the father–infant relationship, and reciprocity is generally considered part of somatic effort (Alexander 1979). An Aka man may be willing to engage in some reciprocity to enhance his mating effort (i.e., keep his mate happy), but I would suggest that most Aka men engage in extensive reciprocity with their wives because they expect to get substantial help from their wives in a wide range of subsistence activities (i.e., somatic effort).

Distinct features about Aka culture and environment help to explain why Aka male–infant care is part of somatic effort. First, as mentioned several times already, husband and wife cooperate frequently in a diversity of subsistence as well as social activities. There are many societies like the Aka in which women contribute substantially to the family diet, but in most of these societies men and women work apart and men do very little childcare (e.g., Hames, this volume). The nature of husband–wife interactions, therefore, is the important factor to understanding reciprocity, not the percentage of calories that males versus females contribute to the diet. Second, the Aka are mobile hunter–gatherer–traders and have minimal (by cross-cultural standards) amounts of warfare and violence. They do not have land or cattle to defend, population densities are low, and game animals are relatively abundant. This means that Aka fathers–husbands do not need to be active protectors and defenders of the family, and can therefore devote more time to providing and caregiving. If Aka fathers had to actively defend resources, it is unlikely that they would be involved with childcare, regardless of the amount of cooperative time that husband and wife spent together. Finally, the demographic and biological features mentioned earlier also contribute to the increased husband–wife reciprocity—high fertility and a relatively high weight of infant/weight of adult female ratio.

CONCLUSIONS

1. Aka fathers provide more direct infant care than fathers in any other known society and provide substantially more direct infant care in the camp setting rather than out on the net hunt when there are good ecological-energetic reasons for increased paternal caregiving due to the unique nature of Aka husband–wife interaction. Aka husband and wife are frequently together, engage in a diversity of tasks together, and often cooperate in these tasks. There is no other known society in which husband and wife relations are as intimate. The nature of husband–wife interaction contributes to extensive generalized husband–wife reciprocity. Infant caregiving is only one of many tasks that are shared by Aka

husband and wife. When husband and wife help each other out frequently in a number of different contexts, fathers help out more with infant care. Fathers provide infant care in the camp setting because it is not energetically demanding and their help is likely to be reciprocated the next day in other contexts.

2. Intracultural and intercultural data demonstrated a relationship between frequency of husband–wife interaction and father involvement in infant care. The more time husband and wife are together the greater the likelihood that the father participates in infant care.

3. Fathers' direct care of infants may be part of somatic effort rather than parental or mating effort.

ACKNOWLEDGMENTS

Research for this chapter was supported by grants from the Wenner-Gren Foundation, University of California Humanities Fund, and the Swan Fund. I would like to gratefully thank the government of the Central African Republic for approving and encouraging the research, especially the Commissioner for Scientific Research, Jean-Claude Kazagui. It is also a pleasure to acknowledge the generous assistance of the Aka families who made this work possible. Finally, I wish to acknowledge the useful comments of Robert Baily, Serge Bahuchet, and Barbara Smuts on earlier drafts of this chapter.

REFERENCES

Adair, L. S., and Popkin, B. M. 1988. Birth weight, maturity and proportionality in Filipino infants. *Human Biology* 60:319–340.
Afifi, Z. E. M. 1985. Determinants of growth of infants in a Egyptian village: Maternal anthropometry, birth interval, solid food and death of siblings. *Human Biology* 57:659–669.
Ainsworth, M. D. S. 1977. Attachment theory and its utility in cross-cultural research. In *Culture and Infancy*. P. H. Leiderman, S. R. Tulkin, and A. Rosenfeld (Eds.), pp. 49–67. New York: Academic Press.
Alexander, R. D. 1979. *Darwinism and Human Affairs*. Seattle: University of Washington Press.
Arensberg, C. 1937. *The Irish Countryman*. New York: Macmillan.
Axelrod, R., and Hamilton, W. D. 1981. The evolution of cooperation. *Science* 211:1390–1396.
Bahuchet, S. 1985. *Les Pygmees Aka et al Foret Centrafricaine*. Paris: SELAF.
———. 1989. *Food Supply and Uncertainly among Aka Pygmies*. Lobaye, Central African Republic. In *Coping with Uncertainty in Food Supply*. I. de Garine and G. A. Harrison (Eds.), 15–27. Oxford: Oxford University Press.

Barry, H., III, and Paxson, L. M. 1971. Infancy and early childhood: Cross-cultural codes 2. *Ethnology* 10:466–508.

Belsky, J., Rovine, M., and Fish, M. 1989. The developing family system. In *Systems and Development, The Minnesota Symposia on Child Psychology*, Vol. 22. M. R. Gunnar and E. Thelen (Eds.). Hillsdale, NJ: Erlbaum.

Broude, G. J. 1983. Male-female relationships in cross-cultural perspective: A study of sex and intimacy. *Behavior Science Research* 18:154–181.

Cosmides, L., and Tooby, J. 1989. Evolutionary psychology and the generation of culture; Part II: Case study: A computational theory of social exchange. *Ethology and Sociobiology* 10:51–98.

Cox, M. J., Owen M. T., Lewis, J. M., Riedel, C., Scalf-McIver, L., and Suster, A. 1985. Transition to parenthood: His, hers, and theirs. *Journal of Family Issues* 6:451–481.

Cronk, C. E., Kurtz, A. B., and Rosenthal, E. 1986. Relationship of fetal ultrasound measurements to postnatal anthropometric variables and maternal measurements. *Human Biology* 58:43–59.

Easterbrooks, M. A., and Emde, R. N. 1988. Marital and parent–child relationships: The role of affect in the family system. In *Relationships within Families*. R. A. Hinde and J. Stevenson-Hinde (Eds.). Oxford: Clarendon Press.

Engfer, A. 1988. The interrelatedness of marriage and the mother-child relationship. In *Relationships within Families*. R. A. Hinde and J. Stevenson-Hinde (Eds). Oxford: Clarendon Press.

Eveleth, P. B., and Tanner, J. M. 1976. *Worldwide Variation in Human Growth*. Cambridge: Cambridge University Press.

Frisancho, A. R., Klayman, J. E., and Matos, J. 1977. Influence of maternal nutritional status on prenatal growth in a peruvian urban population. *Human Biology* 46:265–274.

Gallo, P. G., and Mestriner, M. F. 1980. Growth of Children in Somalia. *Human Biology* 52:547–561.

Goldberg, W. A., and Easterbrooks, M. A. 1984. The role of marital quality in toddler development. *Developmental Psychology* 20:504–519.

Hamilton, A. 1981. *Nature and Nurture: Aboriginal Child-Rearing in North Central Arnhem Land*. Canberra: Australian Institute of Aboriginal Studies.

Heinicke, C. M. 1985. Pre-birth couple functioning and the quality of the mother-infant relationship in the second half of the first year of life. Paper presented at the Biennial Meeting of the Society for Research in Child Development, Toronto.

Hewlett, B. S. 1988. Sexual selection and paternal investment among Aka Pygmies. In *Human Reproductive Behavior*. L. Betzig, M. Bogerhoff Mulder, and P. Turke (Eds.). Cambridge: Cambridge University Press.

Hewlett, B. S. 1991. *Intimate Fathers: The Nature and Context of Aka Pygmy Paternal Infant Care*. Ann Arbor, MI: University of Michigan Press.

Irons, W. 1979. Investment and primary social dyads. In *Evolutionary Biology ahd Human Social Behavior*. N. A. Chagnon and W. Irons (Eds.). North Scituate, MA: Duxbury Press.

Johnson, O. R., and Johnson, A. 1975. Male/female relations and the organization of work in a Machiguenga community. *American Ethnologist* 2:634–648.

Kapalin, V., Kotaskova, J., and Prokopec, M. 1969. *Telesny a Dusevni Vyvoj Soucasne Generace Nasich Deti.* Prague: Academica Praha.

Lamb, M. E. 1981. *The Role of the Father in Child Development*, 2nd ed. New York: Wiley.

Little, M. A., Galvin, K., and Mugambi, M. 1983. Cross-sectional growth of nomadic Turkana Pastoralists. *Human Biology* 55:811–830.

McClung, J. 1969. *Effects of High Altitude on Human Birth.* Cambridge, MA: Harvard University Press.

McGregor, I. A., and Smith, D. A. 1952. A health, nutrition and parasitological survey in a rural village (Keneba) in West Kiang, Gambia. *Transactions of the Royal Society of Tropical Medicine and Hygiene* 46:403–427.

McGregor, I. A., Billewicz, W. Z., and Thomson, A. M. 1961. Growth and mortality in children in an African village. *British Medical Journal* 2:1661–1666.

Malcolm, L. A. 1969. Growth and development of the Kaiapit children of the Markham Valley, New Guinea. *American Journal of Physical Anthropology* 31:39–52.

————. 1970. Growth and development of the Bundi child of the New Guinea Highlands. *Human Biology* 42:293–328.

Meyer, H. J. 1988. Marital and mother-child relationships: Developmental history, parent personality, and child difficultness. In *Relationships within Families*. R. A. Hinde and J. Stevenson-Hinde (eds.). Oxford: Clarendon Press.

Murdock, G. P., and White, D. R. 1969. Standard cross-cultural sample. *Ethnology* 8:329–369.

Neyzi, O., Gunoz, H., Celenk, A., Dindar, A., Bundak, R., and Salgam, H. 1987. Relationships between some maternal factors and pregnancy outcome. *Human Biology* 59:387–398.

Oates, D. S., and Heinicke, C. M. 1985. Pre-birth prediction of the quality of the mother-infant interaction. *Journal of Family Issues* 6:523–542.

Prokopec, M. 1972. *Telesne Charakteristiky Obyvatel CSSR s Prihlednutim k Potrebam Prumyslu.* Institute Hygieny a Epidemiologie, Praha.

Sahlins, M. 1972. *Stone Age Economics.* New York: Aldine.

Vincent, M., Jans, C., and Ghesquiere, J. 1962. The newborn pygmy and his mother. *American Journal of Physical Anthropology* 20:237–247.

Weisner, T. S., and Gallimore, R. 1977. My brother's keeper: Child and sibling caretaking. *Current Anthropology* 18(2):169–190.

West, M. M., and Konner, M. J. 1976. The role of father in anthropological perspective. In *The Role of Father in Child Development*. M. E. Lamb (Ed.). New York: Wiley.

Whiting, J. W. W., and Whiting B. B. 1975. Aloofness and intimacy of husbands and wives: A cross-cultural study. *Ethos* 3:183–208.

Winn, S., Morelli, G. A., and Tronick, E. Z. 1990. The infant in the group: A look at Efe caretaking practices. In *The Cultural Context of Infancy*. J. K. Nugent, B. M. Lester, and T. B. Brazelton (Eds.). New Jersey: Ablex.

Wolf, E. R. 1966. *Peasants.* Englewood Cliffs, NJ: Prentice-Hall.

Chapter 8

Gender Differences in the Perception of Ideal Family Size in an Australian Aboriginal Community

Victoria K. Burbank and James S. Chisholm

In the Bible, Abraham had lots of descendants who split all over the world. It's just in nature to have kids like that.

Aboriginal Father

I am tired of all these children. I tried to run away from them.

Aboriginal Mother

In this chapter we compare Aboriginal mothers' and fathers' expectations and desires about family size. Employing frameworks derived from both evolutionary and sociocultural anthropology, we discuss some of the implications that men and women's contrasting perceptions have for family planning goals, gender relations, and parenting in one Australian Aboriginal community.

In 1988 we initiated a pilot study of the cultural construction of parenting and how this is related to the treatment and health of children aged 0 to 5 in the Australian Aboriginal community that we call Mangrove. The theoretical rationale for this project comes from two sources. One is parental investment theory, which recognizes fundamental differences in male and female reproductive strategies, with males generally adapted to emphasize mating effort and females to emphasize parenting effort (e.g., Betzig 1988; Daly and Wilson 1983; Trivers 1972). The other is Super and Harkness's concept of the "developmental niche" (1986), which provides a multidisciplinary framework for studying the impact of culture on the child's microenvironment of development. In particular, the concept of the "developmental niche" is central to our research and analyses of these data. This new theoretical framework includes (1) the physical and social settings in which development occurs, (2) the culturally regulated patterns of childcare and socialization, and (3) parental psychology—the particular concepts and expectations that caretakers have about what children are, what children can or should become, and what they can or should do to help children get where it is thought they should be (Super and Harkness 1986). We focused especially on the third of these components, that of parental psychology, because a major theoretical goal of our work was to explore the degree of fit between cultural constructions of child bearing and parenting and various predictions from parental investment theory.

The data we present here are derived from conversations and interviews with nearly 30 Aboriginal mothers and fathers. We wish, however, to emphasize that we regard this field study as exploratory, our findings as preliminary, and our results as more suggestive than conclusive.

THE RESEARCH SETTING

Mangrove was established as a Protestant mission in the early 1950s. Situated on half square mile of seacoast, it is located approximately 300 miles from Darwin in the wilderness of the Arnhem Land reserve. Today this settlement is governed by elected Aboriginal officials in consultation with various government agencies and their representatives. But the way of life manifest by its inhabitants reflects, in large part, nearly three decades of effort on the part of missionaries, school teachers, and other government workers to "assimilate" the Aboriginal population into Western society (Cole 1982). Funding for the settlement's school, clinic, housing, and work programs is provided almost exclusively by the Australian government. The majority of adults are unemployed, obtaining cash from pensions, unemployment, and supporting parents benefits. Other sources of food or money include hunting, gathering, fishing, handcraft production, and gambling. Today the people of Mangrove live in Western-styled houses. They eat white flour, tinned beef, and sugar purchased from the local shop; they wash their Western-styled clothing in washing machines, send their children to the local English-speaking school, take their sick to the local health clinic, and amuse themselves with tape recorders, TV, movies, and videos. Still, in large part, their behavior is informed by Aboriginal models of etiquette, religion, kinship, and marriage. Elements of Western culture are incorporated into distinctively Aboriginal schemes. Vehicles, for example, are used for hunting and gathering trips, and chartered airplanes take men to circumcision ceremonies.

To the outside observer this settlement of about 575 Aborigines and 25 whites is a difficult environment in which to raise children. For example, its climate is such that a scratch invites a major infection. It is located on the shore of an ocean inhabited by vicious saltwater crocodiles, hungry sharks, and deadly sea wasps. The surrounding bush is filled with a variety of biting insects and poisonous snakes. The community itself is plagued with litter, backed-up plumbing, and a large domestic dog population that fouls the grounds, acts as a significant disease vector, and makes passage from house to house a sometimes treacherous adventure. Increasing numbers of motor bikes and utility trucks race through the unpaved streets, an occasional spear flies, or someone shoots a rifle into the air. Keeping an eye on young children in these circumstances is an important and full-time job.

In additional to these hazards for children, settlement has brought dramatic demographic change, including what appear to be substantial decreases in birth spacing and increases in family size. Genealogies and reproductive history data indicate that the women of Mangrove may be having more children at shorter intervals than did their grandmothers, or even their mothers. For example, we found that the age at which women first give birth has decreased since the 1930s and the mean interbirth interval has declined from over 50 months between 1925 and 1949 to just 39 months today (Burbank and Chisholm 1989). A residence survey by Burbank in 1981 showed that 27% of the households on the settlement included women with five or more of their biological children living with them. In all but one of these households at least one of the birth intervals was shorter than 3 years. All of this appears to be a radical change from the recent nomadic past. Although there is some disagreement in the literature over whether it is infant and childhood mortality, or low "natural" fertility that account for demographic parameters of precontact Australia, it is generally agreed that Aboriginal families were small, containing perhaps no more than two or three living children (Cowlishaw 1981, 1982; Gray 1985; Hamilton 1975; Reid 1979; see also Campbell and Wood 1988 for hunters and gatherers in general).

According to available reports, childcare among Australian Aborigines, like most hunter–gatherers, is characterized by a high degree of nurturance and indulgence (e.g., Draper 1976; Konner 1976; Hamilton 1981). Many observers, in Australia and elsewhere, have also noted how this pattern of childcare depends on a small number of well-spaced births and how, when women begin to have increasing numbers of children at shorter intervals, the physical and emotional health of children may be compromised because of increased demands on parents' resources, attention, and energy (Berndt 1981; Cowlishaw 1982; Hamilton 1975; Lee 1979; Blurton Jones and Sibly 1978).

GENDER DIFFERENCES IN PERCEPTIONS
OF IDEAL FAMILY SIZE

Given the environmental hazards and the lack of congruence between norms of childcare and family demography, it should come as no surprise to hear that women at Mangrove sometimes complain of their childcare responsibilities. From a Western perspective, these burdens could be ameliorated by use of modern contraception. Although modern contraception is available, however, according to medical records it is rarely used and apparently almost never to space births, but only by older women, to cease their fertility altogether. Nor, according to medical personnel, do men employ Western or indigenous methods of birth control. In 1988, it was reported that some men were requesting condoms from the local health clinic, but they were probably engaging in pre- or extramarital sex, and seemed motivated more by an on-going AIDS education effort than by any desire to limit their fertility.

There have been a number of studies focusing on contraceptive use in Aboriginal populations that have found that although Aboriginal women often wish to control their reproductive lives, a variety of sociocultural factors interfere with their use of modern forms of birth control (Reid 1979; Reid and Gurruwiwi 1979). At Mangrove, at least, we believe that one of these factors is the disparity between men's and women's ideas about ideal family size. For example, all of the women with whom we spoke on this topic wanted no more children than they presently had (which was between two and four). All of the men, on the other hand (who had between one and six children), wanted more. With the exception of one father who said he wanted "lots," the smallest number specified was five children.

We found this difference between mothers' and fathers' views on family size represented in other ways as well. In some of our interviews, for example, we asked mothers and fathers to tell us a story about a mother or a father who had many children. Over 50% of the mothers mentioned problems in their stories. For example, one woman said, "She can't manage to look after them. Two or one would be better than a lot of children." The fathers, on the other hand, did not mention childcare problems at all, but instead related stories we believe reflect their pride or satisfaction in fatherhood. For example, one man said, "I think that married man is a good worker, working for his kids."

GENDER DIFFERENCES IN REPRODUCTIVE GOALS:
AN OVERVIEW

How commonly, we wondered, is this pattern found across societies? Nancy Burley's (1979: 846) survey of 60 HRAF societies revealed only a handful of cases where such information was present, but in all six of these "men had a greater desire for children than did women." She found no data indicating that women wanted more children than men. A review by Mason and Taj (1987a, b) of gender differences in reproductive goals in developing countries, however, paints a different picture. For example,

> Indeed, what is most striking about the results . . . is the variability across social settings. In some settings, women are more likely than men to say they want no more children, while in other settings the reverse is the case. And in many settings (perhaps the majority, if one discounts small percentage differences), the desire to cease having children is on average about equal for the sexes. (Mason and Taj 1987a: 627)

Men, it appears, are not invariably the pronatalist sex. It thus seems likely that explanations for our finding at Mangrove that at least some men want more children than their wives will be found in an examination of aspects of the developmental niche in which the men and women at Mangrove care and provide for their children.

GENDER DIFFERENCES IN THE DEMAND FOR CHILDREN

To organize this examination we follow Mason and Taj (1987a) and employ a "demand framework":

> In this framework, the number or sex of children desired is a function of the perceived value of children (or of sons versus daughters). Whether women and men differ in their fertility desires is consequently a result of the balance between child costs and benefits that each partner perceives. (Mason and Taj 1987a: 613)

According to Christine Oppong (1983: 548) there are three "critical determinants of the demand for children: (1) the perceived value of children, (2) the relative time and material resources available, and (3) the perceived opportunity costs of children. The opportunity costs include the time spent by parents and others in caring for children." In the following discussion we focus on gender differences in the perceived value and costs of children.

In the realm of perceived costs, one basis for differences between mothers and fathers is obvious: Fathers have limited hands-on responsibility for childcare and women have a great deal. Asked, for example, if the fathers of their children helped with childcare, one-third of the women said no, not at all (but none of these women were married to the child's father at the time). But it is also significant that the two-thirds of women who said they did receive help all made it clear that the help they received from their children's fathers was sporadic—for example, a man might bathe or dress a child when its mother was ill. Further, fully 86% of the fathers agreed with mothers, stating that they helped in childcare only a little.

Our structured interviews with 24 mothers and fathers included six questions[1] that we believe are especially likely to reveal basic issues of parenting perceived by the people of Mangrove. A content analysis of the answers reveals both similarities and differences in men's and women's responses. For example, a majority of both mothers and fathers indicated that they regard just having children or being a mother or father very positively. A majority of both mothers and fathers also talked about children's aggression and children's illnesses as issues of concern.

In contrast, obedience (or a lack thereof), correct and incorrect behavior, and accidents were issues raised by a majority of fathers, but by less than half of the mothers. Forty-three percent of the fathers talked about their children's behavior in school, and future jobs that their children might get; only 18 and 29% of mothers raised these topics.

On the other hand, 47% of the mothers talked about children's antisocial activities such as drinking, swearing, and stealing, but only 29% of fathers did. Forty-one percent of mothers talked about separations from their children, but only 15% of fathers did. Thirty-five percent of mothers said that their children made them happy, but only 14% of the fathers raised this topic.

It is not a surprise to find that mothers and fathers emphasize different aspects of children and childcare. Nor, given the particular configuration of the sexual division of labor and gender roles in this Aboriginal community, is it surprising to find men and women emphasizing the things they do. But even given these differences in emphasis, it is not easy to make a strong case for gender differences in the perceived value of children. There were, however, areas of concern raised only by mothers or fathers. Only mothers talked about cuddling babies, children bossing them, and other people making their children happy. Only fathers talked about their responsibility for their children and how they liked to tell their children what to do. Only fathers talked of children's unhappiness, children growing up to take care of parents, and children carrying on the family name. Mason and Taj have observed that "gender differences in the desire for a particular number of children may arise because of differences in the desire for children of a particular sex" (1987a: 630). We believe that differences in men and women's preferences for sons may be a contributing factor in gender differences in perception of ideal family size at Mangrove.

For example, in this society where the division of labor assigns men a preponderant role in valued ceremonial activities and where land "ownership" and membership in significant social categories are derived from the father–child relationship, it is not surprising that men wish to have sons:

> I've got a part to play in ceremony too. I've got songs, ceremonial things. Land too. If I get old I know that I've got a son, he might take responsibility for the ceremony and the Country. Somebody who will take over and my family will go on and on. Instead of just having a family, we could have just lived on with no kids, that would have been the end of [my] family line. Maybe I think different from the other people, but this is the way I think. With out first child we were really happy . . . and we decided to have another. Our real aim was to have a boy, but we didn't have that until we had three girls, then we had a boy, and I think we're finished.

When we spoke to mothers and fathers about gender preferences, however, clear-cut differences did not emerge. It occurred to us that the actual sex composition of our respondents' families might be influencing their answers. We therefore asked the postprimary teachers in the school to ask their pupils (unmarried adolescent girls and boys) to respond to the following question: When you grow up and have children, which would you like to have most, boys or girls? A clear majority of the male students preferred boys, while only one-fifth preferred girls. Over a third of the female students also preferred boys, but a majority preferred girls. We suspect that when students such as these marry and/ or have children, the male preference for sons affects reproductive goals. Women already bearing all the burden of pregnancies and most of the burden of childcare, and not sharing the men's preference for sons, desire fewer children overall.

GENDER ASYMMETRY AND IDEAL FAMILY SIZE

The issue for a woman contemplating limiting her fertility may, however, extend beyond a difference of opinion with her husband. A relationship between the relative power of men and women and fertility has been posited by many (see Beckman 1983, Caldwell 1983; Mason and Taj 1987a, b; Turke 1989 for overviews). It is often assumed that in more egalitarian relationships fertility will be lower because women inevitably want fewer children than do their partners (Beckman 1983; Turke 1989). Mason and Taj (1987b: 18) assert that gender inequality is "probably the most powerful determinant of gender differences in fertility goals," but argue that "patriarchy" can affect women's desire for children in either direction (1987a). Our data demonstrate how gender asymmetries may function to reduce women's power vis-à-vis men when their reproductive goals conflict, and in the particular sociocultural circumstances of Mangrove, increase the number of children that women might otherwise bear.

Mangrove's recent history of polygyny is pertinent here. Just decades ago, polygynous marriage was the norm. For example, in 1981, about 65% of women over 46 years of age had at one time lived as co-wives in polygynous households (Burbank 1988; see also Chisholm and Burbank 1991). This marriage form, however, violated Western law and was discouraged at the mission. Today, though Australian federal law now recognizes plural marriage as a legitimate social arrangement for Aboriginal people, few women share their husband with a co-wife and few appear willing to do so. In 1988, for example, only one man had two wives who lived together in the same household. We believe, however, that the possibility of polygyny nevertheless affects the balance of power between husbands and wives, particularly when it comes to the conflict of their reproductive goals. Indeed, the mismatch of these goals may be a legacy of polygyny. Historically, at least some men of Mangrove had more children than the women of this community; the polygynous father has many more children than any of his wives. Today's monogamous men and women may base their fertility desires on the experiences of their same-sexed parent or grandparent. In a monogamous union, of course, these goals do not match.

Choosing the number two, as it had been mentioned as an ideal number of children by several women, we presented mothers with the following dilemma:

> A married man and a married woman have two kids. Then the woman says she doesn't want any more. But the man wants to have more. What do you think the man will do?

Over half of the respondents said that the man would get another woman. Their answers to the next question "What do you think the woman would do?" indicate that for at least some of them this would not be a satisfactory solution. For example, one woman said, "She'll start to get angry and make a big fight." For a woman unwilling to become a co-wife, this action may signal the end of the union. Thus the possibility that a man may leave a women should she cease to bear children—and this is a time when men do begin looking around for a second wife (Burbank 1980)—may deter any resolve to defer or prevent the arrival of a woman's next child.

An additional pressure to continue rapid child bearing may be the perception, indicated by comments from several women, that men who leave a wife, also reduce or cease support to her children. Analyses of our data indicate, however, that the children of single or separated mothers are at no increased risk for health or development problems, probably because of the support available, through the mother, from her kin (Burbank and Chisholm 1990).

DISCUSSION: EVOLUTIONARY BIOLOGY AND PARENTAL PSYCHOLOGY

This brief look at the differences in male and female ideas about ideal family size suggests that where men desire more children than women and where women perceive that valued relationships with men may be weakened if they cease bearing children, attempts at birth control will be minimal. It also underlines the importance of putting men in the family picture even when their direct contributions to childcare are minimal (see also Kamien 1975; Maynard-Tucker 1989). It also underlines the importance of considering mothers' and fathers' reasons for wanting children, which might help to explain why they want different numbers of children (Mason and Taj 1987a, b).

A reproductive strategy is an inherited and/or learned set of decision heuristics for the allocation of limited resources to reproductive effort. Reproductive effort is held to encompass the traditionally separate components of mating effort and parenting effort. Mating effort consists of the time, energy, or risk costs associated with mating (for humans this includes such activities as the pursuit of social and economic success, courtship, and extramarital affairs). Parenting effort consists of the similar costs associated with bearing and rearing offspring (for humans this includes activities such as breast-feeding, domestic labor related to child welfare—that is, almost any household activity—and resource accumulation). Because female mammals are obligated by internal fertilization, gestation, parturition, and lactation to bear the brunt of parenting costs they become a "limited resource" for mammalian males, who, correspondingly, appear to have been selected to specialize in the expenditure of mating effort (Betzig 1988; Trivers 1972). While it is clear that females of many species expend mating effort (e.g., Hrdy 1981) and males of many species expend parenting effort (e.g., Hewlett 1988; West and Konner 1976), it is commonly—and perhaps uncritically—accepted that effort expended on one component of reproduction cannot be expended on the other. Betzig (1988), for example, in her recent review of theory and research in parental investment, states:

> For any individual female or male, reproductive effort is devoted to parenting at the expense of mating . . . and effort devoted to mating is made at the expense of parenting. (Betzig, 1988: 4).

From looking at human parents' reasons for wanting children, however, we suspect that like many dichotomies, the one between mating effort and parenting effort may sometimes be overdrawn. The biggest difference we found between men's and women's reasons for wanting children was that fathers were much more likely than mothers (p = 0.017; Fisher's exact test) to mention a concern for what appeared to be the survival or longevity of social groups and categories based on patrifiliation. We suggest that one reason for this greater concern among men is that at Mangrove they may think that one way to provide for their children (or grandchildren) is by providing more children. In support of this possibility, consider this father's response to our question about the number of sons and daughters he wanted (he already had one daughter):

> Three boys and three girls . . . [pause]. Or one girl and five boys. [Why?] This is a quiet settlement, but it's a tough place. I'm thinking about if [my daughter]'s the only one, then those other families have help, then she'll have to fight with no hope of winning. If they have trouble then she says, "I've got five brothers—don't pick on me."

In other words, a man's desire for more children, or even for additional wives, may not indicate only his inclination to expend mating effort. Mating effort may occasionally "overlap" with parenting effort. Les Hiatt (1989), citing the work of Smuts (1985) and others, has noted that males may expend parenting effort to achieve mating success, but to our knowledge the reverse seems not to have been suggested. The expenditure of mating effort to achieve parenting success may occur when direct parenting efforts by men are of little marginal value to children (i.e., when such care has little benefit for children and its absence little cost to fathers—as is suggested, for example, by our finding that the children of unmarried women do no worse than the children of married women) and when the only wealth a man can pass on to his children is the "wealth" that comes from the security of sufficient numbers of siblings (or half-siblings) and the inculcation of a sense of group solidarity (see also Rogers 1989). If male fertility itself sometimes constitutes a sort of patrimony, or is at least perceived as such by individual fathers, it is not surprising that men will desire many children, whose mutual support constitutes a form of "delayed" parental investment no father can provide directly. By the same token, when women bear additional children in order to protect their marriages or maintain their husbands' support or interest, they too may be thought of as expending mating effort to achieve parenting success—or at any rate something other than greater fertility.

Many have argued that because only one sex has the ability to bear children, "women's reproductive powers must be socially appropriated" (Harris and Young 1981: 120). Whether this appropriation is in the service of maintaining and reproducing specific social forms or in the services of individual reproductive success, it is men who usually attempt it (e.g., Harris and Young 1981; Hiatt 1985; Mukhopadhyay and Higgins 1988; Paige and Paige 1981; but see also Burley 1979). In this chapter we have tried to demonstrate how important psychological variables are for such models. Gender conflict and power asymmetries, fertility goals and different reproductive strategies cannot be fully comprehended without knowledge of the cultural constructions of reproduction; too narrow a focus on behavior may blind us to what it is that some behavior is intended to achieve and hence to a significant source of its motivation.[2]

ACKNOWLEDGMENTS

We wish to acknowledge the support of the Australian Institute of Aboriginal and Torres Straight Islander Studies, the Fulbright Foundation, the Menzies School of Health Research, and the Northern Territory Department of Health. We also wish to thank the men and women of Mangrove, Drs. Janice Reid, Barry Hewlett, Caroline Bledsoe, and Faye Ginsburg for their comments and assistance on this topic.

NOTES

1. These questions are as follows:

    1. What do you like best about being a mother/father?
    2. What do you not like much about being a mother/father?
    3. What is your best dream/worst fear for your children? Now/when they are grown?
    4. What is the biggest problem that you have with your kids?
    5. Why do women/men want to have children? Why did you want to have children?
    6. How do your children make you: happy, sad, angry, worried, frightened?

2. We wish to point briefly to several works that may presage a greater rapprochement between evolutionary and sociocultural frameworks in anthropology's future. One of these is recent developments in what is called "dual inheritance theory" (the coevolution of genes and culture), which suggests that, for good evolutionary biological reasons, culturally transmitted behaviors—

which necessarily involve considerations of psychology—may be neutral or even maladaptive (in terms of ordinary genetic reproductive success) but still persist (Boyd and Richerson 1985). Another is a new appreciation that it is not behavior, per se, that is selected and evolves, but the cognitive, perceptual, and affective processes that produce behavior (e.g., Tooby and Cosmides 1989; Symons 1989). For more specific discussions of this rapprochement see Chisholm (1992) and Worthman (1992).

REFERENCES

Barkow, J. H., Cosmides, L., and Tooby, J. (eds.). (1991). *The Adapted Mind: Evolutionary Psychology and the Generation of Culture.* New York: Oxford University Press.

Beckman, L. 1983. Communication, power, and the influence of social networks in couple decisions on fertility. In *Determinants of Fertility in Developing Countries.* R. Bulatao and R. Lee (Eds.), pp. 415–443. Vol. 2. New York: Academic Press.

Berndt, C. 1981. Interpretations and "facts" in Aboriginal Australia. In *Woman the Gatherer.* F. Dahlberg (Ed.), pp. 153–203. New Haven: Yale University Press.

Betzig, L. 1988. Mating and parenting in Darwinian perspective. In *Human Reproductive Behavior: A Darwinian Perspective.* L. Betzig, M. Borgerhoff Mulder, and P. Turke (Eds.), pp. 3–20. Cambridge: Cambridge University Press.

Blurton Jones, N., and Sibly, R. 1978. Testing adaptiveness of culturally determined behavior: Do bushmen women maximize their reproductive success by spacing birth widely and foraging seldom? *Society for the Study of Human Biology Symposium 18: Human Behavior and Adaptation.* London: Taylor and Francis.

Boyd, R., and Richerson, P. 1985. *Culture and the Evolutionary Process.* Chicago: University of Chicago Press.

Burbank, V. 1980. Expressions of anger and aggression in an Australian Aboriginal community. Ph.D. dissertation, Rutgers University.

Burbank, V. 1988. *Aboriginal Adolescence: Maidenhood in an Australian Community.* New Brunswick: Rutgers University Press.

Burbank, V., and Chisholm, J. 1989. Old and new inequalities in a Southeast Arnhem land community: Polygyny, marriage age, and birth spacing. In *Emergent Inequalities in Aboriginal Australia.* J. Altman (Ed.). Sydney: Oceania Monographs, No. 38.

Burbank, V., and Chisholm, J. 1990. Maidenhood Revisited: Adolescent pregnancy and parenthood in an Australian Aboriginal community. Paper presented at the Association for Social Anthropology in Oceania meetings, Lihue, Kauai, March.

Burley, N. 1979. The evolution of concealed ovulation. *The American Naturalist* 114:835–858.

Caldwell, J. 1983. Direct economic costs and benefits of children. In *Determinants of Fertility in Developing Countries.* R. Bulatao and R. Lee (Eds.), Vol. 1. New York: Academic Press.

Campbell, K., and Wood, J. 1988. Fertility in traditional societies. In *Natural Human Fertility: Social and Biological Determinants*. P. Diggory, M. Potts, and S. Teper (Eds.), pp. 39–69. London: Macmillan.

Chisholm, J. 1992. Putting people in biology: Toward a synthesis of biological and psychological anthropology. In *Directions in Psychological Anthropology*. T. Schwartz, G. White, and C. Lutz (Eds.). Cambridge: Cambridge University Press (in press).

Chisholm, J., and Burbank, V. K. (1991). Monogamy and polygyny in Southeast Arnhem Land: Male coercion and female choice. *Ethology and Sociobiology*, 12:291–313.

Cowlishaw, G. 1981. The determinants of fertility among Australian Aborigines. *Mankind* 13:37–55.

Cowlishaw, G. 1982. Family planning: A post-contact problem. In *Body, Land, and Spirit: Health and Healing in Aboriginal Society*. J. Reid (Ed.). St. Lucia: University of Queensland Press.

Daly, M., and Wilson, M. 1983. *Sex, Evolution, and Behavior*. 2nd ed. Boston: PWS Publishers.

Draper, P. 1976. Social and economic constraints on child life among the !Kung. In *Kalahari Hunter–Gatherers: Studies of the !Kung San and Their Neighbors*. R. Lee and I. DeVore (Eds.). Cambridge: Harvard University Press.

Gray, A. 1985. Limits for Demographic parameters of Aboriginal populations in the past. *Australian Aboriginal Studies* 1:22–27.

Hamilton, A. 1975. Aboriginal women: The means of production. In *The Other Half: Women in Australian Society*. J. Mercer (Ed.). Hammondsworth: Penguin.

Hamilton, A. 1981. *Nature and Nurture: Aboriginal Child-Rearing in North-Central Arnhem Land*. Canberra: Australian Institute of Aboriginal Studies.

Harris, O., and Young K. 1981. Engendered structures: Some problems in the analysis of reproduction. In *The Anthropology of Pre-Capatalist Societies*. J. Kahn and J. Llohera (Eds.). London: Macmillan.

Hewlett, B. 1988. Sexual selection and paternal investment among Aka Pygmies. In *Human Reproductive Behavior: A Darwinian Perspective*. L. Betzig, M. Borgerhoff Mulder, and P. Turke (Eds.). Cambridge: Cambridge University Press.

Cole, K. 1982. A history of Numbulwar: The story of an Aboriginal community in eastern Arnhem Land, 1952–1987. Bendigo, Victoria: Keith Cole Publ.

Hiatt, L. 1985. Maidens, males, and Marx: Some contrasts in the work of Frederick Rose and Claude Meillassoux. *Oceania* 56:34–46.

Hiatt, L. 1989. The natural history of fatherhood. Paper presented at the First Annual Meeting of the Human Behavior and Evolution Society, Northwestern University, Evanston, Illinois.

Hrdy, S. 1981. *The Woman That Never Evolved*. Cambridge: Harvard University Press.

Kamien, M. 1975. The social psychology of family planning in a part-Aboriginal rural community, 1970 to 1973. *Medical Journal of Australia* 1:25–28.

Konner, M. 1976. Maternal care, infant behavior and development among the !Kung. In *Kalahari Hunter–Gatherers: Studies of the !Kung San and Their Neigh-*

bors. R. Lee and I. DeVore (eds.). Cambridge, MA: Harvard University Press.

Lee, R. 1979. *The !Kung San: Men, Women, and Work in a Foraging Society.* Cambridge: Cambridge University Press.

Mason, K., and Taj, A. (1987a). Differences between women's and men's reproductive goals in developing countries. *Population and Development Review* 13:611–638.

Mason, K., and Taj, A. 1987b. Gender differences in reproductive goals in developing countries. Paper commissioned by the Population Sciences Division of the Rockefeller Foundation, New York, New York.

Maynard-Tucker, G. 1989. Quechua men's role in decision-making concerning reproduction in rural Peru. Paper presented at the Annual Meeting American Anthropological Association, Washington, D.C.

Mukhopadhyay, C., and Higgins, P. 1988. Anthropological studies of women's status revisited: 1977–1978. *Annual Review of Anthropology* 17:461–495.

Oppong, C. 1983. Women's roles, opportunity costs, and fertility. In *Determinants of Fertility in Developing Countries*, Vol. 1. R. Bulatao and R. Lee (Eds.), pp. 547–589. New York: Academic Press.

Paige, K., and Paige J. 1981. *The Politics of Reproductive Rituals.* Berkeley: University of California Press.

Reid, J. 1979. Women's business: Cultural factors affecting the use of family planning services in an Aboriginal community. *Medical Journal of Australia, Special Supplement* 1:1–14.

Reid, J., and Gurruwiwi, M. 1979. Attitudes toward family planning among the women of a Northern Australian Aboriginal community. *Medical Journal of Australia, Special Supplement* 1:5–7.

Rogers, A. 1989. The evolutionary economics of reproduction. Paper presented at the First Annual Meeting of the Human Behavior and Evolution Society, Northwestern University, Evanston, Illinois.

Smuts, B. 1985. *Sex and Friendship in Baboons.* New York: Aldine de Gruyter.

Super, C., and Harkness, S. 1986. The developmental niche: A conceptualization at the interface of child and culture. *International Journal of Behavioral Development* 9:545–569.

Symons, D. 1989. A critique of Darwinian anthropology. *Ethology and Sociobiology* 10:131–144.

Tooby, J., and Cosmides, L. 1989. Evolutionary psychology and the generation of culture, Part I. *Ethology and Sociobiology* 10:29–49.

Trivers, R. 1972. Parental investment and sexual selection. In *Sexual Selection and the Descent of Man*. B. Campbell (Ed.). New York: Aldine.

Turke, P. 1989. Evolution and the demand for children. *Population and Development Review* 15:61–90.

West, M. M., and Konner, M. J. 1976. The role of the father: An anthropological perspective. In *The Role of the Father in Child Development*. M. Lamb (Ed.). New York: Wiley.

Worthman, C. 1992. Cupid and Psyche: Investigative syncretism in biological and psychological anthropology. In *Directions in Psychological Anthropology*. T. Schwartz, G. White, and C. Lutz (Eds.). Cambridge: Cambridge University Press.

PART II

The Cultural Context of Father's Role: Perspectives from Cross-Cultural Human Development and Symbolic Anthropology

Chapter 9

The Cultural Foundations of Fathers' Roles: Evidence from Kenya and the United States

Sara Harkness and Charles M. Super

Although fathers everywhere share a fundamental commitment to the successful growth and development of their children, anthropologists and other observers have documented wide variations in the ways that fathers in different cultures interact with their children and construe their own roles as fathers. Margaret Mead, for example, described a series of contrasts in paternal behavior among three Pacific societies: while some fathers were indulgent playmates with their children, others were feared disciplinarians (Mead 1935). More generally, in polygynous societies where the wives maintain geographically separate households, fathers may be present in the lives of their young children only intermittently. This was the traditional pattern in some East African groups, now recreated by the trend toward urban employment for men while the women and children stay home on the family farm (Abbott 1976; Weisner 1976). At the opposite extreme are "house-husbands," fathers in postindustrial societies who (usually on a temporary basis) are the primary caretakers of an infant or young child.

Sociologists and anthropologists have provided several theoretical frameworks for describing systematic variation across cultures in the ways that parents rear their children. The sociological view of "functions" of the family, as discussed by Popenoe (1988), suggests that with modernization, the basic tasks carried out by the family are increasingly delegated to other social institutions, with the result that the family declines as an institution in its own right. A variation on this view is that certain functions become more elaborated as others are relinquished:

thus, the modern nuclear family becomes socially "specialized" as a context for provision of emotional support, while other functions such as economic cooperation and education are taken over by institutions outside the family. Based on this framework, one would expect predictable patterns of variation in the ways that fathers in different cultures, both historic and contemporary, relate to their children and conceptualize their own roles as fathers.

Another framework for understanding cultural patterns of variation in parenting, particularly in relation to infants and young children, is offered by the anthropologist Robert A. LeVine. In a widely cited essay on parental goals, LeVine (1974) argues that a great deal of variation in parenting behaviors is determined by variations in the health conditions of different populations. He proposes a hierarchy of parental goals, the most basic being assuring the physical survival and health of the child, followed by the development of the child's capacity for economic survival in adulthood, and finally development of the child's ability to represent important cultural values (e.g., morality, prestige). In societies where child mortality is high and the risks to survival great, LeVine suggests, parental practices will focus on the most basic level of the hierarchy (physical survival), while giving little attention to the psychological or behavioral development of the child. In societies where these conditions prevail, such as traditional societies of subsaharan Africa, the cultural pattern of infant care "represents a constant medical alertness, a chronic emergency mobilization effort to save the child at risk" (LeVine 1974:233–234). LeVine stresses, however, that mothers and other caretakers carrying out these culturally established patterns of infant care may not actually feel physically threatened or anxious, and he draws the parallel to "the sentry post, which as an aspect of military structure represents an institutional adaptation to the ever present possibility of intrusion; the sentinel who mans the post, however, may be the picture of drowsy boredom as he holds his loaded gun and scans the horizon for intruders" (LeVine 1974:234). Once the child has survived the period of greatest risk, parenting practices in the same societies will reflect a priority on developing the child's future capacity for economic self-maintenance. LeVine attributes the emphasis on obedience training characteristic of both developing countries and the working classes of industrialized societies to the parental recognition of uncertainty of economic resources, and he contrasts this situation to that of middle class Western parents who, "in an economic environment of stable affluence, . . . can evolve child-rearing philosophies and fashions that are less tightly coupled to the hazards of economic failure; they are relatively free to pursue in their child rearing a wide variety of cultural and personal goals beyond those that appear to be dictated by sheer material survival" (LeVine 1974:237).

A third approach to understanding cross-cultural variation in parenting is the functionalist theory of the Whitings, which suggests that parenting practices are the outcome of the socioeconomic parameters of adult life as represented by the culture's "maintenance systems" (Whiting 1977). As further elaborated by B. Whiting (1980), the constraints on parents' own lives (for example, women's workloads) lead to different styles of parenting as well as different patterns of settings for child life. In East African societies, for example, Whiting and Edwards (1988) describe a pattern of maternal care that they term "the training mother." In interaction with their children, training mothers of East Africa are characterized by relatively high frequencies of assigning chores or infant care and teaching etiquette to young children:

> The training mothers in subsaharan Africa believe that responsibility and obedience can and should be taught to young children. They begin teaching household, gardening, and animal husbandry skill at a comparatively early age. The Ngeca mothers we interviewed are typical: they believe that they should train a child be a competent farmer, herdsman, and child nurse and that a child from age 2 on should be assigned chores that increase in complexity and arduousness with age. They punish their children for failure to perform these tasks responsibly or for stubbornly refusing to do what their elders request of them. They allow much of their children's learning to occur through observation and imitation; only occasionally do they instruct them explicitly. Moreover, mothers seldom praise their children least they become proud, a trait that is unacceptable. They allow the major rewards for task performance to be intrinsic. (Whiting and Edwards 1988:95–96).

In contrast to these training mothers, American mothers in a New England community in the 1950s are described by Whiting and Edwards (1988) as "sociable mothers," distinguished by the relatively high proportion of information exchange and other kinds of reciprocal, friendly interaction with their children. Whiting and Edwards (1988) relate the two contrasting maternal behavioral styles to the parameters of the mothers' own lives. The African mothers must carry out the burden of household subsistence activities, and they rely on the help of their children to accomplish these tasks. In contrast, the American middle class mothers do not need their children to help with basic subsistence (this is being taken care of by the fathers who are off at work), but they do need the children for company as they are isolated in their own homes with no other source of companionship.

Whiting and Edwards' (1988) focus on mother–child interaction in the context of culturally structured daily life leads to recognition of the importance of settings in defining the parameters of social behavior. From this point of view, as Whiting (1980) has suggested, culture can be conceptualized as a "provider of settings," which, in their recurrent nature, encourage the development of certain kinds of behavioral or personality dispositions in preference to others. Although this perspective has been used primarily to compare mothers across cultures, it can equally be applied to fathers.

In this chapter, we explore the issue of cultural variation in fathers' roles as socializers of infants and young children, drawing from our research in a rural Kipsigis community of Kenya and among middle-class American families in the Boston area. We begin with the question of settings, and we ask in what settings of the child's daily life is the father present, and where is he the designated caretaker. Differences in the paternal role emerge from this comparison, as do differences in the ways that childhood itself is structured. Our analysis of settings for father–child interaction in the two cultures also helps to identify culturally constituted customs of care in which fathers do or do not participate. We turn from there to review how fathers actually think about their roles as fathers, as they have expressed these ideas in interviews.

The theoretical framework for this analysis is the "developmental niche" (Super and Harkness 1986), a conceptualization of the culturally structured microenvironment of the child. In comparing fathers' roles in terms of settings of daily life, customs of paternal care, and fathers' ideas about their roles in child rearing, the analysis draws from the three main components of the niche as it has been elaborated in other contexts (Harkness 1991; Harkness and Super, 1983, 1988, 1991b; Super and Harkness 1981). Two major corollaries of the developmental niche framework are that the components of the niche operate as a system, and that each component interacts differentially with elements in the larger culture. We use these corollaries to address the question of how the roles of fathers as socializers of young children vary in relation to major dimensions of difference in the larger environments of families. Finally, we return to reflect again on the sociological and anthropological explanations of child-rearing styles that were introduced above. In doing so, we will necessarily have something to say about the roles of mothers as well as fathers.

THE RESEARCH SETTINGS

Two communities are the sources of comparative data on fathers: A Kipsigis community of western Kenya, which we studied in the early 1970s, and a sample of middle-class American families in the Boston area, whom we studied in the 1980s. The Kipsigis community of Kokwet was the locus of a 3-year field study involving many different aspects of child development and family life (Harkness 1977, 1991; Harkness et al.

1981; Harkness and Super 1983, 1988, 1991b; Super and Harkness 1981). As part of a larger panel of East African communities that were studied under the direction of the Whitings (see Whiting and Edwards 1988), Kokwet has contributed to our understanding of cultural patterns of child rearing in that part of the world (Harkness and Super 1991a,b; Super and Harkness 1986). The more recent American study was undertaken particularly to examine in more detail the dynamics of parental theories of development and their role in promoting it.

The community of Kokwet is located in the western highlands of Kenya, where it enjoys a temperate climate protected by altitude (4000 feet) from the worst of tropical diseases. Consisting of 54 households established on land repatriated from the British at national independence in 1963, Kokwet at the time of fieldwork was a relatively prosperous farming community. As a government-sponsored "settlement scheme," the community was intentionally modern in some agricultural practices, such as the use of hybrid cows for commercial milk production and the marketing of other agricultural produce from household plots of about 20 acres each. This very prosperity, however, had enabled the community to maintain some traditional aspects of life-style, particularly in regard to men's occupations. Unlike other areas where land pressures have been much greater, few men in Kokwet worked away from home, and the organization of the households thus was maintained in its traditional form. Fathers in Kokwet were around to run the political and ceremonial business of the community, settle disputes among their neighbors, direct large, often polygynous households, plough fields with oxen or tractors, harvest maize, mend fences, take care of the cows, and relax with their male friends over a pot of beer in the afternoons. Although none had more than a few years of schooling, these men were for the most part solid citizens, men who had been successful or lucky enough to be able to buy substantial pieces of land, and who had established large families to help them generate the profits. Because their families were built over a period of many years, most of the married men in the community had young children at the time of the field study.

Families in the American sample were recruited through the Cambridge Center of Harvard Community Health Plan, a large health maintenance organization. Thirty-six families participated in the study, with children ranging in age from newborn to 5 years during the 18-month project. The residences of the families included the city of Cambridge itself as well as surrounding suburbs. All families were middle or professional class, intact nuclear families with healthy children. The parents were virtually all American born and the overwhelming majority were of European background. They were all committed parents, interested enough in the daily lives and progress of their children to agree to participate in a study that made real demands on their time over a period of a year and a half. It is notable in this context, however, that of all the parents who were invited to participate in the study (based primarily on the age, sex, and health of their children), about three-quarters agreed to participate and all these remained with the study throughout its duration. In the Cambridge sample, then, we have a set of optimally functioning families in terms of health and stability, but they are not highly self-selected.

FATHERS IN SETTINGS OF DAILY LIFE FOR YOUNG CHILDREN

Father Presence

In comparing the Kipsigis and Cambridge fathers, we first address the question of how much these fathers are present in the lives of their infants and young children, and in what contexts. For the Kokwet fathers, the data for making this comparison are "family spot observations," an adaptation of the technique developed by the Munroes (Munroe and Munroe 1971) for observing social behavior at a given moment in time. In the family spot observations, a research assistant approached the homestead and noted down the activities of all household members who were present, then asked about the location and activities of all others. All families in Kokwet ($n = 64$) were visited in this way approximately 10 times between the hours of 9:00 AM to 6:00 PM, in a pseudo-randomly assigned order, over the course of a couple of weeks (n observations $= 690$). Overall the family observations were spread over a year, in order to capture seasonal variation in activities at the group level. The data for the Cambridge profile of father presence come from "parental diaries," one-page sheets for keeping track of the study child's daily routines in terms of location, activity, caretaker, and others present. The parental diaries were kept by one of the parents (usually the mother) for a week at a time at 6-month intervals, making a total of four sets of diaries for each child over the year and a half of study participation. Because the times for keeping these diaries were established by the child's birthday, the diaries also cover all seasons as well as ages from early infancy to almost the fifth birthday. For the present analysis, we have included all time (both day and night) that the child was awake. Although this time does not correspond to the 9-to-6 hours for the Kokwet observations, it is a fairer basis of comparison for analyzing fathers' roles at home; in Kokwet, the 9-to-6 period is more representative of the full daily cycle that it is in the Cambridge sample. Nevertheless, we also examined the results with a strict comparison of the 9-to-6 hours in the two samples.

As shown in Table 1, the proportions of time that fathers in Kokwet and Cambridge are present with their young children are surprisingly similar, given the differences in ecology. Fathers in both cultures are present with children under 1 year of age about a third of the time (using the whole day for the Cambridge sample), probably reflecting the fact that these infants are likely to be more closely attended by their mothers and that the fathers will thus be in the presence of the infant as a function of spending time at home, with their wives. Thereafter, the proportions of time when the father is present closely parallel each other through age 4, varying from around 25 to 30% of the child's observed time. If we consider only the hours from 9 to 6 for the Cambridge sample, these figures drop by 5 to 10 percentage points, but the pattern across ages remains the same.

Father Caretaking

Given the similarity in overall rate of father presence, an American cultural perspective leads one to ask in what proportion of these times that father and child are together in the same space is the father taking care of the child? The Cambridge fathers' time spent in caretaking, as a proportion of the child's whole day, is reported in Table 1: it hovers around 15%, with no discernible pattern related to the child's age. In attempting to make a comparison with the Kokwet fathers on this measure, we encounter a dramatic difference between fathers' roles in the two cultures. Fathers in Kokwet are virtually never the designated caretakers of infants or young children. In fact, Kipsigis traditions prohibit the father from seeing his newborn infant at all for the first week

Table 1. Fathers' Presence and Caretaking Responsibilities as Percent of Child's Waking Day

	Age of Child (years)				
	0	1	2	3	4
Father present					
Cambridge	34	25	28	25	27
Kokwet	35	23	28	33	30
Father is primary caretaker					
Cambridge	13	15	15	14	17
Kokwet	0	0	0	0	0

Note: Cambridge $n = 16,728$ diary hours while child is awake; Kokwet $n = 748$ spot observations while child is awake.

(formally the first month) after the child's birth, lest the child be damaged by the "strength" of the father's gaze and, conversely, lest the father's masculinity be compromised by close contact with the "dirtiness" (e.g., excreta and vomit) of the baby. Close physical contact between the baby and the father is discouraged during the first year of the baby's life; for example, the baby should not be left to sleep on the father's bed. Despite these restrictions, fathers (like other members of the family) do take great pleasure in their infants and the baby is a frequent center of affectionate attention by the father as well as others. Actual caretaking, however, is left to mothers and siblings.

Along with other researchers whose field data are reported in Whiting and Edwards' comparative study of child rearing, we rated the Kokwet fathers' participation in several specific child care tasks for infants and toddlers (Whiting and Edwards 1988:64–65). The results are summarized in Table 2. As can be seen, fathers in Kokwet rarely played with or entertained their infants, and they were never observed to carry the infant outside the house, dress, feed, or bathe the infant, or take charge of it in the mother's absence. This picture changes only slightly for toddlers: fathers occasionally played with or held these children, and rarely carried them, engaged in physical caretaking, or took charge in the mother's absence. In contrast, the Kokwet fathers frequently disciplined their toddlers verbally, and occasionally taught them chores. Fathers' caretaking involvement for children older than toddlers is not

Table 2. Kokwet Fathers' Participation in Childcare Tasks

Task	Level of father's participation
Child 0–1 years	
Play, entertain	Rare
Hold	Rare
Carry outside house	Never
Dress, feed, bathe	Never
Take charge in mother's absence	Never
Child 2–3 years	
Play, entertain	Occasional
Hold	Occasional
Carry outside house	Rare
Dress, feed, bathe	Rare
Teach chores	Occasional
Teach symbolic material	Never
Physically discipline	Never
Verbally discipline	Daily
Take charge in mother's absence	Rare

Note: adapted from Whiting and Edwards (1988: 64–65).

reported for the simple reason that children over about 2 years of age are not considered to need an assigned caretaker. In this environment where there are always several people of varying ages available, caretaking becomes a diffuse responsibility where even preschoolers are expected to help out in taking care of infant siblings, while older siblings and adults supervise their activities in turn.

Contexts of Father Presence

While fathers in the Kokwet and Cambridge samples can be compared in terms of simple presence or absence and involvement in "caretaking" (as culturally designated), an important aspect of fathers as socializers of young children is reflected in the social contexts that they share with their children. From the child's point of view, the question can be posed first as: What is the child doing when the father is present? As we will see shortly, presence of the father does not imply the same pattern of interaction in different child activity contexts, but this at least provides a

Table 3. Distribution of Chilldren's Major Activities (Percent of Time) While Father Is Present

	Age of child (years)				
	0	*1*	*2*	*3*	*4*
Playing					
Cambridge	39	38	33	27	27
Kokwet	0	7	45	26	17
Eating					
Cambridge	33	24	33	24	21
Kokwet	6	17	13	12	13
Errand, entertainment away from home					
Cambridge	8	19	16	12	20
Kokwet	0	0	0	0	0
Bed and bath routines					
Cambridge	10	11	16	18	18
Kokwet	0	0	0	0	0
Chores					
Cambridge	0	0	0	1	1
Kokwet	0	0	13	26	30
TV or reading					
Cambridge	2	3	7	9	6
Kokwet	0	0	0	0	0
Watch, socialize, "be with"					
Kokwet	94	73	26	35	38
Help/accompany parent					
Cambridge	4	5	5	7	7

starting point for our comparisons. Table 3 shows the percent of time that the child is involved in different activities while the father is present. It will be noted immediately that several of the child activity categories are empty or absent for one sample. This is due partly to different data collection methods (it is not possible to derive the category "help/accompany" from the Kipsigis data), but mainly to the fact that some activity categories that are important in one culture are unimportant or nonexistent in the other. For the Cambridge families, bathing and bedtime routines, watching TV or looking at books, and time away from home (for example, a trip to the doctor, grocery shopping, or a family outing) emerge as distinctive and significant contexts in which fathers and their young children are both present. Among the Kipsigis families of Kokwet, there are no bedtime routines for young children, there are no recreational books or televisions, and errands (which must be done on foot) are usually carried out individually. In contrast, the Kipsigis children from age 2 on are spending a good deal of time doing chores while their fathers are present, and the Cambridge children are doing virtually no chores.

Contexts of Father–Child Interaction

To some extent, of course, the profiles of child activity while the father is present simply reflect the profiles of child activity more generally. The Kipsigis trends in play and chores, for example, are consistent with other data from this community showing that children's play time peaks at age 2, dropping off in subsequent years as the proportion of time children spend doing chores increases (Harkness and Super 1983). To get a better picture of what activities fathers and children might actually be doing together, we turn to further analyses. For the Kokwet sample, the best estimate that can be derived of father–child interaction in the context of different activities is simply the pattern of co-occurrence of the same activities by child and father.

The possible patterns of activity co-occurrence between fathers and children, shown in Table 4, are limited by the fact that some activity categories apply only to babies or children. Most meaningful here is that fathers do not "play" in Kipsigis (nor do mothers, for that matter). The major potentially shared activities are chores, eating, and sociability (including children's play). For each of these, Table 4 lists the shared activity time as a percent of each actor's overall time in that activity, that is, for the child and the father. For 1-year-old children, for example, the concurrent eating time is 57% of all the child's time eating, while it is 67% of the father's overall time eating.

Table 4. Co-occurrence of Father's and Child's Activities, When Father Is Present (Kokwet)

	Age of child (years)				
	0	*1*	*2*	*3*	*4*
Eating					
Percent of child's	0	57	75	88	100
Percent of father's	0	67	50	70	86
Chores					
Percent of child's	—	—	25	71	71
Percent of father's	—	—	8	52	45
Socialize, play					
Percent of child's	25	47	18	49	44
Percent of father's	100	89	80	90	80

It is evident from Table 4 that Kokwet fathers' involvement in the same activities with their children begins in the child's second year of life, when eating becomes a frequent shared activity from the point of view of both child and father. In the next year or two, chores become a second context of activity shared by young children and their fathers in Kokwet. In absolute frequency, chores are the most common activity for children when the father is present, except for general sociability. By the fourth year of life, the child spends most chore time in the context of the father also doing chores (71%). Note, however, that fathers spend a considerable portion of time doing chores while their children are engaged in other activities (45% at age 4). More striking, the percent of eating time is quite high for both fathers and children, suggesting that most of their meals cooccur, although we also know from ethnographic data that fathers and their children often do not "eat together" in the same social space. The pattern of cooccurrence of sociability for fathers and children also suggests that at the very least, a good deal of their sociability is concurrent, although they may not necessarily be socializing with each other.

For the Cambridge sample, we have more direct measures of father–child interaction in the context of different child activities, shown in Table 5. The focus is on the time when the father is the child's caretaker or, even if he is not, when he is specifically the "target" of interaction with the child. Only times when the father is present are included. Two measures for each activity are presented. The "percent interaction with father" indicates the proportion of the time the child was engaged in a particular activity during which father was caretaker or interacting. The second measure, "percent of father's time" indicates the proportion of the father's total caretaking and interacting time that took place during a particular activity.

Table 5. Father–Child Interaction during Major Activities, When Father Is
         Present (Cambridge)

	Age of child (years)				
	0	1	2	3	4
Child eating					
Percent interaction with father	30	41	35	43	47
Percent of father's time	24	18	16	20	18
Bed/bath routines					
Percent interaction with father	48	58	39	46	64
Percent of father's time	12	13	13	15	21
Play					
Percent interaction with father	48	54	61	62	52
Percent of father's time	46	38	41	30	24
TV/books					
Percent interaction with father	50	56	64	44	45
Percent of father's time	2	4	10	10	7
Outside activity					
Percent interaction with father	35	57	41	73	66
Percent of father's time	7	20	14	16	24
Help/accompany					
Percent interaction with father	26	59	52	72	70
Percent of father's time	3	5	5	7	5
Chores					
Percent interaction with father	—	—	—	26	100
Percent of father's time	—	—	—	1	1

The results show that the Cambridge fathers are highly involved with
their children when they are present. For example, they are the caretaker or interactor in a high proportion of the time the children spend in
bed and bath routines (from 39 to 64%). The proportion of father involvement is especially striking in the context of child play, the largest
category of child activity in absolute terms (see Table 3): during the time
that they are home, fathers are interacting with or taking care of their
children nearly half or more of the time the children are playing. From
the fathers' point of view, they are spending from 24 to 46% of their time
home (while the child is awake) actually interacting with or in charge of
their children. Although the proportions in Table 5 fluctuate somewhat
with age, there is a general tendency for father involvement to increase
as the child gets older.

FATHERS' ROLES IN CUSTOMS OF CARE

The analyses of fathers in the settings of everyday life for children in
Kokwet and Cambridge lay the groundwork for an understanding of
fathers' roles in customs of care in the two cultures. For the Kipsigis

fathers, as we have seen, there is a proscription on not only taking care of but even being in the presence of the newborn, and this changes to a pattern of mandated social and physical distance between the father and infant. Following the newborn period and through the first 2 years of the child's life, then, the father is a frequent presence in the child's environment, but he rarely if ever engages in physical caretaking. Fathers' direct involvement in socialization of their children becomes more salient after the age of 2, when children begin to spend significant amounts of time doing chores with their fathers. Other data (not presented here) show that this trend continues to increase over the life span as fathers and sons become partners in work and sociability. The Cambridge fathers' roles in customs of childcare contrast strongly with the Kokwet patterns in several ways. First, fathers are directly involved in caretaking of infants from the beginning of the child's life. This general observation is supported by the fact that rates of father caretaking in the Cambridge sample remain steady at around 15% of the time during the child's first 5 years, suggesting that the amount of time the father spends in caretaking is dictated primarily by other factors such as his own availability rather than by differing cultural expectations in relation to children of different ages in the early years. We can see in the parents' diaries culturally constructed categories of child activity—play, mealtimes, bedtime routines, TV watching and book reading, and outings—that become the contexts for socializing interactions between fathers and their children. It is notable in this regard that the father's participation as "caretaker" or interactor in some of these activities (most notably play and bedtime routines) surpasses that of other potential caretakers (for example, the mother) during the times that the father is present. Even allowing for the fact that the father is undoubtedly the only caretaker present during some of these times, it would appear that fathers are preferentially taking or being given the opportunity to engage in certain kinds of activities with their children. This leads us to focus on the cultural meanings of the activities as vehicles for socialization by the fathers.

FATHERS' CONCEPTUALIZATIONS OF THEIR ROLES

As expressed in interviews, the Kokwet fathers conceptualized their roles as fathers first and foremost in economic terms. They spoke of fathers' obligation to provide food and clothing for the family, to pay for school fees so that all children could attend school at least through the primary level, and to "take care of" (i.e., pay medical costs for) children when they were sick. Beyond this basic role of material provider, the fathers ascribed to themselves the role of moral head of the household.

They should teach their children to obey them, and in cases where there was disobedience, it was the father's responsibility to discipline the errant child. What made them happy, they said, was when children were obedient and responsible, listening to the teacher at school and coming straight home afterward to do chores. What made them unhappy was when a child was disobedient or stole from someone else. Fathers anticipated that following their education, sons would remain to help them on the farm as they themselves grew older, while daughters would move away for marriage. In the meantime, sons would be the preferred social partners: one father said he never sat down to converse with his daughter except when one might have news to share from a visit with far away relatives.

In contrast to the Kokwet fathers, the Cambridge fathers emphasized the importance of developing close affective relationships with their children through activities focused around the child's interests and adapted to the child's developmental capacities. One young father summarized what he thought most important for him to provide for his 6-month-old son: "Paying attention and love. Stimulation, mental and physical." Play, in this context, was taken seriously as a means of enhancing the child's development as well as for building a strong relationship between father and child. As this same father described why he thought it was important for his son to receive stimulation and love: "I feel it might help him to deal with other situations in school, and in life later on. Whereas if he was just sitting in his little chair all the time, he may not adapt as well."

In the context of these general parental goals, the significance of recurrent settings for certain kinds of father–child interaction becomes more evident. In one interview, for example, the parents of a 3-and-a-half-year-old boy described their sense of distress and loss over a change in bedtime routines that had ended up with the child falling asleep watching a movie on the video rather than being read stories and tucked in by his parents. The father described his own feelings about this:

> He didn't like to go to bed, so we would let him watch the movie and fall asleep watching the movie and then carry him to bed. It seemed like a real ugly way of putting a kid to bed. . . . It's really pleasant to sit and read a couple of books and talk about the day, answer questions. It's a great calm time of day, 8:00 at night, 8:30. And so I found that to be really pleasant, compared to leaving him on the sofa with a blanket and letting him fall asleep watching a movie and then going and picking him up and tossing him into bed. There's nothing to that. There's no relationship there.

The father elaborated further on this in terms of his own daily routine:

Well, for me, it's—I catch them very little in the morning. I catch Jonathan because I take him to school now so I see him for a little while, but very little. Then I'm gone all day. And then come home and eat dinner with them, in order to let him lay down and watch a movie; pretty much by 7:30 or so, we would have him on the sofa watching a movie. So that at least I was deprived of any more time. Once the movie is on and he is watching it, then that's it. So I was deprived of a relationship time that I like a lot. I've always liked putting the kids to bed from the time Jonathan was born. So I was losing out on that part. So that's one thing I didn't like about that. It was him and me.

The importance of "special time" or "quality time" emerges as an important element in relationship between each parent and the child, and the Cambridge fathers felt compelled to provide this to their children, sometimes even at the expense of their own time to rest or spend with their wives. Routines around bedtime again emerge as significant in this regard. As one father commented, following a meeting with their pediatrician about their 2-year-old daughter's struggles in going to bed:

Well, I sort of picked it up as my part could be that I could actually start giving Melissa some of that time at night while she was still up, regardless of whatever time it got into. Because I would be sitting down here reading the paper, listening to her upstairs either padding across the rooms or throwing a tantrum or think she's winding down kind of thing. She has in the past wound down by playing—or throwing a tantrum and then she'd be quiet, and the next thing I knew she'd get into bed and fall asleep on her own. It was just something that worked. It wasn't necessarily the best answer. Now—it would be just as easy for me to do something with her and actually give her the attention rather than have her scream for it all the time. That's something—again fighting against I'd like some time too versus her time. I think it's perfectly plausible. The fact is everything gets focused on the older child and she doesn't get too much—or she can't define too much for herself and the only way she has of doing it is kicking and screaming at 9:00 at night.

Ideally for the Cambridge fathers, bedtime, playtime, or other time allocated for exclusive interaction between father and child could serve important educational purposes. One father, who was a lawyer, described how he would talk about almost everything with his son, from his work to the creation. As he explained:

I would talk to him about a case I'm working on and try to explain it to him. If I either won or lost something in court or something along those lines, I'd try to explain to him what I won or what I lost. And then that brings up the consequent winning and losing and the concept of arguing with an attorney in court. It's not just telling him what the argument is about, it's what the argument is.

Sometimes I'll turn to him and say, Do you know what I meant? If I say
we compromised today. It wasn't exactly win or a loss, it was a compromise. I'll say do you know what I meant by compromise? And he'll say no,
always, except if he does know. But he'll say no, what does that mean?
And I'll explain to him and try to bring it to his level of his words. But
there is very little now that you can't translate into his words. Very few
concepts that I can't turn into something that he can hold onto for some
extent.

But I've talked to him about God a little bit and about the creation of the
universe a little bit. Sometimes he sparks it and sometimes I spark it. It had
to do with a tree. We were going for a walk. Well, going for a walk will do
it because you see things. We were on a walk and he said something like,
how did the trees get there? I said I think it starts with a seed and the seed
grows roots and they go downward and the trunk goes up and it spreads.
He said, yeah, they're all going up . . . and I said but you know Jonathan,
the hard question really isn't how the tree got there from the seed. That's
easy. How do you think the seed got there?

In the context of this emphasis on the importance of time spent with
the child and oriented around the child, the reduction of child time and
family time with both parents working at full-time jobs, as was the case
for some of the families in the Cambridge sample, can be stressful for
fathers. As one father of a 3-year-old boy agonized:

I think a lot of problems have come up because of both of us working such
hectic schedules. Time with Michael is very rushed because the time with
Michael is also dinner time, bath time and bed time, brushing teeth and
everything seems to be rammed into the time allotted. It has become a
terrific strain. . . . I feel very strongly about the family unit and when at
dinner time and sometimes the only time we have something that you can
lean on every day because you know your dad will be there. You know
your mom will be there. And I am beginning to be concerned about
latchkey kids. I don't really want Michael to go through that. A friend of
mine once said, "Wait 'til you see some of these kids when they grow up.
Them spending five hours at home alone and Mom and Dad come home at
7:00 and they've been here fending for themselves. They have grown up in
an awful big hurry."

THE CULTURAL FOUNDATIONS OF FATHERS' ROLES

Fathers' roles in Kokwet and Cambridge are constructed rather differently, as manifested in the settings of daily life that fathers and children
jointly participate in, customs of care that involve fathers, and the ways
fathers talk about themselves and their children. While fathers in the
two cultures are present in the environments of young children to a
somewhat similar extent, the Kokwet fathers do not generally "take care

of" infants or young children. In contrast, the Cambridge fathers are involved in caretaking from the beginning of their children's lives, and they seem to share as many kinds of tasks as is physically possible (even, in one example, feeding the baby with breast milk expressed by the mother and stored in a bottle). The settings of father–child interaction that we have described here reflect the cultural construction of childhood in each society: while Kipsigis fathers are with their children in the context of doing chores, eating, and general sociability, the Cambridge fathers play with their babies and young children, take care of bedtime routines, and read books or watch TV with them. Fathers' roles in each society complement childhood roles: while sociability in Kipsigis is often in the context of work, play in the Cambridge setting is taken seriously by parents as a means of education. Thus, the Kipsigis fathers emphasize the importance of their own economic obligations to their children and, paired with this, the children's obligations to be honest, obedient, and diligent in their work. In contrast, the Cambridge fathers speak of building strong affective relationships with their children and providing them with intellectual and social stimulation in the context of activities oriented around the interests and developmental capacities of the child. These are thought necessary for building both self-esteem and the cognitive skills needed for success in later life.

The set of contrasts that can be drawn between fathers in rural Africa and middle-class American resonates to the three theories of cross-cultural variation in the family and in parental roles that we reviewed at the beginning of this chapter. The Kipsigis and Cambridge fathers represent distant points on a sociohistorical continuum in the global family trend from extended families with strong paternalistic authority to small, egalitarian postnuclear families. The trend toward "specialization" of functions in the Cambridge families is interestingly captured by the Cambridge fathers' emphasis on exclusive dyadic relationships with their children—a further step toward the concentration of emotional bonds in smaller and small social units. But what is the explanation for how shifts in the family as a social institution play out in individual roles and relationships within the family?

The Whitings' theory suggests an answer to this question through drawing links from the construction of adult life to the socialization of children through parental assignment of children to different kinds of settings. Families in Kokwet are typical in many ways of East African communities based on subsistence farming by household units. In these families, the characterization of the "training mother" described earlier could equally be ascribed to fathers, and the same contrast could be drawn to the "sociable mothers" (or fathers) of New England. But the Whitings' theory, although it suggests a basis for the different kinds of father–child relationships in different kinds of societies, does not establish a necessary connection. Given the amount of free time that fathers in Kokwet have, they could use some of it to play with their children or have "special time" with them. Given the amount of work that Cambridge parents have to do (especially mothers who are employed outside the home), it is curious that they do not press their young children into helping more. To understand the meaning of culture as a "provider of settings," we must consider not only the practical exigencies of the immediate contexts for family life, but also parental goals for their children's future lives.

Fathers' conceptualizations of their roles and relationships with their children lend strong support to LeVine's idea that childrearing behavior is rooted in parental goals having to do with ensuring the health and future success of their children. It is striking, in both the Kokwet interview material and the discourse of the Cambridge fathers, that these concerns seem to be very close to the surface, easily retrievable on reflection. The Kokwet fathers want their children to be schooled in the work of the household as well as academically, to be ready to take over their own roles as eventual adults responsible for their own families and farms. The Cambridge father plays with his 6-month-old baby son to help him to "adapt" better to school and later life. The lawyer father, while responding to what he sees as his son's natural talent for understanding word concepts, is providing his son with the basic intellectual tools necessary for future success as a lawyer or scholar.

In contrasting fathers' conceptualizations in Kokwet and Cambridge, it is useful to take into account not only what is said but what is left unsaid. Fathers in Kokwet do not talk about building strong emotional relationships with their children, nor do Cambridge fathers talk about economic obligations. LeVine's theory of a hierarchy of parental goals proposes that parents are not free to worry about the psychological development of their children until they have assured their physical survival and future economic viability. The evidence on fathers' conceptualizations presented here, however, suggests a somewhat simpler interpretation: fathers in both cultures talk about what worries them, and do not talk about what they take for granted. Thus, the Cambridge middle-class fathers do not talk about economic support for their children because they take this function for granted. For Kipsigis fathers who are still in transition to a money economy, buying clothes and paying school fees are new and often formidable tasks. On the other hand, the Kipsigis fathers do not talk about building relationships with their children. Given the experience of their culture, they can reasonably expect to have lifelong daily association with their sons, and frequent contacts with their daughters. In contrast, the Cambridge fathers are raising their children with the expectation that they will leave the household permanently within the first 20 years of life, thereafter to visit only occasionally. For both sets of fathers, ensuring future economic viability is seen within the constraints of what is culturally acceptable, and in this regard the Cambridge fathers may face a more uncertain future for their children than do the Kipsigis fathers. Thus, the Kokwet fathers would not have been content to let their children grow up to be hunters and gatherers in the nearby forest, even though this life-style is demonstrated by their neighbors the Ndorobo. In the same way, the Cambridge middle-class fathers would not be happy to raise children who would work on assembly lines or be supported by public welfare funds, even though both options are widely taken in the larger society. The Kipsigis fathers' lack of talk about their children's psychological development may reflect a greater sense of confidence about their children's ability to succeed in the adult life that awaits them right at home; in contrast, the Cambridge fathers' concern about building strong self-esteem would seem to be a realistic reflection of the uncertainties of adult life in an individualistic society.

Thus, while the three theories of culture and the family discussed here each seem to capture important dimensions of contrast, we are left with a continuing sense of mystery about how major sociocultural variables are tied to outcomes for childrearing and the formation of father–child relationships. In attempting to resolve this dilemma, it may be helpful to turn to two corollaries of the developmental niche framework. The first states that "The three components of the developmental niche operate as a system with homeostatic mechanisms that promote consonance among them" (Super and Harkness 1986:559), while the second suggests that "Each of the three subsystems of the niche is also embedded, in different ways, in other aspects of the human ecology; the niche is an 'open system' in the formal sense" (Super and Harkness 1986:560). The Whitings' theory and LeVine's theory each propose direct links from the larger environment (economic organization, demographic conditions) to one or two components of the niche. For the Whitings (to simplify somewhat), the link is from mothers' workload to the settings of daily life (the first component of the niche). For LeVine, the primary connection is drawn from health and economic conditions to parental goals (the third component). Although both theories correspond well to the real differences between family life in different societies, the examples discussed here fail to show the inevitability or necessity of the actual links between the larger sociocultural context and parents' construction of life with their children.

The challenge for understanding how large-scale social and economic change is expressed at the family level, including father–child relationships, is to reconcile the independent influences of the two corollaries of the developmental niche framework. While forces from the outside may directly affect one component of the niche (e.g., settings of daily life) but not another, the press toward internal consistency among the three components (as well as within each one) produces outcomes for the niche's other components that might not seem necessary in their own right. Thus, although the settings of daily life in Kokwet would certainly allow time for fathers to play with their children or spend "special time" with them, this kind of egalitarian, child-centered interaction would be incompatible with the hierarchical helping relationship that is mandated by Kipsigis parental goals and instantiated by the customary activity of doing chores together. Conversely, children's chores among middle class Western families sometimes present difficult issues because they run counter to parents' primary emphasis, expressed in conceptualizations of their roles and in customs of care such as bedtime routines, on adapting their own interests and needs to those of their children. Although the dynamics of these relationships between societal and family forces are most evident during periods of rapid culture change, we believe that they are an important element in the re-creation and acquisition of culture in all societies. Fathers play an important role in the composition of culture for their children, through assimilation of discordant elements from the larger society into a harmonious orchestration of family life.

REFERENCES

Abbott, S. 1976. Full-time farmers and week-end wives: An analysis of altering conjugal roles. *Journal of Marriage and the Family* 38(1):165–174.

Harkness, S. 1977. Aspects of social environment and first language acquisition in rural Africa. In *Talking to Children: Language Input and Acquisition*. C. Snow and C. Ferguson (Eds.), pp. 309–316. Cambridge: Cambridge University Press.

Harkness, S. 1991. A cultural model for the acquisition of language: Implications for the innateness debate. In *The Idea of Innateness: Effects on Language and Communication Research*. C. Dent and P. Zukow (Eds.). *Developmental Psychobiology* 23 (7):727–740.

Harkness, S., Edwards, C. P., and Super, C. M. (1981). Social roles and moral reasoning: A case study in a rural African community. *Developmental Psychology* 17:595–603.

Harkness, S., and Super, C. M. 1983. The cultural construction of child development: A framework for the socialization of affect. *Ethos* 11:221–231.

Harkness, S., and Super, C. M. 1988. Fertility change, child survival, and child development: Observations on a rural Kenyan community. In *Child Treatment and Survival*. pp. 59–70. N. Scheper-Hughes (Ed.). Boston: Reidel.

Harkness, S., and Super, C. M. 1991a. Child care in East Africa. In *Daycare in Context: Historical and Cross-Cultural Perspectives*. M. Lamb, K. Sternberg, C.-P. Hwang, and A. Broberg (Eds.). Hillsdale, NJ: Erlbaum (in press).

Harkness, S., and Super, C. M. 1991b. The "developmental niche": A theoretical framework for analyzing the household production of health. *Social Science and Medicine*.

LeVine, R. A. 1974. Parental goals: A cross-cultural view. *Teachers Collage Record* 76:226–239.

Mead, M. 1935. *Sex and Temperament in Three Primitive Societies*. New York: Morrow.

Munroe, R. H., and Munroe, R. L. 1971. Household density and infant care in an East African society. *Journal of Social Psychology* 83:3–13.

Popenoe, D. 1988. *Disturbing the Nest: Family Change and Decline in Modern Societies*. New York: Aldine de Gruyter.

Super, C. M., and Harkness, S. 1981. The infant's niche in rural Kenya and metropolitan America. In *Cross-Cultural Research at Issue*. pp. 47–55. L. L. Adler (Ed.). New York: Academic Press.

Super, C. M., and Harkness, S. 1986. The developmental niche: A conceptualization at the interface of child and culture. *International Journal of Behavioral Development* 9:545–569.

Weisner, T. S. 1976. The structure of sociability: Urban migration and urban-rural ties in Kenya. *Urban Anthropology* 5(2):199–223.

Whiting, B. B. 1980. Culture and social behavior: A model for the development of social behavior. *Ethos* 8:95–116.

Whiting, B. B., and Whiting, J. W. M. 1975. *Children of Six Cultures: A Psychocultural Analysis*. Cambridge, MA: Harvard University Press.

Whiting, B. B., and Edwards, W. N. 1988. *Children of Different Worlds: The Formation of Social Behavior*. Cambridge, MA: Harvard University Press.

Whiting, J. W. M. 1977. A model for psychocultural research. In *Culture and Infancy: Variations in the Human Experience*. P. H. Leiderman, S. R. Tulkin, and A. Rosenfeld (Eds.), pp. 29–48. New York: Academic Press.

Chapter 10

Fathers in Children's Environments: A Four Culture Study

Robert L. Munroe and Ruth H. Munroe

This chapter has two purposes: first, the presentation of quantitative-descriptive data on father–child contact in agrarian societies in Africa, Asia, Central America, and the Pacific; and second, the presentation of findings from these societies showing an apparent effect of father absence on the behavior of boys but not of girls. We shall see that the results are consistent with a pair of previously derived generalizations, namely, the relatively low degree of father involvement in children's immediate environments in mid-level subsistence societies (Hewlett 1987), and the significance of the absent father for the psychological development of males (Biller 1976; Hamilton 1977; Lamb 1987; Lynn 1974; Stevenson and Black 1988).

The research was carried out in small-scale communities among Black Carib (Belize), Logoli (Kenya), Newar (Nepal) and Samoan (American Samoa) villagers. In all the societies, the father is a policy-maker and figure of authority. External buttressing for this authority is found in patrilineally organized kin groupings among the Logoli and Newars, and in a village council made up of male household heads among the Samoans. Within the family, mothers make most of the day-to-day decisions concerning children and general household activities and, except among the Logoli, exert a degree of influence on their husbands with respect to larger decisions. Mothers seek the father's intercession in matters of serious discipline, and his opinions carry much weight in decisions about children's education and their plans for the future.

Traditional subsistence practices have been supplemented by wage labor activities that engage at least half the fathers in each of the communities. (For descriptive ethnographic background on the traditional systems, see Gonzalez 1969; Holmes 1958, 1974; Mead 1928, 1930; Nepali

1965; Taylor 1951; Toffin 1977; Wagner 1970). When the father's job requires him to reside away from the home community, he is expected to provide support through cash remittances and/or bringing goods home to the family. In this situation, the daily management of family finances falls to the mothers. Few mothers, however, are themselves engaged in wage labor in any of the sample communities.

METHOD

Sample

The sample size for infants, who were studied less intensively than older children, varied from 10 to 13 within each community, totaling 46. Among older subjects, within each community 48 children were selected (6 boys, 6 girls at each of 3, 5, 7, and 9 years of age), yielding a total sample of 192. Since some families had more than one child in the study, a subsample comprised of one child per family was drawn from the larger sample to avoid the use of a parent's score more than once. The resulting partial sample (termed the "reduced sample") was chosen randomly, with two exceptions effected to retain, as closely as possible, the sex and age distribution of the full sample. For the present study, the reduced sample of 133 children was used in one analysis.

Spot Observations

The data were gathered by local personnel who, in each community, were trained to undertake various types of naturalistic observations. The primary technique was the spot observation (Munroe and Munroe 1971; Rogoff 1978), used for both infants and older children in ascertaining levels of father–child contact.[1] The preset observations (likened to still photographs) included information on the place the designated child was located and observed, the activity, other participants in the activity, others present, and location of the parents vis-à-vis the child. Any information not available by means of this visual survey was ascertained through asking those present.

Observations were spread over a 3- to 8-week period for infants and a 6- to 8-week period for older children, and were conducted in a pre-assigned sequence that was rearranged for observers each day. An observer usually checked first to see if the next child on the list (for that day) was in or around his/her home or yard. If not, the observer inquired concerning the child's whereabouts and attempted to locate the child. Infants were nearly always in the home area. For observations of the 3 to 9 year olds, 55% of the protocols were gathered in the child's own home or yard (within 25 feet of home), and 70% were within 75 feet of the home. The remainder were gathered at a greater distance: on paths or roads, in neighboring yards or fields, in the homes/yards of other community members, or in public settings such as playing fields or shops. For infants and non-school-going children, observations were spaced over typical workday hours, i.e., between approximately 8 AM and 6 PM. Schoolgoers were not observed while in school but on afternoons, weekends, holidays, vacations, and occasionally prior to school in the mornings. (For details of procedure within sample societies, see Munroe and Munroe 1989, 1990a,b.) Observations of children in the same household were not conducted simultaneously or sequentially, thereby allowing a wider sampling of the variety of activities and personnel present within any given household.

For the purposes of the observations and the analyses, persons were considered present in the child's immediate social environment if they were participating in the same activity as the child, within the same indoor space as the child, or within 10 feet of the child with no visual barrier. The scores for "Percent fathers present in social environments," reported in Tables 1 and 2, were derived from this information.

Attention to Males

A second observational technique, used only for the 3 to 9 year olds, was concerned with the child's selective attention to others in the social environment (measure patterned after Slaby and Frey 1975). Data were gathered on all sample children except one Black Carib boy, two Black Carib girls, and one Newar girl. On a prearranged schedule, each child was observed only if in the immediate presence of at least two other persons. If this condition was not met, the observer went on to the next-listed child and placed the original child at the end of the list, thus checking at least twice on a given day to see if the observation could be accomplished. Six 10-minute observations were conducted, on the average, for each child at spaced intervals over a 4- to 6-week period in each society. The observer noted the personnel present (by relationship, sex, and age), in columns on an observation sheet. The child's direction of eye gaze was observed for the first 10 seconds of each succeeding 10 minutes, with the remainder of the minute spent recording arrivals and departures and noting whether a child directed his/her attention to each of the individuals in the immediate social environment during the specified interval. For present purposes, we have constructed scores indexing each child's relative attentiveness to males, taking into account the degree to which males were represented (vis-à-vis females) in the environment of the child. For example, a child who directed 60% of his/her attentional gazes at males when the males constituted, say, 40% of that child's social environment would achieve a high score on the measure of "attention to males"; while a child with the same 60% of its attentional gazes directed at males but with a 52% preponderance of males in his/her immediate social surrounds would earn a lower score. Interobserver reliability, obtained through the use of paired observers for some protocols, was at a satisfactory level in all societies: the percentages of agreement between observers (as to whether attention was or was not directed by the child to each of the individuals present during recorded 10-second intervals) were 95.4% for the Belizean sample, 91.4% in Kenya, 80.2% in Nepal, and 80.9% in American Samoa (overall mean = 87.0%).

As might be expected, boys received higher scores overall on the measure of attention to males than did girls ($t = 2.77$, $p < 0.001$). No age trend appeared for relative attention to males; that is, older children did not display a tendency to gaze at males more (or less) frequently than younger children.

Degree of Father Presence/Absence in the Home

Information on current father presence/absence was obtained during census-taking, with corrections and changes noted on the basis of near-daily contact with each sample household throughout the study. Father presence then was scaled in terms of the degree to which the biological father or a father surrogate was residing in the home (i.e., eating main meal and sleeping there). A father surrogate was defined as an individual designated by household members as acting in the social role of father to a given child. The societies varied sharply with respect to the frequency of father surrogates; the numbers (percentages) of children with father surrogates in the community samples were Black Carib, 9 (19%), Logoli, 2 (4%), Newars, 0 (0%), Samoans, 15 (31%). All father surrogates were members of the grandparental generation.

The scale points for father-presence/absence were as follows: 3 points—father (or father surrogate) residing in the home at least 70% of the time (almost all such individuals were resident 100% of the time during the study); 2 points—father (or father surrogate) residing in the home between 10 and 70% of the time (this group was comprised primarily of individuals who were employed away from the immediate home area but who returned on some evenings or weekends); 1 point—father (or father surrogate) residing in home less than 10% of the time (this group consisted primarily of homes with no father resident at any time or with a father who worked and mainly resided elsewhere). Consistent with the operational definition given here, no distinction is made in the analyses between biological fathers and father surrogates.

As will be seen below, two societies were characterized by a high incidence of father (and father surrogate) absence, and two by a low incidence. This relatively sharp disparity between the two sets of societies was not a matter of chance variation but part of the original study design.

RESULTS

Fathers and Infants

Table 1 presents data for three indices of increasingly intimate father–infant contact: the proportion of time that the father was physically present in the immediate environment, the proportion that he was designated as primary caretaker, and the proportion that he was holding the infant. While a drop in the percentages would naturally be expected as more intimate contact is focused on, it is of interest to see the much lower figures for the father's caretaking and holding as compared with his simple presence. Since the infants are being held approximately one-third of the time all told, and are almost always in the charge of a

Table 1. Father Involvement with Infants (3–18 months)

Culture	Number of infants	Fathers present in social environments[a] (%)	Fathers caretaking (%)	Fathers holding (%)
Black Carib	10	11	0	0
Logoli	12	9	1	0
Newars	13	12	9	3
Samoans	11	11	2	0
Total/mean	46	11	3	1

[a] The percentages are based on 2–18 observations per infant. To achieve percentages that are representative for each society, this table includes data from all infants observed, including those without fathers resident in the home (five Black Carib infants, three Logoli infants, and five Samoan infants). If the figures are recalculated to exclude those infants without fathers resident in the home, we find the following for each society (first figure, "Fathers present in social environments (%)"; second figure, "Fathers caretaking (%)"; third figure, "Fathers holding (%)": Black Carib—22%, 0, 0; Logoli—12%, 1%, 0; Newars—12%, 9%, 3%; Samoans—20%, 4%, 0.

caretaker, the father's contribution to these childrearing efforts is obviously not very large.

As Table 1 indicates, the proportion of time the father was present in the social environment of the infant varied around a figure of 11%. (Age of the infant was unrelated to the extent to which the father appeared in the social environment.) The 11% figure is well below those for hunting–gathering societies, for instance the 30% of the !Kung and the astonishing 88% of Hewlett's (1987) Aka pygmies. Similarly, the holding of infants by fathers, which was at zero for all but the Newar infants in our samples,[2] also tends to fall below hunting–gathering peoples, whose percentages vary around 3–4% (again with the exception of the Aka level of 15–20%). For the category of father-as-caretaker, no comparable data are given by Hewlett, but West and Konner (1976) report for the !Kung an average (younger and older infants together) of 4.3%. Thus our mean of 3% is evidence once more for the general point that in agrarian societies the father is, comparatively speaking, involved in very little of the total effort devoted to infant care.

The existence of intercultural variability must not be overlooked. Despite the overall thrust of the data, the Newar fathers, who were both the sole holders of infants and by far the most frequent caretakers, illustrate the fact that some agrarian societies display fairly high levels of father involvement in infant care. It is not clear what sociocultural factors dispose the Newar fathers to close contact with their infants, but the Newars do differ in several ways from the other societies in the sample, viz., the highest level of sociocultural complexity (Kennedy 1987), the least contact with disruptive elements of the urban–industrial world, and the highest proportion of families with a father in residence (see Table 2). The Newars also are one of the two societies (the Samoans are the other) in which the father, mother, and infant sleep together in the early months of the child's life.[3]

Fathers and 3- to 9-Year-Old Children

Table 2 presents data on the degree to which generic father presence/absence in the home was characteristic of the four sample societies, and also data on the extent to which fathers were present in the environments of children during daily activities.

For two of the societies, the Black Carib and the Logoli, the absent-father syndrome characterized the daily life of more than 30% of the sample children, over 50% in the case of the Carib. For the other two, the Newars and Samoans, father absence was at a relatively low level, at only 4 and 15%, respectively. These overall differences are reflected in the spot-observation data, which, as Table 2 indicates, reveal fathers (or

Table 2. Father Presence in the Homes and in the Immediate Social
Environments of Children (3–9 Years)[a]

Culture	Fathers absent from homes (n)	Fathers present or partially present (n)	Fathers present in homes (%)	Fathers present in social environments[b] (%)
Black Carib	25	23	48	3
Logoli	15	33	69	5
Newars	2	46	96	7
Samoans	7	41	85	8
Total/mean	49	143	74	6

[a]n = 48 children per society, six each males and females at ages 3, 5, 7, and 9.
[b]The figures are based on 30 observations per child. To achieve percentages that are representative for each society, these figures include all children who were observed, both those with and those without fathers resident in the home at the time of the study. A 3-way ANOVA (culture × sex of child × age) shows a difference in father presence in observations only for culture, i.e., no differences for children by age or sex. When children with fathers resident in the home are compared, the statistically significant cultural difference disappears although the order of the cultures (lowest to highest percentage of fathers in social environments) is retained almost exactly, with percentages of 6 (Black Carib), 7 (Logoli), 7 (Newars), and 9 (Samoans).

father surrogates) to have been present in their children's immediate social environments less frequently among the Carib and Logoli than among the Newars and Samoans. While these cultural differences are statistically significant, it must be kept in mind that the effect is produced by the complete absence of *any* father for an important segment of the Black Carib and Logoli sample children. As pointed out in Footnote *b* to Table 2, the cultural differences disappear when the comparison is made among only those children who had fathers residing in the home. In such cases fathers were, on an all-culture basis, part of the social environments of those 3 to 9 year olds approximately 7% of the time. (Mothers, by contrast, were present about 20% of the time.) The Whitings' Six Culture data on father availability to 3 to 11 year olds were quite similar, with the mean among the five agricultural societies at 8%, and the range running from 3 to 14% (Whiting and Whiting 1975).

According to the various indices, our infancy and childhood data are of a piece in indicating the father's low involvement in caretaking and his maintaining physical distance. Nevertheless, comparison of Tables 1 and 2 reveals that, on average, in all four societies the fathers were more frequently present in the social environment of their infants than of their older children. One or more of the following factors might account for this regularity. The father of an infant may be around the home area more frequently than is the father of an older child. He may be there intentionally to play a protective role during the 2 years or so after birth when both mother and infant may be more vulnerable, or because his own marital intimacy and desire for closeness to the mother are highest at this time. The father's more frequent presence in the home might be less intentional and result from the fact that he is at an earlier career stage and has less reason to be away from the home area. It is also possible that fathers of infants are not actually home more frequently than are fathers of older children; the effect may derive from the infant's immobility. That is, the father at home is somewhat inadvertently in the immediate social environment of the infant who, unlike the older child, does not have the capability of moving away from the home environment at will.

The Absent Father and Children's Attention to Males

We have seen that father absence from the home occurred at least minimally in all the societies and was widespread in two of those. The measure of "attention to males" allowed investigation of the question of whether father absence was associated with any tendency for children to direct relatively more or less attentiveness to the males in their social environments. Depending on theoretical assumptions about the influence of adult male models, imitative processes, and compensatory strategies in sex-role acquisition, once could mount predictions in favor of either higher or lower relative attention to males on the part of children in father-absent homes, and perhaps differently phrased predictions for boys and girls. Our approach has been to examine the question empirically. The outcomes resulting from a correlational analysis of the degree of father presence/absence and relative attentiveness to males are shown in Table 3.

The findings for boys are clear-cut: In three of the societies and for all boys taken together, absence of the father is associated with higher scores on the attention-to-males variable. The effects, not reaching a relationship as strong as 0.50 in any single case, are moderate, yet unusual for cross-cultural research in that they hold both across cultures and within all but one of the four cultures.

For girls, the relationships vary around zero, and in no case do they reach anything approaching statistical significance. The implication is that so far as attentional behavior toward males is concerned, girls do not differentially respond to the presence or absence of the father.

The results reported in Table 3 are based on scores from all 3- to 9-year-old children. Since a number of sample households in each community contained more than one child, the same score for father

Table 3. Correlations between Father Presence/Absence in the Home
and Children's Attention to Males in Their Immediate Social
Environments[a]

Culture	Boys	Girls
Black Carib	−0.40*	0.16
Logoli	−0.43*	0.03
Newars	−0.46*	−0.18
Samoans	−0.05	−0.02
Total sample	−0.36***	0.00

*$p < 0.05$.
***$p < 0.001$.
[a] n = 24 boys and 24 girls for each culture except Black Carib where n = 23 for boys and 22 for girls, and Newars where n = 23 for girls. Total sample size = 188.

presence/absence would have been applied to all children from a single home. A more conservative approach is to use the reduced sample (described above in the Method section) in which each household was represented by only one child. The outcomes from a reanalysis using the reduced sample are given in Table 4.

The findings, despite reduced sample size, are quite similar to those in Table 3, with boys' attention to males related to the degree of father absence generally across the board, and girls not at all. One interesting outcome is that the Samoan boys, who were an exceptional case in Table 3, now display the same level of correlation as boys in the other societies. For Black Carib boys, however, the relationship has dropped to a nonsignificant level. What this means, though, is that for the two sampling strategies, the association between father absence and attention to males appears at least one time within and across all four societies.

Table 4. Correlations between Father Presence/Absence in the Home
and Children's Attention to Males in Their Immediate Social
Environments: Reduced Sample

Culture	Boys	(n)	Girls	(n)
Black Carib	−0.22	(16)	0.31	(16)
Logoli	−0.45*	(15)	−0.17	(15)
Newars	−0.44*	(18)	−0.01	(18)
Samoans	−0.55*	(17)	−0.14	(18)
Total sample	−0.40***	(66)	0.00	(67)

*$p < 0.05$.
***$p < 0.001$.

We have treated biological fathers and father surrogates as equivalent social figures. Inspection of the data for attention scores indicates a tendency for boys' scores to be affected less strongly by father surrogates than fathers, but with the trend the same in all societies (except among the Newars, where comparison could not be made because all fathers were true fathers). Although further analyses are planned, it will be difficult to reach definite conclusions because father surrogates were present for only one of every six boys in the total sample.

Did father absence have an effect on the attentional behavior of boys not just toward males in general but toward their own fathers as well? The answer is that it did not: Both within and across the cultures, attention to own father was unrelated to degree of father presence in the home. (Obviously this relationship could be investigated only for boys who had either a full-time or a part-time father residing at home.) Another question that can be asked is whether *any* adult male who was resident in the home, not simply the father or a father surrogate, was associated with comparable effects concerning the attention variable. With one qualification, the answer is *no*: Although the all-culture relationship between adult-male absence and attention of boys to males was significant ($r = -0.24$, $p < 0.01$), the association did not appear within any of the four individual sample communities. A final question is whether the frequency of appearance of the father in the course of daily activities. (i.e., during the spot observations) was related to the attention variable, and again the overall answer is negative, with the exception of one within-culture association (in Kenya, $r = -0.55$, $p < 0.01$). Thus these slightly different perspectives fail to add any results that require alteration or reconceptualization of the findings reported in Tables 3 and 4.

DISCUSSION

Our descriptive information on father–child contact seems consistent with the ethnographic background in the four sample societies (Gonzalez 1969; Holmes 1958, 1974; Mead 1928, 1930; Nepali 1965; Taylor 1951; Toffin 1977; Wagner 1970). Nevertheless, the twentieth-century advent of migrant wage labor, with its attendant removal of men from traditional daily rounds, has probably reduced the presence of fathers in many small-scale societies, and what we are seeing in the present data might thus exaggerate the degree of traditional father–child distance. Father–infant proximity ratings for a holocultural sample indicated that traditional agricultural societies did tend to be lower on the whole than foraging groups, but not in a clear and unambiguous way (West and

Konner 1976, based on Barry and Paxson 1971). Therefore, an overall characterization of father–child contact as low in agrarian groups must be seen as provisional and needing further support.

Turning to the association between father absence and attention to males, we feel there are several reasons why the results can be seen as robust despite the modest size of the relationships reported in Tables 3 and 4. First, stable findings across levels of analysis are infrequent in behavioral-science research (DeWalt and Pelto 1985; Shweder 1973); in this instance the all-culture relationship is significant in the two analyses, and the within-culture relationships significant for six of eight correlations. Second, the relationships appear in societies in which father absence is of varying frequency, all the way from the matrifocal Black Carib, where father absence is more common than not, to the Newar situation, where fathers are present in nearly every home. Third, the results have not been affected by the fact that father absence is due to variable conditions, some of these (such as fragile consensual unions and a high rate of separation) being endogenous to the sociocultural system, and others (such as migrant wage labor) being exogenous. And finally, the girls in these societies, living under the same conditions as the boys and experiencing precisely the same degree of father absence, do not display the effects that the boys do.

We might infer, from the low degree of father presence in children's environments, as shown in Tables 1 and 2, that even fathers who are present a small proportion of the time have a relatively strong effect on boys' attentional behavior. This is not necessarily so. The degree to which fathers are in their children's social environments may be underestimated considerably since we did not conduct observations either very early in the morning or during evening and nighttime hours. From the current findings, as reported in Tables 3 and 4, it is clear that father presence in the home is related to boys' attentional behavior, but because we cannot describe the complete-day differences in experience between the father-present and the father-absent boy, we can only speculate on whether total contact time or simple presence in the home is contributing to the outcome.

The results can be discussed in the context of the literature on father absence, the apparent effects of which range from inappropriate sex-typing choices (Biller 1976) through intellectual-performance deficits (Shinn 1978) to institutional modes of expression (Broude 1989; Burton and Whiting 1961). Among the stablest of the outcomes, according to a metaanalysis by Stevenson and Black (1988), are that father-absent boys make cross-sex choices in childhood but display high aggression in adolescence. Although these types of findings seem to have opposite meanings, they are consistent with the idea that inappropriate male sex-role behavior is "behavior that is exaggeratedly male [or] not male enough" (Harrington 1970:86). (Little longitudinal research is available to tell us whether, and to what degree, individual father-absent boys typically transform their responses from "not male enough" to "exaggeratedly male" as they mature.) One way to interpret the research findings is that boys without fathers in the home experience a form of "deprivation" (Biller 1976) that evokes female-like responses at earlier ages and hypermasculine behavior in the adolescent years. Early cross-sex choices by father-absent boys do not seem difficult of explanation, even though there is disagreement about the processes by which these types of choices come to be made (Bem 1981; Chodorow 1978; Kohlberg 1969). More problematic are aggression and the other elements of so-called hypermasculinity that appear in the adolescent years and sometimes earlier (Biller 1976; Whiting 1965). Such outcomes are consistent with the status-envy hypothesis (Burton 1972; Burton and Whiting 1961), according to which the father-absent boy, following a primary feminine identification due to control of resources by the mother, subsequently develops a secondary masculine identification on the basis of perceived control of societal resources by men. (For a recent critique of the status-envy hypothesis, see Broude 1989.)

Another plausible hypothesis arises from recent research on categorization-by-exemplar. This research suggests that categories are differentially created by experts and novices, with experts organizing mental representations by means of examples (exemplars) and novices by means of summarizing concepts (prototypes) (Medin 1989). Deeper experience, as with the expert, avoids the creation of a single summary representation and allows construction of a complex category that is exemplar based. If we apply this reasoning to the present case, the father-present boy, as an "expert" due to the availability of an exemplar, forms a representation of the concept *male* on the basis of exposure to the multifaceted, sometimes contradictory characteristics displayed in the behavior of an actual father. The father-absent boy, as a "novice" without this exposure, forms a representation of the concept *male* that is a simple summary category, namely, a stereotype. It is unsurprising if such a category be centered on aggression, which is so widely bound up with males (Daly and Wilson 1988; Maccoby and Jacklin 1974; Williams and Best 1982). Thus, for father-absent boys over a long period, a disproportionate attention to males—as found in the present sample—would promote construction of a prototypical image of the male role. Additionally, because overt aggression appears more frequently among children than adults, the importance of peers to father-absent boys (Biller 1976) might help link aggression with the concept *male*. This account, resembling in some ways ideas from the emerging gender schema theory (Archer and Lloyd 1982; Bem 1981; Liben and Signorella 1987), is, like those relying on concepts of modeling or sex-role identification (Burton 1972; Burton and Whiting 1961; Harrington 1970; Miller and Swanson 1966; Rohrer and Edmonson 1960), suggestive rather than definitive.

We might suppose that in many societies the presence or absence of a father will not greatly matter, and even that the social category *father* will itself appear in some societies and not others. But powerful regularities exist in this domain, all cultures recognizing a *pater* role (cf. Draper and Harpending 1982), or socially acknowledged father (often but not always identical to the *genitor*, or biological father). A parallel supposition is that gender will be a salient dimension only when it is culturally emphasized, as in the United States (Bem 1981; Jacklin 1989). But as Schlegel (1989:266–267) has pointed out, "the division of human societies into two genders seems to be as pervasive as the division into the two sexes . . . the genders are firmly grounded in the biological reality of sex difference." And biological sex differences in turn are grounded in requisites of human reproduction, the basis for existence. It is then reasonable to hypothesize that in every sociocultural system, gender concepts will be early learned, salient, and laden with significance. In any case, if the universal social category of *father* is tied to pervasive and conceivably inevitable gender distinctions, then the serious psychological consequences of father deprivation for young boys (e.g., Biller 1976; Burton and Whiting 1961; Shinn 1978; Stevenson and Black 1988) may be seen as unsurprising. Furthermore, the present results, which indicate that father-absent boys engage in compensatory attentiveness to males in their social environments, are consistent with the idea that the presence of a father is a critical element in appropriate sex-role development for boys.[4]

This report leaves a number of relevant questions unresolved. As noted above, the extent to which father surrogates exert an effect comparable to that of true fathers is unclear, and further investigation is necessary (cf. Biller 1976). Sensitive-period and cumulative impact hypotheses about father absence can be examined (cf. Burton 1972) if our use of current census data in the home should be supplemented with an analysis of available life-history information on sample children. Although most sample children throughout their lives had experienced a consistent home arrangement with respect to father presence or father absence, this was not true for every child, especially in Samoa where shifting household membership was fairly common. The characteristics of siblings—their sex, age, and number—and their possible contributions to children's attention to males make up another area of needed inquiry (cf. Whiting and Edwards 1988). Further, the data on attention

to males by father-absent boys require continued analysis; we do not yet
know whether these boys are relatively more likely to watch adult
males, adolescent boys, baby boys, or peers. These questions and others
are worth pursuing in the next phase of investigation on the fathers and
children of our four cultures.

ACKNOWLEDGMENTS

Fieldwork among the Black Carib, Newars, and Samoans was supported by
grants from the National Science Foundation, and among the Logoli by grants
from the National Science Foundation and the Carnegie Corporation of New
York. Some portions of the Logoli fieldwork were carried out under the auspices
of the Child Development Research Unit, University of Nairobi (John W. M. and
Beatrice B. Whiting, Directors). Richard N. Tsujimoto made very helpful sugges-
tions concerning the relevance of research on categorization to the father-
absence literature. The authors are indebted to Harold Shimmin, Becky
Thurston and Heather Brown of Claremont Graduate School for their aid in data
analysis, to Sandy Hamilton of Pitzer College for assistance in preparation of the
manuscript, and to Barry Hewlett, Beatrice Whiting, and John Whiting for
comments on an earlier version of this paper.

NOTES

1.   Observations that focused on preselected samples of infants and children
were made in all cases except that of Black Carib infants, for whom a more
indirect mode of assessment was employed. When a Black Carib infant was
present during an observation of an older sibling, the information reported in
such a protocol allowed inferences as to the father's presence and his possible
caretaking behavior. These data for the Black Carib should be taken as less
reliable than the other infant data reported herein.
2.   The scores of zero for father holding of infants among the Black Carib,
Logoli, and Samoans should not be taken to indicate that the event fails to occur.
It must be kept in mind that the scores are based on small sample sizes and a
limited number of observations per infant. The authors have seen infants held
by their fathers in all three of the societies, though very infrequently among the
Logoli.
3.   Among the Black Carib, the modal sleeping arrangement in the first
several months of an infant's life is for the baby and mother to sleep together
while the father occupies a separate room. In some cases, the infant occupies the
same bed with the mother and father, and in others the infant is put into a
separate bed next to that of the mother and father. (For further details on Carib
sleeping arrangements, see Munroe and Munroe 1990a.) Among the Logoli, the
usual pattern is for the father to occupy a different room from the mother and
infant, and a separate sleeping area from them even if in the same room.

4.   Mackey (1985) holds that men associate with children (including boys, of course), in significant numbers in all societies. As evidence for what he terms a "biologically based adult male–child bond," he points to patterns of association in public places in 18 disparate cultures. Among other findings, he reports that the highest degree of association of men-only groups with children occurred during children's mid-childhood stage of life. Mackey's results can be taken as supporting an argument for the importance of contact between developing boys and adult males. But we would need to know the relationships among the people observed to see the relevance of Mackey's findings for our more specific ideas concerning boys and their fathers.

REFERENCES

Archer, J., and Lloyd, B. 1982. *Sex and Gender*. London: Cambridge University Press.

Barry, H., III, and Paxson, L. M. 1971. Infancy and early childhood: Cross-cultural codes 2. *Ethnology* 10:466–508.

Bem, S. L. 1981. Gender schema theory: A cognitive account of sex-typing. *Psychological Review* 88:354–364.

Biller, H. B. 1976. The father and personality development: Paternal deprivation and sex-role development. In *The Role of the Father in Child Development*. M. E. Lamb (Ed.), pp. 89–156. New York: Wiley.

Broude, G. J. 1989. Revisiting status-envy: Does the theory hold up? *Behavior Science Research* 23:146–181.

Burton, R. V. 1972. Cross-sex identity in Barbados. *Developmental Psychology* 6:365–374.

Burton, R. V., and Whiting, J. W. M. 1961. The absent father and cross-sex identity. *Merrill-Palmer Quarterly* 7:85–95.

Chodorow, N. 1978. *The Reproduction of Mothering: Psychoanalysis and the Sociology of Gender*. Berkeley: University of California Press.

Daly, M., and Wilson, M. 1988. *Homicide*. New York: Aldine de Gruyter.

DeWalt, B. R., and Pelto, P. J. (Eds.). 1985. *Micro and Macro Levels of Analysis in Anthropology*. Boulder, CO: Westview Press.

Draper, P., and Harpending, H. 1982. Father absence and reproductive strategy: An evolutionary perspective. *Journal of Anthropological Research* 38:255–273.

Gonzalez, N. L. S. 1969. *Black Carib Household Structure*. Seattle: University of Washington Press.

Hamilton, M. 1977. *Father's Influence on Children*. Chicago: Nelson-Hall.

Harrington, C. C. 1970. *Errors in Sex-Role Behavior in Teen-Age Boys*. New York: Teachers College Press.

Hewlett, B. S. 1987. Intimate fathers: Patterns of paternal holding among Aka Pygmies. In *The Father's Role. Cross-Cultural Perspectives*. M. E. Lamb (Ed.), pp. 295–330. Hillsdale, NJ: Erlbaum.

Holmes, L. D. 1958. *Ta'u, Stability and Change in a Samoan Village*. Wellington, New Zealand: Polynesian Society (Reprint No. 7).

Holmes, L. D. 1974. *Samoan Village*. New York: Holt, Rinehart & Winston.

Jacklin, C. N. 1989. Female and male: Issues of gender. *American Psychologist* 44:127–133.

Kennedy, J. J. 1987. Predictors of experiential learning opportunity for children in traditional cultures. Unpublished Master's thesis, Claremont Graduate School, Claremont, CA.

Kohlberg, L. 1969. Stage and sequence: The cognitive-developmental approach to socialization. In *Handbook of Socialization Theory and Research*. D. A. Goslin (Ed.), pp. 347–480. Chicago: Rand McNally.

Lamb, M. E. 1987. Introduction: The emergent American father. In *The Father's Role*. M. E. Lamb (Ed.), pp. 3–25. Hillsdale, NJ: Erlbaum.

Liben, L. S., and Signorella, M. L. (Eds.). 1987. *Children's Gender Schemata*. San Francisco: Jossey-Bass.

Lynn, D. 1974. *The Father: His Role in Child Development*. Monterey, CA: Brooks/ Cole.

Maccoby, E. E., and Jacklin, C. N. 1974. *The Psychology of Sex Differences*. Stanford, CA: Stanford Univeristy Press.

Mackey, W. C. 1985. *Fathering Behaviors: The Dynamics of the Man-Child Bond*. New York: Plenum.

Mead, M. 1928. *Coming of Age in Samoa*. New York: Morrow.

Mead, M. 1930. *Social Organization of Manua*. Honolulu: Bernice B. Bishop Museum Bulletin No. 76.

Medin, D. L. 1989. Concepts and conceptual structure. *American Psychologist* 44:1469–1481.

Miller, D. R., and Swanson, G. E. 1966. *Inner Conflict and Defense*. New York: Schocken.

Munroe, R. H., and Munroe, R. L. 1971. Household density and infant care in an East African Society. *Journal of Social Psychology* 83:3–13.

Munroe, R. L., and Munroe, R. H. 1989. *Logoli Time Allocation. Cross-Cultural Studies in Time Allocation*, (Vol. 5, Series Ed., A. Johnson). New Haven, CT: HRAF Press.

Munroe, R. L., and Munroe, R. H. 1990a. *Black Carib Time Allocation. Cross-Cultural Studies in Time Allocation*, (*Vol. 6*, Series Ed., A. Johnson). New Haven, CT: HRAF Press.

Munroe, R. L., and Munroe, R. H. 1990b. *Samoan Time Allocation. Cross-Cultural Studies in Time Allocation*, (*Vol. 8*, Series Ed., A. Johnson). New Haven, CT: HRAF Press.

Nepali, G. S. 1965. *The Newars. An Ethno-Sociological Study of a Himalayan Community*. Bombay: United Asia Publications.

Rogoff, B. 1978. Spot observation: An introduction and examination. *The Quarterly Newsletter of the Institute for Comparative Human Development* 2:21–26.

Rohrer, J. H., and Edmonson, M. S. 1960. *The Eighth Generation*. New York: Harper.

Schlegel, A. 1989. Gender issues and cross-cultural research. *Behavior Science Research* 23:265–280.

Shinn, M. 1978. Father absence and children's cognitive development. *Psychological Bulletin* 85:295–324.

Shweder, R. A. 1973. The between and within of cross-cultural research. *Ethos* 1:531–545.

Slaby, R. G., and Frey, K. S. 1975. Development of gender constancy and selective attention to same-sex models. *Child Development* 46:849–856.

Stevenson, M. R., and Black, K. N. 1988. Paternal absence and sex-role development: A meta-analysis. *Child Development* 59:793–814.

Taylor, D., Mac, R. 1951. *The Black Carib of British Honduras.* New York: Wenner-Gren Foundation (Viking Fund Publications in Anthropology No. 17).

Toffin, G. 1977. *Pyangaon, Communauté Newar de la Vallée de Kathmandou.* Paris: Editions du Centre National de al Recherche Scientifique.

Wagner, G. 1970. *The Bantu of Western Kenya* (2 Vols.). London: Oxford University Press.

West, M. M., and Konner, M. J. 1976. The role of the father: An anthropological perspective. In *The Role of the Father in Child Development.* M. E. Lamb (Ed.), pp. 185–217. New York: Wiley.

Whiting, B. B. 1965. Sex identity conflict and physical violence: A comparative study. *American Anthropologist* 67:123–140.

Whiting, B. B., and Edwards, C. P. 1988. *Children of Different Worlds: The Formation of Social Behavior.* Cambridge, MA: Harvard University Press.

Whiting, B. B., and Whiting, J. W. M. 1975. *Children of Six Cultures. A Psycho-Cultural Analysis.* Cambridge, MA: Harvard University Press.

Williams, J. E., and Best, D. L. 1982. *Measuring Sex Stereotypes.* Beverly Hills, CA: Sage.

Chapter 11

Male Care among Efe Foragers and Lese Farmers

Gilda A. Morelli and Edward Z. Tronick

In previous work we described an extensive pattern of multiple caregiving for a group of foragers, the Efe, living in the Ituri Forest of Zaïre (Tronick et al. 1987, 1989). This pattern begins at birth with community members typically holding and/or nursing the infant for several hours before returning him or her to the mother (Morelli et al. 1987). The high levels of care and interaction between infants and individuals other than mothers continue for the infant's first 6 months of life, and provide the majority of daytime caregiving he or she receives. We believe that the Efe infant's early involvement with a variety of community members may foster the development of social capacities for relating to many different individuals, and the development of multiple secure bases for attachment (Tronick et al. 1985).

In this chapter we want to extend our work on forager infants by describing the activities of forager 1 year olds with community members, and by comparing their experiences with a cohort of neighboring farmer children. The research findings raise questions concerning the way fathers' involvement with their young children has traditionally been conceptualized, and it supports the view that the activities children engage in with males, including fathers, and the competencies emerging from these shared experiences, are shaped by features of community life.

CHILDREN'S ACTIVITIES AND COMMUNITY MEMBERS

Our understanding of the role community members play in shaping development owes much to the work of Whiting, Edwards, and their colleagues (see Whiting and Whiting 1975; Whiting and Edwards 1988), who contributed to a perspective that brings to the foreground the importance of children's activities with different community members in understanding development. According to this perspective, community members help create the contexts in which young children develop culturally appropriate thought and behavior by guiding their participation in everyday life.

An important feature of social activity identified by Whiting and Edwards is the "category of person" with whom children are involved. They believe that by interacting with different "categories of people" (classified on the basis of gender, age, and kinship) children practice distinct patterns of behavior. People of a particular "category" share certain behavioral qualities, and as a result model and teach specific behaviors to, and elicit specific behaviors from children. For example, children given the responsibility of caring for infants are likely to practice nurturing behaviors because infants elicit nurturance from those with whom they interact. Mothers, by comparison, elicit dependent behaviors. Thus, the opportunity for children to be actively involved in different categories of people is critical in guiding development, and is shaped by features of the sociocultural system such as the physical and social arrangement of people, male–female roles and responsibilities, and economic work routines.

The model of social development proposed by Whiting and her colleagues focuses on the role community features play in organizing the daily routines of children, features that are critical to shaping the development of skills and competencies. The model pays little attention, however, to the child's role in organizing his or her daily experiences. Rogoff (1990) has introduced the concept of guided participation to capture the child's active role in managing joint interactions with community members. Our own work on the Efe highlights the role of the infant in guiding social experiences. We found, for example, that the degree of infant fussiness correlated with his or her involvement with different caregivers, including mothers (Winn et al. 1989). Thus, children play an active role in constructing reality through their participation in cultural routines with different community members.

CHILDREN'S SOCIAL PARTNERS

Until recently, the infant's developing relationship with his or her mother has been studied by western scientists to the near exclusion of other social categories, such as siblings, peers, or fathers. The decision to focus on the mother–infant dyad is coupled in very complex ways with western views about parenting. In their extreme forms, these views argue that mothers should act as the sole or primary caregivers during their infants' first year of life (see, for example, Bowlby's early work; Bowlby 1969). Few would deny that mothers play an important, and in some communities a central role in guiding the development of their children. However, as research interests broadened to include the study of nonmaternal caregivers, scientists began to recognize the role of other community members such as siblings, peers, and fathers in guiding the development of children's social and cognitive competencies (LeVine et al. 1988; Rogoff 1990; Weisner and Gallimore 1977; Whiting and Edwards 1988; Valsiner 1988; Zukow 1989a).

Siblings and Peers

The role of siblings and peers in development is currently the focus of much research (see, for example, Dunn 1983; Dunn and Kendrick 1982; Weisner and Gallimore 1977; Zukow 1989a). Watson-Gegeo and Gegeo (1989) argue that in the Kwara'ae, a Melanesian people of Malaita in the Solomon Islands, adults' guidance of siblings in activity with children fosters children's understanding of classifactory kinship, seniority, and sibling cooperation. Further, the infant's physical and social mobility, and therefore knowledge of others, is increased when cared for by siblings who often range outside their village. Caregivers, however, are more than babysitters. They facilitate the infant's development of interactional and language skills. And in the context of being with infants, these child caregivers appropriate a variety of competencies themselves. The sibling relationship also fosters social understanding in children. In the course of witnessing or participating in social conflict with siblings, British children's knowledge of social rules and responsibilities, intentions, and feelings, develops (Dunn 1989). Further, in the context of playing with siblings, children often engage in symbolic representation of the social world, an event that rarely takes place in playful interactions with adults.

The contributions of both siblings and mothers to young children's understanding of social events is noted by Zukow in her study of families living in urban and rural Central Mexico (Zukow 1989b). Siblings and mothers guide young children's understanding of ongoing activities. But siblings differ from mothers in that they are more likely to proclaim their competence and, at the same time, their younger siblings incompetence in the activity. Zukow argues that explicitly displaying one's competence has the effect of making known to the young child exactly what event is taking place and what is needed to be successful at it. Concludes Zukow, "knowing what you are doing incorrectly may be quite as informative as gradually getting in right" (p. 98).

Fathers

The role of fathers in guiding their children's developing competencies has also captured the interest of scholars working primarily in the United States and other technologically complex societies (Beail 1983; Belsky et al. 1984; Clarke-Stewart 1981; Lamb 1976, 1987; Lamb et al. 1982a, b; New and Benigni 1987; Power and Parke 1983; Radin and Sagi 1982; Russell 1982). One area of inquiry receiving considerable attention is the skills infants and young children appropriate in the context of playful interactions with their fathers.[1] Play is recognized as an important activity because it provides young children with an opportunity to practice social and cognitive skills (Bruner 1972, 1976; Rubin et al. 1983). Interest in fathers as playmates stems from research suggesting that U.S. fathers' activities with their young children primarily involve vigorous forms of play (Kotelchuck 1976), and that fathers spend a greater proportion of time playing with their young children than mothers (Clarke-Stewart 1981; Yogman 1982). The distinctive play style of U.S. fathers compared to mothers is also believed to foster the development of father–infant attachment relationships (Lamb 1981a).

The view that fathers' involvement with their young children centers around playful interactions may be an artifact of the communities chosen for study. While play may comprise a major portion of U.S. fathers' involvement with their young children (Kotelchuck 1976; Lamb 1981b), it is not the predominant activity characterizing father–child, and indeed adult–child involvement in non-U.S. communities. Whiting and Edwards (1988) observed that, in general, adult–child play was rare in all but one community studied by them and their colleagues—middle-class, U.S. households. Research on paternal care in technologically simple societies also raises questions concerning the prevalence of play between fathers and young children. In Hewlett's (1991) extensive observational study of the Aka, a forager community of the Central African Republic, fathers seldom played with their 1 to 18 month olds. What play was observed was restricted to young infants, 1 to 4 month olds. Aka fathers were more likely to hold infants during the first 18 months of life, and engage them in an intimate and affectionate way. Thus, Hewlett (1987) suggests that fathers in communities outside of the United States may not show the distinctive play style observed in U.S. fathers. Play, therefore, may not be essential to the formation of attachment relationships as proposed by Lamb (1981a).

A second possible result of studying children from primarily western, technologically complex societies is the amount of attention paid to fathers, with little or no attention paid to the role of other adult men and boys (see, for example, Lamb 1987). This is not surprising. In many of the communities examined, fathers are generally the only males available to children on a regular basis. Studies like Malinowski's on the Trobrianders of New Guinea suggest, however, that men other than the father may accept responsibility for the child (Malinowski 1927).

The nature of young children's involvement with their fathers and other males is shaped by features of U.S. middle-class community life. For example, the family constellation in which most young U.S. children are reared consists of the mother, father, and siblings. This arrangement provides few opportunities for children to participate in social activities with males other than their fathers. There is a tendency among U.S. fathers to organize their childcare around monetary-based work routines. Since children do not regularly frequent the work place of adults (including fathers), the time children spend with their fathers may be limited to dinnertime, bedtime, and weekend events, times when the father is not involved in economic activities. It may be well that these settings, along with other sociocultural features such as the perceived roles and responsibilities of males, foster the type of playful interactions reported between U.S. fathers and their young children. It is difficult to know, however, exactly how fathers and other males allocate time with children because of the modest amount of research on this topic.[2]

One of the themes to emerge from the work reported is that children's involvement with their fathers and other males is shaped by sociocultural features, as are the social and cognitive skills they develop in the course of participating in activity with them. We want to explore this theme by examining the forager and farmer 1 year olds' activities with males. By studying children of two different communities we are in a better position to understand how differently their lives are arranged, and how through these arrangements children's social and psychological worlds are constructed.

RESEARCH QUESTIONS

To examine male-care in the forager and farmer community the following questions were asked:

1. What activities do forager fathers share with their 1 year olds and what activities do farmer fathers share with their 1 year olds?
2. To what extent is forager fathers' involvement with their chil-

dren similar to that of other adult males and boys and to what extent is farmer fathers' involvement with children similar to that of other adult males and boys?

3. How do forager and farmer fathers, other adult males, and boys compare in their involvement with children?

THE FORAGER AND FARMER COMMUNITY

The Efe foragers and Lese farmers are sympatric communities living in the Ituri forest of northeastern Zaïre (Figure 1), and are involved in a complex exchange relationship that has been going on for generations. They play an important role in the lives of one another, and inhabit and exploit a similar ecosystem (Bailey and Devore 1989; Wilkie 1988).

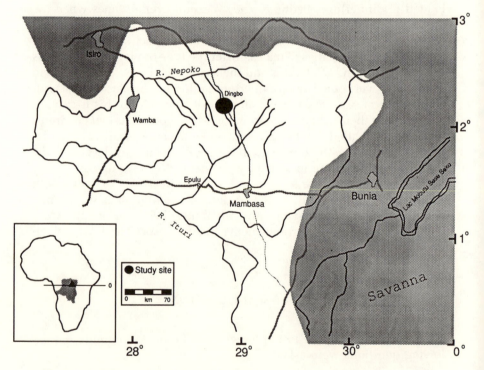

Figure 1. Location of the Efe and Lese communities in northeastern Zaïre.

Efe Foragers

The Efe[3] are a short-statured people who acquire forest foods by gathering and by hunting with bows and mainly metal-tipped arrows. Cultivated foods are also an important part of the Efe diet, and are obtained from the Lese in exchange for forest foods and/or services.

The majority of Efe live in transient camps established in small, forested areas cleared of vegetation. In this study, camp membership ranged from 7 to 21 people, and was made up of one or several extended families. Descent and resident patterns are patrilineal and virilocal. Each family consists of brothers and their wives, children, unmarried sisters, and parents. The Efe build leaf huts that are primarily used for sleeping, food storage, and protection from inclement weather. The huts are typically arranged around the camp's perimeter creating a large, open communal space. Since most day-to-day in-camp activities take place outside, within this communal space, they are in clear view of other camp members.

Camp members do not regularly coordinate their day-to-day activities. During the mid-morning and early afternoon hours when most out-of-camp activities take place, one or several individuals are likely to be found in the camp resting, taking care of children, preparing food, or socializing. The almost continual presence of people in the camp provides mothers with an opportunity to leave their children in the camp while involved in out-of-camp activities such as foraging for food, an opportunity often taken advantage of by them.

Cultural practices concerning the social and physical arrangement of community members make it easy for men and women when in the camp setting to work together, usually side by side, in clear view of children. They also make it more acceptable for fathers to eat with their families, even though each family is never far away from any other family. Indeed, it is quite common for families to carry on conversations with one another while sitting in front of their respective huts.

Many activities are shared by men and women. It is not unusual, for example, to see a man involved in some economic household routine such as preparing food for consumption. However, some activities are considered more appropriate for members of one gender. Women rarely accompany men on hunts, for example, and when they do accompany them, they do not kill forest game with bows and arrows.

Since the amount of time young forager children spend in the camp is considerable, ranging from 80 to 95% of daytime hours (Morelli 1987), they are developing in a community where men, women, boys, and girls are physically and visually available to them. Young children also have the opportunity to be involved in varied ongoing camp activities, and to practice a variety of skills.

Lese Farmers

The Lese are slash-and-burn horticulturalists whose work cycle is entrained to seasonally appropriate tasks such as clearing and burning fields, planting, weeding, and harvesting. The Lese rely on the Efe for labor in their fields.

All Lese farmers live in roadside villages that rarely change location. Each village generally contains several families, but each family's living quarters are often spatially and sometime visually isolated from one another. In this study, membership ranged from 8 to 36 people. Descent is patrilineal, and residency virilocal, with some exceptions. Farmer houses are arranged so that small communal areas are created for members of only one or a few households. A village is more accurately described as a collection of homesteads that varies in social composition and accessibility to others living in the village.

Village houses are primarily used for sleeping, storage, and protection from inclement weather. Most of the activities of women and their children such as cooking, eating, and socializing take place near the house and the cooking area, called the *mafika*, both of which are often set back from the only road in the area. Men's activities, by comparison, take place in a semienclosed sitting area, called the *baraza*, where it is customary for them to wash, eat, socialize, and relax. The men's *baraza* is often located near the road, and separate from the house and *mafika*.

Women are generally found in their fields or *shamba* when not in the village. They are accompanied by their children as fieldwork and child-care is essentially a woman's responsibility. During active agricultural periods most of their time is spent in the *shamba*, leaving men and elderly people in the village. Since fieldwork is often not a communal activity, and fields are separated by some distance, women are often isolated from the company of others, including men, when laboring in the *shamba*.

Men work hard 3 months of the year when land is cleared for planting. During this period, women often visit their relatives, taking their young children with them. Men work very little for the remaining portion of the year, and only occasionally help their wives with fieldwork. It is typical to find men relaxing in their *baraza*, or visiting with friends.

The economic responsibilities of men and women, their scheduling of work, and the cultural practices concerning their physical and social arrangement when in the village influence the amount of time spent in each other's company. Since Lese farmer children spend, on average, over half of their day in the village it is reasonable to assume that time in the company of men including their fathers, and the activities they share when together may be more limited in scope compared to Efe children.

THE STUDY

Children Observed

The social activities of eight forager and eight farmer 12 to 15 month olds were recorded over a 2-year period. Four boys and four girls were observed from each of the communities.

One year olds are the focus of study for several reasons. At this age the majority of forager and farmer children are able to move about their environment with little or no assistance from others, and are therefore able to involve themselves in a variety of activities (Morelli 1987). Further, this age is identified as an important time for the development of social representations, including children's representations of attachment figures. Thus, how children spend their time with males may shed light on the nature of their developing relationships. The results of this work will contribute to our understanding of the relation between sociocultural factors and children's involvement with males, and help put the U.S. father–child relationship into a broader, cultural perspective.

Behavioral Observations

Data Collected. Children were observed using a focal subject sampling technique (Altmann 1974). Each child was observed for six, 1-hour observation sessions evenly distributed throughout the daylight hours. Data were recorded continuously using prepared data sheets. All occurrences of a behavior were coded, and the sequence in which behaviors occurred was preserved. Time was marked at 1-minute intervals.

Behaviors Recorded. Five behaviors commonly occurring between forager/farmer community members and 1 year olds were selected for study (see Table 1 for a description of measures). Care includes holding, dressing, washing and feeding the infant, and supporting the infant in his or her attempts to stand or walk. It does not include nursing, which is almost exclusively a mother's responsibility by the infant's first birthday. Play includes activities involving at least one other person that are

Table 1. Behaviors and Composite Measures

Social engagement	Care	Hold, dress, wash, feed, support
	Play	Recreational
	Groom	Improve health or appearance of another
	Share	Exchange resources
Target of attention	Watching or listening to a person in activity	
Proximity	Within 3 m of focal child	

recreational in scope, usually engaged in for pleasure, joy, or amusement. Groom is any activity meant to improve the health or appearance of another person. Included in this category is searching for head lice, face painting, and hair braiding. Share is the exchange of resources. Finally, target of attention is defined as the child watching or listening to a person participating in an activity.

Two measures were used to compared fathers' and other community members' involvement with the child. The first was target of attention, and reflects the extent to which children eavesdrop on the activities of others who do little to adjust their actions to accommodate the child's watching. The second measure, social engagement, combines the behaviors sharing, play, care, and groom, and reflects community members' and 1 year olds' active involvement with one another.

Social Partners. One year olds' social partners were divided into four categories: father, adult men (excluding father), boys (6 to 15 years), and mothers. Mothers are the only females included in this study on male care because their involvement with children is often used as the yardstick against which to compare the involvement of others.

Conceptualizing Social Partner's Participation in Activity

Given our view that the child's behavior and thought are shaped by his or her active participation in, and observation of, day-to-day cultural activities, we have developed an analytic approach that we think provides are more inclusive measure of the child's social experience[4] than approaches more commonly used. Typically, questions on with whom the child spends his or her time are addressed by taking the proportion of total time (often measured in intervals per hour) the child is with father, mother, other adults, and juveniles/children. Such a measure might indicate that the infant is with mother 30% of the intervals observed, father 20%, other adults 25%, and so on. But obviously these categories are not equivalent from either an analytic or psychological perspective. There is only one mother and father, but there are many adults, juveniles, and children. It is possible, for example, for a child to spend less time with the father compared to other men, but nonetheless to spend more time with the father compared to an individual man. This raises the question of how the infant experiences his or her father relative to another and others. The infants may perceive his or her father as a distinct individual compared to another individual man, even though the infant spends more time with other men. Thus, traditional measures of time with community members compares singular (e.g., father) with multiple classes of social partners (e.g., men), and provides us with one way to make sense of the child's experience of community members. But traditional measures may not capture critical aspects of this experience.

In an attempt to deal with the problems arising from traditional analytic approaches, we developed a measure that compares the time (measured in intervals per hour, and referred to as a rate score) the infant spends with father and mother, and the time he or she spends with the average man (woman, child). The average person score is simply generated by computing the total time the infant is with some category of person (e.g., men or boys) and dividing it by the number of different individuals belonging to that social category who are involved with the child. By comparing the infant's experience of father with their experience of the average man, boy, woman, and girl we are able to evaluate the relative distinctness of the child's experience of these individuals.

The amount of time a child spends with mother, father, other adult men and women, and boys and girls (total person score) is also calculated because the measure provides another way of conceptualizing the child's experience of others. We believe that while the two measures reflect meaningful differences for the child, when considered together they provide more inclusive information about the nature of a child's partnership with different community members.

Behavioral Data Management

Mean hourly partner rate scores were created for each child by calculating the number of intervals in which father, adult men, boys, and mothers were coded as partners in the different activities. The summed score was divided by the number of hours the child was observed. Using this procedure the average and total person scores were determined.

Proximity Measures

People within 3 m of the focal child were identified twice for each hour of observation, coding their presence on the fifth minute before and the fifth minute following the data session. Using this procedure, proximity measures on Efe forager 1 year olds were collected 94 times, and on Lese farmer 1 year olds, 96 times.

Data Analysis

Paired *t*-tests were used to describe forager children's involvement with different categories of people, and to describe farmer children's involvement with different categories of people. Independent *t*-tests were used to compare forager and farmer community members' involvement with 1 year olds.

RESULTS OF BEHAVIORAL STUDY

Proximity to 1 Year Olds

Forager fathers were observed within 3 m of their young children in 40% of the surveys conducted (Figure 2[5]; *t* and *p* values are presented in

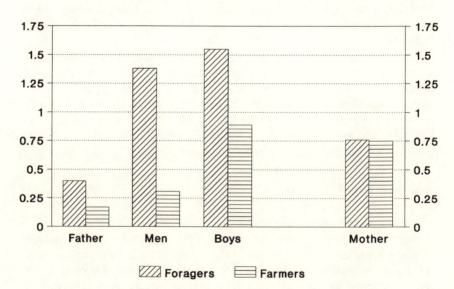

Figure 2. Individuals within 3 m of Efe and Lese 1 year olds.

Table 2. Proximity[a]

	Foragers				Farmers			
	Mother	*Father*	*Men*	*Boys*	*Mother*	*Father*	*Men*	*Boys*
Mother		4.22	3.24	3.26		11.62	3.15	
Father	0.00		4.36	5.14	0.00			3.45
Men	0.01	0.00			0.02			2.66
Boys	0.01	0.00				0.01	0.03	

[a]*t* values are in upper off-diagonal, *p* values are in lower off-diagonal, *df* = 7.

Table 2 for within group comparisons, and Table 5 for between group comparisons). There were consistently more forager adult men and boys in proximity to 1 year olds than fathers. By comparison, adult men and boys were equally likely to be proximal to young forager children.

The percentage of surveys in which forager mothers were in proximity to young children was significantly greater than fathers. But, like fathers, there were more adult men and boys in proximity to 1 year olds.

Farmer fathers were recorded within 3 m of their 1 year olds in 15% of the surveys conducted. The number of adult men in proximity to young children did not significantly differ from fathers. Young farmer children, however, were more likely to be around boys than their fathers and other adult men.

Farmer mothers were more likely to be proximal to young children than fathers, and more likely than adult men as well. In contrast, mothers and boys were as likely to be proximal to 1 year olds than fathers and adult men.

Differences between forager and farmer children in who made up their social space (i.e., within 3 m) were rather telling. Forager 1 year olds were more likely to have males—fathers, men, and boys—proximal to them than farmer 1 year olds.

Paternal Allocation of Time in Activity

The percentage of time fathers spent in different activities with their 1 year olds is illustrated in Figure 3. Forager fathers spent a modest amount of time playing with their children, contrary to what would be expected based on the literature. Instead, they spent a major portion of their time as targets of their children's attention. Sharing also dominated the activities observed between fathers and 1 year olds, as did care-related activities.

The pattern of findings described for forager fathers was similar to that observed for farmer fathers, with one exception: farmer fathers spent as much time playing with, as they did caring for their 1 year olds.

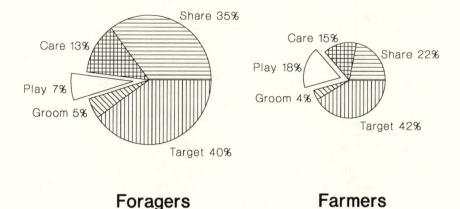

Foragers   Farmers

Figure 3. Allocation of time 1 year olds spend with their fathers.

While forager and farmer fathers were alike in how they allocated time with their 1 year olds, they differed in the total amount of time spent with them. Forager fathers spent more time engaged in activities with their 1 year olds than did farmer fathers as reflected in the size difference between the two pie charts.

*Comparison of Community Members' Activities
with 1 Year Olds*

The next set of analyses compares community members' involvement with 1 year olds. Involvement is evaluated by examining the measures social engagement and target of attention. Each measure is discussed in terms of the total person score and the average person score, permitting us to determine if 1 year olds' experience of categories of people (e.g., men, boys) is similar to their experience of the average person (e.g., man, boy). The discussion centers on male community members—fathers, men, and boys; data on mothers are presented for comparative purposes (*t* and *p* values for social engagement are found in Table 3, and for target of attention in Table 4).

Social Engagement. Forager fathers were as likely to be socially engaged with their 1 year olds as were men (total person score; Figure 4, left-hand side of graph). There was a tendency for forager boys to be more socially engaged than either fathers or men. Forager mothers, by comparison, were clearly more involved than any social category of male.

Table 3. Social Engagement[a]

	Total person score				Average person score			
	Mother	*Father*	*Men*	*Boys*	*Mother*	*Father*	*Men*	*Boys*
				Forager				
Mother		4.98	7.69	2.65		4.98	7.85	3.59
Father	0.00			2.20	0.00			
Men	0.00			2.12	0.00			
Boys	0.03	0.06	0.07		0.01			
				Farmers				
Mother		7.39	7.24	3.96		7.39	7.24	4.79
Father	0.00				0.00			
Men	0.00			2.82	0.00			3.11
Boys	0.01		0.03		0.00		0.02	

[a]t values are in upper off-diagonal, p values are in lower off-diagonal, $df = 7$.

This pattern of engagement changed when the average person score was considered so that fathers were like the average man and the average boy in the amount of time socially engaged with 1 year olds. The average man and boy were also alike (Figure 4, right-hand side of graph). Once again, mothers were clearly more engaged socially with young children than any average male.

How did farmer fathers' engagement with their 1 year olds compare to that of other community members? Farmer fathers were like men and boys in their role as social partners (total person score; Figure 4, left-hand side of the graph). Boys and men, however, were not alike; boys' involvement in social activity clearly exceeded that of men's.

Table 4. Target of Attention[a]

	Total person score				Average person score			
	Mother	*Father*	*Men*	*Boys*	*Mother*	*Father*	*Men*	*Boys*
				Forager				
Mother		6.76	4.28			6.76	5.77	5.22
Father	0.00			6.98	0.00			
Men	0.00			3.26	0.00			2.24
Boys		0.00	0.01		0.00		0.06	
				Farmers				
Mother		9.40	7.46	4.02		9.40	7.41	5.86
Father	0.00			2.96	0.00			
Men	0.00			2.02	0.00			3.05
Boys	0.01	0.02	0.08		0.00		0.02	

[a]t values are in upper off-diagonal, p values are in lower off-diagonal, $df = 7$.

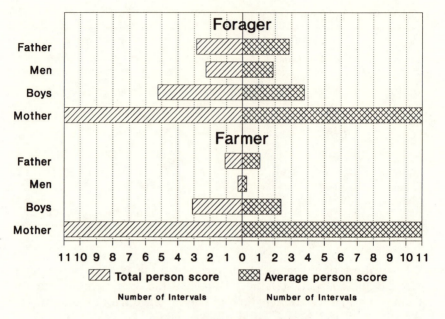

Figure 4. Social engagement.

No differences were observed in the pattern of findings as a result of shifting the unit of analysis from the total person to the average person score.

What can be concluded from an examination of the measure social engagement? Forager 1 year-olds' experience of their fathers as partners in social activities was similar to their experience of other adult men whether the total person or the average person score was considered. Forager boys had a tendency to be more involved than men and fathers, but the average forager boy was as involved with young children as the average man and father. This finding suggests that forager 1 year olds were more likely to have boys as social partners relative to other males because of their numbers. In other words, boys were like other males, there were just more of them involved with young children.

Farmer fathers were like men and boys in the way 1 year olds experienced them as partners in social activity. However, men were less likely to be involved in the activities of young children when compared to boys. One year olds were more likely to be involved with boys, and the average boy was more involved with them than the average man. One can conclude from these findings that boys and men were clearly distinct from one another in their relationship with young farmer children.

Target of Attention. Forager fathers and men were equally likely to be watched by young children. By comparison, forager 1 year olds were more likely to observe the activities of boys than they were the activities of fathers or men (total person score; Figure 5, left-hand side of graph).

Mothers, too, were more likely to be the target of attention for 1 year olds than fathers' and men's. Interestingly, however, mothers and boys were similar in this respect. This finding highlights the relatively prominent role boys played in the lives of young children compared to other male social categories.

What happened when the average score was considered (Figure 5, right-hand side of graph)? Fathers were like the average man and boy. One year olds were still slightly more likely to watch the average boy than the average man, although this difference was not statistically significant. But when the number of boys was taken into consideration we find that the average boy was less likely to be observed than mother.

How did farmer boys and other male community members figure in the life of young farming children? One year olds were as likely to watch the activities of fathers as they were the activities of men. Farmer boys' activities, by comparison, were more likely to be observed by 1 year olds than fathers' and men's, although the difference between men and boys

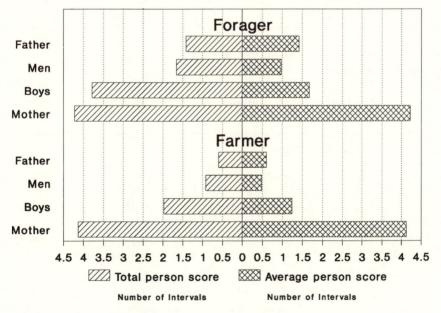

Figure 5. Target of attention.

only approached significance. In contrast, mothers were the target of these young children's attention consistently more often than any social category of male (total person score; Figure 5, left-hand side of graph).

When the average person score was considered a slightly different pattern of results emerged (Figure 5, right-hand side of graph). Now, the average farmer boy was as likely as fathers, but significantly more likely than the average man, to be the target of 1 year olds' attention. The average man and father continued to be similar in this respect.

What statements can be made about the measure target of attention? First, the activities of fathers were as likely to be watched by 1 year olds as were the activities of men in both communities studied. This was true whether fathers were compared to the social category men or to the average man. Thus, fathers' and adult men's involvement with 1 year olds was similar in some respects.

Second, boys as a social class figured prominently in the lives of 1 year olds in the forager and farmer communities. Boys were more likely to be the target of young children's attention compared to fathers and men.

The prominence of boys relative to other males was somewhat diminished when the average person score was considered. The average forager and farmer boy became more like fathers as targets of attention. But the average farmer boy, and to a lesser extent forager boy (the difference approached statistical significance), were still more likely to be watched by young children compared to the average man.

*Comparison of Forager and Farmer Activities
with 1 Year Olds*

The last set of analyses examines the extent to which foragers and farmers were similar in their involvement with young children by comparing the activities of males belonging to the same social class (see Table 5 for *t* and *p* values).

Social Engagement.   Foragers fathers were more likely to be socially engaged with 1 year olds than farmer fathers, and forager men were more likely to be socially engaged with 1 year olds than farmer men. Even when the number of adult men was taken into consideration, the average forager adult man was still engaged significantly more often with young children than the average farmer man (Figure 6).

Target of Attention.   While there was a tendency for forager fathers to be the target of attention more often than farmer fathers, and a tendency for forager men to be the target of attention more often than farmer men, the differences did not reach statistical significance. Forager boys, however, were more likely to be the target of attention than farmer boys

Table 5. Forager and Farmer Pair-wise Comparisons[a]

	Mother	Father	Men	Boys
Proximity				
t		2.39	4.71	2.32
p		.04	.00	.04
Social engagement total person				
t		2.21	2.53	
p		0.05	0.04	
Social engagement average person				
t		2.21	2.58	
p		0.05	0.04	
Target of attention total person				
t		1.96		2.51
p		0.08		0.03
Target of attention average person				
t		1.90		
p		0.08		

[a]$df = 14$.

(total person score, Figure 7, left-hand side of graph). However, this difference disappears when the number of forager and farmer boys are taken into consideration (average person score, Figure 7, right-hand side of graph).

SUMMARY AND CONCLUSIONS

The purpose of this chapter is to extend our knowledge of paternal care, and our understanding of the role of community life in structuring male involvement with young children by studying the social activities of forager and farmer 1 year olds' with male community members (fathers, men, and boys). Our findings raise questions concerning the way fathers' and other males' involvement with young children has been traditionally conceptualized, and bring into focus the importance of everyday life in shaping males' participation in activity with children.

Fathers, Men, and Boys in Proximity

Efe forager and Lese farmer males spent more time around 1 year olds than what would be expected based on accounts of paternal care in

Total Person Score

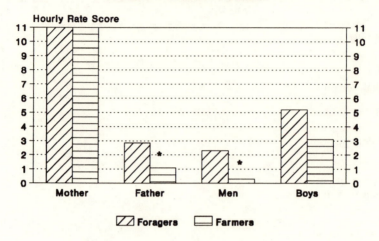

Average Person Score

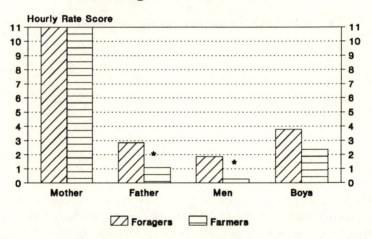

Figure 6. Social engagement.

technologically complex societies. We know that the people who are around young children shape the social and cognitive competencies they develop by guiding their participation in cultural routines (Rogoff 1990; Whiting and Edwards 1988). Children also appropriate cultural knowledge about people—their roles and responsibilities—by watching and listening to them in different contexts. And their chances of survival may be improved by having people near by (Hewlett 1987). Thus, forager and farmer males may be playing a different role, and maybe an

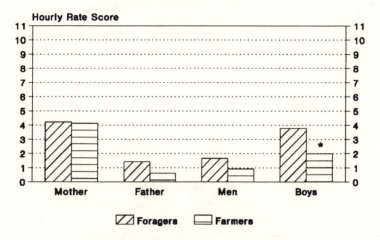

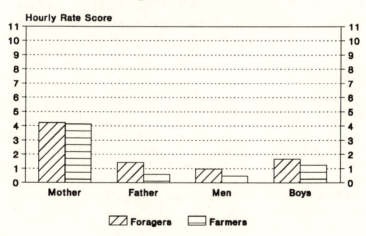

Figure 7. Target of attention.

even more extensive role, in the lives of young children than males of other communities such as the United States.

While having people around may be important for children's survival and development, who spends time in the company of children varies. Why? Community members may differ in their preference to be near children or their caregivers, as the work of Smuts and Guberick (this volume) suggests. Features of community life may also determine who is proximal to young children. Thus, knowledge of the patterning of everyday life among the foragers and farmers can help us understand why Efe forager fathers, men, and boys were more likely to be near 1 year olds than similarly aged Lese farmer males. Aspects of community life that regulate males' availability to children have been described in a previous section, but will be discussed further in the last section of this chapter.

The Role of Fathers in Activity

Forager and farmer fathers shared a wider range of activities with their 1 year olds than what would be expected based on descriptions in the literature that identify play as predominant. Fathers in both communities were three to five times as likely to be targets of their young children's attention than partners in play with them. Indeed, play made up only 7 and 18% of the time in which children and fathers were involved. The importance of appropriating knowledge through observation of cultural routines is not unusual in communities where children actively participate in the social and work world of adults (Rogoff 1990).

The range of activities observed between fathers and their 1 year olds may be a result of the amount of time they spend in each other's company, and the contexts in which their social activities are embedded. The contexts shared by fathers and 1 year olds are varied because forager and farmer fathers rarely adhere to a strict work routine, permitting them to be present all hours of the day and night. Work routines, especially in the foraging community, can take place in and around the camp/village. This offers fathers and young children ample opportunity to be involved in a number of different social activities. Yet, while similarities existed between Efe forager and Lese farmer fathers in how they spent time with their children, it is important to remember that forager fathers spent over twice as much time with their 1 year olds than did farmer fathers.

The Role of Fathers Relative to Men and Boys

The role of forager and farmer men and boys in the lives of 1 year olds prompted us to reevaluate the way males, besides fathers, are portrayed in the parenting literature. The joint involvement of men and boys exceeded that of fathers in both the forager and farmer community, contrary to expectations based on research.

When the roles of men and boys were compared separately to the role of fathers interesting findings emerged. Fathers and men were similar to one another as partners in social activity with, and as targets of attention for 1 year olds. Fathers were also similar to boys, with a few exceptions. These findings cast doubt on the existence of a characteristic "fathering role," and support the view that men and boys are like fathers when given the opportunity to be involved with young children, at least in the two communities studied.

There is some evidence to suggest, however, that a special relationship may exist between forager fathers and their children. For example, proximity data show that forager 1 year olds were two to three times more likely to be near forager adult men than fathers. But the behavioral data show that they were as likely to eavesdrop on the activities of their fathers as they were on the activities of adult men. Thus, insofar as proximity data can be used to make sense of behavioral data, forager 1 year olds may prefer their fathers to adult men (and to a lesser extent boys). A similar analysis can be made with respect to farmer 1 year olds and their preference for their fathers compared to boys as social partners.

The Role of Boys Relative to Men

Forager and farmer boys, as a social class, were more socially engaged with 1 year olds, and were more likely to be a target of their attention than men. When the number of boys was taken into consideration, only the average forager man and boy were alike in the extent to which they were socially engaged with young children.

We can offer several reasons to account for the relative importance of boys in the lives of young children. Boys have few work responsibilities compared to other community members, with the exception of young children. This is particularly true of farmer boys who do not begin to work in earnest until they are married, or until they have reached their late teens. While foragers boys, by their early teens, are invited by men or their peers to hunt forest game, there is little pressure on them to do so, and their survival does not depend on their participation, or success in hunting. Boys are therefore around; and they are around more often in the forager compared to the farmer community.

But why are boys engaged with young children? As boys enter early adolescence, they sometimes receive assistance from other women in the form of food, wood, and water. This is especially true for boys whose mothers are dead, or are no longer living in the camp/village. Thus, boys may be returning favors by helping women with childcare. Furthermore, in the foraging community, infant girls are often "given" to boys (and men) who exchange them for wives when they both reach adulthood. It is possible, therefore, that boys (and men) in the forager community are investing in their future by caring for these young girls. All of this is clearly speculative, yet open to empirical investigation. Perhaps an equally pertinent question is "why wouldn't boys (and men) be involved with young children?" To answer this requires an examination of community life, a task we shall undertake momentarily.

The Role of Forager Males Relative to Farmers Males

Efe forager and Lese farmer males' participation in the activities of 1 year olds differed in interesting ways. Forager fathers and men were socially engaged with 1 year olds significantly more often than farmer fathers and men. While differences were found between the forager and farmer community in the extent to which they were the target of 1 year olds' attention, the differences were not statistically significant.

Forager and farmer boys did not differ significantly in the extent to which they were socially engaged with young children. They did differ, however, in the extent to which their activities were watched; forager boys were watched more often than farmer boys. But these differences disappeared when the average forager and farmer boy were compared. Thus, there was no difference in the extent to which young forager and farmer children observed the average boy, there were just more forager boys available for observation.

The Role of Mothers Relative to Males

While this is a chapter on male care, it is important to put their involvement with children into a broader perspective. One way to accomplish this to compare males and mothers. In doing this we observed that with few exceptions forager and farmer mothers were significantly more likely to be involved with (i.e., social engagement and target of attention) their 1 year olds than any social category of male, total or average person score. This is interesting because in both communities caregiving is a shared activity, and especially in the forager community, males and children spend time in each other's company.

The Role of Community Life in Structuring Male Involvement

When differences between forager and farmer 1 year olds were identified by us, we alluded to the importance of community life in structuring the pattern of results observed. We would like to take the opportunity to highlight aspects of forager and farmer life that we believe put in perspective the differences observed between the two communities in the experiences of young children (for a more detailed description of Efe and Lese life see the section on The Forager and Farmer Community).

The Efe foraging community is structured in a way that fosters the pattern of involvement observed between 1 year olds and males. Cultural practices concerning the social and physical arrangement of people provide children with an opportunity to be involved in the varied ongoing camp activities of fathers, men, and boys.

Forager fathers often eat, work, and relax around their families providing 1 year olds with ample opportunities to be with them. Fathers, men, and boys also share any activities with women, including the care of young children. The active involvement of males in routine childcare is consistent with Efe community members' loose adherence to a gender-based division of labor (Morelli 1990). It is therefore appropriate for males to be involved in the care of young children, and there is plenty of opportunities for them to do so!

In contrast, the Lese farming community is structured in a way that does not easily permit the involvement of young children with fathers and men. In-village activities of farmer men and women are often physically separated, a separation that is promoted by cultural practices concerning the social and physical arrangement of men and women. For example, most of the activities of women and their children take place near the house and the cooking area. Men's activities, by comparison, take place in a semienclosed sitting area often located near the road, and separate from the house and cooking area (see Figure 8 for the layout of a typical camp and village).

Young farming children's access to men other than their fathers is further limited by the fact that farmer houses are arranged so that small communal areas are created for members of only one or a few households. The unavailability of men (excluding fathers) may be partly responsible for young farmer children's rather low rate of involvement with them.

Even when males and females are not in the village their activities tend to be separate. Women are generally found in their fields when not in the village. They are accompanied by their children as fieldwork and childcare are essentially a woman's responsibility. Therefore, women and children are often isolated from the company of fathers and men during these times.

The extent to which farmer males engage in different activities with young children appears not to be the same as that observed in the forager community. In part, this is because farmer males rarely engage in activities considered inappropriate to their gender, especially if such activities are open to the public for scrutiny. One farmer woman told me

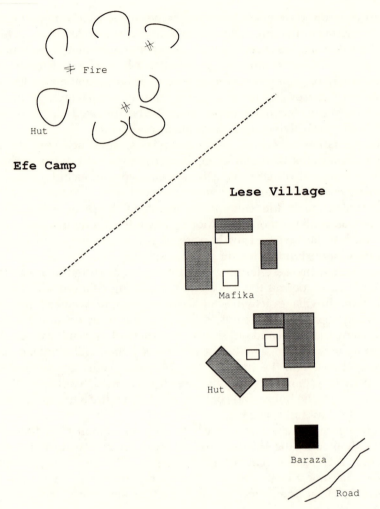

Figure 8. Schematic layout of Efe camp and Lese village.

that "when I work in the fields my husband assists me in childcare by carrying our 1 year old son. But as soon as another person, especially a man, approaches he is quick to return our son to me because he wants to avoid the possibility of being teased." This suggests that when young farmer children observe or participate in activities with males their experiences are likely to be different from those of young forager children, as is their understanding of male/female roles and responsibilities.

One unanticipated finding was the extent to which farmer boys were involved with young children. What might be contributing to the relatively high rate of involvement of boys compared to other males? Unlike the forager community, siblings made up over 50% of the boys with whom 1 year olds were involved. It is entirely possible that their mothers required their assistance, especially when working in the fields. Fieldwork is an arduous tasks; it involves laboring under the hot equatorial sun, often for many hours a day. One year olds cannot tolerate these extreme conditions for long periods of time, and it is the responsibility of children to care for infants in shaded areas while their mothers work. In our experience, women without child caregivers often worked fewer hours each day in the fields, at some expense to the family's food supply. While daughters are preferred caregivers, if they are not available mothers rely on sons for help.

The economic responsibilities of farmer men and women, their scheduling of work, and the cultural practices concerning their physical and social arrangement influence the amount of time they spend in each other's company. This arrangement also influences the activities and social partners readily available to children.

Forager and Farmer Children's Representation of Their Social World

What might these different patterns of involvement mean in terms of Efe forager and Lese farmer 1 year olds' representation of their social world. Efe forager 1 year olds are more likely to "see" a greater number and variety of males as available to them than Lese farmer 1 year olds. Father, men, and boys figure prominently in the way young forager children represent reality. Further, 1 year olds are learning about people's roles in the community, and learning that they can rely equally on community members (males and females) to care for, and to be with them. This broadly based representation serves young forager children well throughout their development by preparing them for the intensely social world in which they participate now, and in which they will participate as adults. As infants, and perhaps as adults, these contacts provide them with many secure bases for attachment, and foster their exploration of the environment.

Lese farmer 1 year olds, by comparison, "see" fewer males as available. Indeed, relative to other community members men are infrequent social partners. Young Lese 1 year olds' representation may be more focused on fewer different individuals. This more narrowly focused representation may serve to prepare the Lese 1 year olds for a more nuclear, family-based social ecology.

We have shown that males' involvement with young children may not be as restricted as previously thought. We have also demonstrated that who the infant is with and what they do together are influenced by a variety of factors including the nature of men's and women's work, the physical layout of the homesteads, and the relations among adults.

In this chapter, we introduced two ways of examining a child's experience of his or her partners in activity; the total person score and the average person score. We believe that each measure taps into different ways of conceptualizing the child's experience, differences which are meaningful to the child. The measures maybe particularly useful when the number of people with whom the child is involved varies, as it does in the forager and farmer community.

Finally, we want to emphasize that the measures chosen to examine 1 year olds' activity with males—social engagement and target of attention—are but one approach that helps us understand the child's sociocultural experiences. Other measures such as the contexts in which activities are embedded or the shared affective state of child and partners play a role in shaping the meaning emerging from the child's social activities.

ACKNOWLEDGMENTS

This research was supported by grants from the National Science Foundation (BNS-8609013), the National Institute of Child Health and Development (1-R01-HD22431), The Spencer Foundation, and Faculty Research Funds from Boston College. The authors would like to thank David S. Wilkie for his critical reading of this manuscript, and Cathy Angelillo for assisting with its preparation.

NOTES

1. The findings on fathers reviewed in this section are based primarily on the study of Caucasian, middle-class, U.S. fathers.
2. There are notable exceptions, for example, Hames's (1988) work on the Ye'kwana and Johnson's (1975) work on the Machiguenga.
3. The Efe are commonly referred to in the literature as pygmies. We have chosen to use this term sparingly. While the term pygmy is informative to the reader, it is considered pejorative by the Efe.
4. A child's experience of a person is measured only by the amount of time (i.e., the number of 1-minute intervals) the child spends in activity with that person.
5. Data on mother and father can be read as the average proportion of time proximal to 1 year olds. Whereas data on men, women, boys, and girls can be read as the average number of people proximal to 1 year olds.

REFERENCES

Altmann, J. 1974. Observational study of behavior. Sampling methods. *Behaviour* 49:227–267.

Bailey, R. C., and DeVore, I. 1989. Research on the Efe and Lese populations of the Ituri forest, Zaïre. *American Journal of Physical Anthropology* 78:459–471.

Beail, N. 1983. The psychology of fatherhood. *Bulletin of British Psychological Society* 36:312–314.

Belsky, J., Gilstrap, B., and Rovine, M. 1984. The Pennsylvania infant and family development project, I: Stability and change in mother-infant and father-infant interaction in a family setting at one, three, and nine months. *Child Development* 55:692–705.

Bowlby, J. 1969. *Attachment*. New York: Basic Books.

Bruner, J. S. 1972. The nature and uses of immaturity. *American Psychologist* 27:687–708.

Bruner, J. S., Jolly, A., and Sylva, K. (Eds.) 1976. *Play, Its Role in Development and Evolution*. New York: Basic Books.

Clarke-Stewart, K. A. 1981. The father's contribution to children's cognitive and social development in early childhood. *The Father-Infant Relationship: Observational Studies in the Family Setting*. In Frank A. Pedersen (Ed.), pp. 111–146. New York: Praeger Publishers.

Dunn, J. 1983. Sibling relationships in early childhood. *Child Development* 54: 787–811.

Dunn, J. 1989. Siblings and the development of social understanding in early childhood. In *Sibling Interaction Across Cultures: Theoretical and Methodological Issues*, P. G. Zukow (Ed.), pp. 106–116. New York: Springer-Verlag.

Dunn, J., and Kendrick C. 1982. *Siblings: Love, Envy, and Understanding*. Cambridge, MA: Harvard University Press.

Hames, R. B. 1988. The allocation of parental care among the Ye'kwana. In *Human Reproductive Behaviour: A Darwinian Perspective*. L. Betzig, M. Borgerhoff Mulder, and P. Turke (Eds.), pp. 237–251. Cambridge, England: Cambridge University Press.

Hewlett, B. S. 1987. The father-infant relationship among Aka pygmies (Central African Republic). Doctoral Dissertation, University of California, Santa Barbara. DAI 48/06A, p. 1486.

Hewlett, B. S. 1991. *Intimate Fathers: The Nature and Context of the Alka Pygmy Paternal Infant Care*. Ann Arbor, MI: University of Michigan Press.

Johnson, A. 1975. Time allocation in a Machiguenga community. *Ethnology* 14:301–310.

Kotelchuck, M. 1976. The infant's relationship to the father: Experimental evidence. In *The Role of the Father in Child Development*. M. E. Lamb (Ed.), New York: Wiley.

Lamb, M. E. (Ed.) 1976. *The Role of the Father in Child Development*. New York: Wiley.

Lamb, M. E. (Ed.) 1981a. *The Role of the Father in Child Development*, Rev. Ed. New York: Wiley.

Lamb, M. E. 1981b. Fathers and child development: An integrative overview. In *The Role of the Father in Child Development*. M. E. Lamb (Ed.), pp. 1–70. New York: Wiley.

Lamb, M. E. (Ed.) 1987. *The Father's Role: Cross-Cultural Perspectives*. Hillsdale, NJ: Erlbaum.

Lamb, M. E., Frodi, A. M., Frodi, M., and Hwang, C. P. 1982a. Characteristics of maternal and paternal behavior in traditional and nontraditional Swedish families. *International Journal of Behavioral Development* 5:131–141.

Lamb, M. E., Frodi, A. M., Hwang, C. P., and Frodi, M. 1982b. Varying degrees of paternal involvement in infant care: Correlates and effects. In *Nontraditional Families: Parenting and Child Development*. M. E. Lamb (Ed.), Hillsdale, NJ: Erlbaum.

LeVine, R. A., Miller, P. M., and Maxwell West, M. (Eds.) 1988. Parental behavior in diverse societies. *New Directions for Child Development*, 40. San Francisco: Jossey-Bass.

Malinowski, B. 1927. *The Father in Primitive Psychology*. New York: Norton.

Morelli, G. A. 1987. A comparative study of Efe (pygmy) and Lese one-, two-, and three-year-olds of the Ituri Forest of northeastern Zaïre: The influence of subsistence-related variables, children's age and gender on social-emotional development. Doctoral Dissertation, University of Massachusetts. DAI 48/02B, p. 582.

Morelli, G. A. 1990. Forager and farmer children's participation in adult-guided activities: appropriating knowledge about gender. Paper presented as part of a symposium at the American Psychological Association. G. A. Morelli (organizer): The Cultural Construction of Gender. Boston, MA.

Morelli, G. A., Winn, S., and Tronick, E. Z. 1987. Perinatal practices: A biosocial perspective. In *Psychobiology and Early Development*. H. Rauh and H.-Ch. Steinhausen (Eds.), pp. 13–22. North Holland: Elsevier.

New, R. S., and Benigni, L. 1987. Italian fathers and infants: Cultural constraints on paternal behavior. In *The Father's Role: Cross-Cultural Perspectives*. M. E. Lamb (Ed.), pp. 139–167. Hillsdale, NJ: Erlbaum.

Power, T. G., and Parke, R. D. 1983. Patterns of mother and father play with their 8-month old infant: A multiple analyses approach. *Infant Behaviour and Development* 6:453–459.

Radin, N., and Sagi, A. 1982. Childrearing fathers in intact families, II: Israel and U.S.A. *Merrill-Palmer Quarterly* 28(1):111–136.

Rogoff, B. (1990). *Apprenticeship in Thinking: Cognitive Development in Social Context*. New York: Oxford University Press.

Rubin, K. H., Fein, G. G., and Vandenberg, B. 1983. Play. In *Handbook of Child Psychology: Vol. 4. Socialization, Personality, and Social Behavior*. P. H. Mussen (Ed.), pp. 693–774. New York: Wiley.

Russell, G. 1982. Shared-caregiving families: An Australian study. In *Nontraditional Families: Parenting and Child Development*. M. E. Lamb (Ed.), pp. 139–171. Hillsdale, NJ: Erlbaum.

Tronick, E. Z., Winn, S., and Morelli, G. A. 1985. Multiple caretaking in the context of human evolution. Why don't the Efe know the western prescription of child-care? In *Psychobiology of Attachment and Separation*. M. Reite and T. Field (Eds.), pp. 293–322. New York: Academic Press.

Tronick, E. Z., Morelli, G. A., and Winn, S. 1987. Multiple caretaking of Efe (Pygmy) infants. *American Anthropologist* 89(1):96–106.

Tronick, E. Z., Morelli, G. A., and Winn, S. 1989. The caretaker-child strategic model: Efe and Aka childrearing as exemplars of the multiple factors affecting childrearing—A reply to Hewlett. *American Anthropologist* 91(1):192–194.

Valsiner, J. (Ed.) 1988. *Child Development within Culturally Structured Environments: Parental Cognition and Adult-Child Interaction*, Vol. 2. Norwood, NJ: Ablex.

Watson-Gegeo, K. A., and Gegeo, D. W. 1989. The role of sibling interaction in child socialization. In *Sibling Interaction Across Cultures: Theoretical and Methodological Issues*. P. G. Zukow (Ed.), pp. 54–76. New York: Springer-Verlag.

Weisner, T. S., and Gallimore, R. 1977. My brother's keeper: Child and sibling caretaking. *Current Anthropology* 18:169–190.

Whiting, B. B., and Edwards, C. 1988. *Children of Different Worlds: The Formation of Social Behavior*. Cambridge, MA: Harvard University Press.

Whiting, B. B., and Whiting, J. W. M. 1975. *Children of Six Cultures: A Psychocultural Analysis*. Cambridge, MA: Harvard University Press.

Wilkie, D. 1988. Hunters and farmers of the African forest. In *People of the Tropical Rain Forest*, J. S. Denslow and C. Padoch (Eds.), pp. 111–126. California: University of California Press.

Winn, S., Morelli, G. A., and Tronick, E. Z. 1989. The infant and the group: A look at Efe care-taking practices. In *The Cultural Context of Infancy*. K. Nugent, B. M. Lester, and T. B. Braxelton (Eds.), pp. 87–109. Norwood, NJ: Ablex.

Yogman, M. 1982. Development of the father-infant relationship. In *Theory and Research in Behavioral Pediatrics*. H. Fitzgerald, B. Lester, and M. Yogman (Eds.), pp. 221–229. New York: Plenum.

Zukow, P. G. 1989a. *Sibling Interaction Across Cultures: Theoretical and Methodological Issues*. New York: Springer-Verlag.

Zukow, P. G. 1989b. Siblings as effective socializing agents: Evidence from Central Mexico. In *Sibling Interaction Across Cultures: Theoretical and Methodological Issues*. P. G. Zukow (Ed.), pp. 79–105. New York: Springer-Verlag.

Chapter 12

Gukwelonone:
The Game of Hiding Fathers and Seeking Sons among the Ongee of Little Andaman

Vishvajit Pandya

Ongee male children from Little Andamans frequently play the game of *Gukwelonone* (hide and seek). Different levels of meaning unfold in this game through the roles played by the fathers of the participants. Using the game of hide and seek as it is thought about and enacted by the Ongees, this chapter analyzes relationships and values of sons, fathers, stepfathers, adopted fathers, and fathers-in-law, within this community of hunters and gatherers.

INTRODUCTION

Fathers are the "culture" and mothers the "nature" (Ortner 1974). A father ruggedly plays with his children to make them adjusted to the social ethos stressing a high degree of individuality and competition. On the other side, the mother has a higher degree of involvement with the raising of a child, mediating her role by playing with "toys." Since she provides the sustenance for the child, she therefore signifies the father as the "breadwinner" of the family—but only in part involved with the raising of child. These formulations are sociologically and ethnologically verifiable only in the context of Western civilization, and the conditions that exist in industrialized societies. Reported observation of "he" and "she" as parents in other cultural contexts questions the validity of these formulations when they apply to "other cultures" (for details, see

263

Hewlett 1987: 295–296). Even the way in which the observer of another culture questions the basic roles of parents and children is predicated on standard Freudian discourse and "our" ideas about childhood and gender.

Beneath everything that can be observed and thought about, there is a history of specific ideas about the child and childhood, and some of these ideas have remained unchanged. Until the thirteenth century adults were raising children within an ideological environment that had little understanding for the needs of children. The child was viewed as a nuisance and an unwarranted burden (and therefore infanticide and selling of children), and casual abandonment of children was tolerated. By the sixteenth and seventeenth century the ideological emphasis had shifted toward an internal suppression, emphasizing the discipline and "training" of the child. From parental efforts aimed at controlling the child's will, the Western ideology of caretaking progressed further in the nineteenth and twentieth century, when the awareness of the sensibilities and needs of children increased. Historically, in Western civilization, there has always been a conflict between "rejecting" and "nurturing" attitudes toward the child and childhood (de Mause 1975).

This is perhaps most evident in Freud's formulation about the Oedipus complex as a source of the feeling of guilt, underlining the beginning of human religion and morality. This formulation was proposed in 1913 (*Totem and Taboo*), and expanded later in the *Introductory Lectures on Psychoanalysis* (1917: Lecture XXI). The Oedipus complex is presented as a major structural factor within the family, generating particular kind of "ambivalence" between the father and the son. Freud (1966: 332–333) develops the idea not only that the son feels the presence of father as a "nuisance," an "egoistic sense of injury," but also regards brothers and sisters with "repugnance and for unhesitatingly getting rid of them by wish" (1966: 334).

There are, however, cultures and societies in which the socialization is not a process of "training," "rearing," or "being brought up." The child has to be taught to confirm the social norms by channelizing its impulses—a model of Western socialization, a historical evolution from the model of disciplining and eventually conquering a child's will. In the South Asian cultural context, especially among the Hindu households in India, children are seen as something nearest to the perfect divine form. And it is the adults that are supposed to learn the child's manner of experiencing the world. In majority of the Indian languages birth of a boy is regarded as god's gift to the parents and in case of a daughter it is expressed as a debt incurred with god. This is not to suggest, however, that the norms and values of adulthood are not conveyed to the child; in fact they are imparted through a clear set of expectations and in a manner that is highly ritualized (for details see Madan 1965; Minturn and Hitchcock 1963; Karve 1968; Buhler 1886; Kakar 1978).

Therefore, in Hindi language (as it is spoken in northern India), "socialization" is *palanposhan*, "protecting and nurturing." The parents are regarded to fit into the child's world. This is inversion of the Western concept, where the emphasis is on the fact that the child should fit into the adults' world. The notion of family is also very different in the two civilizations, and that affects the very construction of the child's world. Within South Asian civilization, children continue to sleep in the same room as their parents until they are 5 or 6 years old (Hobson 1982), with the strong probability of the primordial act being repeated or not repeated at all.[1]

In the Western context the emphasis is on the child not sleeping with parents. Consequently, the children are socialized in all cultures, and their personalities are culturally constructed to fit within their culture, and to relate with their relations and objects that embody these relations. All forms of operating within the child's world do not follow the Freudian presuppositions. For example, the South Asian child grows up with games and toys, representing extensions of his civilization's production of the world, good and evil, with demons and gods, as well as rituals (for details, see Smithsonian 1985; also Berland 1982). Within the context of South Asian culture, the child grows up with siblings in an extended family, and learns to live with many adult male and female role players. This generates the "necessity of oedipal alliance often outweighing the hostility of the Oedipus complex" (Kakar 1978: 130–131). In such an environment, the children in fact grow up using kinship terminology that is much more elaborate than for the Western child, although the basic terminology is a greater degree of transformation of the fundamental "nursery sounds" (Lewis 1964; Kakar 1978:116; Inden and Nicholas 1977:67–84).

Consequently, the ideas and the *ideology* a society has unfold in the way that the children are treated, and they also structure a child's play within childhood. In the small American Midwest town, children can find many toy tractors, but the child in a major big city with numerous TV channels can get plastic movable iconic representations of male models such as G.I. Joe, RoboCop, and Teenage Mutant Ninja Turtles. Toys, games, and children together constitute the area in which one can see the culturally specified roles. This includes the gender roles, which children are prepared to perform, enabling them to function smoothly and to get to the right degree of moral development (Zelditch 1955; Hoffman 1981). Father's interaction with his children orients them to the external world due to the male role being "instrumental"—in contrast to the female role as "expressive" and responsible for the emotional and affectionate home atmosphere (Durkheim 1933). Therefore, it might not be wrong to assume that perhaps Balinese children also learn the same quality about their culture, if not at deep and surface levels, as Geertz did in his observations of the Balinese cock fight. Balinese cock fighting embodies values of the culture, but exists in a form of "crossing of conceptual wires" (Geertz 1973: 447). Because of the values connected with childhood, upbringing in the West is "crossing of" Freudian "conceptual wires." This has affected to a great degree the studies of children and their games. How males remain fathers and interact with sons, and how women interact with children and make them as distinct daughters, may or may not be given the culture's own concern, but certainly it is the concern of the person that studies children, childhood, and socialization. Boys are expected to be assertive and violent—hence in the toy shop the aisles of Barbie Doll and make-believe kitchen with plastic food will frequently be visited only by daughters and mothers. Within Western society, it is possible that boys prefer games with pure physical skill and strategy, whereas girls prefer games of pure strategy, which makes them more obedient than the boys (Roberts and Sutton-Smith 1962). The extension of the Freudian (Western) notions of the child and child-rearing as a paradigmatic perspective for cross-cultural understanding of fathers and boys is problematic because of the differences of the social structures and the cultural meaning of "child" and "childhood." For example, among the Ongees of Little Andaman islands in the Bay of Bengal, men do not only hunt and women do not just gather and raise children. Only men hunt pigs, dugongs, and turtles. Both men and women perform all other activities of day-to-day life, including child-care, cooking, and the gathering of food resources and raw materials.

Gender-specific roles are not as clear-cut as the observer would hope. Ongees are one of the remaining groups of negrito hunters and gatherers of the Andaman Islands, and they consider that men could gather. And they do, just as women do it. Taking care of the child is in the same way seen as much as a male as a female duty. In fact, at the time of delivery, the husband is responsible for being present, attending his wife in labor, and cutting the umbilical cord. The only custom that keeps men and women separate in various activities is the idea that men should not be with women. That is to say, men and women as a group do not undertake any activity, but all men can get together and do what women do as a group activity. Consequently, all men would stay back at the campsite and take care of children, while the women get together and go to the creek, forest, or shore to get some natural resources. Within the Ongee world view, it is said that "all men and women are alike, they together do all that is required to live, the only difference is that spirits first made the women and animals, and therefore women cannot go hunting animals that bleed profusely!"

Western intellectual formulation of what childhood should be within a "behavioral system" has bearings and implications on studying parent–child relations in other cultures (see Whiting 1963: 5, 7). Western formulations about the father and son have influenced the very method of studying childhood (see Lamb 1975). At the expense of understanding how the culture expresses itself within the child's practice and society's construction of childhood, we have imposed our concern of gender and parent role. For a long time, myopically enough, we have taken our notion of what the child is and what Freud has to say about it, and extended it to the other societies. This has resulted in a lack of attention and appreciation of the given culture's own idea of what fathers and mothers have to do for sons and daughters.

For example, the Ongee adult male when finding a crying boy says: "For a man to cry is like seeing one's own wife being a widow! If you do, you will fail as hunter. We men cry only when we are dead and we see our wives as widows or being remarried." Indeed, the Ongee fathers are installing typical male values, as it would be in our cultural context, where crying is seen more as a feminine manifestation of feelings. Among the Ongees the act of crying is very much seen as an orchestrated chorus that only the women initiate and conduct. Hence on occasions such as mourning women come over and ask the mourning men to join in a particular style of crying (see Radcliffe-Brown 1933: 239).

Within such a context of articulation and expression of feelings, the children are raised with an equal amount of attention given by both the parents and all the adults in the campsite. In fact, childcare is seen as an activity in which all the adults are keen on getting involved. So the children in a campsite with a minimum average of about four to six families end up eating every day at all the households. The adults are frequently calling them: "Come! Have some food at my shelter!" The attitude toward providing the food for children and an eagerness to take care of them are evident in the way that daily activities are structured. On the way to the jungle, men and women take with them children who can walk along. In the morning, groups of two to four adult men with a pack of 5 to 10 dogs leave the campsite. As they move toward the forest, they either ask for or receive from different households detachable arrows for pig hunting. While they collect arrows, the boys come to know about the group leaving for the hunt, and they join the group. In the forest, dogs first track down the pigs, and as they get dispersed, the adults and boys also separate in groups. While the men and children are in the forest, the children are told about different plants and their use, about different animals, and about different places and their significance. The presence of tired children and their lack of understanding that in the forest one has to be patient and quiet often result in the group returning to camp empty handed. But the boys are never blamed for the failure, it is attributed to the dogs for being useless. The same event may be repeated next day, and the parents may tell the departing hunting party: "Take our arrows, dogs, and children! They have all rested enough." The procedure is identical during the season of sea—hunting for turtles and dugongs (sea cows), except that the timing of departure depends on the weather and light. It starts with men gathering canoes, ropes, and detachable points for harpoons. As a result, boys learn about the forest and the sea from all the adult males in the campsite. In the same way, the girls are "trained" by the collective effort of all the adult women in the campsite.

After men depart, often women depart with digging sticks and machetes. They collect baskets, and daughters from various households join them. This gathering may range from freshwater fish caught by small hand nets, to fish and crabs picked up at the creek when the tide recedes. Women also dig out and collect different types of tubers. Children who cannot walk stay back. They are the responsibility of the men and women that stay in the campsite. This group later collects the firewood and drinking water, and often it is the only activity when men and women and boys and girls go together. In this way everybody trains the children and educates them about the resources available on the island and ways of using them. This forms the strongest way of installing the Andamanese cultural value of respect toward all the senior members of the community, and acknowledges the influence of elders on junior members of the society (Radcliffe-Brown, 1933).

The socialization of Ongee boys by the fathers and the way in which the adult male relates to the boys show not only the concerns of the Andaman islanders' life (revolving around hunting and gathering), but also reflect the sensitivity of a culturally designed game for the socialization of boys—which should eventually sustain the whole social structure.[2] Much like games and toys provided for the children of the Western world, the socialization reflects culturally constructed values and expectations based on the genders of the children, at the same time upholding the legacy of changing ideas about the nature of children and childhood.

I intend to focus on the pattern of game played by Ongee boys within their culture, and show how the game in fact enables installation of values that are particularly compatible with the social organization of the Ongee hunters and gatherers of the Little Andaman island. The distinctiveness of this game and the interaction of fathers prepare boys for living in a community of hunters and gatherers who have to share everything. Given the small size of the population[3], if we were born as an Ongee boy, we would find that every other adult male in actuality or in expression fulfills one or the other role within a wide spectrum, starting with "father like" and including fathers, stepfathers, adopted fathers, and fathers-in-law. Therefore, when I first witnessed the birth of a male child, a new and proud father told me:

> I don't know how you feel about becoming a father, but I feel very relieved. I am not alone in making or moving the child [*elekolake*][4]. The child moved into the mother's womb because of spirits[5], it came out of the womb because of the mother, but he will become an Ongee hunter and gatherer by all of his fathers teaching him how to move as a hunter without getting hunted by spirits[6].

CHARACTERISTICS OF ONGEE SOCIAL ORGANIZATION

> educational cycle was initiated by parenthood. The problem of Andamanese infancy was less what the parent should do for the child than what the child would do for the parent. Many elements of Andamanese culture were concentrated round a birth, especially that of a first-born. The moral code found expression in a general attitude of kindliness that surrounded childhood. Of these manifestations infant was itself rather the occasion than the cause. (Foster 1930: 91)

When we look at the Ongee ethnographic material and classical descriptions of the Andamanese (Man 1885; Portman 1859; Radcliffe-Brown 1933; Cipriani 1966), it is beyond doubt that the Andamanese have bilateral descent groups. The nuclear family is the major group, around which all the activities (mainly hunting and gathering) revolve. The nuclear family includes a married couple's children, as well as any adopted children. By rule, descent among the Andamanese is bilateral. The kinship system is cognatic and terminology, on the whole, specifies classifactory relations. Prefixes are affixed to classifactory terms of reference, which also emphasize senior and junior age differences.

Children are regarded as an asset because the connection between the world of spirits and the human world is established by them, and they are also desired by the related nuclear families. The practice of foster parenthood and adopting the children strengthens the bonds and links of interdependence among the islanders (Radcliffe-Brown 1933: 72, 77; Man 1885: 57). More than once I have been told by the couples who did not have children that when they get one, they would like to give the child to so and so as that household's adopted child. In 1983–1984 there were 29 children (below age of approximately 15 years) and 69 adults. Of the 29 children 16 were already adopted and a ceremony for three other children's adoption was being planned.

Many families arrange this even before the child is born. Usually the man who would like to adopt a child approaches a recently married man and states his desire by evoking the phrase "We have been *mijejeleh* [friends], we should do *ge-gayetowa-yekamwabe* [for the future of our relation]!" The term *ge-gayetowa-yekamwabe* is frequently invoked, especially on occasions of sharing, or transaction between the two males—and it is this term that also refers to the customs of adoption. Therefore, the Ongees do not see the child as "adopted" or parents as "real" or "social" or "foster," but see both houses connected by the child as something that contributes to the future. The concern for children, therefore, either one's own or another's, is concretized in the language—by which all the adults, male and female, use to refer to all children as *aley*, which means "one that comes." Ongees regard a child as human after its first baby tooth appears. After all teeth have appeared the child may be given in adoption.

When the child is born all the married women congregate at the shelter built especially for the delivery of the child. Even if some married women cannot breast-feed the new baby, the newborn child is passed from woman to woman, and each woman in turn offers her breast for actual sucking or just pacifying. This providing of the prime maternal substance, breast-milk, generates feelings that are "enduring diffuse solidarity (cf. Schnider 1968:50–54; Inden and Nicholas 1977)." Within Ongee culture this treatment expresses value of regarding a child not as one belonging to a particular family, but "one who comes to all." Ongee children grow up addressing all the adult men as *omoree* ("father"), but only after marriage boys can refer to their foster father as *inerare*, which means one who is not an outsider; it is the opposite to the term *ineney*, which implies an outsider. Girls continue to use this term of address for adult men (excluding adult male siblings of any degree) as *omoree* even after marriage. However, one's own mother alone is referred to as *kayree*; all other women are referred to as *maikuta* (maternal women relatives) or *gayekutta* (paternal women relatives).

Marriage is arranged by the elders within the prescribed group, that is, between the turtle hunters and the pig hunters. The island is divided into four major parts and identified with two pairs of mythical birds, each of which is associated with land or water. The four divisions of land represent the four Ongee clans. Each section of the island is further subdivided into sections of land associated with a lineage. These land divisions, known as *megeyabarrota*, are identified with a person's matrilineage and, depending on whether the territory is in the forest or at the coast, with either the turtle hunters (*eahambelakwe*) or the pig hunters (*ehansakwe*). The man's patrilineal relatives receive gifts and demand a daughter from the man's matrilineal group. Among the Ongees, population decline often makes it impossible for a young man to marry his classificatory cross-cousin. An older man or woman who has lost a spouse has priority for marriage. Levirate marriage is also acceptable. In general, we can say that marriage is a highly valued status.

A newly married couple stays with the wife's family at least until a child is born. After a child is born, the couple may move to live with the husband's siblings and their families. The child's matrilineal relatives are responsible for the early socialization. Once a young boy is ready for initiation, his training and education become the responsibility of his patrilineal relatives. After a girl's first menstruation, she is even more closely aligned with her matrilineal relatives. Children of both sexes are taught about the forest while they accompany their elders on different hunting and gathering activities. Through play and the making of toy canoes, bows and arrows, shelters, and small nets, children are introduced to basic requisite skills (cf. Radcliffe-Brown 1933: 76–77).

It is evident that the Ongee boy is being socialized in a place—or, as Ongees would say, "being moved," where it is not just one father, but all adult men who are like the boy's father, or one of them may even be his foster father. It is the world in which all the uncles, initiators, and prospective fathers-in-law are present simultaneously and see to the development of the child and contribute to his childhood. The nature of this specific mode of social organization becomes more clear as the new father says: "I feel very relieved. I am not alone in making or moving the child (*elekolake*)."

Taking the example of how Ongee children play the game of hide and seek, I will show the way in which the relations of fathers and sons along with male–adult and male–children relations are acted out in the game of *gukwelonone*. The pattern of the hide and seek game that was observed is a frequent and regular event throughout the year, and it consistently reflects how the Ongees view raising and socializing the children.

STAGING AND SETTING THE GAME OF HIDE AND SEEK

The heat at the peak of the afternoon makes pig hunting in the dense tropical forest of Little Andamans extremely difficult. Young boys with their elder male relatives end the process of hunting and gathering, which is seen as an act of seeking (*lonone*). In the season of *Mayakangne* (October to February), when the winds blow from the northeast, the Ongee hunters and gatherers are looking for turtles and dugongs (sea cow) hiding in the sea around the island. However, this process is also brought to an end when the sun reaches the top of the horizon or the full moon starts descending. Ongees believe that it is difficult to "seek" hiding (*gukwe*) animals when it gets darker.

Gukwe and *lonone* are the principles around which much of the Ongee world view is organized and explained. For example, the reason for seasonal shift from hunting at the coast in the season of *Mayakangne* and hunting in the forest during the season of *Kwalakangne* (from May to September) is attributed to the presence of the spirits (*tomya*) in the particular season. When the spirits go hunting in the forest, humans hunt in the sea, and vice versa. Not to be in the place where spirits are is seen as a game of *gukwelonone*, by which life continues in the community and generates a virtue known as *gwekekalan*, generating a feeling of interdependence and mutual respect. Ongees explain the term *gweke-kalan* as generation of feeling of togetherness and positive interdependence by which every thing is interconnected, like the winds, which by their quality of permeability go anywhere and everywhere and from everything into everything within nature (see Pandya 1987: 72–116).

As the evening comes, women take the portions of food for cooking toward the periphery of the circular-patterned campsite. Men wake up with other male children after an afternoon nap, but continue lying on the sleeping platforms, facing the central campground. In the middle of the campground some smouldering logs are set up. On top of the fire, a 4- to 5-feet wooden scaffolding is built. It is on this scaffolding that the raw or the semicooked food is kept. The fire protects the food and makes it available to all the households around it. The fire is the collective responsibility of all the campmates, and whenever a particular house wants to set up its own hearth, the fire is obtained from here. When the camp location is changed the fire is also moved, and it is the first thing to be set up in the new campsite.

Men try to awaken the boys by singing or tickling. Once the boys are awake, the instructing and convincing starts. Men intend to send around young boys from the age of 5 to 15 to different shelters within the camp. Once the boys are fully awake they seem to be eager to obey and please elder men and carry small bundles of wild betel nuts and leaves gathered in the forest. While the boys run across the camp-grounds to the house, they often receive some portions of what they are distributing or whatever food the house may have as a special treat— such as a fatty slice of pig or turtle meat. Sometimes men tell all the boys to go to their home and get something that they need or ask for the tools or implements that they may want to borrow or may have loaned out earlier in the day. After some time, the running of the boys from household to household with dogs following them creates shouts from the women who try to control this activity. The Ongee children do not respond to this slowly developing disorderly behavior. Boys start running swiftly across the campground, attracting all the dogs. Since the central campground is a place where the cooked food is kept over a low fire, dogs are not appreciated within the campground. Often the directed visiting becomes a joking game when the boys visit a household and ask for something they were not supposed to, such as boiled turtle eggs in the season of pig hunting, or give an empty basket from a house to another household that did not ask for it. Multiplication of this mischievous behavior is sometimes ended by men not related to the boys, when they get angry and gently grab the children and start tickling them to divert them or even to leave them exhausted and gasping. If the aberrant behavior continues, the men may even slap the children on the upper thighs or pinch them near the groins. Irritated and crying, children then run back to their home.

The men in that household would usually ignore the crying children. They do not check or control the behavior of boys belonging to their own household, and they do not sympathize or console if a boy has been punished by someone from another household. The principle is that men and women from the other households are always entitled to correct a child's behavior, but a child's own household adults give only general instructions, but never punish or correct the child.

As the evening comes, the running from house to house around the campground evolves into a game (*cholo*) of hide and seek, *gukwelonone*. I observed the game at two camp locations. Over a span of about 150 days the game was played 30 times. Men sitting on the sleeping platforms oversee the development of all the activity, including the interaction of boys with each household and interaction of adults with their own children. The Ongee shelter lacks three walls and one cannot escape from experiencing all the sights, smells, movements, and sounds around the sleeping platform.

RELATIONS AND ROLES WITHIN THE GAME

To play the game of hide and seek the boys divide into groups of three to four. Very rarely young girls also play as members of these groups. The oldest boy in the group is appointed the team leader, and he is responsible for conducting the process of going out to seek hiding groups of boys. The seeking group of boys goes to the center of the campground and stands in a circle with their heads bent down, eyes shut, and hands stretched out on each other's shoulders. Sometimes the hiding groups insist that the seeking group should face a particular direction and they should cover their eyes with some leaves. This

covering of eyes with leaves is called *nakwejokobetokabe* and it frequently
is done when the majority of the boys in the seeking group are more
than 5 years old or the seeking group constitutes less than three boys.
The leader tells others not to chuckle and to be quiet. Meanwhile, the
groups that are hiding quickly exit the campground, directed by the
elders who are still on their sleeping platforms. The hiding groups are
instructed to hide in the circular area outside the shelters. Once all the
hiding groups are appropriately scattered, the elders signal the seekers:
"Eehye! Chera ocholo okiyatorankabe!" ("Let's go for the playing of hunting"!) The seeking group, called *gukulobey*, intends to locate the hiding
group, called *nakweyebe*, and the hiding group intends to come out
without being noticed (a sort of staged ambuscade) and surround the
seeking group. The seeking group usually succeeds in surreptitiously
coming up to the hiding group, and then quickly embraces them and
shouts: *"Talabuka! Talabuka!"* The term *Talabuka* means the consciously
caused conviviality or conjunction of the location of something hiding
with the movement undertaken by somebody seeking. Ongees often
use the term to express the success of hunting a pig or a turtle. Meanwhile, the other hiding groups come out and try to catch the seeking
group that has located the first hiding group. If they succeed, they shout
"Malabuka! Malabuka!" *Malabuka* implies a coincidence that happened
without the intention of the seeking party, both within the context of the
game as well as in the context of hunting. When the Ongee hunter fails
in hunting down an animal and even after tracking down an animal if it
escapes, the misfortune is expressed in the use of the term *malabuka*. If
the hiders succeed in their intent before the seekers can locate them,
then the hiding group has to start the game all over again.

As the game starts, the adult males also change and reshuffle their
positions to get involved in the game of *gukwelonone*. Adult men related
to the boys (fathers or fathers' brothers), who are going to look for the
hiding children, turn around and sit looking out from the back of their
shelters. They help in directing the boys to hide in different places
around the campground. Men related to the hiding boys face the center
of the campground and direct the seeking group of boys to proceed in
different locations. This allows the adult men to be involved in the game
without physically moving, but by paying attention to the direction
given for hiding and directing the process of searching for the hiding
group.

The searching group receives help in the form of clues from the adult
males related to the boys that are hiding. Thus the inversion of the role-
play for the adult men takes place as the adult gets into playing the game
of *gukwelonone*.

Some men even step out of the family shelters and come to stand
outside the campground (behind the family shelters). In principle, the

adult men related to the groups of the boys hiding help the seeking group by giving them clues to where they should go, or indicate in a typically recondite and cryptic manner if the direction and location of the pursuit are right or wrong. For example, the message given or the clue given, referred to as *nakwejoko* (knowledge or ability to correlate hearing and seeing especially for successful hunting) could be:

"Look up where the cicadas are not singing and the fireflies are not dancing!"

"Yes! Look at the tree that the civet cat will climb on!"

"Keep walking like a crab!" (Move sideways.)

"Do not walk like a snake!" (Walk straight.)

"Where would you go from there if you were thirsty?" (Go toward the water or nearest coconut tree.)

"Pay attention to where the birds are not making noise!"

"Careful, you might get hot in that place!" (The place is not worth looking.)

Thus the men in the campsite will tell all the boys to whom they are not related the approximate location for seeking out the boys to whom these men are related. After being asked what the game is all about and why they get involved in it, some of the Ongee adults responded: "I want my son to learn how to look for things and if I alone teach him that is no good. We men together all know more about where to look for food in the forests and sea and we all share what we bring back after that process of moving and looking."

BETWEEN HIDING DURKHEIM AND SEEKING FREUD: ONGEE GAME

The game of *gukwelonone* uses the hunting metaphors (*malabuka* and *talabuka*), but it is, in fact, the inversion of the role of adult men and boys involved as teams of those who hide and those who seek.[7]

The game creates the situation that puts the individual boys in a position to relate to the "socially valued" principle of not only learning to look for and moving, but also the technique of looking and learning is to be learned from all the other male adults within the society. The game embodies techniques essential for the Ongee hunters and gatherers and enacts the Ongee socialization that stresses independence in the term *gwekekalan*. Within the context of the game, sharing of knowledge (*nakwejoko*) creates the value for interdependence based on the strong respect for the elders. It also fosters a respect for receiving knowledge pertaining to the requisite skill of an Ongee man, who must hunt and gather. It is this value of the community that Radcliffe-Brown (1933: 264) formulated as something in the mind of the individual existing as a feeling of his dependence on the society, and the value of dependence is not only expressed and related in the game of *gukwelonone*, but is also installed in the participants of the game by its conductors.

Through the game and the issue of "knowledge" involved, as well as the inversion of the roles of adult men related to the boys, Ongee hunters and gatherers instill exactly what Durkheim conceived as education, "a collection of practices and institutions that have organized slowly in the course of time, which are integrated with all other social institutions, and express them" (Durkheim 1956: 65). What Durkheim posited as education being intimately elated to social structure is articulated by the Ongees in the game that functions as a "school" for the future hunters and gatherers. By instilling the value of learning how to look and move (*elekolake*) from all the adult men, the criteria of interdependence within the community, the development and continuation of the game of *gukwelonone* each evening formulate the game into "the image and reflection of the society . . . it imitates and reproduces it in miniature" (Durkheim 1951: 372). The game itself is therefore a strategy designed and played between the elder men and the young boys to instill the required inclination for "collective life" (Durkheim 1961: 239) and transmit the emergent cultural value and social ideal, or, as Radcliffe-Brown formulated, "social-valuable."

The fact that the boys succeed in the game aided by the men who are not related to them creates an interesting Freudian problem. The adult male helpers are also the ones responsible for punishing the boys' misconduct before the game starts. Therefore, the repetition of the events that constitute the game and the repetition of the game within the Ongee boys' childhood construct a history in which none of the fathers is resented. Instead of an Oedipus complex, there is an Oedipal alliance. The game is therefore not a mere model for hunting, transmission of practical knowledge, and looking for other friends—but it is also a situation that makes it possible for the male adults and children to locate the basic values that underlie the roles that every boy and man must play in the future with the same sincerity and intensity. A man who helps a boy in the game may be helping his son-in-law or the child that he is going to adopt. The adults are looking for hiding sons and the boys are locating their fathers.

ACKNOWLEDGMENTS

I would like to thank some of the people who have helped me in thinking about this paper and who have been responsible for my own socialization: the

Ongees of Little Andaman Island, the Government of India, and an American Institute for Indian Studies research fellowship made possible my socialization in Ongee culture as a field worker (1983–1984); my parents in India where I was first socialized; and Roxanna with whom I socialize our son Atayih. These three levels of socialization and understanding of culture would not have been my concern without my discussions with Barry Hewlett who shared with me his "socialization" as an ethnographer among Aka and his socializing of his own children.

NOTES

1. For details refer to Gandhi's idea about sexuality (Fischer 1962: 239–257; Misri 1986) to understand how Indians minimize the Freudian notion of desire or guilt generated in a child by sharing a bed with its parents.

2. All living things are believed to be endowed with power that affects human beings. The universe is a multilayered structure, a configuration of various places through which spirits and the smell and breath of humans, animals, and plants move. Restriction of movement is regarded as a major threat to the order of nature since each place within space is associated with a distinct type of spirit that permits or restricts the movements of all living things. As a consequence the value system is the basic means for maintaining social control. Direct confrontation is avoided and "going away," that is, leaving the source and scene of conflict, for a short time is encouraged. Usually resentment is expressed by breaking or destroying some piece of property at the campsite and then leaving for the forest to stay for a few days. While the offended person is gone, other campmates fix the destroyed property and wait for the return of that person, who returns without recriminations. It is interesting to therefore note that the majority of the myths within the Andamanese culture outline the necessity of conflict between humans and all other forms of life but never within the level of just human society. (For details see Radcliffe-Brown 1933; Pandya 1987.) Conflict is never between father and son or any other relation within the society of human beings. Conflict and resentment are only within the society of different animals and spirits.

3. In 1983–1984 between the two locations of Dugong Creek and South Bay the total Ongee population of Little Andaman Island was 98. Of this 37% was adult male, 34% adult female, 18% male children, and 11% female children. Within the total adult male population 30 men were married and 6 were either awaiting their first or second marriage. Of the 30 married male adults 12 had no children, and within the remaining 18 married men 13 had their own children. Twenty-one of 30 had either one or more adopted sons or daughters and 9 men had either a daughter-in-law or son-in-law.

4. The Ongee language's equivalence for the term socialization is *elekolake*, which means "to make something movable."

5. When a person dies his "body internal" is believed to escape into either the forest or the sea. Thus, a dead coastal dweller becomes a spirit of the sea (*Jurua*) and a dead forest dweller becomes a spirit in the forest (*Lau*). (Radcliffe-Brown 1933: 90–91, 166–75). Those who die in accidents or those whose dead body did not receive the appropriate ceremonial burial become malevolent spirits who cause sickness and death among human beings. Through secondary

burial the bones of the dead person are recovered and made into amulets and body ornaments that attract the spirits of benevolent ancestors who will help and keep safe his living human relatives (Pandya 1990). The Ongees believe that the *tomya* (spirits of dead ancestors) are attracted to the islands and, through a series of events, are transformed into the fetuses of human mothers. Thus the spirits of the ancestors become the children of the Ongees.

6.   Ongees regard the act of hunting as a major danger since in the process of hunting they are also capable of being hunted by the spirits formed out of dead Ongees. Spirits are considered to be like infants since they do not have any teeth to masticate food and eat by sucking the animal or human they hunt.

7.   Like the boys within the campsite, girls also play a game of hide and seek, which is called *gukwelonone-gegi*. The game is very much like the boys game but the difference is that the hiding group hides under some sort of covering such as a pile of dry leaves or even under sand. The hiding girls are regarded as *gegi*, tuber, and the searching group goes around with a stick tapping in different places in an attempt to locate hiding individuals. This game, like the game of the boys, also involves the adult women and recapitulates the principal activity of women—gathering of tubers (or crabs hiding in shallow creek waters) with a digging stick.

REFERENCES

Berland, C. J. 1982. *No Five Fingers Are Alike*. Cambridge, MA: Harvard University Press.

Buhler, G. 1886. *The Laws of Manu*. Oxford: Clarendon Press.

Cipriani, L. 1966. *The Andaman Islanders*. New York: Prager.

de Mause, L. (Ed.). 1975. *The History of Childhood*. New York: Harper Torch Books.

Durkheim, E. 1933. *The Division of Labour in Society*. New York: Macmillan.

———. 1951. *Suicide: A Study in Sociology*. Glencoe, IL: Free Press.

———. 1956. *Education and Society*. Glencoe, IL: Free Press.

———. 1961. *Moral Education: A Study in the Theory and Application of the Sociology of Education*. New York: Free Press of Glencoe.

Fischer, L. (Ed.). 1962. *The Essential Gandhi*. New York: Vintage, Random House.

Foster, T. S. 1930. *From Savagery to Commerce: An Introduction to the Theory of Adult Education*. London: Jonathan Cape.

Freud, S. 1966. *Introductory Lectures on Psychoanalysis*. New York: Norton.

Geertz, C. 1973. Deep Play: Notes on the Balinese Cockfight. In *The Interpretation of Cultures*. C. Geertz (Ed.) pp. 412–453. New York: Basic Books.

Hewlett, B. S. 1987. Intimate fathers: Patterns of paternal holding among Aka Pygmies. In *The Father Role: Cross Cultural Perspectives*. M. E. Lamb (Ed.), pp. 295–330. Hillsdale, NJ: Erlbaum.

Hobson, S. 1982. *Family Web: A Story of India*. Chicago: Academy Chicago.

Hoffman, M. L. 1981. The role of father in moral internalization. In *The Role of Father in Child Development*. M. E. Lamb (Ed.) pp. 359–378. New York: Wiley.

Inden, R. B., and Nicholas, R. W. 1977. *Kinship in Bengali Culture*. Chicago: University of Chicago Press.

Kakar, S. 1978. *The Inner World: A Psychoanalytical Study of Childhood and Society in India*. Delhi: Oxford University Press.

Karve, I. 1968. *Kinship Organization in India*. Bombay: Asia Publishing House.

Lamb, M. E. 1975. Fathers: Forgotten contributors to child development. *Human Development* 18:245–266.

Lewis, M. M. 1964. *Language, Thought, and Personality in Infancy and Childhood*. New York: Basic Books.

Madan, T. N. 1965. *Family and Kinship*. Bombay: Asia Publishing House.

Man, E. H. 1885. *On the Aboriginal Inhabitants of the Andaman Islands*. London: Royal Anthropological Institute.

Minturn, L., and Hitchcock, J. T. 1963. The Rajputs of Khalapur India. In *Six Cultures: Studies of Child Rearing*. B. B. Whiting (Ed.) pp. 203–251. New York: Wiley.

Misri, U. 1986. Child and childhood: A conceptual construction. In *The Word and the World: Fantasy, Symbol and Record*. V. Das (Ed.), pp. 115–132. New Delhi: Sage Publications.

Ortner, S. B. 1974. Is female to male as nature is to culture? In *Women Culture and Society*. M. Z. Rosaldo and Lamphere (Eds.) pp. 67–87. Stanford, CA: Stanford University Press.

Pandya, V. 1987. *Above the Forest: A Study of Andamanese Ethnoanemology, Cosmology and the Power of Ritual*. Ph.D. Dissertation, Department of Anthropology, University of Chicago.

Pandya, V. 1990. Movement and Space: Andamanese Cartography. *American Ethnologist* 17(4):775–797.

Portman, M. V. 1859. *History of Our Relations with the Andamanese*. Calcutta: Government Printing Press.

Radcliffe-Brown, A. R. 1933. *The Andaman Islanders*. Cambridge: Cambridge University Press.

Roberts, J. M., and Sutton-Smith, B. 1962. Child training and game involvement. *Ethnology* 1:166–185.

Schneider, D. M. 1968. *American Kinship: A Cultural Account*. Chicago: University of Chicago Press.

Smithsonian. 1985. *Aditi: The Living Arts of India*. Washington, D.C.: Smithsonian Institution Press.

Whiting, B. B. (Ed.). 1963. *Six Cultures: Studies of Child Rearing*. New York: Wiley.

Zelditch, M. 1955. Role differentiation in the nuclear family. In *Family, Socialization and Interaction Process*. T. Parsons and R. F. Bales (Eds.) pp. 307–352. Illinois: Free Press.

Chapter 13

Fathering in an Egalitarian Society

Karen Endicott

As Hewlett (1987:295, 1991:1) and others have recently pointed out, most anthropological accounts of child development and childrearing contain little information about the role that fathers play in the lives of their children. Research perspectives such as that of Bowlby on mother-infant bonding (1969) that highlight the role of the mother, the high degree of female involvement in childrearing in most societies, and the assumption largely derived from western society that childcare is women's work have influenced anthropologists to ignore fatherhood as a topic worthy of study. Moreover, anthropologists have tended to see males and females as living in separate spheres. Rosaldo goes so far as to push men right out of the family setting. Contending that all societies make a distinction between the domestic and the public, she defines the domestic as "those minimal institutions and modes of activity that are organized immediately around one or more mothers and their children" (Rosaldo 1974:23) and defines public as "activities, institutions, and forms of association that link, rank, or subsume particular mother-child groups" (ibid). She finds that women operate within the domestic and men within the public sphere, yet it is her very definitions rather than empirical data that make this so. In focusing on fathering, anthropology is looking beyond such formulations and assumptions about male and female roles. No doubt the discipline's nascent interest in fathering derives in part from our own society's reevaluation of parenting; regardless of the impetus for these studies, however, inquiry into fathering can only add to our knowledge of human society.

THE CULTURAL CONTEXT OF BATEK CHILDREARING

In this chapter I examine fathering—and fathering's partner, mothering—among the egalitarian Batek, who at the time of my fieldwork, 1975–1976, were living as nomadic hunter–gatherers in the rain forest of the Lebir River watershed in Kelantan, Malaysia. (Widespread logging in that area has changed Batek life considerably in recent years. This chapter presents Batek society as it was in 1975–1976). I consider the Batek to be egalitarian in the sense that adults of both sexes are free to decide their own movements, activities, and relationships; among adults no individual holds authority over others; and neither sex group has power through economic, religious, or social advantage (K.L. Endicott 1979, 1980, 1981, 1984, 1986). As I argue elsewhere (1979), the Batek make little use of gender as a classificatory device or cultural theme, and they do not value males over females or activities done by males over activities done by females. Even their kinship terminology—kinship is reckoned bilaterally—incorporates gender distinctions in only some categories: there are terms for mother, father, grandmother, grandfather, aunt, and uncle. No gender distinctions are made in the terms for children, siblings, cousins, and grandchildren. To specify if one has a daughter or a son, for example, one must say a female child (*awa'yaluw*) or a male child (*awa' temkal*). The Batek do not articulate their egalitarianism as a conscious doctrine; rather, egalitarianism is embedded in their economic, religious, and social practices. This chapter will show that Batek parenting both reflects and reproduces the egalitarian relations of the society.

The Batek De' dialect group in the Lebir River area consists of about 84 people. Usually from 5 to 8 nuclear families camp together, each family in a separate lean-to shelter. The average camp population was 34 persons: 11 men, 9 women, and 14 children below age 15. Often, but not always, the married children of an older couple or individual camp together. There are no corporate groups in Batek society. Camps, as physical entities and as groups, generally last a week to 10 days before people move to find new food or trade resources. Each nuclear family decides where to camp and with whom, a decision often based on the economic plans of like-minded relatives and friends.

Unlike many social environments in which distinct buildings provide settings for different activities, the physical setting of Batek society is simple and largely undifferentiated. The Batek classify the physical environment as either "camp" (*haya'*; literally, "lean-tos") or "forest" (*hep*). There is no evidence that the Batek classify their world into the kind of public and domestic division that Rosaldo (1974:23) suggests is a universal feature of social organization. There are no men's houses or work houses, and no area in a camp is restricted to one sex or the other. The only special-function structures the Batek erect are ritual houses, which are huge lean-tos erected a few times a year to house certain ceremonies, and birth huts, which are lean-tos of normal size built outside of camp and used only during birth. Camps—or homes—are no less public than the forest, and men and women operate within both of these settings. Families erect lean-tos at random locations, rarely more than a few yards from each other. These shelters are open on three sides, thus exposing the activities of camp members to the full view of everyone else in camp. Each nuclear family or unmarried adult occupies a separate shelter. At around 10 years of age children move out of their parents' lean-to and share a nearby shelter with friends. Family members sleep, cook, eat, store their goods, relax, and do much of their work and childcare in and immediately in front of the lean-to. As the living space in these shelters is small—about 32 square feet—parents and their children have frequent physical contact during their at-home activities. A typical at-home scene in a Batek camp is parents sitting in their shelter while several children lounge in their parents' laps, lean against them, or jostle each other.

A fact of life for Batek children is that the groups around them constantly change. With each move, the composition of a camp group may shift dramatically. Sometimes the same group remains together through several moves. Other times each family links up with different groups. Even a child's nuclear family—with whom the child moves and lives—is subject to dissolution through death or easy divorce. Disagreements may lead people to camp in different groups and locations; moving is a common means of handling disputes. Correlated with this freedom to leave social groupings in Batek society is the ease with which individuals can attach themselves to others. Individuals choose who they want to work and camp with, and they select their own marriage partners. Most marriages are monogamous. Occasionally a man decides to marry a second wife, but in the two such cases I heard of, the first wife opted for divorce rather than remaining in a polygynous union. The high degree of individual choice evident in these adult decisions extends to children as well. In cases of divorce, very young children, especially nursing infants, usually remain with the mother, but older children may decide for themselves with which parent they will live. Children may alternate between the parents, live with older siblings, or even live with stepparents who are no longer married to their biological parent. In a sense, divorce enlarges the social world for children as it often brings them into close contact with people other than their parents. Although divorce changes the social world of a child, the sense of loss a child may feel at not having both parents under the same roof may be mitigated by the frequent contact children continue to have with each parent and by the expansion of relationships with others.

The flexibility of social groupings is facilitated by the campwide sharing network that entitles all people in a camp to food. All food—whether vegetable or meat and whether procured by women or men—is shared, unless the quantities are so small as to be considered enough for only one or two people. Parents often give their children plates of food to deliver to other families in camp. This sharing occurs even when each family has procured similar food through their own labors. In addition to ensuring that all people have direct access to foods that they may not be able to procure themselves—because of the division of labor, differences in individual levels of ability, illness, or failure to find food—the sharing network facilitates childcare: raising children does not create overbearing foodgetting burdens on individual caregivers; through the sharing network, the entire camp absorbs responsibility for feeding children.

The Batek organize their foraging activities around (1) blowpipe hunting—mainly done by men, but not prohibited to women; (2) digging for wild yams—which women do on an almost daily basis and men do when hunting fails, when they come across a good find, or when their wives are ill; and (3) collecting rattan—generally carried out by men and by women who do not yet have children or whose children are old enough to help or are grown up. There have been times when the Malaysian government has induced them to grow rice, corn, and manioc, but the Batek tend to abandon their horticultural ventures as soon as they run out of the free food that the government supplies to tide them over until harvest. They trade rattan and other less-frequently collected forest products, such as honey and gaharu wood (*Aquilaria* spp.), for rice, manufactured goods, and money. The Batek share food gained through trade, but the sharing of money and goods that result from trade is left to the discretion of the nuclear family of the trader. The Batek accomplish their food-getting activities within approximately 5 hours of labor per work day. Men averaged 5.6 work days per week; women averaged 5.

BATEK FATHERS' INTERACTIONS WITH THEIR CHILDREN

Men shift into the role of father before their babies are born. Just prior to a birth, the prospective father constructs a special lean-to outside of camp to house his wife during delivery. Usually men do not attend births, but sometimes the attending midwives call in a man to assist with a difficult birth if he is known for his healing skills. Either the midwife or the father names the baby. Birth occasions the renaming of the parents: a man becomes known as Father of So-and-so, the woman as Mother of So-and-so. These teknonyms linguistically emphasize the link between parent and child.

Although babies spend most of their time with their mothers, who carry them in cloth slings and feed them on demand, the Batek do not consider childcare to be the domain of women only. Fathers play an important part in the social life of infants. They hold, cuddle, and chatter to their sons and daughters with as much obvious enjoyment as is evident in mothers' behaviors. Of course, there are individual differences in the interest people take in children. I have seen a range of reactions from both parents. There are fathers who especially dote on their children—some fathers frequently make toys, swings, or other amusements for their young children—and there are some mothers who are easily irritated by theirs. In general, however, people take an active and affectionate interest in babies, admiring and hugging them and reciting rhymes for their amusement. My observation is that Batek parents treat boys and girls the same. There are no overtly observable differences in parental treatment of the sexes: I could not tell the sex of a baby by observing the kinds of interactions adults had with it. For example, all babies are fed on demand; males and females do not receive different amounts of food or time at the breast. Weaning occurs when the child is ready—which may not be until age 4—unless the mother becomes pregnant and tries to wean the child before the next baby is born. Even after the birth of a new sibling, mothers may indulge a child who refuses to be weaned by continuing to breast feed it. When I asked the Batek whether they prefer to have male or female children, they said that they equally desire sons and daughters, a view that is borne out by their affectionate behavior toward infants of each sex, the absence of infanticide, and the absence of differential cultural evaluations of males and females and their activities. The Batek say that they want all children. It appears that women do not seek to lower their fertility rate through contraception, abortion, or protracted post-partum sexual abstinence. Despite prolonged on-demand breast-feeding, some women bear infants every two years, yet many of these children die before the age of 5 from malaria or other diseases.

Infancy is a time of close physical contact—babies are usually held by the mother, father, or another caregiver, and at night nursing infants sleep next to the mother—but mothers try to foster independence in children at an early age. Mothers selectively heed the cries of 2- or 3-year-olds, letting children deal with their own minor frustrations and difficulties and intervening primarily when cries indicate pain, fear, or intense frustration. The father becomes an increasingly important source of attention and comfort for children when the birth of a new sibling displaces them further from their mother's attention and breast. Such children often seek out their fathers when their mothers are occupied with a baby sibling. They may go to sit on their fathers' laps when the men return from work, even when the mothers are nearby. Children thus appear to view each parent as a source of physical contact, comfort, and attention. Sometimes a child who is at home with one parent or another caretaker will wail for the father or mother to return from work, and the sobs will cease only when exhaustion sets in.

Fathers spend much of their in-camp time with their children. Fathers often bathe their children, attend to their excretory needs, and cook for them. And because shelters are so small and open, when a father is at home, he is available to his children. They can be at his side as he makes darts, cleans and dries his blowpipe, butchers meat, or talks to other people in camp. At night children can sleep next to their fathers as the entire family—father, mother, and young children—beds down together in the small space of the shelter. Both parents make sure that their children remain within earshot at all times, calling out for them to return to camp if they think the children have wandered too far off into the surrounding forest. If children who are out of sight suddenly cry out, parents rush to their aid.

In many societies fathers are distracted from close interactions with their children because they play an authoritarian role. Among the Batek neither parent is put in this position. Mothers and fathers share equally in the little authority that Batek adults have over their children—the Batek say that they cannot control much of what children do. Although parents mold their children's behavior through example or verbal correction, neither parent takes on a punitive role. When parents are annoyed with their children, they may tell them that they are angry or upset about the behavior and that they should stop it, but children often ignore them. Fathers have no more effect on their children than mothers. Batek society is highly nonaggressive, and parents rarely strike children or otherwise use physical force to coerce them. The Batek word for "to hit," *sakel*, also means "to kill," and most Batek consider both acts to be abhorrent. Instead of using physical force to influence their children's behavior, parents invoke the third-party figures that Batek culture invests with authority and punitive power: tigers, the thundergod, strangers, and illness. For example, if parents want their children to play closer to camp, they will tell the children that a tiger will come or that a stranger is watching them. Parents teach children to obey the society's religious prohibitions, on pain of punishment by the thundergod who sends specific illnesses or topples trees on the offender (see K.M. Endicott 1979:67–82). Punishment is thus taken out of the parental role. That neither sex group has authority—or is the only one that lacks it—means that fathers and mothers are on equal footing in relation to children.

The only case of physical violence toward children I came across involved a woman who appeared to treat her three young sons with affection and care. According to her mother, however, the woman, in a fit of anger over her husband's supposed (and quite possibly real) advances towards another woman, had struck her baby son over the head with a piece of bamboo, knocking the child unconscious. This boy recovered. But, according to the woman's mother, the woman had killed another son several years earlier through a similar action. When she related this information, the woman's mother was extremely distraught over her daughter's behavior and the condition of her grandson. Several weeks later when I saw the woman, she again appeared to be a kind and affectionate mother toward her children. It seems clear that the woman was emotionally unstable and at times lashed out at her children when she was angry at her husband.

From infancy until around age 10, boys and girls often accompany their mothers on gathering expeditions. Usually several women and their children do their gathering work together, because, as the Batek say, large noisy groups are the best defense against tigers, the predators they fear most. Mothers carry their nursing infants and sometimes the next youngest child as well. They rarely need to walk more than an hour from camp. While the women dig up the wild yams, the children watch, play, and sometimes dig, either as imitative play or—in the case of older children—real work. Adults do not expect children to work at food-getting but welcome any contributions the children want to make. Even when they are not actively working, children who accompany their mothers on gathering expeditions learn how to find and procure tubers, a job that both sexes will do as adults. Batek children see and learn the full range of foodgetting work in which women engage, including digging, collecting fruits and nuts, fishing, and hunting bamboo rats by digging them out of their burrows and killing them.

While the women and children are off on gathering trips, the men either hunt or collect rattan or other trade goods. Some women also work at collecting rattan, but children are not normally involved in these activities. The Batek say that men do not take children with them on hunting trips because the children are too noisy, which scares off the game, and because children would want to be carried over the several miles that men may traverse while hunting.

There are times when mothers want to work without taking their children with them. Mothers occasionally leave children in camp with an older sibling or grandparent or other adult who happens to be remaining there for the day. Frequently, however, there is no one who could look after children in camp, since most people, even the elderly, are engaged in some sort of food-getting activity outside of camp each day. Even if someone is planning to remain in camp, children may not be willing to stay with them. I have heard mothers try to convince children to remain in camp by telling them that there are many leeches in the forest. If children strongly resist being left behind, the mothers usually give in and take them along. When a mother feels the need to work away from her children, she usually arranges to do so when the father is home. In the sense of children being willing to remain with someone other than the mother, fathers are the secondary caregivers in Batek society.

The Batek do not rely on sibling babysitting as frequently or for as long a period as occurs in many other societies (see Weisner and Gallimore 1977:169–180), in part because of the frequent unwillingness of young children to part from their mothers and because older children often are engaged in work or play activities that take them out of camp. Also unlike many societies, the Batek do not give preference to sisters over brothers as babysitters. Any child considered capable of keeping an eye on a younger sibling may be called into action if he or she is available. As noted above, the Batek relationship terms for siblings do not make a distinction between genders—brothers and sisters are referred to with the same term—but the terms do distinguish between older sibling (*to'*) and younger sibling (*ber*). The linguistic focus on the relative age of siblings may well be correlated with the fact that a child has a different relationship with an older sibling than a younger one, for at times older siblings serve as caregivers for younger siblings.

From about age 5 to age 9 children spend much of their time in mixed-sex, multi-age playgroups that ebb and flow according to the imagination of the children involved. In that younger children play with older children, these groups can be considered a childcare situation, but generally children do not spend much time in these groups until they are old enough and self-reliant enough to feel comfortable being away from their parents. Playgroup activities range from pretending to move camp to imitating monkeys to play-practicing economic skills such as blowpipe-hunting, digging tubers, collecting rattan, and fishing. Fathers sometimes intervene in the activities of children to offer advice about how to perform these skills. For example, when several children were pretending that they were harvesting honey by smoking bees out of a hive high in a tree in the middle of camp, a father who often participated in honey collecting showed the children how to properly construct rattan ladders to use for climbing up to the hive. It was the older boys, in the 10- to 12-year-old range, who paid closest attention to this informal lesson.

From the 10- to 12-year age range onward, children spend less and less time in mixed-sex playgroups and more time with same-sex peers and adults. Fathers increasingly take on a more formalized teaching role toward their maturing sons as the boys join men on hunting trips and learn the other economic tasks that men do. At the same time, maturing girls increasingly spend time learning from their mothers and other women how to weave pandanus and perform the economic jobs that women do. Batek children gradually take on these adult work patterns without being overtly pressured by their parents. I have no evidence that girls are actively discouraged from going on hunting trips, for example, but it does appear that the men do not ask them to come along or make a special effort to teach them. Older boys are free to accompany their mothers on gathering trips, but generally have a greater interest in furthering their hunting skills.

Parents do not overtly pressure children into taking up the work patterns of adult men and women. Moreover, the Batek have no initiation rituals to mark—or impose—the end of childhood or entrance into adulthood. What seems to guide children's adoption of adult sex roles is the positive role models that men and women alike provide. Batek men and women appear to be self-confident, enthusiastic about their activities, and generally satisfied with their work and their lives (cf. Draper 1975a:83). Draper gives a similar account of !Kung sex role acquisition:

> Beatrice Whiting (personal communication) has pointed out that since both men and women of the hunting and gathering groups of !Kung have equal power, girls should have little conflict in identifying with the same sex parent. Possibly in this egalitarian setting (and others) learning of sex roles can proceed largely by identification for both sexes and without the need for overt instruction as it occurs in many other societies and ritual guises. (1975b:611)

The positive model that adults present to children extends to their parental as well as their economic roles. Children see that their parents engage in the same range of responsibilities and activities: both parents provide food and take care of sons and daughters. There seems to be little reason that Batek children would not readily adopt the behavior patterns of their appropriate sex group.

In addition to the positive role models that Batek boys and girls receive from their same-sex group, they also receive positive reinforcement from adults of the opposite sex. Various researchers have stressed the influence that positive treatment from the opposite-sex parent has on a person's self-image. In his overview of child-development studies, Lamb writes:

As far as sex role development is concerned, the father's masculinity and his status in the family are correlated with the masculinity of his sons and the femininity of his daughters. However, this association depends on the fathers having sufficient interaction with their children—thus the extent of the father's commitment to childrearing is crucial. One of the best established findings is that the masculinity of sons and femininity of daughters is greatest when fathers are nurturant and participate extensively in childrearing. (1981:20)

As we have seen, Batek mothers and fathers interact with their children in similar fashion and treat their sons and daughters equally in terms of attention, affection, and expectations. Moreover, Batek culture does not downgrade or differentially evaluate the activities of either sex. There is no cultural inducement for fathers to denigrate daughters, and Batek fathers do not do it.

THEORETICAL THEMES AND THE BATEK CASE

Recent concerns in child-development research include such questions as: How much time must parents spend with their children in order to influence their development (see Hewlett 1987)? Is "quality time" more important than the quantity of time parents spend with their children (see Lamb 1981:5)? How does the absence of the father affect child development (Chodorow 1974:49–55; Lamb; 1981:27–30)? What kind of childrearing fosters equal social relations between the sexes (see Chodorow 1974:66)?

The Batek case shows us how one egalitarian society handles childrearing. Batek children below age 10 spend most of their day with their parents. They are usually with their mothers during working hours—5 to 6 hours per day 5 days per week—and with either or both parents for the remainder of the time. There are no commitments other than work that draw either parent away from family interactions, and during their in-camp labors, each parent is available to interact with the children. Both mothers and fathers provide their children with food, housing, physical care, affection, guidance, and informal and formal education for the skills that children must acquire.

Chodorow suggests that in societies in which men work away from their children, sons lack a means of identifying with their fathers. She contends that the absence of the father causes the son to identify

with a fantasied masculine role, because the reality constraint that contact with his father would provide is missing. In all societies characterized by sex segregation (even those in which a son will eventually lead the same sort of life as his father), much of a boy's masculine identification must be of this sort, that is, with aspects of his father's role, or what he fantasies to be a male role, rather than with his father as a person involved in a relationship to him. (1974:50)

Does the fact that young Batek children—boys as well as girls—spend 5 to 6 hours per day 5 days per week accompanying their mothers on food-getting work imply that Batek society is sex-segregated or that Batek children are unfamiliar with the work of the men, and that boys can only fantasize about the male role?

In fact, there are opportunities for even the youngest of Batek children of both sexes to witness men's hunting activities. Occasionally, a wife and children accompany a man on a hunt. Sometimes when people travel through the forest to move camp, they come across game. If so, men take up their blowpipes and dispatch the animal in full view of the children. At times people sight game close to camp, providing yet another opportunity for children to witness men's hunting activities. Older children, usually boys but some interested girls as well, spend many hours practicing with blowpipes near camp. Younger children can observe them shooting dirt pellets in attempts to bring down squirrels and birds. Hunters carve darts, prepare poison, and produce and repair their blowpipes—tasks necessary for hunting—during their time in camp, where their efforts can be observed by anyone. Children of both sexes carve darts for fun or to use. Thus, even though children do not usually accompany men on the hunt, they are well aware of the kind of activity that their fathers do.

So it is with rattan collection as well. There are enough times when young children witness rattan work that even though they do not constantly accompany rattan workers, they know what these workers do when they are away from camp. Children even incorporate this knowledge into their play; one of their many activities is pretending to collect rattan.

The economic activities of men do not appear to constitute a realm of mystery and fantasy for Batek children in the way that Chodorow suggests is the case when men work away from their families. Moreover, the economic activities that both boys and girls learn during early childhood from accompanying their mothers and other women on their gathering work become part of their adult work repertoire.

Batek fathers' involvement with childcare is similar to fathering in some other hunting and gathering societies. For example, Hewlett shows that among the Aka Pygmies men play a major role in childcare. Not only do they carry children back from net-hunts when mothers transport meat back to camp, but fathers also hold and tend to children's physical needs with such frequency that they are the "secondary infant and child caretakers" (Hewlett 1987:323). He attributes the Aka organization of childcare to "male and female overlapping subsistence patterns, and the great distances traveled by women while engaged in subsistence activities" (Hewlett 1987:323), which, he says, favors fathers rather than sisters as secondary caretakers. Estioko-Griffin writes of childcare among the Agta of the Philippines, "Mothers and females in general are most decidedly the major child tenders in Agta society. Mothers do the greatest share, followed by elder sisters and grandmothers. Fathers are fourth, but still spend a significant amount of time caring for their children. Young fathers of two or three children assist their wives in child care every day. These fathers often carry older children, aged about three to eight, on foraging trips outside of camp, tending the children while mothers spearfish or gather" (1987:237). Katz and Konner discuss the interrelationship of childcare and socioeconomic factors. They write:

> Using a scale of father-infant "proximity," variations found in a sample of 80 nonindustrial societies are related to family and community organization and economic adaptation. Fathers are more likely to be in proximity to their infants in monogamous, nuclear-family, and nonpatrilocal cultures and in subsistence adaptations in which the mother makes a large contribution to the resources of the family. On this scale, fathers are relatively "close" among foragers, who represent the sociocultural adaptation that existed for 99 percent of human history. (Katz and Konner 1981:181)

Katz and Konner's correlations provide evidence that economic and social factors influence the parental division of labor. The "close fathering" that is found in some foraging societies suggests that except for their biological inability to breast-feed infants, males are as capable as females in caring for children, a notion that challenges long-held stereotypes in many cultures.

As we are well aware, our own culture largely views childcare as women's work, in part because the culture regards women as nurturing, caring, and other-oriented while men are regarded as more distant, even to the point of being unable to sustain the emotional closeness attributed to women (see Chodorow 1974:54–60). Lamb outlines Parsons' child-development schema that holds that during the pre-Oedipal phase of childhood, mothers played "expressive (nurturant, empathic) and instrumental (competence-directed, achievement-focused) functions in relation to the child" but that after that period fathers become the instrumental parent (Lamb 1981:10). Lamb's overview of western-oriented child-development studies concludes:

> On the whole, the empirical evidence is consistent with the theoretical predictions. Fathers and mothers both appear to be psychologically salient to their children from the time the children are infants, and they appear to

adopt differentiable roles from this point on. Mothers are consistently assigned responsibility for nurturance and physical childcare, whereas fathers tend to be associated with playful interaction as well as with demands that children conform to cultural norms. Fathers do appear to be more demanding and exacting, as social learning theorists, psychoanalysts, and Parsonians assumed. Whether or not they have more influence on them, fathers are more involved in the socialization of sons than of daughters. (1981:16–67)

Although this assessment of parental behaviors may be accurate for our own culture, it does not hold true cross-culturally. For example, Hewlett's observations of the Aka present a very different view of parental roles. He notes, for example, that Aka fathers do not engage in the rough-and-tumble play that characterizes the style of playful interaction in which western fathers engage (1987:311). Instead, Aka fathers' interactions with their infants included holding, kissing, hugging, transporting, and taking care of their physical needs. Hewlett writes: "Fathers also offered their nipple to the infant when the infant tried to nurse, often cleaned dirt from the infant's nose, chest, and hair as they held the infant; picked lice from their hair; cleaned mucus from their nose; and cleaned them after they urinated or defecated (often on the father)" (1987:326). Similarly, Batek men carry children who are too young to walk distances on their own but have been displaced by a younger sibling, they bathe their children and tend to the excretory needs, and serve as sources of comfort.

These behaviors cut across the western associations cited above: that mothers nurture while fathers instruct, demand, and engage in specific sorts of play with their children. Profoundly influencing parental behaviors in a society are that society's beliefs about the physical, intellectual, or emotional attributes of the sexes. The kind of fathering that occurs among the Aka and the Batek would be unacceptable among Bimin-Kuskusmin of New Guinea, for example, a society that considers the bodily substances of women to be so polluting that fully initiated men avoid direct contact with unweaned children (Poole 1981:138–9; see also Douglas 1966:149,173). The Batek say that men can run faster and blow darts more strongly than women, and they say that the blood of men and women smell different. Although the Batek do not symbolically elaborate these perceived differences or use them as the basis for evaluative judgments about the sexes, their division of labor in parenting is affected by them. The Batek association of males' greater speed and breath strength with men's responsibility for blowpipe-hunting affects the availability of men for childcare. While the Batek believe that male and female blood smells different, it is usually the mother rather than the father who performs the blood sacrifice on behalf of a child—male or female—who breaks a prohibition that can only be righted by making this retribution to the punitive thundergod. To perform the blood sacrifice, transgressors draw a few drops of blood from their leg, mix the blood with water, and throw the liquid upward toward the thundergod. Rather than subject young children to the bloodletting, parents usually cut their own legs and smear the blood on the child's leg to trick the thundergod into believing that it is the child's own blood. While the Batek statement that male and female blood smells different would suggest that fathers would make the blood sacrifice on behalf of their sons and mothers would perform it for daughters, the Batek leave it to whoever saw a child act in a manner that may have earned the wrath of the thundergod. As it is the mothers who spend the most time with children, they are more likely than fathers to observe children's transgressions. (One woman offered a simple explanation: women usually do the blood sacrifice for children because the men are too scared. She punctuated her statement with a howl of laughter.)

The cross-cultural variability of parental roles should lead us to question how much of our own categorization of western parental roles has to do with cultural belief rather than scientific reality. For example, are women really more nurturing, emotional, and caring than men, or does the cultural expectation that that is how mothers should act influence women to fit themselves to these stereotypes? Are men really stronger, more independent, and rational, or does our culture expect them to fit these patterns? Is western fathering geared toward fulfilling these expectations? Do western fathers engage their children in rough-and-tumble play, for example, because it fits western stereotypes of how men should behave?

Our difficulty in separating our beliefs about the sexes from our ideas about the nature of mothering and fathering suggests that the division of labor in parenting is a powerful phenomenon. It not only reflects cultural ideas about the sexes, but effectively reproduces them by shaping the very interactions that mothers and fathers can have with their children and molding a child's earliest views of what it is that men and women do.

REFERENCES

Bowlby, J. 1969. *Attachment and Loss*. New York: Basic Books.

Chodorow, N. 1974. Family structure and feminine personality. In *Woman Culture, & Society*, M. Z. Rosaldo and L. Lamphere (Eds.), pp. 43–66. Stanford: Stanford University Press.

Douglas, M. 1966. *Purity and Danger: An Analysis of Concepts of Pollution and Taboo*. Harmondsworth: Penguin Books.

Draper, P. 1975a. !Kung women: Contrasts in sexual egalitarianism in foraging and sedentary contexts. In *Toward an Anthropology of Women*, R. R. Reiter (Ed.), pp. 77–109. New York: Monthly Review Press.

――――. 1975b. Cultural pressure on sex differences. *American Ethnologist* 2(4): 602–616.

Endicott, K. L. 1979. Batek Negrito sex roles. Unpublished M.A. thesis, The Australian National University, Canberra.

――――. 1980. Batek Negrito sex roles: Behavior and ideology. Paper presented to Second International Conference on Hunting and Gathering Societies, Quebec (printed in proceedings of the conference).

――――. 1981. The conditions of egalitarian male-female relationships in foraging societies. *Canberra Anthropology* 4(2):1–10.

――――. 1984. The Batek De' of Malaysia: Development and egalitarian sex roles. *Cultural Survival Quarterly* 8(2):6–8.

――――. 1986. Batek socialization and kinship. Paper prepared for the Fourth International Conference on Hunting and Gathering Societies, London (printed in proceedings of the conference).

Endicott, K. M. 1979. *Batek Negrito Religion: The World-view and Rituals of a Hunting and Gathering People of Peninsular Malaysia.* Oxford: Clarendon Press.

Estioko-Griffin, A. 1987. Daughters of the forest. In *Anthropology: Contemporary Perspectives*, 5th ed., P. Whitten, and, D. E. K. Hunter (Eds.), pp. 234–237. Boston: Little, Brown.

Hewlett, B. 1987. Intimate fathers: Patterns of paternal holding among Aka Pygmies. In *Father's Role in Cross-Cultural Perspective*. M. E. Lamb (Ed.), pp. 295–330. New York: Erlbaum.

Hewlett, B. 1991. *Intimate Fathers: The Nature and Context of Aka Pygmy Paternal Infant Care.* Ann Arbor: University of Michigan Press.

Katz, M. M., and Konner, M. J. 1981. The role of the father: An anthropological perspective. In *The Role of the Father in Child Development*, M. E. Lamb (Ed.), pp. 155–185. New York: Wiley.

Lamb, M. E. 1981. Fathers and child development: An integrative overview. In *The Role of the Father in Child Development*, M. E. Lamb (Ed.), pp. 1–70. New York: Wiley.

Poole, F. J. P. 1981. Transforming 'natural' woman: Female ritual leaders and gender ideology among Bimin-Kuskusmin. In *Sexual Meanings: The Cultural Construction of Gender and Sexuality*, S. B. Ortner and H. Whitehead (Eds.), pp. 116–165. Cambridge: Cambridge University Press.

Rosaldo, M. Z. 1974. Woman, culture, and society: A theoretical overview. In *Woman, Culture, and Society*, M. Z. Rosaldo and L. Lamphere (Eds.), pp. 17–42. Stanford: Stanford University Press.

Weisner, T. S., and Gallimore, R. 1977. My brother's keeper: Child and sibling caretaking. *Current Anthropology* 18(2):169–190.

Chapter 14

Fathers and Childcare among the Cagayan Agta

P. Bion Griffin and Marcus B. Griffin

Fathers' caregiving to children among the Agta foragers of the Philippines is especially interesting because of the participation of women in hunting wild pig and deer. The lack of a pronounced gender division of labor in many areas of life places fathers in a context in which their attention to children may be critical to mothers' success in food provisioning and in bearing and rearing children. Among the Cagayan Agta resident in the early 1980s around the Nanadukan River of coastal Cagayan, women hunting in teams secured one third the wild pigs and one-fifth the deer. Joining parties of men, they helped kill even more (Estioko-Griffin 1985; Goodman et al. 1985a). The predilection of women to contribute to animal protein acquisition and to be active in all subsistence efforts places them at one end of the forager scale of female food-getting efforts, contrasting with perhaps the other extreme, Ache foragers of Paraguay (Hurtado et al. 1985). Initial analyses of childcare among the Agta suggested that mothers predominate in the in-camp care of children (Goodman et al. 1985a) despite their engagement in all subsistence activities. The importance of women's hunting and seeming effectiveness of parenting has led to the interests in the present chapter: understanding variables that affect the parenting behaviors of Agta fathers and mothers. We will examine Agta caregiving with a focus on the men.

THE AGTA

The Agta are foragers scattered throughout the range of mountains that parallels the Pacific Ocean coast on the eastern side of the main island of the northern Philippines (Griffin 1989). Diversity in habitat is typical of the Agta natural environment. The Sierra Madre is a semi-seasonal tropical rain forest, extremely broken and rugged, and cut by innumerable streams and rapidly falling rivers. The coastline is equally rugged, fronting the rough Pacific. Few coral reefs shelter the beaches or provide easy littoral zone fishing. Along much of its length the mountains drop through narrow foothills into the ocean. Even the valleys of the East running rivers afford few alluvial flats, excepting those adjacent to the two or three major rivers. Still, the rivers and lower elevation streams are abundant in fish and shellfish. The forest is, or was, very rich in faunal resources.

Agta are in a sense typical Southeast Asian foragers, with a dependent economic relationship with neighboring nonforaging peasants and proletarians (Griffin 1991; Rai 1990; Headland 1986; Peterson 1978). The social environment of neighboring groups is one of increasingly numerous near-subsistence level farmers, poor fisherfolk, and wage laborers, the latter numerically dominated by loggers. Traditional swidden horticulturalists are few, although in past decades they comprised the bulk of the non-Agta population. Non-Agta provision Agta with the bulk of their plant foodstuffs, especially rice. They also sell consumer goods, tobacco, liquor, and tools. Subsistence activities and the gender division of labor revolve around extraction of forest and aquatic resources and their exchange for rice, maize, root crops, and the materials of daily life: cloth, metal, tobacco, medicine, and consumer goods.

Agta are not in a position to dictate the terms of their exchanges, being dominated by their nonforager neighbors. Non-Agta can usually do without Agta goods; meatless meals are the rule, hence forest game may be refused unless the price is right. Fish may be procured from sources other than Agta. Other forest products are even less necessary. Agta labor may be useful, even critical, on rare occasions, but Agta need the payment more than non-Agta need the product. Agta hunt wild pig and deer for exchange and consumption, usually selling the highest quality portions. Wild pig fat is favored by non-Agta and Agta, being most needed and most available in the cold rainy season. Fish are caught primarily in the dry season and make up an important component of exchange because of low price and favored place in non-Agta diets.

Agta men are all hunters and fishermen. In the Southeast Cagayan region they may occasionally engage in labor for peasants or proletarians, but they prefer to exchange meat and fish for needed food and goods. Men also collect rattan for sale and clear and plant small swidden plots of upland rice and root crops. Women undertake the same work, consuming or exchanging their production in much the same manner as the men. The gender division of labor, flexible as it is, emically places primary responsibility for childrearing on mothers, yet enables women to engage as actively as they choose in subsistence efforts. They allocate less time to hunting than do men and usually undertake less fishing in dangerous water, but do participate differentially according to family demands, health, and place in the life cycle. The Agta, like many foragers, may be directly involved with subsistence efforts only a few hours per day, but engage in maintenance activities at a leisurely pace much of the day and into the evening hours.

The Agta settlement system involves residential clusters of related kin and a flexibility in household location. Movement to and from the cluster is easy and common. Each nuclear family, occasionally polygynous in marriage, resides in its own small house, placed close to extended family members within the residential cluster of the local group (Figure 1). A local group is always an aggregate of family members, all closely related through consanguinity or marriage. Typically an elder parent or parents will be senior members, but the local group tends to be built around sibling bonds. Sisters favor living together, but the ideal is met only in a transitory fashion. Size of the local cluster fluctuates within a range of 15 to 35 members. Dry season cluster tend to be often at or below 15, while rainy season residential groups may sporadically reach 50 members. Entrance to a group depends on having

Figure 1. An Agta residential cluster; father and mother build a house while a son plays.

a kinsperson to bond to and to a certain degree on adequacy of local food resources. Departure stems from choosing to seek more favorable resources elsewhere, tensions of the moment, and desire to visit other kin. The entire group moves occasionally, either together or splitting into separate families. Movement is partly seasonal, since rainy season clusters must be located carefully, taking account of possible typhoon, flooding, and food resource conditions, as well as ease of access to trade partners. The dry season allows a greater dispersal, and sees the cluster often breaking into smaller clusters that locate near specific resources. Only exceptionally do nuclear families split up, for example, during foraging trips of several nights duration undertaken by men.

As noted, polygyny is an option for Agta and is seen in about 20% of the marriages. It is nearly always explained as a necessity due to infertility of the first wife. No cases of three wives were observed, although one polyandrous marriage was seen and one other reported. Divorce is frequent before a child is born, but discouraged by family members after. Remarriage of widows and widowers is usual for reproductively active men and women. Elderly people who cannot provide for a family most often assist their children and grandchildren, who in turn care for them in infirmity. Postmarital residence is flexible; usually the groom joins his young wife at her parents' cluster until after the first child survives its first year. Then a visit to his family is made. After that, about 2 years residence alternating between families is the ideal pattern.

Kinship is bilaterally organized and little differentiation of mother's and father's kin is made; in-laws are accorded respect through deference and assistance. The kinship terminology follows the "eskimo" system, or a terminology of reference basically like Americans use. The biological father is called *amang* ("father"), mother *ina* or *inang*, all parents' siblings *amai* "uncle," *manay* "aunt," and siblings are divided on the basis of older or younger than ego, but not on the basis of gender. Cousins are simply cousins *pensan* or *kasinsin*, and nieces and nephews are lumped in one gender-free category.

An adult Agta is fortunate to have surviving parents. Grandparents are rare. Childhood mortality is high, although not atypical of foraging people. Census data collected in southern Cagayan and northern Isalela Provinces indicate approximately 49% of prepubescent children die, usually of respiratory and digestive system disease, perhaps exacerbated by poor nutrition. Women have many children, have short birth intervals, and lose many infants. The average birth interval over all orders for 143 live births among the Agta where an infant survived until the birth of the next sibling was 2.85 (SD 1.35). If only birth intervals where the infant survived to the birth of the next sibling are considered, the average spacing in 56 cases among Agta women over 45 at the time of the survey was 3.05 years (SD 1.53) (Goodman et al. 1985b: 176).

The average completed parity for these latter women is 6.53 live births. While the mean number of live births for the whole group was 4.39 (SD 3.62), the mean number of still living children was only 2.91 (SD 2.90) (Goodman et al. 1985b: 172). These data suggest a major childcare burden on mothers and, as we shall see, the need for fathers to provide care in those cases of several closely spaced living children.

AGTA INFANCY AND CHILDHOOD

The Agta infant joins a compact and intimate family unit, one spatially segregated but still close to other units. Agta children are born into a space that includes the father. From the first day the father, unless he dies, is within touching distance. He sleeps beside his children at night, eats from the same pot at meals, and is present during illnesses and hunger. The baby remains against the body of the mother nearly constantly in its first weeks, but is also in contact with father, siblings if any, and other kin that may drop in to visit, nap, or play. Dogs may as well be warm bodies tucked nearby at night. Babies sleep by mothers' breasts, between mother and father. Older children, depending on ages, position themselves to the other sides of their parents or curl in clusters among themselves and close to the hearth. Grandparents may take in toddlers and older children on a "drop-in" basis or in the case of the parents overnight departure for hunting and fishing. During the first 12 months an infant is usually carried in a sling at the mother's back, side, or front. Since Agta travel frequently, the baby is accustomed to lying quietly during travel or work. Nursed on demand, it is returned to the back for sleeping after suckling. Women are quite comfortable thus engaged in collection of forest materials, and some sporadically hunt and kill game while transporting the baby. As the baby grows in its first year, it is increasingly handled by others, albeit in brief episodes. The Agta follow the widespread Philippine custom of giving much attention to infants and toddlers, and an infant under 1 year may be passed among several adults and youths, being returned to its mother if it becomes fussy.

During childhood, from the stage the toddler of 1 to 2 years until about 10 years, Agta become increasingly independent of adult supervision, competent in dealing with the environment, and responsible in family matters. The small child is accorded an amount of freedom of movement that would frighten a non-Agta Filipino mother and perhaps horrify a Euro-American. Playing near open fires, with large knives, and in rivers is commonplace. On the other hand, the mother or any attendant is charged with very serious responsibility in caring for a child and is strongly and openly criticized in the event of errors in care. Children continue to sleep with parents, although as they grow they increasingly overnight with friends (usually cousins) and their parents. Sometimes a vacant dwelling is commandeered by a cluster of children, often accompanied by a teenaged sibling.

Children are left in camp by mothers at increasingly frequent and lengthy intervals. Late in the first year an infant may be left for an hour or two; sisters or mother's mother or father are acceptable caregivers. At Nanadukan (see discussions of Agta individuals below), one sister sporadically nursed her sister's infant as well as her own, permitting the young mother time outside the camp. More frequently, however, babies are carried by mothers until the age of 2 or slightly more, when they are considered heavy for carrying on longer trips. Mothers of two or three small children usually work in teams in the forest, assisting each other with the children. Older girls are involved also.

Economic demands on children of 10 and under are minimal. Fetching items, including water and firewood, or simply running errands may be expected. Children do forage in play groups, killing and consuming birds, fish, and shellfish. Fruit collection, sometimes in the company of a grandparent or adult women, is a frequent affair. As children approach the age of 10, they are more often seen in babysitting tasks themselves, assisting mothers with younger siblings or just guarding them from mishap. Play groups are not age or gender segregated, but made up of most children in local group, or by whoever is inclined to join in play. Teen-aged girls bring toddlers on their hips to observe or join play. When not playing outside the home, children often sit, crawl, and run around in or about the house. Children groom each other, and rest as elder children and adults, usually mothers, delouse them. No Agta in our acquaintance has admitted to a gender preference in children, other than desiring a mix of girls and boys. Pedicide of newborns is known but is considered inappropriate behavior. Few cases were found in Agnes Estioko-Griffin's reproductive history research (Goodman et al. 1985a,b). We believe but cannot quantitatively demonstrate that adopted orphans receive care inferior to that given one's own children. Orphans are always close kin, the children of siblings or cousins. Aside from orphans, very occasional adoption is known. Among our host residential cluster, the eldest son of an eldest daughter was adopted by grandparents and treated as a son. Since the parents were sometimes within the group the caregiving lines were vague. When the "grandfather" was killed, the adopted boy returned to his biological parents [in turn, his father was killed, and he returned again to his grandmothers (co-wives/co-widows)]. Adoption, then, serves to support orphans of close kin or to give one of several siblings to still strong older adults.

AGTA FATHERS

Two sources of data are used to describe and understand Agta fathers, as well as children and mothers; one source relies on spot focal samples of community members general activities ("Daily Activity Record") and childcare ("Childcare Record") events as well as subsistence activity-related data. The other uses less systematically, or at least quantitatively collected data, and is built from field observations found in daily notes concerning Agta behavior. While one research goal of the 1980–1992 project concerned childcare, caregivers, and activities of children, we did not as fully record fathers' actions while with children as we now see possible (Hewlett 1987, 1988). The childcare record involved randomly selecting infants and small children for eight spot observations again randomly selected for on the hour observations, beginning at 0500 and ending at 1900. At each of the observations the kinship category of the attended was recorded, and the appropriate codes for the activities of both the attendant and the child were entered on the form. The randomized top-of-the-hour observations were designed to reveal variations in activities over the course of the day. As seen in the pattern of attendants for all children, no marked variation existed throughout the day (Goodman et al. 1985a). In this chapter the hourly observations are consolidated into simple percentage vis-à-vis children's caregivers. Observations were made of 21 children, although in uneven numbers relative to age and to total per child. This is an artifact of the changing presence within the local cluster of given children and their parents. Age division membership includes under 6 months (1), 6 months to 1 year (3), 1 to 2 years (5), 2 to 3 years (1), 3 to 4 years (2), 4 to 5 years (4), and 5 to 8 years (5). Sixteen boys and five girls were present. (This male to female ratio is only accidental; no excessive female mortality can be discerned in our data to date.)

The record of adults' general activities was also a spot focal recording of coded observations, but done by 15-minute intervals. The bulk of these data come from dawn to early evening observations, and in this chapter include those from 0500 to 2000. In addition to subsistence tasks, a variety of maintenance, leisure, and childcare activities were recorded. From these data we gain a second glimpse at fathers' activities and the ability to compare them with mothers.

Analysis of the childcare record (Table 1) indicates that within an "at home" context, that is within the residential cluster, mothers of children from age 10 to 8 years are caregivers slightly more than 50% of the time. Grandmothers and elder sisters come in at a modest 7.5 and 10.4%, and fathers follow with only 4.4%.

Table 1. Childcare Provided by Attendant Number of Observations over 282 Person-Days, 8 Observations/Day: Children ages: Infant–8 Years

Attendant	Percent	Number
Mother	51.7	1166
Father	4.4	99
Grandmother	7.5	170
Grandfather	1.4	34
Elder sister	10.4	225
Elder brother	1.1	25
None	18.8	424
Other[a]	5.1	115
Total	100.0	2256

[a] In descending importance: aunts, cousins, anthropologists.

Examination of the daily activity record data (Table 2), arranged by spouse couples, suggests general patterns of father and mother attention to infants and small toddlers. The activities are limited to those within the residential area, and subsume a variety of acts under the several categories. For example, "babysitting" may involve holding a child, or keeping it within reaching distance. Most likely the child is either asleep or playing adjacent to the sitter (Figure 2). Carrying in camp is "overrecorded" in the sense that the Daily Activity Record does not detail carrying, or any childcare during subsistence work or other travel. In any case, the pattern between men and women, and among men, is indicative of childcare emphases at home. As will be developed later in biographical sketches of fathers, we see Tomba aged 30 and father of four, a much more active caregiver than Sikel, aged 42 and father of two, one a girl of 15, or than Heting, aged 53, and father of six, ranging from teenagers to an infant. Table 3 also compares Tomba and Heting.[1] Maymayan's new infant, born during data collection, accounts for the relatively high babysitting events within only 5 days of observation. As with most young first time fathers, Hurere helped with the infant. Lakop, an experienced father, saw little need to babysit, especially since his wife Dagew did little else, seldom undertaking any subsistence or maintenance activities. Aking, aged 36, and father of a toddler and a boy of 6, occasionally babysat, or tended the children when his wife Ogay joined her sister Iring and mother Abey in work. Both Iring and Ogay availed themselves of childcare from their mother Abey as needed, and as reflected in Table 1. She was one of two or three grandmothers in the sampled group, Taytayan, the mother of Paola and Maymayan being the principal other. Angaden and Kuya were newlyweds with their first child. Angaden, a very active hunter–fisher,

Table 2. Father–Mother Pairs and Respective Childcare Activities from the Daily Activity Record[a]

Spouse set	Babysitting	Carrying	Feeding	Nursing	Playing
Fa: Tomba (9)	62	1	—	—	—
Mo: Paola (5)	91	—	4	5	—
[1–2]					
Fa: Hurere (7)	23	23	—	—	—
Mo: Maymayan (5)	120	24	—	26	5
[<1]					
Fa: Aking (4)	11	—	—	—	—
Mo: Ogay (1)	19	—	—	—	—
[1–2]					
Fa: Lakop (1)	2	1	—	—	—
Mo: Dagew (1)	15	—	—	5	1
[<1]					
Fa: Angaden (2)	2	1	—	—	—
Mo: Kuya (2)	37	12	—	10	—
[<1]					
Fa: Sikel (10)	—	—	—	—	—
Mo: Iring (8)	155	11	11	7	—
[1–2]					
Fa: Heting (5)	—	—	—	—	—
Mo: Leti (8)	136	66	1	18	—
[<1]					

[a]The number of days observed is given next to the name of each mother or father. The age of the child is given in brackets under the parents' names. The number under each column is the total number of observations for the given number of days observed (60 observations per day).

neither emphasized nor disparaged tending his infant. While both Tomba and Hurere were active hunters, they chose to spend time with wives and children. Tomba's several children necessitated both parents' care. Any birth is believed to necessitate that careful attention be given to mother and child, because of the high mortality rate of babies under 2 years of age (Goodman et al. 1985b). The data on carrying reflect the standard behavior observable throughout any day among the Agta. Infants are carried in a cloth sling much of the time before exploratory crawling and first walking begins. Carrying does not cease then; usually a toddler is carried frequently by the mother. Toddlers are always carried over distances of more than 50 or so meters. Not infrequently, when families travel together, the mother carries a heavy weight of

Figure 2. Agta fathers relaxing with their families.

household belongings while the father carries hunting and fishing tools and a small child. Two forms of carrying might be noted: the regular carrying of infants and the carrying of older children, ages 1 to 6 or so on travels. Even around camp, young are carried when, for example, going to the beach to play, or to the river to fetch water, and on firewood collection trips, if the child is not left with the father or other caregiver. The in-camp carrying may be done by elder sisters or occasionally by an elder brother as well as mother, grandmother, and others. Fathers are not frequent in-camp carriers. They are most often seen carrying toddlers and older children on subsistence trips and on residential moves (Figures 3 and 4). Table 2 suggests the importance of carrying infants, since all have a high count per days of observation. Recall that spot checks were made on the first minute of each 15-minute interval. The carrying variation among fathers relates to the family life cycle characteristics as well as personal preferences. Iring did not need much help from Sikel since their 13-year-old daughter was available. Likewise, Leti relied not on her older husband, but on her daughters (see also Table 3). Concerning feeding, the low counts may be a result of the rapid, brief eating episodes typical of most Agta dining as well as the propensity of quick snacks to occur. In addition, the children observed in Table 2 breast-fed more than they consumed solid foods. Playing with infants and children is not a frequent Agta practice, although girls, not adults, pass much time in play activities with infants and small children. Agta fathers and mothers may fondle or simply hold a baby. A mother, unlike

Table 3. Comparison of Caregiving Events in Two Families with Infants and Older Children, Featuring Contrasting Fathers

Couple One:
  Father: Heting age 53
  Mother: Leti age 35
  Infant: Bebe age <1 year
  Child: Luming age >3<5
  Child: Tuhan age >5<9
  Elder sister: Ebi age 13
  Elder sister: Anay age 11
  Elder brother: Ulak age 16

	Observations by caregiver and carereceiver (n = total observations)[a]		
	Bebe (n = 168)	Luming (n = 152)	Tuhan (n = 184)
Mother	125	69	40
Father	—	4	8
Elder sisters	43	74	18
Elder brother	—	1	4
None	—	4	114

Couple Two:
  Father: Tomba age 30
  Mother: Paola age 25
  Toddler: Bondying age >1<2
  Child: Lalokin age >3<5
  Child: Maribet age >5<9
  Grandmother: Taytayan age 43
  Grandmother: Littawan age 45
  Grandfather: Galpong age 50

	Observations by caregiver and carereceiver (n = total observation)[a]		
	Bondying (n = 160)	Lalokin (n = 48)	Maribet (n = 116)
Mother	105	15	44
Father	27	6	8
Grandmothers[b]	16	2	21
Grandfather	2	—	6
None	4	24	37

[a]Small counts by rare caregivers, such as the anthropologists, are not indicated above.
[b]These are "co-grandmothers," sisters, and co-wives of Galpong. Taytayan is the biological grandmother.

a father, will engage a fussing, crying, or upset baby by play attempts and fondling, including rubbing or kissing genitals. Fathers were never observed in this pacification play.

A view of two cases of Agta families' caregiving to both small and larger (up to age 8) children is available in Table 3. Tomba and Heting,

Figure 3. Tomba carrying a son.

who are profiled at length later, were chosen as roughly representative
of the young father with several closely spaced children and as an older
man with several children. Heting is an older man still producing young
children. Leti joined the family as a second wife since the first wife, now
deceased, was infertile. In Tomba's case we note that his caregiving was
supplemented by the maternal grandmothers. Tomba's caregiving,
mostly babysitting at home, decreased slightly proportionate to the
increased age of the child, but the attention to Maribet, a girl of about 8
years, is atypically great. The attention to the toddler son is considerable
and certainly at one end of the range of variation observed. One should
note that Maribet was occasionally herself a caregiver, watching over her
younger brothers (with great concern, empathy, and skill). The case of
Heting and Leti is perhaps another end of the Agta caregiving spectrum.
Tuhan and Luming were young enough to need attention, although
they could join unsupervised play groups nearly at will. In this family

Figure 4. A father helping two children mount his back for carrying.

we see two daughters, the elder already skilled in childcare. Ebi with some help from Anay gave Leti much support in care of the infant Bebe and of her brother Luming. Ulak, by comparison, was a teenage boy and only helped carry a sibling if so instructed. Teenage boys, unlike girls, have minimal caregiving duties. Heting was absent from infant care, but paid more attention to sons as they matured. Tuhan, for example, could accompany Heting and Ulak on brief subsistence excursions and often joined his father and brother on line fishing efforts made a few hundred meters from the houses. Maribet joined Tomba only on subsistence trips when the whole nuclear family went. More often, she stayed at home tending children in concert with Taytayan and Littawan while Tomba, Paola, and Bondying went on upriver on spearfishing trips of a few hours duration.[2]

The question of what fathers do outside of camp is of interest, partly because I argue that, in a way, they do more. Already published data indicate that mothers may hunt, and kill, game while carrying infants and toddlers (none under 6–8 months). Instances of fathers hunting with children or with wives and children were seen (Goodman et al. 1985a; Estioko-Griffin 1985, 1986). Data from the data record of subsistence activities and nonquantitative observations provide the means of describing fathers in the forest. Of 155 hunting events analyzed from the subsistence record, 43 game kills were realized, and of these six involved the presence of children (Table 4). Young mothers, however, are not the major women hunters; mature women with self-sufficient children secure most of the game animals considered by both number and weight. For example, in Table 4, 23 of 29 kills were made by senior women, either singly, with other women, or with men. Only six kills were made by women accompanied by men. Reference to field notes indicates that these five kills were of immature animals, hence less dangerous, less difficult to kill, and less heavy to carry.

The curious condition is not the low counts of women hunters, or the lower counts of hunts involving children, but the success in killing wild pig and deer when children are present. In addition, we see that mothers appear to not be relieved of most childcare, even though they are active in subsistence. Fathers' activities with their children may be examined in this light and through considering the range of activities of children outside the home and in the forest.

The Agta are a very mobile people. Residential locations are sporadically shifted, depending on season and resource availability. Most subsistence efforts necessitate foot travel to collection and processing areas. The forest, streams and rivers, and coastline all yield food and materials for maintenance and exchange. Agta vastly enjoy the forest and highly value human skill in its exploitation. Prospective spouses are judged not so much on physical attractiveness but on ability to collect forest and aquatic foods. Spouses and other lovers retreat to the forest for their most enjoyable lovemaking. New infants are taken into the forest as

Table 4. Agta Quarry by Composition of Hunting Party[a]

	Wild pig	Deer	Monkey
Single male	5 (27.8%)	4 (25.0%)	4 (44.4%)
Team male	1 (5.6%)	—	—
Single female	—	2 (12.5%)	—
Team female	6 (33.3%)	3 (18.8%)	—
Male and female	4 (22.2%)	4 (25.0%)	4 (44.4%)
Male, female, and children	—	3 (18.8%)	1 (11.1%)
Female and children	2 (11.1%)	—	—
Total kill	18 (100%)	16 (100%)	9 (100%)

[a]Taken from Goodman et al. (1985b: 1204).

soon as mothers are up and about following delivery. Nuclear families often make 1 day or overnight foraging trips during the dry season; on these trips some fathers are especially visible in their caregiving. Using qualitative data from field notes, an understanding of fathers' relationships with children may be possible.

Residential moves or visits to other local clusters usually involve carrying all belongings on one's back. Everybody carries, although often women take the bulk of the household effects: mats, blankets, cooking gear, clothes, and food supplies, and infants. Men carry hunting and fishing gear, ready for instantaneous use, and sometimes packs of food such as rice, maize, or roots. They also may carry one, sometimes two children (Figures 3 and 4). If the family composition permits, mothers may hand over children to older girls for carrying; fathers may not carry, or may infrequently carry toddlers or small children. Children of seven and up usually walk and often carry small packs themselves, boys by backpack and girls by trumpline. Little girls carrying puppies in miniature clothslings, reminiscent of adults and infants, may be seen. Travel is slow, rests and snacks frequent compared with subsistence travel, and fathers relaxed.

Subsistence trips may be just that—a rapid trip to hunt, fish, or gather, or it may take on aspects of the residential move as a nuclear family moves for one or a few nights in a forest or beach camp near special resources. The latter replicates much of the larger move, except belongings are left at the residential cluster of the extended family. Fathers carry children and help babysit once the campsite is reached. Usually the wife and older children enter the forest for collection of house-building materials, return, build the house, and cook. The father watches the small children, chews betel nut, and readies his gear for hunting and fishing. On the rapid subsistence trip, a husband and wife often work as a team. Young and old wives are the most frequent participants, but a wife and infant may join the shorter trips, traveling only up to 6 or 7 km over a few hours. Return to camp of older children is expected whether or not the trip is successful. On these trips the husband may carry the infant (not younger than 6 months) until close to the hunting terrain, when he returns the baby to its mother, who follows. She often controls the hunting dogs, running with them, directing them in their search and pursuit of game. The father works to reach points from which he may shoot, either in ambush or in close quarters to cornered game. Should the mother corner the animal, she will seldom set aside the child as might the Aka mother (Hewlett 1987: 303), instead assuming it to be safe and secure on her back. She would attempt to stab the animal with a long-bladed knife or with a knife lashed to a pole on the spot. Not infrequently the woman kills the animal, since the man with the bow hesitates to shoot for fear of hitting one of several dogs caught in the turmoil. In fishing, as is noted below in the discussion of Tomba, men and women usually alternate underwater fishing and warming up while babysitting. Family fishing expeditions are an Agta favorite since the entire family can participate without the rigors of the hunt. All subsistence trips of over 2 or 3 hours duration bring periods of rest and relaxation. Adults chew betel or drink coffee, nap, chat, and watch the children play. Families sit close together, although the children may run in and out of the rest spot.

THE MEN OF NANADUKAN

During major portions of 1980, 1981, and 1982, a local cluster of Agta resided adjacent to the mouth of the Nanadukan River, on the Pacific Coast of Cagayan Province. Two brothers and some of their children remained with the cluster most of the time, and relatives came and went over the years, some staying days or weeks, other months. The principal members of the group were two brothers, Galpong and Heting. Both men were in their fifties and had adult or nearly adult children. Part of 1980 and 1981 Abey, their sister, and her husband and their daughters' families joined the local group. Sibling groups ideally build the core of Agta local groups, although a single parent couple or cousins may suffice when siblings cannot reside together. The Nanadukan core is somewhat unusual in the presence of three relatively old siblings together with their spouses. A fourth, a brother, joined in early 1980, leaving late in the year due to conflicts over relationships with non-Agta. A fifth visited briefly, but regularly resided 2 days walk distance.

Galpong, identified by the Agta as the long-term stable resident of Nanadukan and nearby Malibu, was the husband of Taytayan and Littawan (Estioko-Griffin 1986). Taytayan had two grown and married daughters, discussed in tabular form above, Paola and Maymayan. Littawan was childless. Maymayan, whose husband was Hurere, gave birth to her first child in January 1981, while Paola, married to Tomba, had borne four living children, ranging in age in 1980 from infancy to about 9 years. Paola's eldest, Maling, had been adopted by Galpong, Taytayan, and Littawan and was treated as a son, not a grandson.

Heting had been recently in a polygynous marriage, but his first and childless wife had died, while her co-wife, Leti, was both fertile and relatively successful in keeping her children alive. Her six children ranged from Ulak, a boy of 16, through the infant Bebe. Leti's elder sister, Beting, joined the group for most of 1981, accompanied by her husband Kupel and their two adolescent children, Romi and Adingel, plus an infant boy.

In early 1981 Galpong and Heting's sister and her daughters' families left and were replaced by Sinebo, the brother of Taytayan, and by his two wives Babey, with no surviving children, and Sela, with a daughter, Nati, aged five. These members were among the longer residents in the local group and will illustrate the fathers and their relationships with their families. They seem fairly representative, although the incidence of polygynous marriages associated with female infertility or childhood deaths is high compared with a much larger sample of Agta (Rai 1990; Goodman et al. 1985b).

Galpong was a remarkable man, a charismatic, intelligent, hard working, politically astute senior person. As the principal resident of the area, he exerted influence on the movement of kin to and from the group, and his strong personality both attracted and repelled. Married to two sisters, one equally exceptional, he favored close kin living with him under his direction. Galpong was a grandfather, but in a sense remained a father through having adopted Maling. Maling and his playmates enjoyed sporadic trips with Galpong, especially for honey collection. Net and line fishing with Galpong was a favorite activity for the boy and for Tuhan, Heting's son. Galpong, as tends to be the case for many senior men in polygynous marriages (Hewlett 1988), no longer interested himself directly with infants and toddlers (beyond an occasional and brief embrace, kiss, or cuddle). His wives, however, often had grandchildren with them and they devoted much time to childcare. In their mid-forties, they often verbalized desire for a pregnancy (even inquiring about fertility drugs!). The household and its caregiving clearly demonstrates a strategy that erases lines between grandchildren and children and that maximizes attention to the well-being of offspring. A Darwinian perspective adds some insight into the effectiveness of Galpong's subsistence and caregiving behavior. In addition, Galpong was a kind and loving man.

Tomba (Figure 3) was an extreme in fathering; he had to be and wanted to be. He was a devoted family man and his three younger children loved him dearly. He babysat daily, carried children often, and worked together with Paola. For example, he helped in the rice husking, pounding with a long mortar in concert with Paola. Many men, like most rural Filipinos, considered rice pounding as women's work. Food preparation, cooking, and even (really Agta women's work) collecting firewood was acceptable to Tomba. On fishing trips Tomba watched the children as Paola spearfished. When she became too cold and tired, Tomba fished and Paola warmed herself and babysat. Turns were so taken until a new foraging activity was in order. A man of great patience, he strived to help Paola with her burden of several closely spaced children. Herein lies the critical consideration: young men whose wives have borne several children who lived must assist in caregiving. A woman cannot adequately tend closely spaced children alone. Since the lactation period is briefer than some forgers and birth spacing is shorter, Tomba's situation is not aberrant (Goodman et al. 1985b; Howell 1979; Lee 1979; Blurton Jones 1986). Galpong, on the contrary, had no need to carry children, even as a young man. His two wives or a younger person was always at hand. Tomba, in addition to his caring personality, had no choice. Heting, the older brother of Galpong, exemplifies a senior father with children who invest in caring for younger siblings.

Heting had his surviving children late in life. His first wife died with no surviving children. Long before her death, Heting took Leti as his second wife. Leti lost one child, her first, but that one not to usual illness but to raiders. Raiders are, or were, Agta from different dialect groups who, on long distance raids, killed as many men, women, and children as possible. They are reported to have sporadically kidnapped children who they adopted into their group. (Genealogical investigations reveal deaths and abductions, but no adoptions. The abductions may be a fiction for death by other means. Raiders, however, are genuine, having been known by the writers.)

Heting did not care to play the part of the young, helping father. His elder daughters, Ebi and Anay, were the caregivers and transporters of Leti's younger children. Heting was old and although strong had to concentrate his energy on hunting and other food production. He was friendly with his children, but was an effective disciplinarian. Should Ebi or Anay neglect the little children, strong words or even a blow could result. The junior author remembers, during his many days in the Heting–Leti house, Heting's advice, commands, and his sense of responsibility, but beyond laughs and jokes, little hands-on caregiving. Heting certainly could speak clearly, even kindly, about proper behavior, Agta values, and the human frailties in meeting the values. Physical attention however, was Leti's charge. Heting was neither the source of affection as was Tomba nor the constant humorist as was Galpong. He represented industry and providence in the way that, however, his nephew Kupel did not.

Kupel was married to the sister of Leti. He certainly had rights to claim residence at Nanadukan and Galpong suffered his presence. Kupel represents a rare type in Agta society, yet one that anthropologists should remember exist among all people. To one of Darwinian persuasion, Kupel exemplifies the person likely to have minimal inclusive fitness. To another, he is simply a man less intelligent and successful than are the good hunters and fishers. Perhaps he suffered nutritional deprivation due to his parents' early deaths; orphans *appear* sometimes to fare poorly nutritionally. In any case, Kupel did little to care for his two near-teenage children and infant son. He sat about while Romi and Adingel foraged for *his* food; he hated to work, disliked the rigors of forest and river, and produced little meat, fish, or cultivated food. One of Galpong's favorite "Kupel stories" involved Kupel sitting on a big rock in the middle of the river, taking the sun, while everyone else fished in the cold water. Kupel gave his children little food, little affection, and no praise. He did not teach by example, nor did he counsel wisely. His wife Beting was no improvement. The elder children, however, absorbed proper behavior from Galpong, Heting, and others.

Sinebo (Figure 5), Galpong's brother-in-law, was a loving father but was plagued by the all-too-frequent problem (as the Agta view it) of seeing most of his children die. His two wives had managed to keep only one daughter alive. Others died of malnutrition, illness, and bad luck. Although the observation period was too brief to be certain, Sinebo may have been less than a skillful hunter. He hunted frequently but his catches were poor.

Figure 5. Sinebo helping Nati nock her arrow on a play bow.

Sinebo was an average father in intensity of caregiving. He did not need to help much since both wives poured their attentions on the daughter. A proud father, however, he began taking Nati to the forest on brief hunting trips when she was younger than 10 years. He tried to buy her clothing, although he badly neglected such needs of his wives and himself. Sinebo's lack of success in foraging, in childrearing, and in maintaining the health of his wives dampened his spirits, but he continued to work hard at providing. In 1984 his new baby daughter suffered from serious malnutrition because Sela's milk failed. At considerable cost Sinebo procured milk—but sweetened condensed milk—and the little girl slipped from hunger to retardation. By 1986 she was dead; by 1989 Nati was a young woman engaged to be married. Sinebo hoped that Sela would conceive again, giving him one more chance.

SUMMARY AND CONCLUSIONS

Agta fathers conform to general patterns of human male parenting behaviors in affection, handling, and bodily contact (Eibl-Eibesfeldt 1989: 224–233), to environmental variables affecting humid tropics foraging peoples, and to characteristics in the family composition and life-history events. Their behaviors are best understood in relation to their wives participation in both subsistence work and in childcare. They perform the needed parenting depending on their family situations, based on cultural values seated in a specific environment, and with the knowledge that considerable effort is needed to reduce the high childhood mortality and to keep one's children alive. Fathers and mothers, along with members of the extended family in the local group, strive to daily obtain adequate food resources. They fit their childcare around food-getting options and around the abilities of each other at a given moment.

Fathers' caregiving predictably varies according to the life-history of each family. Most basically, young couples with two or more closely spaced children find fathers' care of children mandatory. Until a daughter is old enough to carry and wisely care for a younger sibling, the father must assist. Men in polygynous families are less likely to be serious caregivers, since seldom would both wives be bearing young children. The presence of teenage girls relieves men from most direct caregiving, although indirect attention still obtains. Throughout our observations, the Agta assigned the caregiver as the mother, even in the usual situation when the father was present and aware of the family activities.

The participation of women in hunting, fishing, and other subsistence and maintenance work originally suggested that men must devote a concomitant amount of time to childcare. On the other hand, Cagayan Agta are unique primarily in the participation of women in hunting. Mothers, therefore, are not atypically demanding of childcare, since they combine hunting with other forest activities. The issue is that the entire range of forest and water subsistence activities favors involvement of women, and mothers are not excluded. Fathers assist women in their forest work when joining themselves. Fathers therefore take their turns caring for small children.

The Agta fathers are not particularly active with children when compared with the !Kung, the Aka, and even the Ache (Maxwell-West and Konner 1976; Hewlett 1987; Hill et al. 1985; Hurtado et al. 1985). Agta young fathers may be especially frequent caregivers, similar to the Aka father, but the Agta case may be striking in the relative withdrawal of grandmothers from major caregiving. Young grandmothers, such as Taytayan and Littawan (Estioko-Griffin 1986), are frequently in the forest. They explicitly and overtly chose hunting and fishing over enhanced childcare. These behaviors place more caregiving time on mothers and fathers.

Cagayan Agta women hunting and fishing are part of group efforts to gain adequate animal protein, fats, and other nutrients and calories. Today the effort is related to gaining meat to exchange for carbohydrate staples—grains and roots.[3] In the past, according to the life-histories collected by Agnes Estioko-Griffin (1986), consumption of fat played an important dietary role and women hunted more than is seen today. Many women, it was recounted, carried bows and arrows during the search for wild roots, abandoning digging for hunting whenever the opportunity arose. The forests may be improvident in wild roots and other starch sources (Griffin 1984; Headland 1987), or the mammalian food resources may be especially provident. In any case, female participation in hunting and fishing is economically and nutritionally advantageous. As women are active in food getting, so men adjust to helping with child care. Women with several small children do not frequently hunt, nor are they especially productive in kills. They must, however, engage in fishing, collection of food, in gathering shellfish and plant foods, and planting small swidden plots. As they feel the burden of tending children, the fathers come to their assistance.

The main conclusion to be drawn from the study of Agta subsistence contributions and child care is that fathers do not assume an unusual amount of parenting duties despite their wives input to the economy. Mothers are still allocated the major responsibilities in childrearing. Fathers remain affectionate, giving care as most fathers do, but they do not as a rule become significant caregivers so that mothers are relieved of the bulk of caregiving. Only in the cases of economic necessity, when wives have several small children, do fathers expend greater parenting efforts. In this they are not unlike other foraging fathers. The Agta case further supports the biological foundation of mothers' special abilities and propensities for child care. Even when Agta women are major food providers they remain the mothers—and fathers do not become mothers.

NOTES

1. For age estimation techniques see Goodman et al. (1985b).
2. Some complexities of these observations have been smoothed over. For example, another brother younger than Anay and older than Luming is included in Heting's family. Paola's eldest son, as discussed elsewhere, was adopted by Galpong, Taytayan, and Littawan and was treated as a son. The caregiving of other local group members, as they came and went, is not discussed herein.
3. Women are very active in the collection of nonfood economic resources. Clark (1990) quantitatively describes the Cagayan Agta women's collection of rattan and wage labor at a time hunting was less feasible.

ACKNOWLEDGMENTS

The families of Nanadukan, now widely scattered and decimated due to the military conflicts between the Armed Forces of the Philippines and the New Peoples' Army, were the hosts and friends of Agnes, Marcus, and Bion Griffin on several occasions from 1980 to 1989. We thank them for their caregiving, hospitality, and interest. Nick Cerra and Pat Jackson of Goodwood Management Corporation Ltd. and Alfonso Lim Jr. of Acme Plywood and Veneer Inc. made our work possible and provided help and friendship; we again thank them. The National Museum of the Philippines approved and supported the research. The National Science Foundation (Grant BNS80-14308), the National Endowment for the Humanities (Grant RO-00168-80-0123), and the University of Hawaii funded the research. We thank these institutions. Special thanks are due Irenäus Eibl-Eibesfeldt and the Max Planck Institute for Human Ethology, Andechs, Germany, for providing the facilities and support for the senior author to work on this paper. Polly Wiessner is thanked for her comments. This paper is dedicated to the memory of Tomba, killed by members of the New Peoples' Army in 1988.

REFERENCES

Blurton Jones, N. 1986. Bushman birth spacing: A test for optimal birth intervals. *Ethology and Sociobiology* 7:91–105.
Clark, C. D. 1990. The trading networks of the Northeastern Cagayan Agta Negritos. Masters Thesis, Department of Anthropology, University of Hawaii, Manoa.

Eibl-Eibesfeldt, I. 1989. *Human Ecology*, Hawthorne, NY: Aldine deGruyter.

Estioko-Griffin, A. 1986. Daughters of the forest. *Natural History* 95(5):36–43.

———. 1985. Women as hunters: The case of an eastern Cagayan group. In *The Agta of Northeastern Luzon: Recent Studies*. P. B. Griffin and A. Estioko-Griffin (Eds.), pp. 18–32. Cebu City, Philippines: San Carlos Publications, University of San Carlos.

Estioko A. A., and Griffin, P. B. 1975. The Ebukid Agta of northeastern Luzon. *Philippine Journal of Culture and Society* 3:237–244.

Goodman, M. J., Griffin, P. B. , Estioko-Griffin, A., and Grove, J. S. 1985a. The compatibility of hunting and mothering among the Agta hunter-gatherers of the Philippines. *Sex Roles* 12(11/12):1199–1209.

Goodman, M. J., Estioko-Griffin, A., Griffin, P. B., and Grove, J. S. 1985b. Menarche, pregnancy, birth spacing and menopause among the Agta women foragers of Cagayan Province, Luzon, the Philippines. *Annals of Human Biology* 12(2):169–177.

Griffin, P. B. 1991. Philippine Agta forager-serfs: Commodities and Philippine Agta Forager-Serfs: Commodities and Exploitation. In *Cash, Commoditisation and Changing Foragers*, edited by Nicolas Peterson and Toshio Matsuyama, Senri Ethnological Studies no. 30, National Museum of Ethnology, Osaka, Japan, pp. 199–222.

———. 1989. Hunting, farming, and sedentism in a rain forest society. In *Farmers as Hunters: The Implications of Sedentism*. Susan Kent (ed.), pp. 60–70. Cambridge: Cambridge University Press.

———. 1984. Forager resource and land use in the humid tropics: The Agta of northeastern Luzon, the Philippines. In *Past and Present in Hunter Gatherer Studies*. C. Schrire (ed.), pp. 95–121. Orlando, FL: Academic Press.

Headland, T. N. 1987. The wild yam question: How well could independent hunter-gatherers live in a tropical rainforest ecosystem? *Human Ecology* 15:463–491.

———. 1986. *Why Foragers do not Become Farmers: a Historical Study of a Changing Ecosystem and Its Effects on a Negrito Hunter-Gatherer Group in the Philippines*. Ann Arbor: University Microfilms International.

Hewlett, B. S. 1988. Sexual selection and paternal investment among the Aka Pygmies. In *Human Reproductive Behavior: A Darwinian Perspective*. L. Betzig, M. Borgerhoff Mulder, and P. Turke (Eds.), pp. 263–276. Cambridge: Cambridge University Press.

———. 1987. Intimate fathers: Patterns of paternal holding among Aka Pygmies. In *The Father's Role: Cross-Cultural Perspectives*. M. E. Lamb (Ed.), pp. 295–330. Hillsdale, NJ: Erlbaum.

Hill, K., Kaplan, H. Hawkes, K., and Hurtado, A. 1985. Men's time allocation to subsistence work among the Ache of eastern Paraguay. *Human Ecology* 13:29–47.

Howell, N. 1979. *Demography of the Dobe !King*. New York: Academic Press.

Hurtado, A. M., Hawkes, K. and Kaplan, H. 1985. Female subsistence strategies among Ache hunter-gatherers of eastern Paraguay. *Human Ecology* 13:1–28.

Lee, R. B. 1979. *The !Kung San: Men, Women, and Work in a Foraging Society*. Cambridge: Cambridge University Press.

Maxwell West, M., and Konner, M. J. 1976. The role of the father: An anthropological perspective. In *The Role of the Father in Child Development*. M. E. Lamb (Ed.), pp. 185–217. New York: Wiley.

Peterson, J. T. 1978. *The Ecology of Social Boundaries: Agta Farmers of the Philippines.* Urbana, IL: University of Illinois Press.

Rai, N. K. 1990. *Living in a Lean-to: Philippine Negrito Foragers in Transition.* Anthropological Papers No. 80, Museum of Anthropology. Ann Arbor: University of Michigan.

Chapter 15

Perceptions of Parenting among the Nso of Cameroon

Bame A. Nsamenang

INTRODUCTION

This chapter is about the perception of parenting by fathers and mothers in a West African community, the Nso of Cameroon. Prior to delving into the core concern of the chapter, however, two pertinent topics will be briefly discussed. Accordingly, in the first part of the chapter, a critique of social science research of parenting in African societies is attempted. In the second part, I endeavor to present an Afrocentric view on parenting. Finally, in the third part, the majority and primary focus of the chapter, I report and discuss a case study of maternal and paternal perceptions of parenting in Nso, one of several Fondoms (Kingdoms) in the Grassfields of Cameroon.

PARENTING RESEARCH IN AFRICAN CULTURES:
A CRITICAL VIEWPOINT

"Cultural scripts no less than biology and phylogeny contribute to the ways in which societies perceive parenthood and the task of raising children. These ways are rational in that they contain information about environmental contingencies previously [cognized and] experienced by the population and assimilated into its cultural tradition" (LeVine, 1974: 227). Despite the apparent universality of these forms of parental knowledge, it seems that social science research, particularly developmental research, is a science of exclusion; it excludes most non-Western sources of human knowledge in a universe that exists to be discovered. For instance, my starkly illiterate aged mother recognizes three broad categories of humans—**Wir Nso** (the Nso person), **Wir Kitum** (the stranger), and **Kimbang** (the White person)—each of whom she believes possesses certain traits and peculiarities. Unfortunately, the social sciences have tended to disregard, ignore, and stubbornly refused to incorporate social representations such as my mother's into the mainstream of the discipline's scientific knowledge. The social sciences tend to ignore such major kinds of knowledge as "sensuous penetration, loving participation, ecstasy, and transcendent aspiration" (Nchabeleng 1982:162).

Because sociocultural research on parenting has typically been framed in Eurocentric terms, social scientists seldom view the human person as a global species. Consequently, they rarely ask what the version of parental cognition of non-Western people signify for the universal condition of human parenthood. If such questions are not asked or if answers are not carefully construed by considering all patterns of parenting, then, only a lopsided picture of parenting is portrayed. But who cares: who, for example, really needs an Afrocentric viewpoint on parenting? Wright's (1984: xiv) wisdom in this regard is as insightful as it is instructive:

> We must begin to look for alternatives to the traditional views, not so that those views may be necessarily displaced, but so that we may come to wider, fuller understanding of man qua man. We must be willing to look at all views, no matter how diverse, and learn what we may from them.

We ought to cease behaving as if the current "scientific" sources of knowledge represented "the last word" in the epistemology of human knowledge, particularly parenting knowledge.

Scientists are not insentient, uncommitted, neutral fact-finders. Scientific choices and target "facts" tend to be consistent with the value and motivational systems of the scientists and their sponsors. Thus far, the "facts" researchers obtain are characteristically presented and interpreted using Western "looking glasses." When Western scientists (and some of their African counterparts) do not understand or subsume African traditional thought under Western models, they do not hesitate to stigmatize Africans as functioning at the "prelogical" level of cognitive development.

One reason for this "arrogant" scientific posture—why African and other non-Western forms of knowledge are excluded from the corpus of scientific knowledge—is that African (or other) folk thought and Western scientific thought are framed by different world views and are oriented towards different consequences; hence the fallaciousness of equating the two systems of knowledge. A major criticism of the sociocultural research on parenting in African societies is that it is typically defined, conducted, and interpreted in Eurocentric terms. In fact, psychological and "Anthropological studies are almost always formulated within the framework of Western academia rather than as participatory research with the target group's interests in mind" (Sponel, 1990: 32).

In this light, Goody's (1978: 228) insinuation that "the giving up of parental rights" in fosterage is a form of parental rejection becomes meaningless and distortional for Africans whose cultures permit and encourage the practice of collective responsibility in raising offspring. There is a lively and widespread belief in Africa that parents alone cannot raise wholesome and competent children. Furthermore, in Nso as in much of Africa, only the unborn baby belongs to the parents; from the moment of birth, the child belongs to the kin group whose members readily share in childcare. Kinsmen are subject to pressures and sanctions if they depart too widely from the expected role as surrogate or foster careproviders. Thus, in much of Africa, kin retain some responsibility for the socialization and care of children, a role that may mean grandparents, in-laws, uncles, cousins, even fictive kin may have, and frequently do have, authority to make important decisions affecting kin's children (Nsamenang 1991).

The ideas of parents concerning children, their development, and their upbringing have become the focus of research attention in recent years. Scientific emphasis on parental beliefs highlights an essential distinction between folk notions and scientific or professional conceptions of human reproductive ideology, human parenthood, and child development. Unfortunately, however, both African and their foreign peers are guilty of the scientific neglect of the African father's role. Among foreign scholars only the work of a few (Draper 1976; Fortes 1950; Goody 1975; Hewlett 1997; LeVine et al. 1967, among others) refer to the African father as a parenting figure. However, in comparison to the relatively comprehensive nature of literature on Western fatherhood, most of their discussions (with the possible exception of Hewlett's) of the father's role in African cultures are undertaken more from social anthropological perspectives rather than from the viewpoints of fathers as titular parents, influencers of family life, and anchors for child development. More seriously, most accounts of family life, human development, and parenting handle and treat African ideas and knowledge as "more or less wrong about the facts" (Riesman 1986) of life. African scholars fare no better than their Western counterparts. Only a few African scholars, among them Ayisi (1979), Bekombo (1981), Ekpere et al. (1978), Kaye (1962), Uka (1966), and some novelists (e.g., Achebe 1958; Laye, 1977; Soyinka, 1981) make passing mention of the father in their various discussions of childrearing or growing up in different African communities. Thus, there has not been sufficient research attention on paternal contributions to parenting and child development in African societies. But "To consider the status of either sex without reference to the other is to distort the reality we are trying to understand" (Fortes 1980: 363); hence the focus of this chapter is on maternal and paternal ideas about children and parenting in a West African community.

The neglect of the African father's role notwithstanding, preliminary reports by Nsamenang (1987a, 1983) and Nsamenang and Laosebikan (1981) highlight the significance of West African fathers to their children. These authors traced the incidence of filial emotional disturbances and academic underachievement to inadequate or pathologic fathering and unknown paternity.

The predominance of patrilineal over matrilineal societies and the esteemed social representation of men in Nso (as in other African) folklore and social circles betray their scientific neglect. Scientific devaluation of the paternal (men's) role probably derived from the fact that the social scientists who inaugurated parenting research in African societies spuriously brought, adopted, or inherited matricentric research models. Moreover, since African traditions do not sanction, much less encourage, "paternal involvement," fathers seemed to have unwittingly been considered to be insignificant entities or peripheral figures in the lives of their children. Fathers thus became invisible to sociocultural scientists and imperceptibly slipped out of parenting research in spite of their overbearing social status and presence.

Although the depictions of Africa and Africans by most Westerners are done in "good faith," the sore point is their inability, reluctance, or obsessive "refusal" to transcend the blind spots inherent in Western perspectives. By paying much attention to research methodology and the pronouncements of their disciplines, researchers of parenting in African contexts "ignore the subject-matter: the theories and concepts through which the owners of the culture see their cultural world" (Anyawu, 1975: 149), their parental role, and parenting activities. In this sense, research paradigms wherein scientists "set out to show how social action in one world makes sense from the point of view of another" are fundamentally faulty (Agar 1986: 12). The flow of information is typically unidirectional: how African patterns fit Western models. That is, African ideas and knowledge have to be explicable in Western terms. Western researchers and scholars do not readily acknowledge the truth of African knowledge because Western symbols and knowledge-bases are different than Africa's (Riesman 1986).

The excessively domineering impact of Eurocentric scientific viewpoints therefore makes it difficult to present an Afrocentric perspective convincingly. This becomes more fastidious because the "acceptable" logic of discourse flows out of other-than-African world views and conceptual systems. Nevertheless, this is not an apologia for not attempting to articulate an unexplored Afrocentric perspective on parenting.

PARENTING RESEARCH: AN AFROCENTRIC INPUT

To get a glimpse of an Afrocentric prespective, it is but essential to take a short look at Africa and its sociocultural frame of reference.

Globally, Africa has the distinction of sheltering the least literate and most rural populations, but is the continent with the fastest rate of urbanization. Africa may also be the one spot in our planet where emphasis on the acquisition of the appropriate gender roles and notions of seniority and locus of authority, which reside mainly in parents, especially the father, are quite pervasive and most forceful. In addition, what first strikes even a casual observer of the African sociocultural landscape are the strong desire for children by both men and women, men's high social visibility particularly the revered status of the father, and women's heavy workloads. Furthermore, African customs "put women in a subordinate position to men" (Nsamenang 1987a: 285).

African cosmology posits a hierarchical, three-tier universe with the "Supreme One" at the apex, followed by a spiritual world of deities and dead ancestors, and a profane world that the living inhabit. Africans fervently believe that the whole universe and the human person are interrelated in multiple ways. In more specific terms, human link to God is via filiation rather than through creation. This viewpoint connotes God's infinite ability to give or deny fertility to individuals or couples. Although all children have a divine origin, societies like the Nso attach special socioreligious significance to one class of offspring referred to as **woon-ah nyuy** ("children of God"). Just as the ancestors are thought to have gone from the land of the living, though not far, the newborn are regarded as not fully and securely with the living and are thought to have special links with the spirit world" (Ellis 1978: 42). That is, children are not considered to belong to "this" world until hey have been incorporated into the community of the living through naming.

In addition, a frame of reference that focuses on the individual does not come to the African readily. In African conception "man is not man on his own; the individual gains significance from and through his relationships with others" (Ellis 1978: 6); hence the developmental implications of the systematic incorporation of children into various social statuses at different life stations. Without adequate socialization and incorporation into "this" or "that" human community, individuals are considered mere "danglers" to whom the designation "person" does not appropriately and fully apply.

Armed with this view of the universe, Africans attempt to construct parenthood and the human life cycle in "their own terms." Accordingly, the human neonate, in lay, mundane terms, is a biological framework that shelters a spiritual selfhood onto which a social selfhood begins ontogenetic development on the assignment of a name; hence the critical importance of the naming rite. Both fathers and mothers are expected to "guide" the development of the social selfhood from the moment of birth, but African traditions do not actively sanction routine paternal involvement, much less the provisioning of care to children, especially to neonates and infants. In spite of the apparent lopsidedness of paternal and maternal involvement in caregiving, a strictly matricentric focus of parenting and developmental research is unjustifiable. Although the bulk of childcare and homekeeping in Africa is undertaken by women, with the assistance of older siblings and peers, African fathers cannot, however, be assumed to be peripheral or insignificant figures in the lives of their children. They deserve scientific attention and research scrutiny if only as social entities (even when absent) in their children's social worlds. Research focus on the African father's role is therefore the more compelling in face of Lamb's (1987: xiii) insightful remark that "fathers play multiple roles in the family, and that one needs to consider them all even when concerned narrowly about paternal effects on young children." Unfortunately, however, as stated earlier, fathers have virtually been excluded from most accounts of childrearing in African cultures. The most glaring example of scholarly neglect of the role of African men is Oppong's *Male and Female in West Africa*, which undermines, ignores, or slights men's, particularly fathers', critical role in their children's lives. The discussion thus far emphasizes the point that the African world view differs markedly from the world views contained in the contemporary parenting and developmental literatures, In fact, it reveals an African conception of the universe and of the child that is so native, intricate, and systematic than previously suspected, much less acknowledged. It is therefore absolutely essential to ground any sociocultural research designed to foster a genuine and deeper appreciation of parenting and developmental pathways in African societies in a thorough understanding of the sociocosmic "reality" and social structure of African people. For instance, parenting research in African contexts must conceptualize the child as a "plant" growing up in the middle of a field—the kin group (Nsamenang 1987a). Furthermore, the child's social world must be seen to include multiple caretakers of either sex and socialization or caregiving as a collective enterprise in which older siblings and peers are active participants. It is also noteworthy that the most significant persons in the lives of many Africans may not necessarily be their biological parents. The typical caretaking picture is one in which parents either lurk in the background or may be only partially available, the "actual parenting" of children who have been weaned being provided by someone (foster parent) other than the parents. The lurking possibility that the African child may be "attached" to multiple caregivers—the mother, sitter, elder sibling, or peer, for example—at the same time undoubtedly carries weighty implications for parenting research in general and attachment theory in particular.

Considering the foregoing, the major task of the next section is to attempt a descriptive account of how Nso fathers and mothers perceive the parental role, albeit in the language coined by Westerners. The focus of attention is on the ideas of beliefs that may illuminate how the Nso view and experience childbearing and the task of parenting, that is, the parenting or reproductive ideology of the Nso. As a concept, parental ideas or beliefs carry crucial theoretical and practical importance since an understanding of the value of children (VOC), for example, "is a key to developing insights into family dynamics, sex role, social norms" and "childbearing motivations" (Kagitcibasi 1982: 2–3).

PERCEPTIONS OF PARENTING: A CASE STUDY OF THE NSO OF CAMEROON

In examining the parenting ideology of the Nso, one is emboldened by the fact that parenting is a universal as well as an ecologically niched phenomenon. As such, it varies greatly across ecocultures. In the words of Draper and Harpending (1987: 218), children "can succeed under a variety of caretaking regimes." Nso ideas about children and parenting, "far from being an isolated phenomenon, are interwoven with the life-patterns and ways of thinking characteristic of" (Palacios 1990: 139) the Nso.

In Nsoland as in other communities in Africa, the desire for children is passionate; it is deep-rooted in the hearts of both men and women. Parenthood, then, is the core purpose of marriage. The ideas parents hold about children reflect both the needs of parents and the place of children in the family and society. Thus, the key question of the study was to explore the multidimensionality of the value of children to Nso parents as the motive force behind the perceptions of the parental role and what parents wished to accomplish in parenting. Accordingly, the study focused on three fundamental themes in Nso reproductive or parenting ideology: why Nso people want children, how Nso view children; and what Nso people hope to achieve in raising children. These questions revolve on ideas or beliefs about child development and parenting, the so-called "parents' cognitive processes" (Palacios 1990: 137).

There is considerable variation in the notions scientists use in reference to parental beliefs about child development and parenting. The plethora of conceptual routes and belief-referent labels—ideas, values, perceptions, concepts, attributions, internal states—in the literature points to the disagreement and confusion in the conceptualization of parental beliefs and the problem studied. The present study simply conceptualized parental beliefs as cognitive phenomena, the perceived parental ideas, values, and expectations that accord meaning and direction to the status of parent. We assumed that beliefs influence parenting decisions and behaviors only if they are perceived by the parent to be significant. In our study, these beliefs were assessed as self-reported verbalizations in response to interview questions. To contextualize the study and introduce its socioanthropolocial background, it seems expedient to present a cursory picture of the setting.

A PROFILE OF THE NSO OF CAMEROON

The history of the numerous ethnic polities of the Bamenda Grassfields in what today roughly corresponds to the Northwest Province (NWP), one of Cameroon's 10 Provinces, reveals population movements, the adjustment of cultural patterns, and adaptation to the savanna ecology. As a result of similarity in the physical ecology, patterns of migration and frequent culture contacts, the people of the Bamenda Grassfields evolved "common political and social institutions with only slight variations" (Nkwi 1983). The Nso Fondom (Kingdom) is the largest and said to be the most powerful of the NWP Fondoms. The bulk of the Nso population lives in villages in Nsoland, but some Nso migrants have settled outside the ancestral land, the majority in Bamenda (capital of the NWP) 65 miles to the south. Residence in Nso villages, which vary in territorial size, population, and importance, is patrivirilocal and clustered around a lineage or family head. Social ties to extensive networks of kin and affines provide anchorage for supportive fellowship, especially in childrearing and emotional security.

Over 90% of food in Nso, as in much of Cameroon, is homegrown. About 85% of all income is produced through the sale of produce and crafts rather than wages or salaries. In the family economy, each sex semispecializes in the production of particular types of crops and/or services. Generally, women's labor is allocated to childcare, homekeeping, and food processing, whereas men concentrate on the cultivation of industrial crops and the performance of ill-defined community-oriented roles. Typically, an adult is responsible for a particular activity or service and is usually assisted by younger persons and children of the same sex. That is, "a horizontal distribution of work between the sexes is combined with a 'vertical' distribution of work between adults and the young" (Boserup 1970: 140). However, children's labor—men's and women's valuable resource—"is diminishing, as increasing numbers of the young attend school" (Oppong 1983: 283).

Like most West African women, Nso women "are highly prolific—mothers of many children—and at the same time heavily engaged in productive work both inside and outside the home" (Oppong 1983: 4). For example, Nsamenang's (1989) report of 4.7 siblings per Bamenda Grassfields family seems to be consistent with Ware's (1983: 18) finding that the total fertility in West Africa varies "from just over 4.5 in Cameroon to something close to 7.0 in most countries of the region." Most women, especially rural mothers, "work longer hours and engage in more physical labour than men" (Ware 1983: 17). This is because Nso mothers combine the care of many children with the brunt of producing food crops and preparing the family's daily menu. Because tradition places the responsibility to feed the family on mothers, the Nso father is not, and has never been, the sole provider. As a result, Nso mothers, especially in polygynous homes, do not expect nor wish to be totally maintained by their husbands. Instead, they find independent ways to support themselves and their children. It is not that Nso men "are uninterested in the welfare of their families, but rather that they are not socially held responsible for the family's daily food security" (Goheen 1989: 10). Although there is considerable economic individualism, most men attempt to monitor the use of their wive's income in what resembles a deeply ingrained male obsession to retain control of the proceeds of female labor (Kaberry 1952; Nsamenang 1987a).

Nso is a male-dominated culture, but male dominance may be a matter of appearance rather than reality. For instance, Nso women organize themselves into several "women's houses." During crises or situations of perceived social injustice, the combined force and influence of "women's houses" have usually overwhelmed the authority of the most powerful patriarch, monarch, or State power.

METHOD

Subjects

The sample consisted of 389 parents (211 fathers and 178 mothers) grouped in terms of the following criteria: experience as parents, place of residence, and religious background. As regards experience in parenthood, we simply made a distinction between parents (persons who had at least one child 10 years of age or younger) and grandparents (persons with at least one grandchild). In relation to religious background, we considered whether subjects affiliated to the African, Christian, or Islamic faith. With regards to habitat, a distinction was made between residence in Nso villages (rural subjects) and residence in the town of Bamenda (urban subjects). Subject distribution is given in Table 1. The selection of subjects was based on the voluntary participation of one parent per family.

Table 1. Distribution of Subjects by Variable

Variable	Number of subjects	% of total
Religion		
African	95	24.4
Christian	226	58.1
Moslem	68	17.5
Experience as parents		
Parents[a]	191	49.1
Grandparents[b]	198	50.9
Habitat		
Rural	263	67.6
Urban	126	32.4
Gender		
Fathers	211	54.2
Mothers	178	45.8
Education		
No schooling	234	60.2
Some schooling[c]	155	39.8
Elementary education	102	26.2
Postelementary education	53	13.6
Total number of subjects	389	

[a]Person with at least one child, ten years of age or younger.
[b]Person with at least one grandchild.
[c]At least one year of formal, institutional education.

The Questionnaire

To study Nso beliefs regarding children and parenting we used the **Lamnso** (Nso language) version of the Parent Interview Guide (PIG) (Nsamenang and Lamb 1988) to collect the data. During the development of the English version of the PIG, it was progressively "refined" after extensive discussions with colleagues, visiting scholars, and several trial interviews with five Cameroonians and three Americans. The fact that the first author is a native-born Nso with first-hand knowledge of the culture helped in the generation of "culture-fair" items and phraseology of the questions (particularly those pertaining to sex, taboos during pregnancy, and reasons for procreation), to reflect and ensure their relevance to the Nso culture. Although knowledge of Nso cultural traditions was input into the generation of items for the English version of the PIG, it was translated into **Lamnso** with special care so that the respondents could interpret the questions correctly. The translation was done by a Nso member of the team that compiled a **Lamnso**–English dictionary and translated the Bible from English into **Lamnso**. His translation was later critiqued, revised, and tried out twice on Nso parents in Bamenda by seven interviewers and trainer, native speakers of **Lamnso**, before the final **Lamnso** version was produced.

The PIG is an open-ended interview schedule that explores 16 core dimensions of the concept of child, perinatal concerns, and parenting issues. Although the selection of areas included in questionnaires generally implies a certain degree of arbitrariness, those selected for the PIG are distributed among the areas most frequently explored in the research literature as well as those of special import in Nso culture. Each area is identified below, together with a representative example of the type of question used within it:

1. Information regarding pregnancy: Can you tell me the significance of pregnancy to Nso people?
2. Taboos during pregnancy: Identify for me the most important or the most severe Nso custom or taboo associated with pregnancy?
3. Prenatal care: How do Nso people usually care for women with first time pregnancies from the moment of conception until they give birth?
4. Ideas about labor and delivery: What is usually done to make the laboring woman give birth safely and without difficulty?
5. Immediate postnatal care: Explain to me what was done to— (target child's) placenta and umbilical stump?
6. Celebration of birth: In Nso, is the birth of a baby formally celebrated?

7. Naming of children: Now let us discuss the ways in which the names of babies are chosen and assigned in Nso. I am interested in knowing: Some reasons for giving children names.

8. Nature of children: Tell me if Nso believe that children inherit or are born with some behaviors, traits, or characteristics?

9. Value of children: Can you explain to me some of the reasons why Nso people want children?

10. Weaning: Could you describe for me how 6-month-old babies are usually fed in Nso?

11. Caretaking team: Who usually cares for babies from birth until they are (i) 3 months old; (ii) 1.5 years old; (iii) 5 years of age?

12. Practices of upbringing and discipline: Could you describe for me the various ways Nso parents train their children so that they would grow up to become the kinds of adults they admire and want?

13. Parental aspirations and expectations: Let us discuss the expectations parents have of their children: What parents want children to do to or for their parents?

14. Children's attributes: What actions, habits, or qualities of children do Nso parents consider misbehavior or wrongdoing?

15. Gender differences. Do Nso parents usually give the same kinds of punishment to boys and girls? If no, give some of the reasons why they punish boys and girls differently?

16. Parenting difficulties: Are you sometimes bothered by the things parents do to their children today? If yes, please tell me what some of them are?

Procedure. Five literate native Nso fathers from different villages in Nsoland and two from the town of Bamenda were recruited and trained as interviewers. The first training session, which lasted 14 days, focused mainly on correcting and mastering the reading of the **Lamnso** PIG; interviewing techniques; practice interviews; criteria and strategies for subject selection, fieldwork, and scheduling interviews. During the second 7-day training frame, interviewers rehearsed interviewing techniques, role-played, carried out trial interviews, and the tape-recording of interviews.

The seven interviewers went to designated villages in Nso and neighborhoods of Bamenda to explain the nature and purpose of the study to parents. They selected volunteers who conformed to the criteria stated above and drew up an interview timetable at the parent's convenience. Interviewers were expected to adhere strictly to a 10-point code-of-conduct drawn up together. This code included the item: "Parents or our subjects and members of the public will have mixed-feelings and reactions about our work. It is therefore important that we uphold acceptable standards of good behavior and not engage in activities or behaviors that will give a poor impression of ourselves and our work." The parents were interviewed in their homes in January and February of 1989 in a friendly, open-ended format using the PIG. The duration of interviews ranged from 1 to 2 hours.

Coding. On the PIG Code Book there were series of possible response options that an insider's knowledge of Nso culture and the previous pilot interviews had revealed as common. Four female native Nso played back the audiotapes and carefully listened to and coded each of the 389 tapes. If a parent's response corresponded to any of the expected categories, the codifier simply registered it. There was an "other" option under which were registered doubtful answers or those not contained in the prepared format.

RESULTS

Although the present study yielded a dataset on parental beliefs about children and parenting, the findings reported here pertain only to maternal and paternal ideas about pregnancy, what happens during the perinatal period, the value and nature of children, and parenting goals.

Table 2 contains the percentage of the "yes" responses scores for Nso fathers and mothers on beliefs about and practice during pregnancy and the perinatal period. From an insider's position, the face validity of the contents of Table 2 seems to indicate that the ideas held about pregnancy or the practices undertaken during the perinatal period were of two broad categories: those anchored on the endogenous culture and those shaped by acculturation or cultural adaptation. The view of pregnancy as divine gift, the use of potions and **amakooy** (traditional birth attendants), the burial of the placenta, and pregnancy taboos, for instance, are indigenous cultural concepts or practices. Whereas the leaving of the placenta in the hospital and the use of drugs and the "modern" health care system signify acculturation, cleaning the baby and concern with nutrition, labor, the umbilical cord, and the health of the mother and baby may be a function of either native knowledge or external cultural influence. But they are better thought of as evidence of indigenous cultural inheritance because such concerns have always been integral to customary practices. Thus, on the basis of numbers and face validity of the response categories, the answers Nso parents gave seemed to have been inspired more by native knowledge bases than by the effects and dynamics of acculturation or cultural adaptation.

Table 2. Percentages of the "Yes" Responses on Beliefs and Practices about Pregnancy and the Perinatal Period (*N* = 323)

Item	Fathers	Mothers
Significance of pregnancy to Nso		
Increase in family size	52	41
How a Nso woman knows when she has become pregnant: Cessation of mensis	92	95
How Nso people prepare for the birth of babies		
Performance of ritual during pregnancy	31	32
Adequate nutrition during pregnancy	98	97
Reduction of labor during pregnancy	86	85
Financial support of pregnant woman	41	50
Use of modern health care system	48	70
Use of modern drugs	26	65
Why Nso people care for the pregnant woman		
Concern about baby's health	57	53
Concern about mother's health	58	60
Most severe Nso custom or taboo associated with pregnancy		
Taboos regarding sex during pregnancy	39	45
Taboos related to supernatural element	61	45
How babies are delivered in Nso		
Use of potions to facilitate childbirth	96	73
Severing the umbilicus at birth	71	74
Burying the placenta outside the house	86	82
Leaving the placenta in the hospital	62	64
Disposal of placenta as customary practice	53	37
Use of **amakooy** (traditional midwives)	75	77
Is childbirth celebrated: Yes	95	97
How birth is usually celebrated: By feasting	58	51
The ways in which the names of babies are chosen and assigned in Nso		
Deriving names from circumstance of birth	72	62
Names as form of identification	53	49

The percentages and weighed totals of the "yes" scores for the value of children (VOC) are presented in Table 3. Although the VOC to parents is usually expressed as a unidimensional economic concept, the variety of response categories displayed in Table 3 suggests the multidimensionality of the VOC concept, at least for Nso parents. Thus, the value Nso parents attach to children comprise spiritual, psychological, social, and economic or utilitarian dimensions. The spiritual component of the VOC derives from the Nso view of children as "divine gift" or "ancestral blessing." Undergirding this is a lively faith in "God's use of humans" to propagate the species and in the divine decision to "give" or "not give" fertility to individuals or couples. That is, fecundity is not conferred simply because one is born of human progeny. Because infer-

Table 3. Percentages and Weighted Totals of the "Yes" Responses on Value of Children by Variable (*N* = 323)

Variable	Fathers	Mothers	Weighted total
Why Nso people want children			
Continuation of the lineage	63	33	48.0
Source of happiness	34	16	25.0
Obedience to parents	37	35	36.0
Respect parents get	27	26	26.5
Running errands	34	26	30.0
Performing domestic chores	52	60	56.0
Enjoyment of children	15	17	16.0
Mark of social prestige	15	15	15.0
Inheritance	15	6	10.5
Proof of one's virility	7	6	6.5
Wish to raise children	2	2	2.0
"Other"	7	3	5.0
Where children come from			
God's precious gift	25	32	29.0
Mark of ancestral blessing	11	15	13.0

tility is abhorred and having children implies escape from a detestable social stigma, children therefore confer a deep sense of personal fulfillment and accomplishment. In addition, parents not only "enjoy watching children grow" but also "want to raise children." The significance of the social VOC lies in the fact that "The social position of a married man and woman who have children is of greater importance and dignity than that of a bachelor or spinster" (Kenyatta 1965a: 158). Because having children helps "to carry on the family blood," a person's blood does not become extinct. Economically, children are useful because of the need "to have a child to send and to help around the house," but more importantly to have "someone to assist you in old age" in a society where centrally organized social security services are conspicuous by their absence.

Table 4 contains the response categories regarding the nature of children (NOC). It indicates that more than half the "yes" responses for both fathers and mothers supported the idea that children are born with innate traits and that more fathers than mothers held innatist perceptions. Whereas more mothers than fathers reported a need for the differential socialization of boys and girls, more fathers than mothers expressed the necessity of enforcing discipline in children through punishment. On the other hand, belief in the notion of the weaker sex and the protection of girls from exploitation was more characteristic of mothers than fathers. Overall, the results pertaining to the NOC seem to

Table 4. Percentages and Weighted Totals of the "Yes" Responses on
the Nature of Children for Nso Fathers and Mothers (*N* = 323)

Variable	Fathers	Mothers	Weighted total
If Nso believe in?			
Innateness of traits: "Yes"	63	50	56.5
Instilling discipline	44	37	40.5
Discipline via punishment	39	32	35.5
Do Nso parents make a distinction in the way they raise boys and girls?			
Notion of weaker sex	38	34	36.0
Differences in socialization	38	40	34.0
Protection of girls	28	36	32.0

point to the fact that whereas fathers were more likely to attribute
children's traits to nature and to employ more punitive disciplinary
measures, mothers tended to be more conscious of and to emphasize
gender differences, to be less punitive in discipline, and more protective
of daughters. These sorts of ideas are likely to foster differences in
maternal and paternal orientations, at least in some aspects of childrearing. They may also affect what fathers and mothers expect from children
as well as the goals and strategies they set for raising children. Regarding maternal and paternal differences, Table 5 contains the chi-square
comparison of the ideas of fathers and mothers on some aspects of
pregnancy and the perinatal period. Table 5 reveals significant differences between fathers and mothers in several domains. The implication
of this finding is that mothers and fathers are likely to approach parenting with different frames of reference and may set varying parenting
goals or hold differing expectations.

In relation to differences in goals and expectations, the percentages in
Table 6 point to the possibility of similarity and differences in the
parenting goals and expectations of Nso fathers and mothers. That is,
there were possibilities for agreement as well as disagreement in the
ideas of Nso mothers and fathers on some aspects of pregnancy and
perinatal concerns. The chances for conflict in maternal and paternal
goals and expectations may somehow be reduced by an overriding
interest to raise obedient children who are committed to upholding the
family name and ensuring the cohesion of the lineage. According to
Table 6, there are basically two response modes: child-directed concerns
and parent-focused preoccupations. In other words, the goals and expectations reflect the place of children in Nso society and the parenting
wishes or needs of Nso parents. Among both fathers and mothers, the
most frequently cited concern was the development of proper character.
Progress in school, success in life, and the attainment of parenthood
were also highly rated, in that order. Concern with academic progress

Table 5. Chi-Square and *p* Values of Nso Fathers and Mothers by Variables
about Pregnancy and the Perinatal Period (*N* = 389)

Variable	χ	p value[a]
Can you tell me the significance of pregnancy to Nso people		
Increase in family size/strength	7.80	0.007
Sign of divine gift/Ancestral blessing	4.78	0.029
How the Nso prepare for the birth of babies		
Emotional support of pregnant woman	7.09	0.008
Use of potions for prenatal care	22.89	0.000
Use of the modern health care system	11.54	0.007
The most severe Nso custom or taboo associated with pregnancy		
Visit to tabooed places/sites	5.08	0.024
How are babies delivered in Nso		
Use of potions to facilitate childbirth	14.83	0.000
Use of biomedical means to ease childbirth	16.12	0.000
Customary disposal of placenta/umbilical stump	8.44	0.011
Fertility adversely affected if placenta or umbilical stump is not properly disposed	15.88	0.000
How is the baby handled and treated at birth		
Cleaning the baby at birth	7.45	0.006
Covering/wrapping the baby at birth	9.41	0.002
"Other" forms of postpartum care of neonate	8.96	0.008

[a]Significant values are after Yates correction.

suggests cultural adaptation because formal schooling is not an endogenous cultural tradition in Nsoland. A general implication of the results in Table 6 is that Nso parents were overly concerned with filial success in life because failure connotes children's inability to provide the assistance and social security parents need, especially in old age.

Table 6. Percentages and Weighted Totals by Variable for Parental
Goals/Expectations of Nso Fathers and Mothers (*N* = 323)

Variable	Fathers	Mothers	Weighted total
Tell me the responsibilities of Nso parents to their children			
Training in proper character	75	64	69.5
Filial marital arrangement	25	24	24.5
What do Nso parents generally expect from their children			
Good progress in school	55	44	49.5
Success in life	37	53	45.0
Attainment of parenthood	37	42	39.5
Filial service	28	26	27.0
Vocational competence	17	22	19.5
Social competence	16	17	16.5

Taken together, the results suggest that mothers tended to report more externalized beliefs than fathers. That is, the ideas of fathers more than those of mothers derived more from native perspectives than from the influence of alien cultural fragments or notions.

DISCUSSION

Parenting knowledge is not a prerogative of any one human society. Every culture constructs its own parenting knowledge according to its ecocultural imperatives and existential history. Consequently, there is considerable cross-cultural variation in the pattern and impact of parental knowledge. In discussing the remarkable diversity in human parenting patterns, Draper and Harpending (1987: 218) stated that "Children clearly can succeed under a variety of caretaking regimes." But Ellis (1978) alleged that "proper" childrearing among West Africans "is axiomatic" and that caregivers do not question the basis of their actions. The data presented in this chapter unambiguously indicate that the Nso, one group of West Africans, are clearly guided by "their own ideas" of children and parenting. In the article cited above, Ellis (1978) contradicts his own assertion by acknowledging that "punishment and close surveillance" in West Africa occur "within an accepted framework." Perhaps Ellis wished to point out that West Africans do not employ or apply identical childrearing concepts and principles as do Westerners, specifically the British.

Although most respondents in the present study claimed that the interview was the first time they were ever asked to introspect and verbalize their views of children and parenting, their beliefs are discernible by anyone who is sufficiently motivated and genuinely interested in exploring them. The responses obtained in the present study represent what Piaget (1929) referred to as "liberated convictions." That is, "answers that are elicited for the first time by new content but that grow out of preexisting thought structures" (Miller 1988: 265).

Draper and Harpending (1987: 218) questioned the implicit assumption in the literature and scientific circles "that the western pattern [of parenting] is inherently superior." In claiming the superiority of one set of parental know-how over all others, it is perhaps instructive to reflect on the point that the variety of views of childhood and parenting in the extant scientific literature are not always in agreement with formal or professional psychology (Goodnow 1988; Maccoby and Martin 1983; Miller 1988). The nonexistence of universal criteria for human parenthood is self-evident in the submission that

> The process of becoming a parent in any culture includes learning how to apply general cultural models to specific sequences commonly presented by children at different ages, in ways that feel consistent with one's cultural goals and definitions of personhood. (Harkness et al. nd)

In other terms, parenting knowledge emanates largely from world views and ecocultural realities.

Ellis (1978: 7) further noted that all African cultures have been exposed to external cultural influences, the "effects of which should not be underplayed." This fact notwithstanding, Nso ideas of the parental role do not seem to manifest excessive exteriority or extensive modification by or adaptation to alien cultural influences. The reason is that the face validity of most of the responses obtained in this study seems to indicate that they are more deeply rooted in Nso cosmology, endogenous traditions, and knowledge bases than in alien cultural traditions and world views. For example, parental concern with school progress, though not originally an indigenous motive, derives from a cultural belief in social competence and realization that since "Education and farming appear to be incompatible" (Ohuche and Otaala 1982: 17), contemporary realities demand that raising children be focused on what provides the basic requirements for functional and meaningful citizenship. A plausible explanation for the tenacity of Nso parenting beliefs in the face of potent modifying forces is Uka's (1966: 29) claim that childrearing beliefs "are never amendable to easy changes because beliefs about the origin of life are not held on a rational basis."

The existence of both similarity and differences in maternal and paternal ideas is potentially interesting because it has to do with the incidence of conflict, or the lack of it, within the parenting environment. In other areas, such as the awareness of the need for adequate nutrition and reduction of labor during pregnancy, fathers' responses seem to point to greater role awareness than mothers'. The crux of the matter, however, is the extent to which the inferred paternal role awareness translates into "paternal involvement." In this direction, Nsamenang (1987b: 12) hinted that in the Bamenda Grassfields of Cameroon, "Mothers accused fathers for not performing their traditional roles in the family production line." Nsamenang (1987b: 12) further noted the likelihood of parental conflict since one area where fathers and mothers differed was on "how the proceeds of women's economic activities should be utilized." In some areas mothers' responses more than fathers' favoring the use of drugs and the modern health care system, and disfavoring the use of potions imply that paternal ideas were more the outcome of "the influence of a well-defined cultural background that has strong roots" (Palacios 1990: 150) than maternal. The finding that mothers, more than fathers, tended to manifest less traditional views on some dimensions is plausible because, mothers far more than fathers, are exposed to external modifiers of cultural knowledge and norms in prenatal and antenatal clinics where they receive instructions and lectures from staff trained primarily in Western orientations and value systems.

To summarize and conclude, the first part of this chapter attempted to point out that idiosyncratic attributes, cultural blind spots, and ideology are inherent facets of the scientific enterprise that render researchers more or less unremittent ideologues. By using only the knowledge and conceptual systems of their own cultures to interpret sociocultural phenomena in other cultures, cross-cultural researchers ought to be aware that their interpretations may be radically different than those of owners of the culture. The second part of the chapter endeavored to argue for the authenticity and intricate nature of the African world view and concept of the child and caregiving, which ought to be considered in parenting research with African subjects. In the third section, evidence from the perceptions of parenthood by Nso parents was presented to illustrate the point that, though perceived in diverse terms in different cultures, parenting is a universal phenomenon rooted in the ecoculture. In reality, every human culture possesses a unique profile of parental roles, parenting knowledge, and parental stereotypes, few or many traits or elements of which may be found in other cultures. Armed with "their own" ideology about desirable childstates and the parental role, Nso parents reported that they try to "develop" good character in their children to ensure their academic progress and success in parenthood in particular and life in general. Thus in Nso, as elsewhere, there are competent mothers and fathers who, in their own way, have raised culturally competent children who have excelled in learning and character to earn recognition in other cultures, notably European and North American cultures.

An unfortunate but noteworthy point is that in spite of their enormous power and high social esteem, African fathers are "forgotten contributors to child development" (Lamb 1975). Initial empirical evidence in West Africa indicates that African fathers are significant to their children (perhaps even when absent). Another point worth critical consideration in cross-cultural research is the use of technology. We increasingly see research reports based on videotapes of parent–child interactions recorded in the most "remote" parts of our planet and mailed to some of the most "civilized" cities for analysis, interpretation, and publication by the foremost sociocultural scientists of the modern era. From the viewpoint of social sciences as the science of humanity carried out by humans, how is such technologically "advanced" research superior to the ethnographic reports of participant observers or the introspective verbal records of owners of the culture? In the interest of science as one of the tools for the generation of human knowledge, it seems essential to involve owners of the culture under study in all phases of the cross-cultural research effort.

REFERENCES

Achebe, C. 1958. *Things Fall Apart*. London: Heinemann.

Agar, M. H. 1986. *Speaking Ethnographically*. Beverly Hills: Sage.

Anyawu, K. C. 1975. African religion as an experienced reality. In *Africa: Thought and Practice, Journal of the Philosophical Association of Kenya* 2 (2).

Ayisi, E. O. 1979. *An Introduction to the Study of African Culture*. London: Heinemann.

Bekombo, M. 1981. The child in Africa: Socialization, education and work. In *Child Work, Poverty, and Underdevelopment*. G. Rodgers and G. Standing (Eds.), pp. 113–129. Geneva: WHO.

Berger, P. L. 1974. *Pyramids of Sacrific: Political Ethics and Social Change*. New York: Pelican.

Boserup, E. 1970. *Women's Role in Economic Development*. London: Allen & Unwin.

Draper, P. 1976. Social and economic constraints on child life among the !Kung. In *Kalihari Hunter-Gatherers*. R. Lee and I. Devore (Eds.), pp 199–217. Cambridge: Harvard University Press.

Draper, P., and Harpending, H. 1987. Parent investment and the child's environment. In *Parenting Across the Life Span*. J. B. Lancaster et al. (Eds.), pp. 207–271. New York: Aldine.

Ekpere, J. A., Oyedipe, F. P. A., and Adegboye, R. O. 1978. Family role differentiation within the Kwara nomadic Fulani. In *Marriage, Fertility and Parenthood in West Africa*. C. Oppong, G. Adaba, M. Bekombo-Priso, and J. Mogey (Eds.). Canberra: The Australian National University.

Ellis, J. 1978. The child in West African society. In *West African Families in Britain*. J. Ellis (Ed.). London: Routledge & Kegan Paul.

Fortes, M. 1950. Kinship and marriage among the Ashanti. In *African Systems of Kinship and Marriage*. A. R. Radcliffe-Brown and D. Forde (Eds.). London: Oxford University Press.

Fortes, M. 1980. "Informants." *L'Uomo* IV(2).

Goheen, M. 1989. The ideology and political economy of gender: Women and land in Nso, Cameroon. In *Women and Structural Adjustment in Africa*. C. Gladwin (Ed.). University of Florida: Carter Lecture Series.

Goodnow, J. J. 1988. Parents' ideas, actions, and feelings: Models and methods from developmental and social psychology. *Child Development* 58(2):286–320.

Goody, E. 1978. Some theoretical and empirical aspects of parenthood in West Africa. In *Marriage, Fertility and Parenthood in West Africa*. C. Oppong, G. Adaba, and J. M. Bekombo-Priso (Eds.). Canberra: The Australian National University.

Goody, J. 1975. Religion, social change and the sociology of conversion. In *Changing Social Structure in Ghana*. E. Goody (Ed.), pp 227–271. London: International African Institute.

Harkness, S., Super, C. M., and Keefer, C. H. (nd). The acquisition and application of American parents' theories about child behavior and development. Unpublished manuscript.

Hewlett, B. S. 1987. Intimate fathers'. Patterns of paternal holding among Aka Pygmies. In *The Father's Role: Cross-Cultural Perspectives*. M. E. Lamb (Ed.). Hillsdale, NJ: Erlbaum.

Kaberry, P. M. 1952. *Women of the Grassfields*. London: H. M. Royal Stationary Office.

Kagitcibasi, C. 1982. *The Changing Value of Children in Turkey*. Number 60-E, Papers of the East-West Population Institute.

Kaye, B. 1962. *Bringing-Up Children in Ghana*. London: Allen & Unwin.

Kenyatta, J. 1965. *Facing Mount Kenya*. London: Heinemann.

Lamb, M. E. 1975. Fathers: Forgotten contributors to child development. *Human Development* 18:245–266.

Lamb, M. E. 1987. Preface. In *The Father's Role: Cross-Cultural Perspectives*. M. E. Lamb (Ed.). Hillsdale, NJ: Erlbaum.

Laye, C. 1977. *The African Child*. Douglas, Isles of Man: Fontana.

LeVine, R. 1974. Parental goals: A cross-cultural view. *Teacher's College Record* 76(2)226–239.

LeVine, R. A., Klein, N. H., and Owen, C. R. 1967. Father-Child relationships and changing life-styles in Ibadan, Nigeria. In *The City in Modern Africa*. H. Miner (Ed.). London: Pall Mall Press.

Maccoby, E. E., and Martin, J. P. 1983. Socialization in the context of the family: Parent-child interaction. In *Handbook of child psychology: Vol 4: Socialization, Personality and Social Development*. E. M. Hetherington (Ed.). New York: Wiley.

Miller, S. A. 1988. Parent's beliefs about children's cognitive development. *Child Development*, 59(2):259–285.

Nchabeleng, J. M. 1982. The concept of play: Its relationship to social science methodology in Africa. Ph.D. thesis, Free University of Amsterdam, The Netherlands.

Nkwi, P. N. 1983. Traditional diplomacy, trade and warfare in the nineteenth century Western Grassfields. *Science and Technology* 1(3–4).

Nsamenang, B. A. 1991. Kinship networks and the socialization of children: A Bamenda Grassfields profile. *Science and Technology* (submitted).

Nsamenang, B. A. 1989. The social ecology of Cameroonian childhood. A poster presented at the Tenth Biennial Meetings of the International Society for the Study of Behavioral Development, 9–13 July, 1989, Jyvaskyla, Finland.

Nsamenang, B. A. 1987a. A West African perspective. In *The Father's Role: Cross-Cultural Perspectives*. M. E. Lamb (Ed.). Hillsdale, NJ: Erlbaum.

Nsamenang, B. A. 1987b. Parental education and socialization of children in the Bamenda Grassfields: A research report. Unpublished manuscript. Bamenda: Institute of Human Sciences.

Nsamenang, B. A. 1983. Experimental improvement of the quality of fathering among a group of Cameroonians. Ph.D. thesis, University of Ibadan, Nigeria.

Nsamenang, B. A., and Lamb, M. E. 1988. *Parent Interview Guide.* An unpublished interview schedule.

Nsamenang, B. A., and Laosebikan, S. 1981. Father-child relationships and the development of psychopathology: Two clinical examples. A paper read at the Nigerian Psychological Society Conference, April 1981, Jos, Nigeria.

Ohuche, R. O., and Otaala, B. 1982. *The African Child in His Environment.* Oxford: Pergamon.

Oppong, C. (ed.). 1983. *Female and Male in West Africa.* London: Allen & Unwin.

Palacios, J. 1990. Parents' ideas about the development and education of their children: Answers to some questions. *International Journal of Behavioral Development* 13(2):137–155.

Piaget, J. 1929. *The Child's Conception of the World.* London: Routledge & Kegan Paul.

Riesman, P. 1986. The person and the life cycle in African social life and thought. *African Studies Review* 29(2):1–138.

Soyinka, W. 1981. *Ake: The Years of Childhood.* New York: Aventura.

Sponel, L. E. 1990. Commentary: Does anthropology have a future. *Anthropology Newsletter* 31(3):29–32.

Uka, N. 1966. *Growing Up in Nigerian Culture.* Ibadan: Ibadan University Press.

Ware, H. 1983. Female and male lifecycles. In *Female and Male in West Africa.* C. Oppong (Ed.). Boston: Allen & Unwin.

Wright, R. A. 1984. Preface to first edition. In *African Philosophy.* R. A. Wright (Ed.), pp xiii–xv. Lanham, MD: University Press of America.

Chapter 16

Father–Child Relations in Urban China

William Jankowiak

The pervasive assumption in studies of the history of the family is that there is a close relationship between the process of urbanization and industrialization, and the reorganization of familial bonds of affection. These processes, it is pointed out, steadily undermine the prevailing conventional wisdom until the new understandings and the accompanying sentiments are institutionalized within a "new" style of family organization (Goode 1963; Parsons and Bales 1955; Whyte 1988). Much of this research builds on the work of William Goode, who found that within large urban centers there is a worldwide pattern of a shift from arranged marriages to marriages based on free choice and mutual affection. The husband–wife relationship, in short, shifted from a purely instrumental posture toward one organized around idealization, affection, and companionship (Macfarlane 1987; Stone 1977, 1987; Whyte 1988).

Surprisingly, neither Goode, his colleagues, nor admirers have examined what effect, if any, this historical process has had on the style of parenting toward their children. Thus it is unclear if and in what way the historical transformation of the husband–wife relationship also affected the intensity of men and women's commitment and daily involvement with their children.

In this chapter I will discus the level, context, and style of paternal versus maternal caregiving in urban China, and describe some of the emerging features of the interaction styles the Chinese adopt toward their children in Huhhot, the capital of the Inner Mongolia Autonomous Region, in the People's Republic of China.[1] Some concomitent questions I want to explore are: What has been the effect of urbanization on the Chinese on parent–child relations? Has the overall quality of parent–child interaction been undermined in favor of developing closer more intimate husband–wife relationship? Have women deemphasized their

345

"traditional" role of caretaker in favor of a greater involvement and intimacy with their spouse? Has the organization of the modern family around a notion of mutual affection resulted in greater warmth and involvement between a father and his children? Or do fathers remain, by and large, uninvolved with their young children? If so, at what age to fathers become more active in the parenting process. Since no one within an urban context has broached these questions, our understanding of the intensity with which men and women are active or indifferent participants in the creation and re-creation of domestic reality has been impoverished.[2]

The reevaluation of customary kinship obligations, conjugal expectations and duties, and parent–child interaction did not begin with the socialist transformation of China's urban infrastructure. It had been unfolding in China's largest cities for over 50 years (Wu 1987; Tan 1988). In this way, the changes in the contemporary urban Chinese family's organization are typical of a worldwide pattern that tends toward the formation of a nuclear family, a decline in fertility, and the decreasing power of the aged. Whyte and Parish's urban survey found that many of the domestic changes were already under way prior to the 1949 Communist Revolution, asserting that the changes were gradual and not radical (1984: 191–192). Still there have been a number of striking changes within the urban household's organization (Wolf 1985). The elimination of most family property has forced the urban populace to rely on bureaucratic agencies for housing and other critical resources, thereby weakening the traditional patrilineal and patrilocal forms in favor of a more flexible system organized around the principles of neolocal resident and bilateral descent: In the process, the politics of kinship have been transformed. Because urban women, unlike their rural counterparts, have gained full participation in the labor force, a salary that is of paramount importance for the family budget as well as for management of family finances, and equal access to educational opportunities, they have a greater opportunity to achieve parity with men in the family decision-making process. Hence they are able to more readily achieve independence and security within the domestic sphere. Wolf (1985) found that as a consequence women are less concerned with protecting their personal interest against the interest of a hostile mother-in-law and an indifferent or threatening husband. In addition, love, marriage, and spousal intimacy are widely regarded as important and worthwide aspirations (Cao 1987; Hoing and Hershatter 1988; Whyte and Parish 1984; Wolf 1985). Although the current research is exceptional and has identified numerous changes in the urban husband–wife relationship, there are few accounts exploring the impact of socialist reorganization has on the idea of the "good parent" and the overall style of urban Chinese parent–child interaction.

China scholars stress that the father–child relationship, throughout much of Chinese history, was organized around an ideology of filial piety that encouraged total obedience, respect, and loyalty toward the father (de Groot 1882–1910; Hanan 1985; Freeman 1965). It was understood that the "father had obligations far beyond that of providing food and clothing and shelter for his [children]," he also had to provide, especially in the case of his sons, sufficient funds to obtain a wife and receive an inheritance (Levy 1968: 169). Fathers, for the most part, undertook their duties seriously and strove to economically support and morally instruct their children (Wolf 1968). However, Chinese fathers, as a counterpoint to the role of mothers, did not strive to develop a warm emotionally charged parent–child relationship. Rather they believed that their role should not encourage or tolerate emotional indulgence. They assumed instead the ideal and expected role of a stern disciplinarian (Fei 1935; Ho 1987; Wilson 1974; Wolf 1972; Yang 1945). This posture did not mean that fathers were without compassion or love for their children. Most Chinese fathers, in fact, felt a warm deep sentiment toward their children (Solomon 1971; Li 1969). The articulation of that sentiment was estrainèd by their traditional parenting role, and its expectations (Levy 1968). Solomon quotes a Qing dynasty scholar-official who wrote that a "father loved his child with all his heart, but he would not express it" (Solomon 1971: 60). Solomon further adds that this parenting posture sometimes produced resentment and acute anxiety for the child in later life (Solomon 1971: 39–61). In this way, a Chinese ethos emerged that justified complimentary parenting postures: the father facilitated a child's entry into the outside world, whereas the mother provided a secure and loving environment within the home. It was assumed that these roles were inevitable and unchangeable. In addition, it also was assumed this sexual division in parenting roles contributed to producing a more responsible and ethical person (Solomon 1971).

The sex-linked parenting roles were sustained, if not developed, because men and women occupied different positions within the social structure. By controlling the distribution of the family inheritance, a father could effect a special, if not psychological, dependency on the part of the child. On the other hand, a mother's parenting style was seen as much a result of being considered an "outsider" as it was of a "natural" attachment fostered through childbirth and early childcare (Bowlby 1951; Daly and Wilson 1987). Given her lower status in her husband's family, the mother needed a friend, an ally, and what better one than her own child (Wolf 1972). In this way, the different access to and use of economic and psychological "resources" contributed to the elaboration of the two complementary parenting styles: the father as a disciplinary provider and the mother as an intimate nurturer.

Huhhotians have a very clear sense of gender-specific childcare duties, and this sense is patterned by the setting, timing, and manner of parental interaction with the child. Although young Huhhotian fathers, especially the more educated, often spoke enthusiastically about their desire to increase the frequency of their parent–child interaction, observations in the home, neighborhood, and public park found that the child's age and sex influenced the frequency and style of that interaction.

THE LEVEL AND CONTEXT OF FATHER INVOLVEMENT

In Huhhot there are several development stages of parent–child interaction, but I will describe only three: the early and late infancy (yinger) and the childhood stage (ertong). For analytical reasons I have divided childhood into an early (birth to 6 months) and late (7 to 12 months) phase. Each phase demands that a different parent become more actively involved. During the infant stage, Huhhotians agreed that the mother is the more involved parent, whereas the father becomes so when the child reaches the late childhood stage of (3–6 years old). Men and women stressed that a fathers' important responsibility began, however, once the child, around 7 years old, enters school. Fathers, especially college and high school educated, believed that they should oversee the child's studies, stressing diligence. I found that in every household ($n = 23$) where the mother was educated, it was she, and not the father, who oversaw and helped shape the child through his or her studies. For the most part, the educational level of the spouses is more or less equivalent, it is the mother, therefore, who is actually responsible for the child's educational development. Nonetheless, fathers insisted that they did participate in their child's educational development, if in no other way then by accompanying them to the museum, or special exhibition, or by instructing the child on how to accomplish some particular task. Moreover, as the child matured and entered middle school many educated father's did become more actively involved with their child's education. Significantly, Huhhotian men and women did not assess a father's actual value or contribution by the frequency of father–child interaction. Rather, that value is typically assessed through the expression and quality of fatherly concern, advice, and support.

Infant Care

In urban China women give birth in hospitals. It is expected that their husband accompany them to the delivery room and wait outside until labor has been completed and birth given. Because women usually are granted a 6-month pregnancy leave to recover and care for their infant, there is no pragmatic or ideological reason for men's immediate involvement in infant care. Furthermore, Huhhotian women generally believe that men are incompetent and ignorant in infant care, and cannot be trusted to properly respond to very small infants. One 55-year-old woman told me that if "a man held an infant, he might become confused and drop it." Another asserted that "men have no ability to do small things. Thus women were better." Another woman noted that men are unskilled in the art of swaddling, that is, they wrap the infant so tightly in a cotton quilt that it cannot move either its arms or its legs.[3] During both field seasons, I never once observed a man cradling an infant in his arms under six months of age! I did, however, observe on two separate occasions a young father sitting motionless in the Park with a swaddled infant asleep across his legs. Both fathers remained immobilized until their wives returned, whereupon the mothers promptly craddled the infant in their arms. Such is the force of cultural assumptions that, at different phases of childhood, women are deemed more qualified than men to perform certain tasks. In these two instances the young fathers were so physically and metaphorically paralyzed by this belief that they were incompetent to interact in an other than cursory fashion with their new-born child.

Late Infancy (7–12 Months)

Although women in this phase continue to perform most tasks, men are no longer prohibited by cultural convention, which patterns their own assumed sense of incompetence from interacting with their child. One young educated father, initially very excited about becoming a father, acknowledged that he was "very involved with his child." He added, in a complete misunderstanding of Chinese tradition, that "it is a Chinese tradition for fathers to be involved with their child." Observation found him only incidentally involved. For example, during my four visits to his home, he only held his 7-month-old infant once. Nevertheless, he characterized himself as "a modern father" who was active with his child. Besides a new father's enthusiasm, there is also a practical need for men's involvement in childcare: their wives return to work and husbands thus are initiated into caretaking tasks (such as holding the child while their wives prepare dinner or go to a store to buy something) much sooner and more frequently than they might have in fact preferred. For example, in one home a man whose wife worked the night shift performed routine childcare functions. He regularly changed soiled clothes, bathed, and fed his child. During casual conversation, he admitted that he did not enjoy the tasks and preferred that his wife perform them. Since she had to work, however, there was no other means to cope with what was for him an obviously onerous task.

Early Childhood (13–36 Months)

This is a period when men begin to be more actively involved in their child's affairs. As the child starts to walk and talk, a father's involvement increases. Men consistently told me that the phase they enjoyed the most was when their child reached approximately 3 years of age. For the father, the child is more playful and can carry on a conversation, a conversation that the fathers frequently found amusing. Fathers will regularly take their child on short trips to the store or peasant market and for walks in the neighborhood before and, sometimes, after dinner. Significantly, women, too, indicated that they enjoyed the years when their child could speak. They differ from men, however, in also finding infancy just as satisfying. Not one man expressed satisfaction in the infant phase of development. It could be speculated that one reason is their lack of involvement. This interpretation was borne out, to some extent, in observations made in several local neighborhoods and city parks in July and August 1987. Every evening around 6 PM roughly 145 men and 120 women by themselves would be outdoors either holding, or walking with, a young child (between 1 and 3 years old). Men clearly outnumbered women. However, by 9 PM, the ratio was reversed: 100 men and 165 women with their children. During the earlier evening hours men are performing childcare duties while women are preparing dinner. After dinner, women start to interact with their child. What is most striking about this pre- and postdinner trend is that it is an individual parental affair and not one engaged in by the couple together. This changes on Sunday, the day of family gatherings and communal events. Over a 2-month period I systematically observed, in the public park over 2162 brief parent–child interactions. Of 461 single father–child interactions, 180 interactions involved fathers with a young child, and 281 interactions with older children. On the other hand, 331 of a total 436 mother–child interactions involved a young child, while only 105 involved older children. In addition, I observed only six infants brought to the park. In every case, it was the mother who held the infant in her arms while the couple strolled through the park.

Overall, there were 1265 couples with a child. Of these only 53 involved both parents holding a child's hand. However, this was not characteristic of most couple–child interactions. The typical couple–child interaction saw one parent assume the more immediate and direct contact with the child. This contact was more or less equally divided between both parents. I observed 608 fathers, accompanied by their wives, touching or holding their child and 657 mothers, accompanied by their husband, doing the same. If the age of the child is considered, an interesting pattern emerges. Mothers interact in this manner more often with young children than with older ones. Fathers, on the other hand, interact with equal frequency with both young and older children. For example, 306 of the 608 fathers interacted with a child between 1 and 3 years old, while 301 did so with a child between 3 and 6 years old. On the other hand, 499 of the 657 women interacted with a child between 1 and 3 years old, yet only 103 women did so with a child over 3 years old. The older the child, the less frequent the mother–child interaction in public. One possible explanation is that the older the child the more the child actively sought out the father, the parent it interacted with least during the work week. Since Sundays are culturally defined as a family day, it is reasonable to suspect that children look forward to interacting and playing with their father. Although I did not systematically count the frequency, I noticed that whenever a couple was seated, the child, particularly one over 3 years old, tended to sit next to the father. This occurred even if the couple was actively engaged in conversation: the child remained content to quietly play next to his or her father.

STYLES OF PARENTAL CAREGIVING

There are gender differences in parent–child caretaking styles. For instance, whenever women hold a child, it is typically held close to their body, while men's holding style is the reverse: the child is held usually with arms extended either upward or outward away from their body. Mothers and fathers differed in the patience shown toward a stubborn child who refused to move. The common response of the Chinese parent is to call out the equivalent of "good-bye" (zou) and walk off. Usually the child panics over the threat of being abandoned and quickly follows. Although both men and women strove not to use force in motivating their child to move, they are also not above abruptly picking up the child. Significantly, men and women differed in the patience and, therefore, ability to wait out a stubborn child's refusal to move. In the 27 incidents of child stubbornness I observed that mothers ($n = 18$)

were able to wait longer than fathers ($n = 9$) who never waited more than 5 and usually 3 minutes before they returned and picked up the child, whereas mothers would wait at least twice as long.

Men and women also differ in the style used to walk with their child. Women, for example, rarely walked ahead of their child. Rather they preferred to stand 3 to 4 feet behind the child and coach it. The few instances where a mother walked ahead was when the child refused to move forward and the mother wanted to move it along by threats of abandonment. Men, on the other hand, use a different walking style. They usually walk ahead, and not behind, the child, thereby allowing for greater physical distance to grow between the child and himself. The emphasis is on the independence of the child. One father allowed a 3-year-old child to wander more than 30 yards behind him, something a Chinese mother would not do. The age and sex of the child did not affect the parents' walking style. Fathers allowed young girls to wander just as much as boys, whereas mothers stood just as close to a boy as they did to a girl.

The style of conversation also differs between mothers and fathers. If a mother is holding a young child, for example, she rarely talks to it. However, as soon as the mother starts walking with the child, she breaks into a continuous mode of verbal coaching and pattern addressed toward the child. The verbal stream acts to "hold" her child in check. Unlike mothers, fathers talk to the child when they are holding it. They converse with the child when walking with a child, however, the conversation revolves around teaching the child something or commanding it to hurry up. The style in which a father issues commands differs from mothers, who typically never stop talking. The father issues commands in rapid bursts, two or three times, to signal the child to move faster. Fathers, in short, do not attempt to use a cradle of sound to communicate closeness or authority. Instead they point out and comment on specific features around them. Regardless of social class, mothers use a harsh and abrasive tone, whenever they address a child (from 1 to 6 yards old, in contrast to a father's tone, which is softer. Fathers are especially affectionate and openly express this affection to an older infant. For instance, fathers frequently repeatedly kissed an infant on its exposed buttocks (the Chinese do not use diapers but prefer to dress the child in pants that have an opening in its crotch). As a child enters late childhood (3–6 years old) parents become sensitive to possible gossip over expressing physical affection toward their child. Thus fathers in public, but not necessarily within the home, are reluctant to actually hug a child over 6 years old. This is especially true in father–daughter interactions. A father told me that "sometimes I might like to but I am afraid that people might think I like [i.e., sexually] my daughter too much." Another father admitted that he sometimes hugs his 10-year-old daughter but only in the privacy of his home. On the other hand, I observed mothers repeatedly hugging a son or daughter within the home. For example, mothers, whenever they are reading a book and their child is lying next to them, will periodically lean over and brush their cheek next to their child's cheek, say something, and then return to their book. In contrast, once the child enters the first grade, fathers follow social convention, begin gradually to restrict the frequency of physical affection shown toward their child. However, once a boy or girl passes puberty, even mothers become more restrained in their expression of physical affection.

Although men and women differ in the frequency in which they perform caretaking duties, there is no noticeable difference in the way they perform routine maintenance functions. I observed countless instances in the public park when a father, alone with his child, aptly performed the basic childcare duties: wiping a dirty face, slicing food and feeding the child, unwrapping a popsicle, or buttoning and unbuttoning a child's clothes. Whenever a child was with both parents, it was assumed and expected that the mother would perform all the necessary caretaking acts, the same acts she performed within the home. This is especially so if the child becomes cranky and starts to cry, a behavior that immediately activates the mother's involvement as it rapidly disengages the father's interest. During the summer of 1987 I never saw a father, in a home or in public, holding a crying child in the presence of his wife.

Men's and women's caretaking styles do not change noticeably within the more private domestic setting. Whenever a child is sick, for example, it is the mother who cares for it. It is the mother who dresses the child for school and it is the mother who scolds the child when it is bad. The father remains aloof and enters into the disciplinary role only when something very serious occurs. However, fathers are involved in subtle yet psychologically important ways. I saw, for example, two long-time friends, on two separate occasions, wash their child's legs and arms, after their wives had whipped the child's bare legs or arm with a small stick. The fathers did not utter a word nor did they protest the punishment. What they did communicate was a love and concern for their child's well-being.

In public, Chinese fathers prefer more action-oriented activities (such as playing pool, rowing a boat, going to the zoo) that encourage creativity and independence; in the domestic sphere, they adopt a more reserved yet involved stance. For example, they often discuss, tease, and occasionally wrestle with their child inside the house. In addition, they are not above helping their wife, if she is momentarily overburdened by work or beside herself in anger with the child. On the other hand, mothers' parenting style in both the public and domestic spheres does not change. She remains the primary caretaker who is, however inconsistent, always the nurturer (Lamb 1987). Furthermore, mothers organize activities designed to protect and nurture the child against unseen yet potentially harmful forces, thereby promoting and securing an intensely close emotional bond that normally continues well into adulthood. Significantly, although women often vociferously complained about their husband's lack of support and assistance in performing household chores, they seldom complained about their more numerous parental duties. The childcare duties are sex-linked duties considered natural, normal, and beyond critical discussion or evaluation.

MOTHER–CHILD VERSUS FATHER–CHILD BOND

One of the primary means whereby traditional Chinese women attempt to secure and protect themselves from a hostile mother-in-law and often unsympathetic husband is to foster an intense emotional dependency with her children so that, once grown, they will take care of her (Wolf 1972). It was the mother who is the primary educator of very young children. She sets the goals, moulds behavior, and forges the intellectual and ethical identity of the culture's next generation. In Margery Wolf's study of contemporary urban life in the PRC, she observed that recent socialist changes no longer make it necessary for women to foster this type of parent–child dependency. She adds that: "The uterine family has disappeared because the need for it has disappeared. Urban women do not express the same degree of anxiety about their old age that they used to. Young women work and expect pensions, older women who do not have pensions are assured by the government that they are cared for " (Wolf 1985: 207). I found that in Huhhot it had not disappeared. It is persistent, however, for a different reason: the continuing preference and habit to cultivate bonds of intense emotional dependency. Mothers continue to exercise tremendous psychological control over their offspring. In fact, the mother–child relationship is the most admired parent–child dyad. For example, in 58 cases that I collected of parental intervention in an offspring's mate selection, it was, inevitably, the mother who was the deciding force. Middle-aged men and women frequently confided to me that their emotional involvement with their mothers remained remarkably strong after their marriage and throughout their adult lives.

Although the Chinese respect their fathers, they adore their mothers. It is culturally understood and accepted that a son or a daughter will exchange, at some point, harsh words with one's father, but it is considered very bad, very regrettable form, that this would ever happen with one's mother. The intensity of the emotional adoration was expressed to me by several college students, in their twenties, who permitted me to read sections of their diaries. One 26-year-old female student wrote: "I love my mother very much, from my heart. She has given me too much, both knowledge of society and science, and knowledge of life. She has taught me how to encounter difficulties. Now she is ill, I wish it was me instead." A 20-year-old young man wrote that "In the evening I write to my mother. I miss her very much, and I can imagine how much she misses me. I've just received a letter from my mother. She told me she is very healthy and pleased. She said she misses me and hopes I can go back home on the holidays." A 23-year-old, extremely articulate, female worker from Nanjing told me that "Since I came to this city, I've missed my family, especially my mother. I cried while I read my mother's letter. I often dream of my family and getting together to eat dinner and watch television or go to the movies. I often say to myself: 'You aren't a child; you're a grown-up.' I do not know why I can not overcome my weakness. Maybe my mother gave me too much love." A 24-year-old male stated that when he is at home, he often goes for evening strolls with his mother because "I like to talk to my mother. She is a teacher and she knows young people. We talk about studying and about life. If I meet some problems, I would ask my mother and she would tell me what I should do." A 19-year-old student who was suffering from a cold acknowledged that "I think of my dear mother. If she was here, she could cook delicious food for me and comfort me. But here 5,000 miles away from home, who could be as dear as my mother?" Finally a 21-year-old male student recorded rather bleakly in his diary "another Sunday of loneliness and restlessness. I'd rather be a bird, then I could fly back home and see my mother."

Adoration is probably not too strong a word to describe the emotional connections between mother and child. The extent to which Chinese symbolically extend this connection was vividly and dramatically revealed to me when I asked my informants ($n = 29$) to respond to the following hypothetical situation. I asked them to imagine walking across a bridge with their mother and father. Suddenly the bridge collapses and everyone is thrown into the water. If they could save only one person, who would it be? Of the 29 informants (19 males and 10 females), 20 selected their mother for saving while the remaining 9 refused to answer.

The Chinese mother is the glue that binds the family together. She is the center of the communication network. Through visits she becomes the focal point for news and a pivot for influencing various kin opinions and actions.

For reasons other than simple fear of a vengeful mother-in-law or hostile spouse, the emotional bonds between mother and child formed during infancy and the early childhood years are maintained. These bonds are sustained, in large part, through a Chinese tradition that legitimizes and promotes in practice an intense lifelong emotional bond between mother and child (Solomon 1971: Pye 1985). It is a bond that is idealized in literature and in conversation as a celebration of harmony, rememberance, and enduring love (Link 1981). Moreover, the intensity of its expression signifies to every Huhhotian the continued importance, influence, and power of the Chinese woman.

THE EMERGENT URBAN CHINESE FATHER–CHILD RELATIONSHIP

The "traditional" Chinese conception of the parenting process is similar to Parsons and Bales' (1955) typology, which posits that, within the domestic sphere, men perform an instrumental or competence-directed role, whereas women perform the more expressive or empathetic role. The typology is an accurate representation of how the Chinese peasant views parent–child relations (Fei 1939; Gallin 1966). It is also strikingly similar to the parenting style found in both Taiwan and Hong Kong (Ho 1987). However, in Huhhot, the emergence of a new urban infrastructure has fostered a supportive environment for the expression of warmer sentiments and closer interaction between father and child. At present, it is an emerging sentiment that is more strongly, but not entirely, articulated by Huhhot's college-educated stratum. The expression, as such, is a refinement of Chinese tradition and constitutes a new attitude that stresses the importance of intimate father–child interaction within a variety of social settings. By insisting that fathers should not adopt an aloof posture but rather should continue to demonstrate care and affection toward their child, it is a notion that challenges the traditional father–child role, a role and style of interaction that is, in fact, seen by the previous generations' fathers as no longer satisfying or necessary.

There are three factors that contribute to the increasing intimacy of father–child interaction in both public and private settings. First, women work outside the home—a fact that compels even the most reluctant father to become more involved in caretaking activities. Second, the ecology of domestic space. The typically small one-room apartment places the father in constant and close proximity to his child, thereby enabling easier, albeit causal, parent–child interaction. Third, a new folk notion promoting fatherly involvement has emerged within many urban households. Although it has yet to receive official endorsement in state publications (Honig and Heshatter 1988: 181), this notion nevertheless is readily articulated in conversations across Huhhot. As such it suggests a fundamental shift in the criteria used to access the relative importance of sons over daughters.

FATHER–DAUGHTER LOVE: A NEW DOMESTIC REALITY

The core of Chinese kinship has been the father–son relationship (Hsu 1967). The homage to that relationship and the patrilineal tradition that spawned it continue to be expressed in a variety of social settings. One example is the many ad hoc folk theories of conception. Throughout Chinese history the mother was considered primarily responsible for determining the sex of the child. Thus whenever a child was born, it was not the man's but rather the woman's doing or, in the case of a girl, her "fault." (The word "fault" is used to indicate the traditional preference for a male child.) Mongolian herders also believe that the mother supplies the child's blood and flesh while the father is the source of its bones or essence.

Today educated Huhhotians seem to possess a slight understanding of basic human anatomy. Unlike the less educated Huhhotians who continue to embrace traditional notions of fetal development, the educated strata do not and, yet, have not replaced them with any solid scientific explanation. They are as uninformed as their uneducated peers and, contrastingly, emphasize the father's role in conception. When I asked 17 college students, for example, where a baby's genes come from, their response was mixed. Some thought that, if the baby was a girl, the mother contributed 40% of the child's make-up and the father 60%, however, if the baby was a boy, the ratio was reversed. Others thought that the baby's sex was not important and that the father contributed 60% while the mother contributed 40% of the baby's genes. Although the sample is small, it suggests that educated Huhhotians ($n = 13$) have not been instructed in this matter and hold a variety of ad hoc explanations. Thus a female student noted that "your mother gives you 60% genes and your father gives you 40%. But those genes of your father are stronger than your mother's. They usually win. That is why you look more like your father." A college-educated man told me that "the father's and mother's genes are mixed. But your father's genes are stronger. He determines [for both the son and daughter] the blood and character." The following dialogue between two male students aptly reveals the propensity to associate character traits with the father.

> First Student: "Your father's reproductive role is more important."
> Second Student: "Who told you?"
> First Student: "I know."
> Second Student: "Well, my mother has red hair and my father does not."
> First student: "O.K., your mother gave you a little but your father influenced your character."[5]

Although each person interviewed asserted a slightly different opinion, everyone shared a common assumption: the father, and not the mother, has the greater impact on the formation of both physical appearance and character.[4]

Publicly Huhhotians speak continually about the importance of "having a son," an obsession so acute that relatives and friends closely watch a pregnant woman's every step whenever she enters a door. It is believed that if the mother-to-be's left foot enters first, she will give birth to a girl; if it is the right foot, then it will be a boy. Moreover, whenever people ask a pregnant woman about the expected delivery date, they seldom use the gender-neutral word "child" (haizi) but, instead, use the word "son" as the generic term for pregnancy. Hence, they ask "when are you going to have your son?" The obsession is so complete that everyone interviewed on the topic publicly hoped for a son. However, my research assistant found in private interviews with the college-educated women that daughters were thought to be more loyal, easier to raise, and more pleasant to interact with. As a consequence, half of those interviewed admitted that they wanted a daughter, a fact that suggests that women's public comments are more a social form than an accurate expression of personal conviction. At least among the college-educated, it also suggests that the linguistic terminology used to speak of pregnancy might be more traditional than true evidence of a continued preference for a son.

Although Huhhotians, as elsewhere in urban China, continue to publicly value sons over daughters, I found that parents were also very happy with the birth of daughters. In fact, even in those families that unreservedly wished for a son, parents rapidly adjusted and came to value their daughter. As previously shown in the section on mother-in-law and daughter-in-law relationships, sons are increasingly regarded as unreliable in fulfilling family obligations. They are seen as easily lost to their wives and her family, while daughters are thought of as more considerate and faithful in continuing to visit their natal home. Sons are viewed as less of an asset than before. Huhhotian fathers indicated they were more demanding with their son than their daughter. They interacted with their daughters more openly, more warmly. Fathers, for example, tended to speak less harshly to their daughters. Whenever fathers discussed their children, it was common to stress "how wonderful little girls are." Moreover, fathers seldom wrestled or teased their daughters as often as they did with their sons. This is not new. Peasants demonstrate similar sex-linked postures toward childcare. What is a new occurrence is the greater valuing of daughters within a growing number of urban households. As such, it constitutes an enormous shift in a patrilineal tradition that valued sons and grandsons over daughters and granddaughters.

The socialist transformation of urban society has had a corresponding impact on men's conception of themselves as husbands and fathers. Young fathers continue to assume a firm and somewhat formal posture toward their sons, while paradoxically insisting they did not want to be as formal and reserved as their fathers had been with them. In Huhhot, I often heard men insisting (much as in traditional China) that, while they "loved their father, I did not like him." I never heard women express in causal conversation or in direct interview a similar resentment or disappointment with their mother's parenting style. Women were adamant in insisting that they wanted to be exactly "the kind of mother their mother had been." Huhhotians felt strongly that it was improper for a child to grow up and not like his or her father. Although contemporary Huhhotian fathers wish to become a close friend with their child, as opposed to striking the more traditional note of a stern moral authority ever ready to criticize shortcomings, they remain uncertain and confused as how to express this wish. Warmth and immediacy of affection are not easily achieved. It is easier for them to accomplish this with a daughter than with a son. Significantly, fathers are more ambivalent than mothers in balancing their obligations as both spouse and parent. This ambivalence was profoundly articulated by many college-educated fathers who voiced concern that their child loved their mothers more than them! Although the male desire to become more involved in feeling and thought, as I have demonstrated, is far from achieved, it is a desire frequently heard in conversation among close friends. As such, it has enormous implications for the quality of future parent–child relations. For example, one 37-year-old man told me that "I do not want my child to dislike me." Another 29-year-old man admitted that "it is bad for a son to resent a father. That is why you must respect your children, so that they will not resent you." A 48-year-old man who had four children told me that he had changed his parenting style with his youngest son. He explained that "I had been very reserved with my older children, but with my youngest I do not think that is such a good idea." Another middle-aged man acknowledged that "I want my child to love me, not fear me, so I am kind to him."

More and more often, the popular Chinese press and magazines are filled with stories of urban parents complaining that their child has become a "little emperor" who is spoiled and no longer listens to them. The blame for this has been placed chiefly on a doting, an overindulgent mother (who has only one child) and two sets of grandparents who also tend to smother the child in love and kindness. In effect, the child is not provided with a sense of structure and is, therefore, developing without any self-discipline. These attitudes toward mother–child and grandparent–child interaction are not new. What is new is that fathers, much more than mothers, are wavering in their role and have become inconsistent in their interacting style. They are ambivalent, torn between two competing viewpoints, and the behavioral signals that they send their children because of this are mixed, if not outright contradictory. The immediate result is a cohort of children who have become more unruly than the previous generation of children. The full impact can be seen in interviews that I had with two elementary school teachers in 1983. Both teachers freely admitted that approximately half their students' parents (20–40) visited them and requested that the teachers lecture on proper behavior and respect toward their parents. It is clear that parents are beginning to feel a loosening grip on their children's upbringing and behavior.

CONCLUSION

The gradual transformation of the urban Chinese family organization has resulted in a shift from arranged marriages to marriages based on free choice and mutual affection. At present this change has not significantly altered the traditional instrumental versus expressive parent–child interaction and caregiving styles. Although Goode examined the effect that the historical process has had on men and women's parenting style, my data suggest that the emphasis and value on mutual affection between spouses may cause both parents to prefer closer, warmer more frequent involvement with the child. The Goode model is less useful, however, in accounting for the continuation of gender differences in caretaking styles or the timing of when men prefer to become more involved with their child. For instance, the child's age and gender continue to affect the style and frequency of the father's overall involvement. Mothers continued to be responsible for infant and early childcare, whereas fathers remain only nominally involved. Fathers expressed a clear preference with interacting with more mature children who could speak and play in more action-oriented activities; mothers found different kinds of satisfaction depending on the child's age. Fathers also tended to demonstrate kinder and more nurturent (or expressive) behavior toward a young daughter compared to a young son, whereas mother's preference for a daughter did not result in a noticeable different in parenting style. Moreover, there is no noticeable difference in the way men and women perform routine childcare maintenance functions. In this way, the Parson–Bales typology is misleading as it does not account for specific settings in which fathers perform nurturing and caretaking tasks. In addition, the urban transformation of society has had a corresponding impact on men's conception of themselves as husbands and fathers. Many fathers, especially college-educated, remain uncertain over the nature of their parenting responsibilities. Their confusion has, in turn, affected the overall discipline posture within many households and has contributed to fostering the "spoiled child" syndrome. Consequently, the urban father is caught in a dilemma that each father must resolve individually; a desired resolution that some have aptly achieved, others less satisfactorily, and other, perhaps, never will. The full implications of these changes and conflicts for parent–child and husband–wife relationships will be played out in succeeding generations.

NOTES

1. The material that forms much of this research was collected in two different field seasons in Huhhot, capital of Inner Mongolia Autonomous Region, People's Republic of China. The first field season was between 1981 and 1983 and, most recently, between May and August of 1987. Huhhot is a city with over 491,000, of which 80% are Han and the remaining 20% are either Chinese Moslem (Hui) or Mongolian. Unless otherwise noted, all comments about Huhhotians apply to both Mongolia and Han.

2. This study is the first observational study of frequency and style of Chinese parent–child interaction. There is no comparable study. Consequently, it is difficult to determine which Huhhotian behaviors represent cultural continuity and which are recent innovations. I have relied on older Huhhotians observations and comments that suggest that there has been a gradual shift toward more frequent father–child interaction. However, until there is an observational study of the frequency of the father–child interaction in the countryside, it is difficult to access the reliability of senior Huhhotians remembrance. My study is far from comprehensive. My interest in this domain grew out of repeated promptings from Barry Hewlett to investigate this facet of Chinese life. In 1987 I undertook this project as a secondary project that could be concluded while I investigated other topics. As a consequent, I had neither read widely nor thought through some of the more intricate research problems. Thus my study is

an exploration into a largely unexplored domain. The analysis that follows is suggestive, and not conclusive. I will focus on the difference and similarities in mother–child and father–child behavioral style within three domains: the home, semi-public arena of four neighborhoods, and two different public parks. The frequency and style of public interaction were recorded through a series of unobtrusive spot observations conducted throughout July 1987.

3.   Tumote peasants, unlike Huhhotians, restrict men from entering a room with a newborn infant. The restriction lasts for a month. In Taiwan it is thought that the mother and the baby are a polluting substance and thus can harm the man. In Tumote countryside it is reverse. It is men, the outsiders to the event, who are regarded as potentially harmful agents. If a man enters the room, he must shout out that he is coming in so the woman can cover the child. Not to do so might result in the baby becoming sick.

4.   It is believed that the failure to swaddle results in soft bones that are easy to break. In Huhhot, the period of swaddling varies between households, but usually ends after 12 months.

5.   Significantly I found a consensus among uneducated women. Their position was similar to that which was articulated in the countryside where it is believed that 100% of the baby's blood and, therefore, its sex is a product of the mother. As one 54-year-old woman noted "It came from me, so it is mine."

REFERENCES

Bowlby, J. 1951. *Maternal Care and Mental Health*. Geneva: WHO.

Cao, J. 1987. Single women and men over 30 in China. In *New Trends in Chinese Marriage and the Family*. Women and China (Eds.). Beijing: China International Book Trading.

Daly, M., and Wilson, M. 1987. *Homocide*. Hawthorne, NY: Aldine De Gruyter.

DeGroot, J. 1882–1910. *The Religious System of China*, 6 Vols. Leiden: Brill.

Fei, X. 1935. *Peasant Life in Rural China*. Shanghai: Shanghai Press.

Freeman, M. 1965. *Lineage in Southeastern China*. London: University of London Press.

Gallin, B. 1966. *Hsin Hxing, Taiwan, a Chinese Village in Change*. Berkeley: University of California Press.

Goode, W. 1963. *World Revolution and Family Patterns*. New York: Free Press.

Hanan, P. 1988. *The Invention of Li Yui*. Cambridge: Harvard University Press.

Ho, D. 1987. "Fatherhood in Chinese society. In *The Father's Role: Cross-Cultural Perspective*. M. E. Lamb (Ed.). Hillsdale, NJ: Erlbaum.

Honig, E., and Hershatter, G. 1988. *Personal Voices Chinese Women in the 1980's*. Palto Alto: Stanford University Press.

Hsu, F. 1967. *Under the Ancestors' Shadow*. New York: Doubleday Anchor Book.

Macfarlane, A. 1987. *The Culture of Capitalism*. Oxford: Basil Blackwell.

Lamb, M. E. 1987. *Father's Role: Cross-Cultural Perspective*. Hillsdale, NJ: Erlbaum.

Levy, M. 1968. *The Family Revolution in Modern China*. New York: Atheneum.

Li, Y. C. 1969. *Against Culture: Problematic Love in Early European and Chinese Narrative Fiction*. Microfilm. Ann Arbor: University Microfilm International.

Link, P. 1981. *Mandarin Ducks and Butterflies*. Berkeley: University of California Press.

Parsons, T., and Bales, R. 1955. *Family, Socialization and Interaction Process.* Glencoe, IL: Free Press.

Pye, L. 1985. *Asian Power and Politics.* Cambridge: Harvard University Press.

Solomon, R. 1971. Mao's Revolution and the Chinese Political Culture. Berkeley: University of California Press.

Stone, L. 1977. *The Family, Sex and Marriage in England 1500–1800.* New York: Harper & Row.

———. 1987. Passionate attachments in the west in historical perspective. In *Passionate Attachments.* W. Gaylin and E. Person (Eds.), pp. 14–27. New York: Free Press.

Wolf, M. 1968. *The House of Limi.* Englewood Cliffs, NJ: Prentice-Hall.

———. 1970. Child training and the Chinese family. In *Family and Kinship in Chinese Society.* M. Freeman (Ed.). Standord: Standord University Press.

———. 1972. Uterine families and the women's community. In *Women and the Family in Rural Taiwan.* M. Wolf (Ed.). Palo Alto: Stanford University Press.

———. 1985. *Revolution Postponed.* Stanford: Stanford University Press.

Tan, M. 1988. Changing views of marriage. *China Reconstructs.* December 8–9.

Whyte, M. 1988. Changes in mate choice in Chengdu. In *Center for Research on Social Organization, the Working Paper Series.* Ann Arbor: University of Michigan.

Whyte, M., and Parish, W. 1984. *Urban Life in Contemporary China.* Chicago: University of Chicago Press.

Wilson, R. 1974. The moral state: A study of the political socialization of Chinese and American children. In *Normal and Abnormal Behavior in Chinese Culture.* A. Kleinman and T. Y. Lin (Eds.), pp. 1–13. Holland: Reidel.

Wu, R. 1987. The urban family in flux. In *New Trends in Chinese Marriage and the Family.* Women and China (Eds.). Beijing: China International Book Trading.

Yang, M. 1945. *Chinese Village.* New York: Columbia University Press.

Author Index

Subject Index